D0712742

Encounters with Islam in German Literature and Culture

Studies in German Literature, Linguistics, and Culture

Encounters with Islam in German Literature and Culture

Edited by
James Hodkinson and Jeff Morrison

CAMDEN HOUSE
Rochester, New York

First published 2009
by Camden House

Camden House is an imprint of Boydell & Brewer Inc.
668 Mt. Hope Avenue, Rochester, NY 14620, USA
www.camden-house.com
and of Boydell & Brewer Limited
PO Box 9, Woodbridge, Suffolk IP12 3DF, UK
www.boydellandbrewer.com

ISBN-13: 978-1-57113-419-6
ISBN-10: 1-57113-419-0

Library of Congress Cataloging-in-Publication Data

Encounters with Islam in German literature and culture / edited by James
Hodkinson and Jeff Morrison.
    p. cm. — (Studies in German literature, linguistics, and culture)
Includes bibliographical references and index.
ISBN-13: 978-1-57113-419-6 (hardcover : alk. paper)
ISBN-10: 1-57113-419-0 (hardcover : alk. paper)
    1. German literature—History and criticism. 2. Islam in literature.
3. Orientalism in literature. 4. Orient—In literature. 5. Other (Philosophy) in
literature. 6. East and West in literature. 7. Islam—Relations—Christianity.
I. Hodkinson, James R., 1973–. II. Morrison, Jeffrey.

PT143.O75E63 2009
840.9'38297—dc22

2009021015

A catalogue record for this title is available from the British Library.

This publication is printed on acid-free paper.
Printed in the United States of America.

Contents

Acknowledgments

THE EDITORS OF THIS VOLUME wish to thank the President and staff of the National University of Ireland Maynooth for their assistance in hosting the March 2007 conference that gave rise to this volume. We acknowledge with thanks the financial support provided by the National University of Ireland, which enabled publication of this volume, and thanks are due to the Humanities Research Fund at the University of Warwick for similar financial assistance. As ever, our thanks are extended to Jim Walker, Jane M. Best, and Sue Innes at Camden House for their close and careful attention and support during the preparation of the volume.

James Hodkinson wishes to extend thanks to the Directorate of the Topkapi Palace Museum, Istanbul, for granting the rights to reproduce the image on the front cover of this volume and to Kadriye Özbiyik in particular for her assistance in this matter. Dr. Karin Yeşilada (Paderborn) must be thanked for her assistance in liaising with Istanbul and enabling "first contact." Especial thanks are also due to my friend and colleague Dr. Birgit Röder (University of Warwick) for tracking down the cover image in Istanbul in the first place, and for sharing her wealth of knowledge on matters Islamic, Arabic, Persian and Turkish, for the illuminating discussions on E. T. A. Hoffmann, and for encouragement and support in general. I also thank my colleagues in the Department of German Studies, Warwick University, for allowing me to present to them, prior to publication, the work that has gone into this volume in a supportive and constructively critical environment.

Jeff Morrison wishes to express his gratitude for the support offered by his colleagues in the German Department at NUIM during the *Encounters with Islam* conference and the financial assistance provided by the Dean of Research of the university. He would also like to thank the Sabbatical Committee at NUIM for providing him with the time to work on this volume.

Introduction

James Hodkinson and Jeff Morrison

THE VOLUME *Encounters with Islam in German Literature and Culture* developed out of the conference *German Encounters with Islam*, which took place at the National University of Ireland, Maynooth, in March 2007. The conference raised a number of important issues, issues that not only are interesting in their own right but also seem particularly pertinent, given the prevailing global political — and, sadly, military — situation. The relationship between Europe and the Islamic world once more appears undeniably strained, and so it has become the subject of serious reflection for political, church, and intellectual leaders as well as for the ordinary citizens who find themselves at the troubled interface of two cultures. Yet despite obvious points of geographical, military, and political tension, the model of a fundamental clash of civilizations is as much a product of existing tensions as it is evidence of absolute and insurmountable division between Islam and Europe. Indeed, as the Maynooth conference showed, talk in general of two monolithic cultural blocks, opposed or not, is increasingly inadequate as an approach: contemporary reality is far more complex. Whereas in earlier times any European engagement with Islam would have meant substantially engagement with a remote "Other," it now involves also looking within at the developing Islamic presence within European culture. Islamic self-definition is likewise increasingly colored by global influences that problematize a simple sense of Islamic self.

The conference illuminated a range of largely germanophone literary and theoretical responses to Islamic culture and revealed important aspects of the dynamics of cultural interaction. The texts discussed were many and varied and included travelogues based on first-hand encounters with Islam; literary, essayistic, and theological writing on Islamic religious practice; texts incorporating characters, situations, or locations from the Islamic world into prose fiction or drama; and writing in German by Muslims, or those of a Muslim background. Each of these categories of writing, of course, revealed as much about the European "home" culture as it did of Islamic culture. The contributions cover an extraordinary chronological range — from the Middle Ages to the present day — a variety of genres, and a wealth of attitudes; the theoretical premises of the contributions also vary widely. Fascinating continuities also exist, however, between texts across all periods: there are tendencies both to conspire in and reject the Western exploitation and exoticization of Islam; there is both the suppression of the autonomous Muslim voice within the German language, and the struggle to rehabilitate that voice; and there is implicit and explicit theological debate on Islam, be it of progressive or reactionary character. Of particular interest are the instances in which texts demonstrate how spurious the stark divisions between the Western, ostensibly Christian, world and Islam really are, together with the ongoing debate about how the division of the faiths relates to the political, ethnic, and social identity of the individual.

Until the fairly recent past it would have been possible to maintain the position that German (-language) culture was peripheral to the project of "Orientalism" analyzed most tellingly by Said.[1] While it required the wearing of historical blinkers, it was possible to see the German-speaking lands as only marginal participants in the history of colonialism and as less obviously represented in the process of intellectual ostracization or domination of the constructed "Orient" depicted in Said's influential text. Clearly, many have identified the flaws in this analysis over a long period, but the most substantial revision of the German position has taken place in the wake of the massive transformation of German society brought about by the arrival of Muslim, usually (though not exclusively) of Turkish *Gastarbeiter* to drive the German industrial resurgence after the Second World War. It had previously perhaps been possible to see Germany as quintessentially European, whether in its geographical location, its ethnicity, or its cultural traditions; indeed it would have appeared most actively European, whether in introducing Protestantism or providing the genetic backbone of the ruling dynasties of Europe. Even in its most sinister manifestation, under Hitler, German culture clearly saw itself in European terms; the Germania embraced by the National Socialists may have been based on a bizarre, mythical understanding of tradition, but it was robustly, if perversely, European.

In the twentieth and twenty-first centuries, however, German self-understanding and the outsider perception of Germany have been radically transformed by the increased visibility of a Muslim presence at the heart of German culture. At its simplest, it is difficult to ignore a Muslim population now numbering something in the region of 2.6 million. It is furthermore difficult to see Muslim communities as marginal any longer. Some groups, particularly those of Turkish origin, have already been present for several generations. Muslim communities have often moved beyond the physical boundaries of ethnic minority suburbs, crossed linguistic and professional boundaries, and thus taken a more visible role in the shaping of "German" culture generally. In fact, it has become nonsensical to talk in terms of homogenized and utterly distinct "immigrant" vis-à-vis "German" cultures when talking of the geographical space Germany (the same principle applies to a lesser extent to other German-speaking countries). The hybrid cultures produced within Germany's physical borders and discussed in this volume often articulate the complex experiences and literary voices of Germans of non-European extraction.[2] What is true of these migrant communities in terms of their complex sense of national and ethnic identity is also true in terms of their identity as Muslims. The Muslim population as a whole has become increasingly diverse in its ethnic composition, given the arrival of further economic immigrants, refugees, and asylum seekers, and now includes Kurds, Afghans, Iranians, Bulgarians, Bosnians, and North Africans among others. Naturally, different Muslim communities in Germany approach Islam from differing, often culturally determined perspectives, which can entail radicalizing and secularizing tendencies, as well as from mainstream Shiite, Sunni, or other ways of life. To this must be added that German-born Muslims are not only Muslims but also the "hybrid" inhabitants and citizens of a historically non-Muslim German state.

Several contributions in this volume are dedicated to contemporary cultural manifestations of the German-Islamic encounter and demonstrate the multitude of themes and perspectives on the topic existing in German-language culture. Margaret Littler's powerful chapter examines how Turkish-German writers have sought to fight against the homogenizing ideas of Turkish Islam within the medium of the German language. Littler uses texts by Emine Sevgi Özdamar, Feridun Zaimoğlu, and Zafer Şenocak to show how writers seek to render Islam heterogeneous, evoking traditions of Anatolian Sufism that make fluid the boundaries between the categories of the "sacred" and the "profane" through their provocative erotic content, and also offer critical warnings on the violence underlying fundamentalist thinking. All three writers' works are shown to demand a nuanced understanding of Islam and of Ottoman poetic traditions.

Karin Yeşilada is concerned to explode the category of "German Muslim," reminding us of the limitations of herding together diverse cultures and traditions under so crude a term. She focuses on a particular strand of Turkish-German thought represented by Şenocak, beginning with his essayistic work, before moving to contrast this with a "German" perspective offered in a novel by Christoph Peters. What interests Yeşilada is the way in which both authors construct real and imagined dialogues with Islam from differing perspectives and represent these as succeeding and failing to differing degrees: Şenocak writes against the dogmatic dimension of fundamentalism, calling for modern Muslims to adopt a more self-critical posture and appealing to earlier traditions of more flexible and "enlightened" Islam. Peters, on the other hand, writes of a fictional German protagonist who has converted to Islam and is arrested for becoming involved in terrorist activities in Egypt. The German ambassador, who has past leftist-terrorist leanings, attempts to have his likely death sentence commuted. While the novel shows the mutual perceptions of European Christians and Muslims in terms of a complex series of differing attitudes—the "Muslim" Egyptian authorities oppose Islamist terrorism, for instance—the dialogue fails both ideologically and literally.

German perceptions of Islamic radicalism are dealt with in this volume by Monika Shafi's chapter, which seeks to make subtle distinctions between differing responses. Shafi discusses H. M. Enzensberger's controversial essay "Schreckens Männer: Versuch über den radikalen Verlierer," in which he tried to explain how the "radical loser" can be co-opted into violent terrorist activity by a powerful ideological and religious force, Islamism. Shafi reviews the reception of the essay, both the praise it gained and the criticism of the model of a clash of civilizations that it ostensibly reproduces, before offering a contrast with Ian Buruma's analysis of the assassination of the outspoken Dutch critic of Islam, Theo van Gogh, by a radicalized young Dutch Moroccan. For Shafi, Buruma's essay offers a wider, "postmodern" survey of the complex forces acting upon young terrorists, and her aim is to illuminate the productive insights offered by Enzensberger, while demonstrating that only discussions taking into the account the full range of "social contexts and historical legacies" (257) offer a corrective view and help avoid the drift toward binary conceptions of Islam and the West.

The other issue touched upon briefly by Karin Yeşilada, namely that of European (and German) converts to Islam, is given a full examination by Edwin Wieringa. The author examines Michaela M. Özelsel's *Pilgerfahrt nach Mekka; Meine Reise in eine geheimnisvolle Welt* (2005), making Wieringa's chapter a unique discussion of popular literary treatments of Islam within this collection—though one with serious cultural implications nonetheless. Özelsel's text is a journey narrative in various senses: it tells of the voyage of religious conversion and the physical journey of the *hajj* to Mecca undertaken by the narrator. These transitions, however, are also set in the context of the author's own psychologized quest for self-development, and this is what makes Wieringa ultimately cynical about the narrative's value. Özelsel chooses to pursue certain Sufi lines of thought, though in so doing she propounds a Western view of that tradition. Her take on Islam is placed in the context of Western "New Age" culture more generally and is thus in danger of re-projecting a vision of spiritualized otherness onto Islam, all of which render the author a kind of neo-Orientalist and not the most reliable of informants on contemporary forms of Islam.

A less polemical approach is adopted by Frauke Matthes in her study of *Zu den heiligen Quellen des Islam: Als Pilger nach Mekka und Medina* (2004) by Ilija Trojanow, a German speaker of Bulgarian descent. Matthes does not deal with conversion as such but with how the author-narrator reconnects with his Muslim heritage, follows his own particular pathway, spiritual, cultural, and physical, to Islam, and recounts this (in part as a travel writer) in this travelogue on the hajj. Trojanow sought to see travel not as movement into alien or foreign territory but as an attempt at assimilation into the alterity of different cultures, and Matthes shows that he has a fascinatingly plural and flexible perspective on Islam. Theories of travel writing that refute the possibility of experiencing or writing a wholly authentic account of another culture will be elucidated later in this introduction: Matthes uses such theory as a lens through which to view Trojanow's text and sees it as a multi-layered narrative on Islam, in which the faith is both universal and communal and, simultaneously, part of the author's own relative, subjective experience.

However important these contemporary manifestations of German-Muslim encounter are, they must be viewed as part of a historical process of working through (if not out) the questions of that long-standing relationship. Although we do not seek to reduce the history of the German-Muslim to that of a transnational relationship between Germany and Turkey, we cannot overlook Germany's close historical involvement with Ottoman and post-Ottoman Turkey, as a number of contributions in the volume demonstrate. If the postwar German-Turkish encounter is well known, then the prewar flight of German liberals and leftists to Turkey after 1933 is less familiar. Few are aware that German refugees had a key role to play in the development of Turkish industry and institutions, particularly universities, at this time. This could, of course, be seen in terms of conventional colonialist discourse, with the Western imports having a formative, controlling role in producing a culture in the image of their own. It is, however, difficult to overlook the power structure at play there: Turkish Muslims were acting as host to these people, and they were dependent upon its charity; the Germans are clearly the representatives of the decadent culture in this case, and Turkey is identified with the positive alternative. So even this short journey back in time sees a shift in the dynamics of our encounter.

If we move back to the period around the First World War, then another dynamic emerges. We see the German Empire and Austro-Hungary in alliance with the Ottoman Empire: a perhaps unlikely union pitted against other more obviously European, Western nations. This was a pragmatic political alliance, designed to suit the German-speaking countries in the first instance, but it simultaneously offers proof that perceived barriers between cultures can be lifted where a need arises; if economic and institutional pragmatism allowed the presence of Germans in Turkey after 1933, then political and military necessity enabled compromise before the First World War. In her contribution, Rachel MagShamhráin investigates precisely this period, focusing on the dynamic that enabled an unlikely, and perhaps unholy, "Holy War" against France and England on the part of unlikely allies. Her highly original study touches on the pro-Turkish (anti-Catholic) sentiments in the journalism of Hans Barth and in the Imperialist travel writings of Alfred Körte, before exploring how German military strategy ultimately embraced a form of this apparent Islamophilia: the diplomat Max Freiherr von Oppenheim is shown to have persuaded Wilhelm II to cease his attempts to control the spread of Islam and to seek instead to agitate for Islamic Revolution in the colonial territories of Germany's enemies. The great subtlety to emerge from MagShamhráin's piece is, however, that this German functionalization of Islam was not an instance of the unidirectional model of Orientalism, whereby a Christian West simply functionalizes a Muslim East: in seeking to "align" themselves with Turkey, the Germans had to negotiate the horrific issue of the Turkish oppression and massacre of (their fellow Christian) Armenians within Ottoman territory from 1915 onward. Barth, for instance, sought to make this more palatable by "Othering" Armenians, by passing them off as the sly instigators of apparent Kurdish barbarism—the Kurds themselves having been shown to represent a cruder form of Islam than that of the more culturally refined Turkish allies. Thus, as author shows "the mechanism called Orientalism . . . is a discursive missile that can be directed as easily at and by a German and a Christian as at and by a Turk and a Muslim."[3]

Earlier periods show similarly complex relationships between German-speaking and Ottoman, Christian and Muslim territories—relationships exhibiting both instances of political and economic compromise and periods of heightened tension. One might take a look at the broad pattern of exchange between the houses of Habsburg and Osman, between Austro-Hungary and the Ottoman Empire, as an instance of sustained, if fraught and sometimes violent, encounter. From the establishment of a shared border in 1526 after the substantial conquest of Hungary and Croatia by the Ottoman Empire after the Battle of Mohác, until the disappearance of that same border in the wake of the Balkan Wars (1912–13), there was constant although largely negative interaction between the two opposing power blocs, which were to re-emerge as allies in the First World War. Silke Falkner makes an all-too-rare contribution on the period between the 1453 Ottoman conquest of Constantinople and circa 1700, a point at which earlier European understandings of the so-called "Orient" were transformed by the changing political, military, and cultural relationships between Ottoman Turkey and Europe. Falkner examines German-language literature on Turkish Muslims, known collectively as *turcica,* examining both Dionysius von Rickell's refutation of the *Koran* of the 1540s and Stephan Gerlach's diaries chronicling his travels in Ottoman territory between 1573 and 1578. While von Rickell's text seeks to distinguish between the uncontaminated truths of the Bible and the allegedly corrupted half-truths of the Koran, Gerlach's text represents Turks as sexually perverse practitioners of sodomy and bestiality. Both texts are complicit in practices that establish boundaries and transgress them: von Rickell seeks to delineate between Christianity and Islam, which he sees as a bastardized religion impinging on the "true" faith, while Gerlach depicts Turkish-Muslim transgressions from normal/moral to abnormal/ immoral forms of sexuality: such images of violation form the basis of the main two negative stereotypes about Muslims prevalent in the period: religious fraudster and sexual pervert.

In studying the Christian-Muslim encounter before 1526, however, we find that it no longer maps so directly onto the history of German-Turkish relations. In this period we have to acknowledge German participation in the Crusades, particularly the role of the Teutonic Knights and their antagonistic encounters with Middle Eastern, Arabic Muslims. Initially our contributions in this area acknowledge the fundamental crudity of many medieval European perspectives on the Muslim Other. Timothy Jackson's opening chapter, for instance, surveys medieval religious writing, which ranges widely in genre and mode to include narrative, didactic, gnomic, homiletic, and allegorical texts. The authors dealt with are in no doubt that Christianity alone provides the means of salvation, and the more orthodox locate Muslims along with Jews and heretics as an inferior (and on occasion demonized) group hierarchically below Christians. However, the medieval Christian/Muslim encounter can produce unexpectedly differentiated responses, with instances of polemical skepticism toward certain forces within the church being found alongside a degree of tolerance toward the representatives of Islam.

Cyril Edwards's chapter, however, focuses more exclusively on Wolfram von Eschenbach's major works, the Grail romance *Parzival* and the most likely unfinished epic *Willehalm*. Edwards shows how in the former text the figure of Gyburc/Arabel, a convert from Islam to Christianity, preaches an extraordinary message of tolerance, given that Wolfram is writing during the Crusades and contemporaries such as Hartmann von Aue and Walther von der Vogelweide were writing poetry encouraging knights to crusade against the infidel. Interesting for different reasons in *Parzival* is the figure of Feirefiz, the other son of Parzival's father Gahmuret and the black queen Belacane, who is literally and symbolically of black-and-white, magpie countenance. He appears as an adherent of a falsely polytheistic vision of Islam and is shown as a burlesque figure, redeemed later by his conversion to Christianity. Edwards shows Wolfram to have certain sympathies with Feirefiz, despite the fact that he represents yet another Muslim convert to Christianity—a view not as surprising as one might think.[4] Edwards does not contend that Wolfram offers a wholly egalitarian treatment of Islam, but rather that he has subtle (if Christian) sympathies with the other faith. Complementing each other thus, the contributions by Jackson and Edwards in this volume offer a treatment of medieval manifestations of the encounter more nuanced than non-medievalists might have thought.

This volume does not, however, offer a solely chronological reconstruction of German Islamic encounters. Katherine Roy bucks the trend toward strictly periodized studies to offer an innovatively transhistorical chapter that connects the culture of Imperial Germany, in the form of the memoirs of a national of Oman and Zanzibar who emigrated to Germany, Salme/Emily Ruete (1844–1924), with the contemporary writing of the well-known German-Turkish writer Emine Sevgi Özdamar. What connects the two women for Roy and makes them a point of comparison across history is that both have chosen German as the language of their literary expression, and both provide literary responses to Islamic culture in a German setting that problematize understandings of "Islamic heritage." Both writers also complicate the dynamics of intercultural communication, though they do so differently, with Ruete being thought to "pare down" her language in comparision with other memoir writers of the time, while Özdamar "overloads" her language.[5]

Almost any snapshot of the history of the German-speaking lands will reveal an instance of real encounter between Christian-European and Muslim cultures. Although these encounters are generally remembered in terms of faith, politics, or institutions, they clearly had more intimate aspects, were processed (multi-) linguistically, and led to cultural cross-fertilization at a microcosmic, familial, individual level; it is often at this level that the encounter manifests itself in literature. Indeed, the encounter with Islam is not necessarily predicated upon an instance of concrete commercial, political, or military encounter, or even upon personal experience. The contributions to this volume show many examples of motifs, themes, characters, and genre traits that have been derived remotely from literary, philosophical, or theological traditions rather than from any "literal" source. Often enough the deployment of these motifs in germanophone literature was essentially decorative, constituting the application of a gloss of (alternative, exotic) culture; one might look, for example, at the deployment of oriental motifs in popular journals and literature of the nineteenth century for evidence of how aspects of a literary culture can be downgraded to fashion accessories. However, this brand of intercultural intertextuality need not necessarily be trivial in its implications, be they positive or negative. This is made very clear in contributions on the late eighteenth and early nineteenth centuries, a period in which such intertextual encounters were rife. The Enlightenment and Romantic periods produced increasingly sophisticated, philosophically derived conceptual tools with which they could grapple with concepts such as "ethnic identity" and "religion," yet they also reacted in an overtly and covertly emotional way to Islam, being both fascinated and appalled by it, feeling its allure though seeking also to categorize it and control it through writing. Writers and thinkers from this period examine the faith through some incredibly limited, though in some cases also remarkably refined, lenses and this diversity is reflected in the varied findings of this volume's contribution on the period.

Daniel Wilson continues, for the most part, the tradition of critiquing German Enlightenment thought on Islam, examining the works of Meiners and Herder. Wilson finds that the works of these prominent figures not only propounded an image of Muslims as collectively passive, treacherous, and in need of civilizing, but also displayed another alarming trend: anti-Semitism. The writers in question propose expelling the partly Europeanized though essentially "Oriental" Jews from Europe and returning them to Palestine, where they would cause no further damage to Europe and might, in part, civilize Muslims. Indeed, in Wilson's view there is a "secret Other in these German discussions of Islam, just as Muslims are the unseen Other in the project of 'resettling' Jews in Palestine" (85). Wilson's contribution resonates with that of Jackson, which shows how the radically prejudicial formation of Muslim identity in much medieval German writing is predicated upon a simultaneously loaded treatment of the Jews, among others. These chapters point to the fact that historical discourses that appear to stereotype one particular group are often also complicit in reductive thinking about others. Both discussions thus serve as a reminder to other contributors and to readers that methodologies conceiving of cultural encounters in terms of the oppressive treatment of one grouping by another must not disregard the hidden oppression of other Others, those groups that may, temporarily, go unremarked given a particular thematic focus.

Seeking out less one-dimensional manifestations of the German-Islamic encounter in the period are the contributions by Yomb May and James Hodkinson. May accepts the received view that Goethe's *West-östlicher Divan* is a formal and thematic literary experiment synthesizing Western and Eastern culture across religious, cultural, and linguistic divides. The experiment, though, has mixed results. Building on existing scholarship, May warns that the modern reader risks overlooking the colonial tendencies of Goethe's endeavor, given contemporary enthusiasm for the poet's apparently enlightened stance on matters intercultural. The Enlightenment, however, was itself complicit in the process of devaluing non-European cultures and religions, while flying the flag of ostensible universalism: May reminds us that Goethe is part of this tradition, as the poet's own comments in his notes on the *Divan,* his lectures on the subject, and other letters from the period show. The work is still of value for us today, particularly given its openness to its apparent Other in the form of Islam and the modern world's apparent anxiety about an alleged clash of civilizations. That value is only to be found, however, if postcolonial techniques are used to demonstrate both the strengths and the weaknesses of Goethe's poetic achievement.

James Hodkinson examines how Romantic thought and literature thinks and rethinks the Christian-Islamic encounter with varying outcomes. Romantic theoretical writing might seem to promise a more flexible image of Islam, given its apparent distaste for static, dogmatic categories of thought, though in practice both (the later) Friedrich Schlegel and, perhaps disappointingly, the theologian Schleiermacher ultimately stereotype and subordinate Islam to their own vision of Christendom-cum-Christianity. It is rather in the realm of literary practice that Romanticism becomes more progressive, through poetic experimentation with concepts such as "identity" and "intersubjective communication," and so the prose fiction of Novalis (*Heinrich von Ofterdingen*) begins to open out a dialogue between Muslim and Christian subjects. Yet even then Hodkinson returns to the later Romanticism of E. T. A. Hoffmann to find in his story *Das Sanctus* a less dialectical narrative of Muslim-Christian conflict, in which Christian Europeans triumph on various levels: Romanticism offers a typically ambivalent vision of the encounter.

Of course, there is a brand of literature that is predicated upon actual experience of the alternative culture, namely travel literature. For someone writing about Turkey, the Middle or Far East, or North Africa in the nineteenth century or earlier the act of travel was a serious, perhaps life-threatening enterprise, as becomes clear in the contribution by Jeffrey Morrison, who deals with the often undercover travel of a Swiss agent of the British Africa Association. Surprisingly, given the disturbing implications of exotic travel, the reports and itineraries produced often betray a striking lack of serious engagement with different cultures. Morrison's findings sensitize us to a wider issue, for many of the writers dealt with throughout this volume exhibit narratorial attitudes that mirror the common prejudices of their age, apparently in an unreflecting manner unmediated by positive experience. Once again, however, this is not always the case and in the chapters that follow a number of works come to light, which demonstrate varying degrees of serious engagement with Islam, despite the fact that their authors, eras and ideological origins might lead one to expect otherwise.

The one certainty is that almost any view of the German-Muslim encounter, whether synchronic or diachronic, whether at the level of politics or at the level of literature, reveals a highly problematized moment of interface. What methods are scholars to use, though, to examine such complexity? German Studies has equipped itself with the theoretical tools that enable a more differentiated understanding of such encounters as they manifest in culture. Fine work has been conducted by scholars both in German-language *Germanistik* and in anglophone German Studies dealing critically, for instance, with German-language treatments of eighteenth- and nineteenth century European colonial experiences, and studies have been made into how contemporary German-language culture is codetermined by the works of immigrant writers not seen as conventionally German.[6] The subject matter of this collection has required many of its contributors to pursue a number of theoretical refinements.

The history of encounters between European cultures and the Islamic world has been placed within various theoretical frameworks by cultural historians since the late 1970s. Within this tradition, Islam has been subsumed, both helpfully and unhelpfully, into the wider concept of the "Orient." In this context, the "Orient" refers to a vast sprawling set of geographical, cultural, ethnic, and religious associations generated by eighteenth- and nineteenth-century European cultures, generally understood as including the regions of the Middle East, Africa, and the Far East, with their exotic, darker-skinned peoples, who were in essence culturally and racially "Other" to Europeans and for the most part adherents of other fanatical or heathen religions. The seminal work in this field—one to which many contributors in this volume refer both critically and with admiration—has to be Edward Said's *Orientalism* (1977). Those interested in German-language discourses on the so-called Orient have been generally critical of Said's lack of attention to this area, self-confessed though this may be (*O*, 17–19). Of course, he does engage with some of the more obvious points of interface between German culture and Middle-Eastern and Asian culture in *Orientalism*. Goethe, for instance, whom he presents as a "gifted enthusiast" among Orientalists, receives the fullest treatment, particularly his collection of poems the *West-östlicher Divan*. Said, of course, applies his model to Goethe, emphasizing within the collection the positive mysticization of the Middle East (particularly Persia), as cradle or origin of humanity, to which one "always returned" (*O*, 167) and which functioned as a "form of release" for the Western mind, an opportunity for Westerners to experience the "completion and confirmation of everything one had imagined" (*O*, 167). But Said has by no means had the last word on his subject.

A swath of Germanists continue to enrich the debate on how German thinkers and writers engaged with and represented their fantasy of the Orient. This involves both broadening the scope of German culture to be considered and refining the approach, such that idealized representations of the East are not simply seen as homogeneous products of Western colonial power. Most recently, Todd Kontje's *German Orientalisms* (2004) places itself directly in dialogue with Said, self-consciously building on Said's *Orientalism* yet offering, according to the book's sleeve notes, a "more nuanced version as seen through the lens of German literature of the last thousand years." Not only is Kontje's scope specifically German, but it also stretches from the medieval to the contemporary period. Acknowledging Said's obvious point that, given its diffuse political structure prior to 1871, Germany had no colonial interest in Asia or the Middle East, he asserts that the "very lack of a unified nation-state and the absence of empire contributed to the development of a particularly German Orientalism. German writers oscillated between identifying their country with the rest of Europe against the Orient and allying themselves with selected parts of the East against the West" (*GO*, 2–3).

Indeed, for Kontje it is often the more cultural-scholarly leanings of German Orientalist traditions that allowed for the development of such divergent forms of Orientalism, rather than the political and economically driven encounters of Britain and France. Kontje's readings of these tendencies in the Enlightenment and post-Enlightenment periods, for example, reveals a "compensatory Eurocentricism" (demarcating a European Germany from the East), yet also emergent traditions of "anti-semitic Indo-Germanicism" (*GO*, 2–3) growing throughout the long nineteenth century. The author can thus map out a plurality of specifically German "Orientalisms," free of geographical specificity, whereby each serves a differing function at different points throughout the history of German nation-building. The breadth of the study is impressive, examining in chronological order Wolfram's *Parzival*, Grimmelshausen's *Simplicissimus*, then Herder, Novalis, Goethe, and later Thomas Mann's *Zauberberg*, though also looking at themes in German writing on the (Middle) East across epochs, taking in Eichendorff, Gustav Freytag, and Günter Grass and even looking at migrant writers, such as Özdamar, working within contemporary Germany.

In all of these increasingly subtle studies of German constructions of the "Orient" the encounter with Islam has often remained within that wider category and has not developed as a focus of study in its own right.[7] Edward Said looks at a range of manifestations of Islam, examining a number of Western responses to Islam, from among others Napoleon's perhaps impressionistic admiration for the faith to the serious European philological engagements with the religion of the nineteenth century, including William Robertson Smith's attempts to demythologize the religion (*O*, 235–36). There may well be a case for examining how European encounters with Islam are marked by the same broader idealizing and demonizing tendencies inherent to Orientalist discourses and traditions. In focusing, for instance, on one particular eighteenth-century attempt to move beyond the non-dialectical image of Islam-as-Other, namely Herder's *Ideen zur Philosophie der Menschheit* (1784–91), Said shows how that text advances the notion of the author as a sensitive observer who has "sacrificed his prejudices to *Einfühlung*" (*O*, 118)—a kind of "historical sympathy"—who can in fact "breach the doctrinal walls erected between the West and Islam and see hidden elements of kinship between himself and the Orient" (*O*, 118). This approach Said identifies with other forms of ostensible Western sympathies for Islam, which he criticizes for being "usually selective" and ultimately difficult to disentangle from the "entire range of pre-Romantic and Romantic representations of the Orient as exotic locale" (*O*, 118). This may well be a fair assessment of the brief and still arguably Eurocentric snapshot of Western-Islamic relations offered to us by Herder, but this reading, typical of Said's process of argument, seems bound always to identify representations of Islam with a wider and ideologically charged product of Western discourse.

Kontje also considered representations of Islam as a function of larger historical discourses, examining for instance how medieval texts sought to construct a notion of a Christian Europe vis-à-vis a heathen Muslim East (*GO*, 15–32). In doing so, however, he started to unravel the notion of Islam from Orientalist discourse and look at ways writers such as Wolfram von Eschenbach and later Novalis represented religious difference with some subtlety and sophistication (*GO*, 33–101). To consider European, or, specifically, German representations of Islam solely as by-products of a larger Orientalist project is to run the risk of overlooking those instances, however scarce they might be, in which Western discourse attempts to represent Islam as evolving beyond stereotypical "functions," attempts to enter into dialogue with Muslims and to afford them communicative rights of their own. Kontje's approach of considering representations of Islam both within an Orientalist concept, and as a discourse in its own right, represents a welcome refinement of the debate—one that has become characteristic of many of the contributions in this volume. This introduction, then, does not seek to belittle the findings of critics working on European Orientalism in the broader sense or to rail against the Foucauldian method they often employ.[8] Indeed, throughout the volume, Said's work remains a useful reminder of how easily discourses produced in the (German-speaking) West can relapse into modes of writing that functionalize the Islamic world—even with apparently benevolent purposes. Used in the contemporary context the term "Orient," together with the adjective "oriental," is highly problematic, for it seems hopelessly outdated, generalizing, and crassly ideological, especially when used indiscriminately, seemingly without an awareness of historical contextualization. In many cases though, our contributors use the term frequently: Cyril Edwards refers to it, and Yomb May's chapter on Goethe is littered with references. It should be noted, however, that all of our contributors are acutely aware of the provenance and problematic nature of the term: they choose to use it if it was used explicitly by the authors they are dealing with and seems in certain cases inseparable from their writing about Islam.

This introduction does not seek to open out a theoretical meta-debate, nor does it seek to forge some spurious ideological or methodological unity between the volume's chapter. In fact, the chapters display a quite divergent set of approaches to their common theme, some of which might be usefully mapped out here. While certain contributions privilege the close hermeneutic reading of primary texts in historical context over any form of theoretical discussion at all, others make reference to Said and Kontje[9] or mobilize other contemporary theoretical trends within scholarship. Where the focus is on aspects of Islam in travel writing, it is no surprise that appeals are made to a number of theorists. Clifford Geertz's insights from the field of ethnography are mentioned on a number of occasions.[10] Geertz's work highlights the importance of the notion of "thick description," the move by twentieth-century Western ethnographers to develop a theory and method of writing about encounters between cultures in a mode that includes a multitude of perspectives and copious detail (hence "thick") in an attempt to move beyond the limiting, ideologically selective writing about culture that characterized colonialism: insights offered by Geertz help enrich Yomb May's criticism of Goethe's quasi-ethnographic aspirations, for example.[11] The cultural-theoretical work of anthropologist James Clifford is also of importance for this collection.[12] Clifford not only explodes the myth that traveling to encounter another culture grants the traveler special access to an essence of the culture observed but also asserts that both the home culture of the writer and the target culture written about are not fixed and essential structures but constructed and contingent upon language (67). Encounters between cultures involve identities that are constantly in flux; they demand a more complex understanding of the literary self, be it Christian, Muslim, or otherwise, as it conceives and represents both itself and the "target" culture that it is observing though travel.[13]

As the focus of the chapters shifts toward contemporary culture, there arises a range of complex issues, which at times require theoretical underpinning. There are the questions of the hybridity of German-Muslim identity, the poetic agency of Muslim writers within the German language, the status of Muslim writers as artists working within so-called "minority literatures," and the poetic strategies they employ to articulate themselves in that context. In examining these issues our contributors appeal to a range of theoretical approaches. Homi K. Bhabha's work receives several mentions: his much-lauded though not uncontroversial book *The Location of Culture* has become synonymous with this notion of cultures in "hybrid" forms.[14] When applied to (post)colonial culture, this model allows us to think of the identities of colonizers and colonized as already complex and in flux at the point of encounter: thus we need no longer think of such encounters as collisions of simple opposites such as black and white, Eastern and Western—or think of encounters as a unilateral process whereby one party exercises power over another.[15] On other occasions appeals are made to the twentieth-century French thinker Giles Deleuze and the notion of "minor" authors in his work with Félix Guattari. A range of Muslim writers are treated in this way by Margaret Littler, who does not suggest that they are "representative" of a minority community or, indeed, of minor canonical relevance but rather points out that their writing can be seen to challenge dominant paradigms of German identity and culture. In chapter 9 Kate Roy uses Deleuzian thought as a means of examining how certain Muslim writers opt for (and against) making German work for them by "overloading" their use of the language; she describes overloading as a process in which "the grammatical constants of the major language are repeated and varied, sometimes under the influence of other languages, to the extent that their dynamics create a multitude of voices that deterritorialize German."[16]

Despite the range of approaches and material dealt with in this volume, the chapters nevertheless show certain unities of purpose and approach. First, they address the need in scholarship to continue focusing on representations of Islam within German-language cultures, and to do so in a context that is distinct from, if at times related to, the process and canon of what has become called "Orientalism." Second, where the chapters seek to use theory to illuminate their material, they do not privilege that discussion in a manner that neglects aesthetic texts; indeed, close readings of primary textual sources are in the forefront of the argument. The volume's aim as a whole is to show how German-language cultural representations of Islam neither uniquely misrepresent, nor indeed uniquely favor, that faith vis-à-vis other European traditions. The chapters seek to shed light on the pluralist nature of the relationship between Islam and German culture, highlighting its continuities and discontinuities, its traditions of mutual antagonism and its ideals of peaceful coexistence, and reconstructing, where they exist, dialogical relationships between the two worlds, though also showing how limited, monological thinking and writing is rarely far away. It aims not only to offer an addition and a corrective to scholarship but also to demonstrate the inadequacy of those contemporary media, political, and intellectual discourses that would have us believe in a "clash of civilizations"[17] between the West and Islam: a model that can sometimes be appropriate but certainly is not sophisticated enough to convey the complex relations involved.

Notes

[1] See Edward W. Said, *Orientalism*. 3rd ed. (London: Penguin, 2003). A critique of Said's methodology and findings, as well as his tendency to subsume Islam into his notion of the Orient, follows later in this introduction. Further references to this work are given in the text of the introduction using the abbreviation *O* and the page number.

[2] The process of assimilation and the associated processes of cross-fertilization between cultures have not been unproblematic. The relationship between Germany and Turkey as nation states, and between German-Turkish Muslims and ethnically German citizens of the Federal Republic, is an interesting example. It would be nice to claim with confidence that the naming of Essen and Istanbul as European capitals of culture for 2010 will mark a watershed in relations between

Germany, Europe, and the Islamic world. After all, Essen, at the heart of the Ruhrgebiet, is strongly identified with the postwar rise in German industry, and as that industry developed it became the most powerful magnet for Turkish (and other) guest workers. Essen became an interculture. Istanbul for its part could once be seen as marking the frontier between East and West. Although one part of the city was located geographically in Europe and the other in Asia, it was viewed from Europe as culturally unequivocally Eastern, exotic. Now the government based there sees itself substantially, particularly economically, in European terms and desires greater financial and political integration with the EU. There is a multicultural, hybrid future implicit in the naming of these two cities as European capitals of culture.

[3] Rachel MagShamhráin, chapter 8 in this volume, 159.

[4] See Todd Kontje, *German Orientalisms* (Ann Arbor: U of Michigan P, 2004). Kontje briefly examines Feirefiz and feels that Wolfram's treatment of the figure reveals "a utopian Christianity that simultaneously effaces and embraces difference; one that is at once a totalizing vision of a Christian world that transcends history, and one that recognizes and accepts existing differences" (32). Further references to this work are given in the text using the abbreviation *GO* and the page number.

[5] See Katherine Roy's chapter in this volume (chapter 9). The concept of "overloading" language in this way is a term adduced by Roy from Giles Deleuze and Félix Guattari: see also the overview of theoretical approaches adopted by contributors to this volume, later in the introduction, 13–15.

[6] Notable scholars have shown how the project of constructing German national identity in the eighteenth century was in fact reliant upon fantasies of colonial experience—fantasies that in some cases would provide the blueprints for Germany's "real" colonial escapades in Africa and the Americas. On this see Susanne Zantop, *Colonial Fantasies: Conquest, Family and Nation in Precolonial Germany, 1770–1870* (Durham, NC, and London: Duke UP, 1997). Many fine discussions of the role that migrant writers have played in the complex formations of contemporary German culture have appeared in print. On the role of Turkish writers in German language culture, see David Horrocks and Eva Kolinsky, eds., *Turkish Culture in German Society Today* (Providence, RI: Berghahn, 1996). For a collection of essays dedicated to more complex transcultural issues involved in reading migrant literature in German, see *GLL, Special Edition: Crossing Boundaries,* ed. James Jordan, vol. 59, issue 4, Oct. 2006.

[7] See also: Andre Polaschegg, *Der andere Orientalismus. Regeln deutsch-Morgenländischer Imagination im 19. Jahrhundert* (Berlin/New York: de Gruyter, 2005). In this wide ranging study of nineteenth-century German Orientalism, Andrea Polaschegg was concerned to move beyond Said's findings, which she feels propounded a view of the Orient dominated by the Arabic-Islamic world, arguing instead that German culture envisaged a culturally and geographically much wider Orient also embracing the Far East (82–83). As a result, the Islamic world played a lesser role in the nineteenth-century, German consciousness of the Orient than had been thought hitherto: such thinking, argues Polaschegg, is much more a function of our current obsession with finding Western representations of Islam

from earlier periods (96–97). Whilst Polaschegg's attempt to construct a wider Germanic Orient is certainly convincing and well-researched, her argument does not preclude the existence of an important, nineteenth-century German language discourse on Islam which exists in its own right, whether connected to debates on Orientalism or not.

⁸ Perhaps it was the Foucauldian methodology underlying Said's earlier work that helped to produce a more static vision of Islam as the disempowered and misrepresented object of Western cultural power. For Foucault the history of culture is a history of discourse, more particularly a history of the use of language from a privileged position of power to construct norms of culture. The discursive agent is empowered to represent itself and its others, a state of affairs that renders those groups without power as limited stereotypes. Said applies this model directly through reference to Foucault's *The Archaeology of Knowledge* (1969) and *Discipline and Punish* (1975) (*O*, 3), and applies it to the processes that gave rise to the construction of the Orient by Western discourse and resulted in precisely this "disempowerment" of its peoples: ". . . because of Orientalism the Orient was not (and is not) a free subject of thought or action" (*O*, 3). Although, unlike Foucault, Said does believe more in the "determining imprint" of individual authors upon the history of discourse (*O*, 23), that is, the power of writers to change the history of cultures in representation, he does tend to homogenize his findings, finding diverse forms of Orientalism, including an Islamic Orient, though presenting these traditions as functioning as the product of an overarching Western Orientalist project.

⁹ See, for instance, Dan Wilson's key essay, chapter 4 in this volume, 73–75.

¹⁰ Clifford Geertz, *The Interpretation of Cultures: Selected Essays* (New York: Basic Books, 2005).

¹¹ See Yomb May's essay, chapter 5 of this volume, 97.

¹² James Clifford, *Routes: Travel and Translation in the Late Twentieth Century* (Cambridge, MA: Harvard UP, 1997), 66. Certain of Clifford's ideas resonate with those of Iain Chambers, whose work is also cited in this volume. See Iain Chambers, *Migrancy, Culture, Identity* (London and New York: Routledge, 1994).

¹³ On this see Clifford's earlier work: James Clifford, *The Predicament of Culture: Twentieth-Century Ethnography, Literature and Art* (Cambridge, MA: Harvard UP, 1988), 10.

¹⁴ Homi Bhabha, *The Location of Culture* (London: Routledge, 1994)

¹⁵ See Bhabha, *The Location of Culture*, 159–60. The ramifications of this notion arguably allow critics to conceive of migrant Muslims working as minority writers within majority cultures as complex individuals, simultaneously empowered and disempowered by diverse traditions.

¹⁶ Both Margaret Littler and Katherine Roy make good use of Gilles Deleuze and Félix Guattari, *A Thousand Plateaus: Capitalism and Schizophrenia*, trans. Brian Massumi (London and New York: Continuum, 2004).

¹⁷ Samuel P. Huntington, *The Clash of Civilizations and the Remaking of World Order* (New York: Simon & Schuster, 1996).

1: "cristen, ketzer, heiden, jüden": Questions of Identity in the Middle Ages

Timothy R. Jackson

AN INTERESTING ASPECT OF THE MIDDLE AGES is the way in which big theological or philosophical ideas (at that time the distinction is not always clear-cut), find their way from the Latin discourse of scholars into vernacular texts intended for a very different audience, non-scholarly and frequently made up of members of the laity. The discursive and narrative texts that will be discussed below are mainly spiritual in orientation, were produced by a mixture of lay and religious authors, and demonstrate a wide range of approaches: didactic, gnomic, homiletic, and allegorical. It is also interesting to see how, while the broad parameters of a big idea may be laid down by ecclesiastical orthodoxy, the details that fill out the resulting schema can vary widely. In this instance, while the Middle Ages may be characterized by an acute awareness of religious differences, explicit reactions to these were less monolithic and more nuanced than one might expect.

Samuel Beckett, when asked whether he was an Englishman, is said to have replied, "Au contraire." Nor do Canadians like to be taken for Americans, New Zealanders for Australians, Austrians for Germans. We attach emotional importance to differences that distinguish us from other people. Similarities are important too of course, but we seem in particular to use all kinds of differences between ourselves and other people, not just to establish the otherness of the Other, but also more positively to define our own place in the world, in a way that Hall associates with the thinking of Saussure: "'Difference' matters because it is essential to meaning."[1] Differences can thus be a means to self-understanding, building-blocks in the construction of an identity. But for some of us the need to define ourselves in terms of what we are *not* seems to be particularly strong. A dependence on distinctions between ourselves and others, defined say as contrasting religious and/or ethnic groups, can acquire neurotic proportions, such that the distinctions are drawn in the starkest terms and religion or ethnicity becomes the basis for social and political divisions. This has potentially disastrous consequences, be they the massacres suffered or perpetrated by the Crusaders or the horrendous events of the Shoah. Gilman refers to "the distinction between pathological stereotyping and the stereotyping all of us need to do to preserve our illusion of control over the self and the world."[2]

Of course every religion, and every subgroup within each religion, defines itself at least partly in terms of the distance between itself and others. Hence the use of terms like "non-Catholic" or "gentile." Heresies arise when the gap between personal beliefs and the prevailing orthodoxy is so great that it cannot be bridged—though of course it is the forces of orthodoxy that decide what is indeed heretical. Individuals must decide for themselves how important such religious differences are—and it may be that to exaggerate their importance is no more dangerous than to ignore them. For to be Catholic or Protestant is not the same thing; to be Christian or Muslim is not the same thing; to be Sunni or Shia is not the same thing.

From the twelfth century on, Western European philosophy "was characterized by extraordinary concern with boundaries, definitions, self-definitions, and classifications."[3] Moreover, as Krings writes, "Der Begriff der Ordnung schließt den der Unterscheidung ein; d.h. es ist keine Ordnung ohne eine Unterscheidung der Glieder denkbar."[4] And he refers to Bonaventura's assertion, "ubi ordo ibi distinctio" (where there is order there is distinction),[5] which in turn echoes Augustine from many centuries before, "ordo absque distinctione non est" (without distinction there is no order), which suggests that the awareness of the connection between difference and meaning long predates Saussure. When combined with the medieval preoccupation with patterns, particularly patterns that can be rendered numerically, this leads to statements like Freidank's: "Got hât drîer slahte kint, / daz kristen, juden, heiden sint" (God has three kinds of children; that is, Christians, Jews and heathens).[6] He concedes that all three religions believe that they possess the true faith—"sie wellent alle haben reht" (they all wish to be right; 10,22)—but is in no doubt as to where the truth lies: "swer mit gote wil bestân / der muoz kristen glouben hân" (Whoever wishes for the support of God must possess the Christian faith; 11,1–2).

At one point in his *Goldene Schmiede*, a poem in praise of the Virgin, Konrad von Würzburg interprets the four rivers of paradise (Genesis 2:10–14) allegorically as representing the fourfold consolation of Mary that is available to "cristen ketzer heiden jüden."[7] By adding heretics to the pattern he produces a tetrad that delineates the horizon of the religious world as it was understood by Western Europeans in the Middle Ages. But whereas Konrad does not overtly call attention to distinctions here, Brun von Schonebeck orders the tetrad differently in his allegorical interpretation of the two children, Esau and Jacob, struggling in the womb of Rebekah (Genesis 25:21–23). He identifies them as two peoples, "of whom one shall be stronger than the other," on the one hand the Christians and on the other:

di ketzer di juden di heiden,
di wil ich nicht von in scheiden,
wen si sin an dem ungelouben ein,
dar an ist zwivel dokein.[8]

[heretics, Jews, heathens,
whom I do not wish to distinguish from one another,
for they are one in their unbelief—
of that there is no doubt.]

Occasionally, evaluative distinctions are made within the non-Christian group. Thus in the *Millstätter Exodus* the heathens are explicitly subordinated to the Jews, for example where God distinguishes between the latter and the Egyptians with the words, "ich gibe diseme liute / gnâde uor heidinisker diete" (I bestow my grace upon this people rather than the heathens).[9] And regarding the same text, Gutfleisch-Ziche points to "die Charakterisierung des jüdischen Volkes als adelige Kriegerkaste, die sich im Kampf mit den militärisch beeindruckenden, aber diabolischen Heiden befindet."[10]

For purposes of comparison and contrast all four members of the tetrad will be considered below, but with a concentration on the "heiden." However, the term "heathen" will be understood not in its modern sense of "polytheistic," but, following the texts, as meaning everything that was not Christian or Jewish. And within "heidenschaft" Muslims in particular will be considered, rather than, say, the Greeks or Romans. It is true that for medieval Europe Islam was not yet a political threat but a military opponent in a distant theater of war[11]—though one text or another may have been intended as direct or indirect propaganda for the Crusades. Nor was Islam, any more than Judaism, a serious religious threat: the likelihood of conversion was small. And yet for producers of Christian literature such as the author of the *Millstätter Exodus* Muslims are frequently the target of outright hostility.

That said, however, vernacular Christian texts of the Middle Ages show an alarming lack of knowledge about heathens and/or a cavalier readiness to misrepresent their belief systems. There are admittedly scholarly writers, such as Peter the Venerable, Gulielmus Durandus, and Ralph Higden, who take a genuine interest in the realities of paganism—Durandus and Higden, for example, were aware that Muslims did not worship idols.[12] However, in the German-language texts that are under discussion we regularly find inappropriate and/or confused lists of the gods in whom the monotheistic Muslims are alleged to believe. Bruder Philipp in his *Marienleben* tells the reader/listener that when, on the flight from Herod, the infant Jesus destroyed a number of Egyptian idols,

Jupiter und Saturnîus,
Mars und her Mercurîus
und ander göter lesterlîche
lâgen ûf dem esteriche [*sic*].[13]

[Jupiter and Saturn,
Mars and Sir Mercury,
and other shameful gods
lay on the floor]

In the Spanish setting of Charlemagne's struggle with the heathen in Pfaffe Konrad's *Rolandslied* there is mention of Mars, Jouinus, Saturnus, and Appollo, as well as Machmet and Teruagant;[14] and in the Palestine of Reinbot von Durne's *Der heilige Georg* the heathens pray to Apollo, Ercules, Tervigant, Jupiter, and Mahmet.[15] Rudolf von Ems, in his *Barlaam und Josaphat,* offers the standard division into Jews, Christians, and heathens and then subdivides the heathens into Chaldeans, Greeks, and Egyptians.[16] But, while he ascribes an unexpectedly accurate list of divinities to the Egyptians — "Typhôn unde Îsis, / Ôrus unde ouch Ôsiris" (6425–26) — the Greeks are said to worship a jumble of (mainly) Roman deities, Greek heroes, and mythical figures like Hercules and Adonis, Medusa, and Thetis. Nor was there even unanimity as to who the heathens were; for example, in Konrad von Würzburg's romance *Partonopier und Meliur* the Irish king Fursin — doubtless on account of the geographical remoteness of his origins — is described as "ein edel Sarrazîn, / gar hövesch unde kurteis" (a noble Saracen, most courtly and chivalrous).[17]

In other words, whatever the interest in distinguishing between Christian and heathen, texts intended for non-scholarly circles show little interest in making accurate distinctions within heathendom. Nor was the categorical distinction between heathen and Jew always seen as clearly as it might have been. Camille illustrates this with a French instance: in his *Jeu de Saint Nicolas* Jean Bodel refers to non-Christian places of worship indiscriminately as "synagogue" or "mahommerie" — the latter term being derived from the name of the Prophet (*GI,* 130). A quite different religious and historical context offers a comparable misnomer: in 1595 a raiding party of Spaniards attacked and destroyed a number of villages in Cornwall. On their return home it was reported that they had forborne to sack a "mosque" because mass had previously been celebrated in it; this will have been an originally Catholic place of worship taken over by the reformed Church of England, which had been established some decades earlier. It is difficult to know whether in such cases one is dealing with genuine ignorance, or an inability to think in new categories, or a deliberate, polemical attempt to deny the validity of an institution or grouping by asserting its irreducible otherness.

For whatever reason, the claim that Muslims worshipped idols was widespread in the Middle Ages. Thus in his *Marienleben* Wernher der Schweizer recounts the same episode from the flight into Egypt.[18] The Holy Family is forced to spend the night in front of a heathen temple ("abgot hus"; 4040), and the next morning it is discovered that the idols that it contained (no fewer than 350, none identified by name) are lying smashed on the floor of the building. At first the local inhabitants suspect that the gods of the sea have defeated the gods of the land in a battle. However, despite the fact that in the Judaeo-Christian tradition part of the definition of graven images is that "They have mouths, but they speak not" (Psalms 135:16), when the fallen idols are interrogated they are able to explain that the God of all gods is among them and "Er ist war und wir gelogen" (4126; He is true and we false).

Once the assumption of Muslim idol-worship is made, then the Christian imagination goes to work, and we are presented in text and image with idols possessing human bodies and animal heads, idols with three heads, idols that require child sacrifice, and the like. In a manuscript of the *Expositio in Apocalypsim* by the Franciscan Alexander von Bremen, Mohammed himself is represented as a dog-headed god. It is likely that such accusations of polytheism and idol-worship will have owed less to contemporary empirical observation than to Old Testament narratives (*GI*, 138, 141, and 158). They were inaccurate and unjust, but from the Muslim perspective they were also perverse. Freidank asserts that Jews and heathens are unable to comprehend the concept of the unity of the Trinity—though he concedes that for Christians too it is nothing less than a "wunder."[19] However, Muslims in their turn not only insisted on their own monotheism but regarded their opponents as worshippers of a trinity of false gods. Their own resistance to the Crusaders could thus be characterized by the Arab historian Ibn Al-Qalanisi in the mid-twelfth century as a "battle against the polytheist and heretic Franks."[20] And another historian, Imad ad-Din, recording the slaughter of Christian prisoners (members of the hated orders of Templars and Hospitallers) by Saladin's forces in 1187, interpreted the actions of one of the execution-ers thus: "I saw how he killed unbelief to give life to Islam, and destroyed polytheism to build monotheism" (*AH*, 139). Moreover, it was not they themselves but the Christians who produced countless graven images for veneration, as observed by the same Imad ad-Din in his description of the Church of the Resurrection: "pictures of the apostles conversing, Popes with their histories, monks in their cells . . . effigies of the Madonna . . . of the ox and the ass" (*AH*, 148–49). But here too Durandus is ready to acknowledge that not all Christians recognize the vital distinctions between signifier and signified (for example, between statue and saint) and thus between an acceptable *figura* and an unacceptable idol—distinctions without which Christian iconographic practice is indeed rendered idolatrous (*GI,* 207–8).

According to Christian orthodoxy salvation can not come without belief in Jesus, but in medieval texts the expression of this doctrine could vary widely. The image of the four rivers of paradise as presented by Konrad von Würzburg is potentially positive: through her son, Mary makes the possibility of divine grace available in principle to all four religious categories. But not every text is so clear-cut. At the start of his sermon *Von drin mûren* Berthold von Regensburg declares unequivocally:

> Ez gêt niht weges zem himelrîche ûz der heidenschaft noch ûz der jüden ê, noch ûz der ketzerîe gêt niht weges zuo dem himelrîche.[21]

> [No path leads to the kingdom of heaven from heathendom, nor from Judaism, nor does a path lead from heresy to the kingdom of heaven.]

The three allegorical walls of the title—one made of silk, one made of iron, and a heavenly wall—defend the allegorical field ("acker"; 357,9) of Christianity from the other three groupings. The silken wall represents the church, which enables Christians to protect themselves spiritually,

> ob in jüden oder heiden oder ketzer den kristenglouben leiden wolten, daz sie den künnen widerstên unde sich vor ungelouben gehüeten künnen (361,7–9)

> [if Jews or heathens or heretics wished to damage the Christian faith, that they may resist them and defend themselves from faithlessness]

The second wall is the iron sword of secular justice. This the Pope grants to the emperor, so that if anybody should be so disobedient as to break through the silken wall of the church,

> daz diu îsenîniu mûre dannoch dâ vor sî unde den acker schirme vor jüden unde vor heiden unde vor ketzern (362,28–30)

> [the wall of iron is still before it to protect the field from Jews and heathens and heretics]

Finally, as regards the third protective wall, God has given everybody a guardian angel:

> Er hât ze . . . einem iegelîchen kristenmenschen sunderlîchen einen hüeter und einen engel gegeben, unde halt ieslîchem heiden unde ketzer unde jüden unde slafênen unde tatânen [. . .] (365,22–34)

> [To each individual Christian he has given a guardian [and] angel, and indeed to each heathen and heretic and Jew and Slav and Tartar.]

On the other hand, however,

Dâ hât ouch iegelîchez einen tiuvel: der bræche im sâ zehant den
hals abe wan diu huote des engels, swenne er eine tôtsünde getæte.
(365,36–38)

[Each one has a devil as well, who, but for the protection of the
angel, would instantly break his neck, should he ever commit a mortal sin.]

The reason for this equality of treatment lies in the fact that not just
Christians but heathens, heretics, and Jews "menschen sint unde nâch gote
gebildet sint" (366,2; are humans and made in God's image). It would also
seem to suggest, along with Konrad von Würzburg, that none are categori-
cally excluded from God's grace. And indeed Karl's first victory in Pfaffe
Konrad's *Rolandslied,* the capture of the Spanish town of Tortolose, is followed by mass conversion and baptism (349–60); and in Reinbot's *Georg,*
Queen Alexandrina exhorts a heathen crowd to convert by claiming that,
when asked on his deathbed how Jews, Christians, and heathens would fare
in the future, Mohammed replied, "mit wazzer muoz man genesen" (4287;
one must be saved by water), which she interprets as baptism.

Hugo von Trimberg tells an exemplum — *Von einem künige, der
hete vier süne* (Concerning a king who had three sons) — that treats similar themes, but with less generosity.[22] When a wise and virtuous king
dies, leaving four sons, the eldest wishes to inherit the throne, but he is
opposed by the others. The late king's privy councillor proposes to settle
the dispute by having the corpse exhumed and set up against a wall, and
whichever son shoots an arrow at it most accurately will be king. The
first son's arrow strikes the right hand of the dead king, the second the
mouth, the third the heart. The fourth son, in an act that recalls the judgment of Solomon, refuses to shoot at his father, whereupon the princes of
the realm install him as king.

Here too an allegorical interpretation is offered. The king is God, who
is continually being martyred by three kinds of people, namely "Juden,
ketzer und heiden" (24317), who are children of an inconstant mother
("unstête muoter"; 24325), that is to say unbelief, and are therefore not
his true inheritors ("niht rehte erbe süne"; 24319). Then we are told:

Kristen, ketzer, juden, heiden,
Der liebe gein gote ist underscheiden (24331–32)

[Christians, heretics, Jews, heathens
Are differentiated in their love for God]

for it is the heathens who have struck the father's hand, in that they have
always mutilated and hanged the messengers of God (24333), while the

Jews have shot him in the mouth by rejecting his teachings (24337), and heretics have shot him in the heart by defiling Christian belief (24347). Only faithful Christians, who have drunk the milk of true belief, are thereby his true inheritors (24353).

Yet this same Hugo von Trimberg has no problem in recognizing the wisdom of a heathen philosopher like Aristotle (24381). More striking, though, is the case of Brun von Schonebeck, who, as he begins the sixth part of his lengthy and pious allegorical interpretation of the Song of Solomon, invokes, not the aid of the Holy Spirit or Mary or some other saint, but that of "Lachtasis."[23] It is clear from the context that he means Lachesis, the Greek Fate who spins the thread of life, and he wishes her to ensure that he will live long enough to complete his book. This allusion illustrates something of the profoundly ambiguous attitude of the Middle Ages toward specific phenomena of heathen history, mythology, and culture. The wholesale rejection of heathen religious beliefs exists side by side with a keen appreciation of many of the achievements of pagan peoples, be they literary or philosophical, military or political. And in a process referred to allegorically as the "spolia Aegyptorum," in line with phrases from the book of Exodus such as "ye shall spoil the Egyptians" (3:22, cf. 12:36), there was a readiness, if not indeed eagerness, to plunder items of that culture and accommodate the resulting booty within the Christian tradition.[24]

One example of this process is the number of cathedral portals that are decorated with the pagan signs of the zodiac and, related to these, the widespread practice of astrology with its Babylonian associations. A second example: while many early Christians thought it appropriate that a rustic style should characterize the writings of a religion fostered in its infancy by unlettered fishermen, others were sensitive to the criticism that their writings were unsophisticated and crude, and so they cultivated a stylistic elegance based on pre-Christian Roman models. And a third: a number of these classical Roman writers were also pressed into unlikely service as prophets of the coming of Christ (with, for example, passages from Virgil's fourth eclogue serving the purpose), not to mention the exploitation of the extensive Greek and Roman Sibylline prophetic traditions in the same interest. One suspects, however, that such tactics were intended to assert and buttress the claims of Christianity rather than illustrate the prescient wisdom of pagans.[25]

None of these figures are Muslims, but let us return briefly to Brun von Schonebeck. He, as one would expect from a commentator on the Song of Songs, quotes patristic and high medieval Christian authorities, such as Augustine, Ambrosius, and Bernard of Clairvaux. However, he also refers in wholly positive terms to the wisdom of Latin writers, such as "her Seneca" (2275), "meister Virgilius" (10310), "der wise meister Oracius" (Horace; 3490), and "der vil wise heide Ovidius" (2940). An interesting passage (10218–357), in which he points to the deceitfulness of the world, contains a series of rhetorical questions based on the "Ubi sunt?" topos and then explicitly brings together exemplary Christians, Jews, and heathens: "Tell me, where is the beauty of Absalom . . . the power of Pharaoh . . . the chivalry of Nero . . . ?" He goes on to praise heathen men of science, first, astronomers. He does not name them but will almost certainly have had oriental Muslim scholars in mind:

> wa sint di heiden di in den buchen
> beide tag und ouch di nacht
> di maniche stunt han irdacht?
> si waren der wisheit ein kerne,
> si larten irkennen an dem sterne,
> waz geschen wolde von geschichte,
> daz sahen si mit der ougen gesichte.[26] (10299–305)

[Where are the heathens, who studied in books night and day for many an hour? They were a kernel of wisdom, they taught how to see from the stars what Fortune would bring—they saw that with the sight of their eyes.]

And then:

> wa ist der wise heide Boecius,
> Avicenna Galyen und Johannicius?[27]
> di vunden der physiken kunst,
> si irwarben der werlde gunst. (10306–309)

[Where is the wise heathen Boethius, Avicenna, Galen, and Johannicius? They discovered the art of physic, thereby earning the gratitude of the world.]

With the mention of Avicenna as a significant contributor to the medical tradition, Brun is referring to a medieval heathen and Muslim. Earlier in the text, in an exposition of the four elements and, associated with these, the qualities of hot and cold, wet and dry, he places him as his first authority (7061).

In his *Alexander*, Rudolf von Ems asserts that history offers examples of Jews, Christians, *and* heathens who "nâch êren strebten / die wîle daz si lebten" (12949–50; who strove after honour as long as they lived) and kept to the precepts of their respective religions. They are thus models of virtuous behavior whom his contemporaries might imitate.[28] And so, as Avicenna appears as an exemplum of the Muslim scholar, Saladin (the sultan of Egypt) can be presented as an idealized Muslim ruler. In one of his *Sprüche* (35,27) Walther von der Vogelweide advises that in order to know people you must look inside them and not judge them by mere outward appearance, for, as he assures us, "vil manic môre ist innen tugende vol" (35,35; full many a Moor is inwardly full of virtues).[29] In another *Spruch* (19,17) he links Saladin and Richard Lionheart as exemplars of generosity, in contrast to the allegedly stingy Philipp von Schwaben, to whom the poem is addressed. Similarly, Bruder Werner uses Saladin to hyperbolic effect when he claims that nobody, not even Saladin, was ever more generous than Graf Wilhelm von Heunburg.[30] However, it is equally true that Saladin could be seen, for example by Joachim de Fiore, as a figure who will wage war on God's elect in the last days[31] or could be joined with Mohammed to form the apocalyptic pair Gog and Magog (*GI,* 139). A similar ambivalence can be seen in the figure of Avenier, king of India, in Rudolf's *Barlaam;* he is wise and virtuous, yet a persecutor whom the devil has led into idolatry (238–40).

Saladin was a heathen whom some of the recipients of courtly literature had met and against whom many more had fought. And if among those recipients and within the literature of their secular culture he enjoyed a reputation for chivalrous behaviour, then this can be seen to parallel the use of heathen prophets within ecclesiastical culture to support the theological claims of Christianity. It is true that the role of heathens in a text like Pfaffe Konrad's *Rolandslied* is to be cut to pieces to the greater glory of God and that the cruel heathen authority figure—king, emperor, father[32]—is a stock figure in many a legend of martyrdom, say Emperor Maximian in Konrad von Würzburg's *Pantaleon.*[33] But in a romance such as Konrad's *Partonopier und Meliur* a figure like Fursin is a dashing and sophisticated exemplar of an exotic culture, and to distinguish a worthy heathen opponent as an exemplary knight adds further luster to the European concept of chivalry; idealization of the Muslim can be a form of self-idealization.

It seems therefore that the presence and presentation of heathen figures in a text may sometimes be intended not solely to mirror important religious differences in real life but also to serve more narrowly narrative strategies, such as the clearer delineation of two sets of opponents. The cruelty of the heathens in a text like the *Rolandslied* allows the Christian heroes to appear even more heroic; the cruelty of Maximian makes clear the unshakeable faith and superhuman courage of the martyred Pantaleon. Within secular literature, on the other hand, distinctions can be minimized to the extent that an unconverted heathen—particularly if he can be presented as having been assimilated to an ethically informed code such as chivalry—can play an entirely positive role. In Rudolf von Ems's *Alexander,* the narrator reports that the young men under the command of Mazeus of Babylon are "mit zühteclîchen hovesitn / ritterlîche wol bekleit" (13234–35; chivalrously clothed in the courteous customs of the court). Thus the labels "Christian" and "heathen" are not always exclusively religious or ideological concepts: to some extent they identify motifs that can be fitted into narrative patterns.

One of the more unexpected aspects of the Christian–heathen nexus is the way in which it provides opportunities for polemics directed at Christians, both lay and clerical. Jews lived, and heretics might be suspected of living, within Christian communities in Germany and elsewhere in medieval Europe, but the overwhelming proportion of contact between Christians and heathens will have taken place in the Holy Land. In yet another *Spruch* (10,9) Walther calls on God to avenge himself on Christians and heathens, both of whom are "iuwers erbelandes vînde"[34] (enemies of the land of your inheritance), both equally deficient in their love for him — except that the heathens are at least open in the impurity of their opposition ("offenlîche unreine"; 10,14), whereas the Christians are the more impure for being surreptitious about it.

Freidank has a series of deeply pessimistic reflections on the events of the Crusade of 1228–29, led by Emperor Frederick II. He does not see the Holy Land in simplistic religio-political terms as territory from which the infidel must be driven. Rather it is a country to which deceit is innate, where neither God nor man ever experienced fidelity ("dâ got noch man nie triuwe vant"; 158,25), and this subverts every relationship within the crusading enterprise. Christians who are already there vie with the heathens in exploiting new arrivals (154,24–155,12; 156,6–15). Indeed, Freidank says, in Acre Christian and heathen cannot be told apart, for all speak heathen tongues (156,10–11); already in the previous century the Arab historian Usama had recorded the assimilation of some Franks to the surrounding culture, their practice of "living like Muslims" (*AH*, 78–79). The "Welschen" (those from Romance-speaking countries) would rather that the country remained in heathen hands than be subjugated by the Germans (163,7–12). Moreover, the Emperor's efforts are opposed not just by the heathens but by the clergy too (159,15–17), headed by Pope Gregory IX himself, for, as Freidank asks rhetorically: When previously did an emperor go on crusade under excommunication and without an army of princes? "Wâ gefuor ê keiser über mer / im banne und âne fürsten her?" (158,22–23 — cf. 157,17–20). Despite all this Frederick has redeemed the Holy Sepulchre, yet still remains excommunicate (160,16–23) — a use of ecclesiastical sanction that is so unprincipled that it puts faith itself at risk and fosters unbelief (162,4–7, 23–25). It is known that his contacts with the Sultan al-Malik al-Kamil eventually led to a guarantee of Christian access to the holy places, but all the whispered negotiation puts even the loyalty of Freidank's gnomic "ich" under strain:

Dem keiser wol gezæme,
daz 'z rûnen ende næme,
daz zer unde der soldân
nû lange hânt getân. (158,4–7)

[The emperor would do well to put an end to the whispering that he and the Sultan have long carried on.]

Gabrieli draws attention to Frederick's tolerance, "his pro-Islamic bias in political matters and his religious scepticism" (*AH,* 267). His open-mindedness is attested on the Arab side by Ibn Wasil's striking confirmation of the respect accorded to Islamic religious practice by Frederick and his nephew Manfred (271–78), while his skepticism is not unreasonable, given the evidence that the Templars and Hospitallers plotted to betray him to the Saracens. In Freidank's view, the only relationship to remain unspoiled in the Holy Land is that between man and God: the pious crusader can still reckon that his service will bring forgiveness of his sins and, should he die there, salvation: "swer dâ rehte stirbet, derst genesen" (164,2).[35]

This survey concludes with a brief consideration of the fate that awaits the different religious groups in the Last Days. For Hugo von Trimberg the outlook for three of them is bleak, for in the exemplum of the four sons they are excluded from the kingdom of the late king: "Juden, ketzer und heiden / Von dem rîche sint gescheiden."[36] According to one understanding, mankind will be divided into four categories on the Day of Judgment: two will go to heaven or hell after being judged and two will go to heaven or hell without the necessity of their even coming before the Judgment seat. While the saints will belong to the third category, the *Lucidarius* affirms that the fourth will be made up of "die ane reht gesundet hant, alse heiden, unde juden die sit Cristes geburte sint" (those who have sinned without law, such as heathens and those Jews who have lived since the birth of Christ).[37] But, as has been shown, other writers make it clear that redemption is potentially no less available to Muslims than to Christians, heretics, and Jews, albeit on the basis of conversion. Thus the gospel story of the Canaanite woman—she who pointed out that "the dogs eat of the crumbs which fall from their masters' table" (Matthew 15:27)—was interpreted as meaning that the Word was sent to the Jews first, then to the heathens.[38] Augustine had written that the Jews would ultimately be converted, and of the medieval German writers Berthold von Regensburg, for example, preached that as many Jews as survived the predations of the Antichrist would become Christian;[39] and Brun von Schonebeck offers assurance that even if at the end of time there is only one believer left—and he says that as he writes there are only a handful—all unbelievers will nevertheless embrace the Christian religion.[40] The anonymous author of *Die Erlösung* gives a list of the peoples that will be involved in this conversion; it includes "Iuden, Sarrazîne / und allez volc, waz sprâche iz kan" (Jews, Saracens and all peoples, whatever their language).[41] Heinrich von Neustadt asserts that the universal adoption of Christianity—"ein glaube gantz"[42]—will be achieved by the end of the forty-five days separating the death of the Antichrist from the Day of Judgment.

When Walther warns that a day is approaching that should fill every Christian, Jew, and heathen with dread (21,27), he is emphasizing an essential commonality rather than distinct groups. Heinrich von Neustadt similarly describes the wailing of all four confessional categories on that day, though their trepidation has varying causes: for the Jews it is their false accusations against Jesus; for the heathens their scorn for a cruci-fied God and their idolatry; for sinful Christians their bringing disgrace upon that name; for heretics their peddling of false beliefs. Heinrich sug-gests that of those who end up in hell Christians will suffer most, for they have failed to benefit from hearing daily of the works of Christ—an opportunity denied to heathens (6478–561). This idea had been dealt with more systematically by Mechthild von Magdeburg: the deepest part of hell, where the torments are greatest, will be occupied by the Chris-tians, as punishment for their willfulness. The middle section will house the Jews, lamenting that the law of Moses did not lead them to God. The heathens will fare best: bewailing the fact that they did not have a religion (by which they might have been saved) they will be assigned to the upper part, where the suffering will be least.[43]

This survey has shown how, in its treatment of heathens, medieval German literature oscillates between a cautious tolerance and outright hostility. On the one hand Walther von der Vogelweide concedes that Christians, Jews, *and* heathens serve him who sustains all living won-ders ("im dienent kristen juden unde heiden / der elliu lebenden wunder nert"; 22,16–17).[44] On the other hand, God declares to Charlemagne at the beginning of Pfaffe Konrad's *Rolandslied* that any heathens who oppose his campaign in Spain are children of the Devil and therefore damned (59–61).[45] Despite its heathen origins astrology was practiced by many in the West, yet Heinrich von Neustadt finds it as reprehensible as idolatry.[46] Nevertheless, for Walther, Konrad, and Heinrich equally, religion—whether one is Christian or Muslim—would have been an absolute distinction, whereas the twenty-first-century readiness to con-struct a personal belief system from components taken from more than one faith represents an eclecticism that the Middle Ages would have found incomprehensible.

Christianity perceived itself, or at least (in a way that perhaps does parallel aspects of early twenty-first-century experience) portrayed itself, as under constant threat. Muslims were one of a range of histori-cal or contemporary countertypes to Christians, which also included the Greeks, Romans, Chaldeans, Jews, and heretics. The protection of belief was paramount, and anything other than adherence to strict orthodoxy could be painted in the most lurid terms: the idolatry of the heathen; the ritual murder practiced by the Jew; the sexual depravity of the heretic. Moreover, the correlation between ethnicity and religion that character-izes most of the encounters between Christian and non-Christian will, in the case of the clash between Christianity and Islam, have been exacer-bated by the crusading experience. Indeed, given that only the Muslims, as instanced by the Saracens, represented a significant opponent to the interests of medieval Christendom, it is the more remarkable that the tolerant view found expression at all.

Notes

[1] Stuart Hall, "The Spectacle of the 'Other,'" in *Representation: Cultural Representations and Signifying Practices,* ed. S. H. (London: SAGE Publications, 1997), 223–90; here 234–38.

[2] Sander L. Gilman, *Difference and Pathology: Stereotypes of Sexuality, Race, and Madness* (Ithaca, NY, and London: Cornell UP, 1985), 18.

[3] Caroline Walker Bynum, *The Resurrection of the Body in Western Christianity, 200–1336* (New York: Columbia UP, 1995), 215.

[4] Hermann Krings, *Ordo: Philosophisch-historische Grundlegung einer abendländischen Idee,* 2nd ed. (Hamburg: Meiner, 1982), 62. All translations in this chapter are my own unless otherwise noted.

[5] All translations in this chapter are my own.

[6] Freidank, *Bescheidenheit,* ed. H. E. Bezzenberger (Halle: Verlag der Buchhandlung des Waisenhauses, 1872), 10, 17–18. This refers to the page and line number of the earliest edition, and the system has been maintained in subsequent editions (thus these lines are actually not on page 10 of Bezzenberger's book).

[7] Konrad von Würzburg, *Die goldene Schmiede,* ed. Edward Schröder, 2nd ed. (Göttingen: Vandenhoeck & Ruprecht, 1969), 543.

[8] Brun von Schonebeck, *Das hohe Lied,* ed. Arwed Fischer, BLVS 198 (Tübingen: Der Litterarische Verein in Stuttgart, 1893; repr. Hildesheim and New York: Olms, 1973), 11094–97. Noah's curse upon his son Ham (Genesis 9:20–27)—that his descendants should be the servants of his brothers' descendants—which was traditionally used to account for the division of society into free and unfree, is extended by Hugo von Trimberg to cover "Juden, ketzer, heiden / Und kristen, die unbescheiden / Sind und unordenlichen lebent" (Jews, heretics, heathens, and Christians who lack understanding and lead disordered lives). Hugo von Trimberg, *Der Renner,* ed. Gustav Ehrismann. 4 vols., BLVS 247, 248, 252, and 256 (Tübingen: Der Litterarische Verein in Stuttgart, 1908–11; repr., Berlin: de Gruyter, 1970), 1352–1406; here 1401–3. Cf. Klaus Grubmüller, "Nôes Fluch: Zur Begründung von Herrschaft und Unfreiheit in mittelalterlicher Literatur," in *Medium aevum deutsch: Beiträge zur deutschen Literatur des hohen und späten Mittelalters: Festschrift für Kurt Ruh zum 65. Geburtstag,* ed. Dietrich Huschenbett, Klaus Matzel, Georg Steer, and Norbert Wagner (Tübingen, Germany: Niemeyer, 1979), 99–119.

[9] *Die altdeutsche Exodus: Untersuchungen und kritischer Text,* ed. Edgar Papp, Medium Aevum 16 (Munich: Fink, 1968), 671–72. Cf. Siegfried Stein, *Die Ungläubigen in der mittelhochdeutschen Literatur von 1050 bis 1250* (Berlin: Eisner, 1933; repr., Darmstadt: Wissenschaftliche Buchgesellschaft, 1963), 20.

[10] Barbara Gutfleisch-Ziche, "Die Millstätter Sammelhandschrift," in *Die Vermittlung geistlicher Inhalte im deutschen Mittelalter: Internationales Symposium, Roscrea 1994*, ed. Timothy R. Jackson, Nigel F. Palmer, and Almut Suerbaum (Tübingen: Niemeyer, 1996), 79–96; here 95.

[11] Hans Eberhard Mayer, *The Crusades*, trans. John Gillingham (Oxford: Oxford UP, 1972), 221, points out that, for example, from the 1220s there was an awareness in the West of non-Muslim peoples like the Mongols, but such groups rarely feature in the texts that I have considered.

[12] Michael Camille, *The Gothic Idol: Ideology and Image-making in Medieval Art*, Cambridge New Art History and Criticism (Cambridge: Cambridge UP, 1991), 140 and 206. Further references to this work are given in the text using the abbreviation *GI* and the page number.

[13] *Bruder Philipps des Carthäusers Marienleben*, ed. Heinrich Rückert, Bibl. d. Nat. Lit. 34 (Quedlinburg and Leipzig: Basse, 1853; repr., Amsterdam: Rodopi, 1966), 3342–45.

[14] Pfaffe Konrad, *Das Rolandslied des Pfaffen Konrad: Mittelhochdeutscher Text und Übertragung*, ed. Dieter Kartschoke (Frankfurt am Main: Fischer, 1970), 2647–52; 4683; 7273–74.

[15] Reinbot von Durne, *Der heilige Georg*, ed. Carl von Kraus, Germanische Bibl. 3, Abt. 1 (Heidelberg: Winter, 1907), 2366–75.

[16] Rudolf von Ems, *Barlaam und Josaphat*, ed. Franz Pfeiffer, Dichtungen des deutschen Mittelalters 3 (Leipzig: Göschen, 1843); repr., Dt. Neudrucke, Reihe: Texte des Mittelalters (Berlin: de Gruyter, 1965), 9251–57.

[17] Konrad von Würzburg, *Partonopier und Meliur*, ed. Karl Bartsch (Vienna: Braumüller, 1871; repr., Berlin: de Gruyter, 1970), 6514–15.

[18] *Das Marienleben des Schweizers Wernher*, ed. Max Päpke and Arthur Hübner, DTM 27 (Berlin: Weidmann, 1920; repr., Dublin and Zurich: Weidmann, 1967), 4031–4126.

[19] Freidank, *Bescheidenheit*, 24,24–25,2.

[20] Francesco Gabrieli, *Arab Historians of the Crusades*, trans. E. J. Costello (London: Routledge & Kegan Paul, 1969), 65. Further references to this work are given in the text using the abbreviation *AH* and the page number.

[21] Berthold von Regensburg, *Vollständige Ausgabe seiner Predigten*, ed. Franz Pfeiffer, 2 vols. (Vienna: Braumüller, 1862/80; repr., Berlin: de Gruyter, 1965), 1:357–71; here 357, 6–8.

[22] Hugo von Trimberg, *Der Renner*, 24239–396.

[23] Brun von Schonebeck, *Das hohe Lied*, 10428–34.

[24] See Michael Stolz, "Körper und Schrift: Wissensvermittlung im *Psalterium glossatum* von Wilhelm Müncher (1418)," in Jackson et al., *Die Vermittlung geistlicher Inhalte*, 97–117; here 111 and n. 33.

[25] When Hugo von Trimberg writes that his *Renner* contains honey and beeswax he intends us to understand Christian doctrine and heathen writings respectively (24504–15).

[26] Among the Indians and Chaldeans who assemble for the disputation in Rudolf von Ems's *Barlaam und Josaphat* are "wîser sternewarter vil" (8931; many wise astronomers).

[27] Boethius was neither a doctor nor a heathen, but one of the themes of his *De consolatione philosophiae* was precisely the mutability of human fortunes.

[28] Rudolf von Ems, *Alexander: Ein höfischer Versroman des 13. Jahrhunderts,* ed. Victor Junk, 2 vols., BLVS 272 and 274 (Leipzig: Der Litterarische Verein in Stuttgart, 1928/29; repr., Darmstadt: Wissenschaftliche Buchgesellschaft, 1970), 12941–60.

[29] *Die Gedichte Walthers von der Vogelweide,* ed. Karl Lachmann and Hugo Kuhn (Berlin: de Gruyter, 1965).

[30] Bruder Werner, *Spruch* 56, in *Politische Lyrik des deutschen Mittelalters: Texte I; Von Friedrich II. bis Ludwig dem Bayern,* ed. Ulrich Müller, GAG 68 (Göppingen: Kümmerle, 1972), 36. Dante places Saladin in a limbo of his own: "*e solo in parte vidi il Saladino,*" such is his respect for him. *Opere di Dante Alighieri,* ed. Fredi Chiapelli (Milan: Mursia, 1974), *Inferno* 4, 129.

[31] See Bernard McGinn, *Visions of the End: Apocalyptic Traditions in the Middle Ages* (New York: Columbia UP, 1979), 137.

[32] Stein, *Die Ungläubigen,* 21–22.

[33] Konrad von Würzburg, *Die Legenden III: Pantaleon,* ed. Paul Gereke and Winfried Woesler, ATB 21 (Tübingen: Niemeyer, 1974).

[34] In his so-called "Palästinalied," Walther, in a manner that recalls Freidank's reflections on the competing religions, accepts that Christians, Jews, and heathens all lay claim to the Holy Land, but he is in no doubt that God should recognize the Christian claim: "reht ist daz er uns gewer" (16,35).

[35] The author of the *Gesta Francorum* also assures us that those who died in the course of the First Crusade, be it in battle, be it from starvation, entered heaven as martyrs—cf. Karl Bertau, *Deutsche Literatur im europäischen Mittelalter,* 2 vols. (Munich: Beck, 1972/73), 187.

[36] Hugo von Trimberg, *Der Renner,* 24317–18.

[37] *Lucidarius, aus der Berliner Handschrift,* ed. Felix Heidlauf, DTM 28 (Berlin: Weidmann, 1915), 70,11–12—cf. Romans 2:12.

[38] *Altdeutsche Predigten,* ed. Anton E. Schönbach. 3 vols. (Graz, Austria: Styria, 1886–91), 2:62–63.

[39] Berthold von Regensburg, *Vollständige Ausgabe seiner Predigten,* 1:363,15–16.

[40] Brun von Schonebeck, *Das hohe Lied,* 11106–59.

[41] *Die Erlösung: Eine geistliche Dichtung des 14. Jahrhunderts,* ed. Friedrich Maurer, DLE: Geistliche Dichtung des Mittelalters 6 (Leipzig: Reclam, 1934), 6496–97.

[42] Heinrich von Neustadt, *Appolonius von Tyrland, Gottes Zukunft, Visio Philiberti,* ed. S. Singer (Berlin: Weidmann, 1906; repr., Dublin and Zurich: Weidmann, 1967), *Gottes Zukunft,* 6000.

[43] *Offenbarungen der Schwester Mechthild von Magdeburg, oder: Das fließende Licht der Gottheit,* ed. Gall Morel (Regensburg: Manz, 1869; repr., Darmstadt: Wissenschaftliche Buchgesellschaft, 1976), 82–83.

[44] Hall points out the importance for the anti-slavery movement of the concept of a "common humanity" ("The Spectacle of the 'Other,'" 249).

[45] One suspects that in such thinking the ethnocentrism to which Hall refers ("The Spectacle of the 'Other,'" 258–59) is combining with the fundamental religiocentrism of the text.

[46] Heinrich von Neustadt, *Gottes Zukunft,* 6507–8.

2: Wolfram von Eschenbach, Islam, and the Crusades

Cyril Edwards

THE VIEW OF THE ORIENT that obtains in Wolfram von Eschenbach's Arthurian romance, *Parzival,* and in his final, unfinished epic, *Willehalm,* is unlikely to have stemmed from first-hand experience. While Wolfram had access to Arab learning, probably through the medium of Latin translations, there is no evidence that he ever went to Arab lands. Nevertheless, the Orient and oriental characters play a major role in both narratives, and there is a notable conformity of attitude between the two works, which points to a greater degree of compassion and understanding than might be expected at a time when the crusading ethos was prevalent. Wolfram's use of place-names and proper names that may or may not derive from the Arabic, and the problems of geography, have been tackled elsewhere.[1] The aim of this chapter is to attempt an overview of Wolfram's portrayal of oriental characters and their religion, and the implications of this in the context of the politics of the early thirteenth century.

The first book of Wolfram's *Parzival* has no parallel in his main source, Chrétien de Troyes's *Conte du Graal* or *Perceval.* It sees Gahmuret, Parzival's father, setting off for adventures in the Orient. Gahmuret's goal is to serve "die hœhsten hant," (13,13; "the Highest Hand on this earth").[2] He is told of the powerful "bâruc," the caliph resident in Baldac (Baghdad), to whom two-thirds of the earth are subject, or even more. Later Gahmuret's son will come to know that the Highest Hand is that of God; this new awareness symbolizes the way Parzival outgrows his father.

Wolfram draws a parallel between the "bâruc" and the Pope, a parallel drawn again in *Willehalm.* The "bâruc" "gives absolution's proof" to the heathens "for their sins" (14,1–2). The heathen "ê" (order) is seen very much in Christian terms. The pagans are not criticized overtly, nor is there any sense that the heathen world is in direct opposition to Christendom. This is in itself surprising, given that *Parzival* was composed in the first decade of the thirteenth century.

Gahmuret duly establishes his reputation in heathen lands, fighting in Morocco, Persia, Damascus and Aleppo, Arabia and its capital, Araby. The plot propels him forward to the kingdom of Zazamanc, a Moorish land under siege. His train of pages is by now composed partly of Saracens. Gahmuret makes the acquaintance of the land's queen, Belacane, and a love-relationship develops between them:

> Gahmureten dûhte sân,
> swie si wære ein heidenin,
> mit triwen wîplîcher sin
> in wîbes herze nie geslouf.
> ir kiusche was ein reiner touf (28, 10–14)

[Gahmuret's immediate thought was that, although she was a heathen, a more womanly and loyal disposition had never glided into a woman's heart. Her chastity was a pure baptism]

Wolfram's praise of the Moorish queen is very much in Christian terms. As for Belacane,

> si kunde ouch liehte varwe spehen:
> wan sie het och ê gesehen
> manegen liehten heiden. (29, 3–5)

[She knew how to judge pale complexions, for she had seen many a fair-skinned heathen before.]

Evidently Wolfram knows that not all pagans are dark-skinned. His patron for the writing of *Willehalm* and probably for *Parzival*, Margrave Hermann of Thuringia,[3] had been to the Holy Land and must have talked to him about his experiences.

Gahmuret successfully defeats the invaders and marries Belacane, but, like his son after him, he suffers from restless ambition, "linge." Wolfram takes pains to make it clear that Gahmuret's dissatisfaction has no basis in color bias:

> daz er niht rîterschefte vant,
> des was sîn freude sorgen phant.
> Doch was im daz swarze wîp
> lieber dan sîn selbes lîp. (54, 19–22)

[That he found no deeds of knighthood caused his joy to be sorrow's forfeit. Yet the black woman was dearer to him than his own life.]

Gahmuret sneaks away. His master mariner is more racist than Gahmuret, warning him that he must conceal his departure from all with black skins there. Wolfram is voicing a problem that, while not becoming a major theme in *Parzival* as it was to do in *Willehalm*, figures largely in the closing stages of the work. Race, color, and religion play their part in binding the thematic structure of *Parzival*.

Gahmuret (again prefiguring the actions of his son, Parzival) deserts his wife. He sends her a letter that the modern reader, and perhaps his medieval predecessor, finds less than satisfactory:

> frouwe, in mac dich niht verheln,
> wær dîn ordn in mîner ê,
> sô wær mir immer nâch dir wê . . . (55, 24–26)

[Lady, I cannot conceal from you that if your religion were within my law, then I would always long for you]

Yet the issue never seems to have been raised openly between them, as far as the narrator lets us know. Gahmuret has made his getaway. Belacane's response, voiced in a monologue (56,28–57,8), states that she would be fully willing to be baptized and accept Gahmuret's God, but she is denied the opportunity.

Belacane gives birth to a son, who is of two colors. The magpie hue of Feirefiz echoes a theme voiced in the enigmatic prologue to *Parzival:*

> gesmæhet unde gezieret
> ist, swâ sich parrieret
> unverzaget mannes muot,
> als agelstern varwe tuot. (1, 3–6)

[There is both scorning and adorning when a man's undaunted mind turns pied like the magpie's hue.]

Feirefiz's complexion is linked with the opposition between heaven and hell as expounded in the prologue, and anticipates his eventual conversion to Christianity, his ultimate redemption. Color works symbolically here.[4] Yet in the story of Belacane and the portrayal of Feirefiz there is no direct correlation between blackness of color and damnation. Wolfram holds back here, compared with the binary opposition in the prologue, which unequivocally equates blackness, inconstancy, and hell.

In Waleis, in Book 2, Gahmuret thinks back to the girl he's left behind him in Patelamunt, Zazamanc's capital, and again the theme of color is broached:

> nu wænt manc ungewisser man
> daz mich ir swerze jagte dane:
> die sah ich für die sunnen ane. (91, 4–6)

[Now many an ignorant man believes it was her blackness drove me away—that I would look on rather than the sun!]

Wolfram is placing in Gahmuret's mouth anti-racist words. It would be hard to find a parallel for this in Arthurian romance.

Towards the end of Book 2 of *Parzival,* Gahmuret hears that the Baruch is in difficulties, and again Gahmuret deserts his wife, this time the Christian Herzeloyde, the queen whom he had won by his victory in a tournament, in order to go to the Baruch's aid. He fights in Alexandria, is killed by a poisoned spear, and is buried in Baghdad, a bejeweled cross placed over his grave. The heathens, we are told, worshipped Gahmuret as a god (107, 19–20); the supposed polytheism of the Arabs is evident here, as later in *Willehalm*. Nevertheless the Baruch gives Gahmuret a costly Christian burial; the two faiths are mutually acknowledged:

er truoc den touf und kristen ê:
sîn tôt tet Sarrazînen wê (108, 21–22)

[He bore baptism and Christian faith. His death grieved Saracens]

From Book 3 onwards, Wolfram's plot clings closer to Chrétien for a time, and it is only towards the end of Book 6 that the Orient re-enters the story. Feirefiz, so Cundrie tells Parzival and Arthur's court, has won in battle the fabulously wealthy city of Tabronit and the hand of its queen, Secundille. The magpie theme recurs: Cundrie emphasizes the fact that Feirefiz is both black and white (317, 9–10). This is the lowest point in Parzival's fortunes, for he is, if Cundrie is to be believed, destined for hell (316, 7); Feirefiz, his heathen half-brother, stands higher in repute. His wealth, too, is unsurpassed, save by that of the Baruch. This is acknowledged by a guest at Arthur's court, Ekuba, the heathen Queen of Janfuse, another pagan figure who is portrayed positively. She is praised as being wealthy and wise, and for her fine command of French (329, 11–13). She tells Arthur's court that like his father before him, Feirefiz is regarded by his people as a god, and again his mixed color is emphasized:

man bett in an als einen got.
sîn vel hât vil spæhen glast:
er ist aller mannes varwe ein gast,
wîz unde swarz [ist er] erkant. (328, 14–17)

[They worship him as a god. His skin has a most mysterious sheen; he is a stranger to all other men's hue. He is known to be black and white.]

The color difference is a matter for wonder, but there is no hint of a negative view here. The motif is entirely lacking in Wolfram's source. It can only derive from Wolfram's rich imagination.

The interwoven tales of Parzival's two heroes, Parzival and Gawan, are linked on various levels: by motifs such as the accusations of rape leveled at them both and the heroes' quests to aid their kindred; by the use of keywords such as "zwîvel" (doubt, despair) and "helfe" (help); but also by means of the various personages they meet on their travels. These include Cundrie la Surziere, the Grail messenger in Books 6 and 15, and Malcreatiure, her brother, encountered by Gawan in Book 10. These two deformed creatures, with their teeth sticking out like those of a wild boar, hail from the land of Tribalibot (i.e. India), by the river Ganges, which is the land of Feirefiz's wife, Queen Secundille. Here Wolfram introduces one of many motifs that will recur with much greater prominence in his final work, *Willehalm:* the monstrous races of the East, a motif that has its origins in the classical world.[5] Wolfram traces the deformities to the wilfulness of Adam's daughters:

> dô sîniu kint der jâre kraft
> gewonnen, daz si berhaft
> wurden menneschlîcher fruht,
> er widerriet in ungenuht. . . .
> vil würze er se mîden hiez
> die menschen fruht verkêrten . . .
> diu wîp tâten et als wîp: . . .
> sus wart verkêrt diu mennischeit . . . (518,11–29)

[When his daughters had reached such years' number that they were capable of giving birth to human fruit, he counselled them against immoderation. . . . seldom omitting to advise them to avoid many herbs that disfigure man's fruit . . . The women, however, acted as women do. . . . Thus mankind was deformed. . . .]

These deformed descendants of Adam have lived in Secundille's land ever since. She has sent two of them, Cundrie and Malcreatiure, as presents to Anfortas, the Grail King. As Roy Wisbey has shown, Wolfram is incorporating into *Parzival* a tradition established in German in the *Wiener Genesis* and the *Lucidarius,* both of which contain the motif of forbidden herbs.[6]

One of the many masterstrokes in Wolfram's adaptation and continuation of Chrétien de Troyes's unfinished romance is the employment of the oriental theme as a symmetrical framing device. Feirefiz, though born toward the end of the first book of *Parzival,* does not appear in person as an adult until near the beginning of Book 15, the work's penultimate book. Several motifs that will recur when heathens are depicted in *Willehalm* are employed to characterize him when he is introduced. He is fabulously wealthy; he is motivated by courtly love; many lands are subject to him, in which many different languages are spoken; they are populated by Moors and other Saracens (737, 1–4). Not knowing that they are half-brothers, Feirefiz and Parzival undertake a joust against one another. Here at last we come closer to Islam, in that the two knights now come to be seen as representative of each other's faith; the terminology is identical to that used later in *Willehalm*. Parzival is "der getoufte" (the baptized one); Feirefiz is "der heiden" or "der heidenische man." Recurring almost as a refrain is the line: "Der heiden tet em getouften wê" (739,23; 741,1; The heathen hurt the Christian hard).

Disaster is averted by divine intervention, and by the generosity of Feirefiz, so that Parzival does not, having slain his distant kinsman Ither, now kill another member of his family. The two brothers reveal their identity to one another. Feirefiz, rejoicing at this, names some of his gods. Wolfram attributes to Muslims the polytheism of the ancient world, and the gods he names are from classical antiquity:

> al mîne gote des gêret sint.
> mîn gotinne Jûnô
> dis prîses mac wol wesen vrô.
> mîn kreftec got Jupiter
> dirre sælden was mîn wer.
> gote unt gotinne,
> iwer kraft ich immer minne. (748, 17–22)

[All my gods are honoured by this! My goddess Juno has good reason to rejoice at this honour! My mighty god Jupiter was my guarantor of this blessing. Gods and goddesses, I shall love your power forever!]

Jupiter and Juno are frequently on Feirefiz's lips. When he lists the knights in his train, he compares them with the armies at the siege of Troy (768, 1–9). Parzival then leads Feirefiz into King Arthur's court, where again Feirefiz's color is a subject of amazement.

In Book 16, the final book of *Parzival*, Feirefiz accompanies his half-brother to the Grail Castle. The theme of color and race resurfaces in a discomforting moment. Parzival's young son Loherangrin—later to degenerate into Wagner's Lohengrin—is carried over to his uncle:

> dô der was swarz unde wîz,
> Der knabe sîn wolde küssen niht.
> werden kinden man noch vorhte giht.
> des lachte der heiden. (805,30—806, 3)

[He being black and white, the boy did not want to kiss him. Even today, fear is reported of noble children. At that the heathen laughed.]

The disconcerting moment is passed off lightly, and Feirefiz becomes an increasingly burlesque figure. Not being baptized, he is incapable of seeing the Grail. He falls in love with the Grail-bearer, Parzival's (and

Feirefiz's) aunt, Repanse de Schoye, sister-in-law to Gahmuret. Wolfram supplies a comic variation on the Ovidian symptom of pallor: "des plankiu mâl gar wurden bleich" (811,19; his white marks all grown pale). In order to marry Repanse de Schoye, Feirefiz agrees to be baptized and make the shift from polytheism to monotheism:

> bruoder, hât dîn muome got,
> an den geloube ich unt an sie . . .
> al mîne gote sint verkorn. (*Parzival* 818, 6–9)

[Brother, if your aunt has a god, I believe in him and in her . . . All *my* gods are renounced!]

Conveniently, the Indian queen Secundille, Feirefiz's first wife, is killed off by Wolfram, greatly to the relief of Repanse de Schoye. She and Feirefiz have a son, Johan or Prester John, and they establish the Christian religion in India. Thus, through Feirefiz and his family, the salvatory message of Wolfram's work is extended to the Orient, and the symmetry of the work is given its finishing touch.

There is only one reference to the crusades in *Parzival*, a tenuous one at that, but it is vital for the dating of the work, and for the relative dating of many of the texts of the *höfische Blütezeit*. In Book 11, in the Land of Wonders (*Terre Marveile*), Gawan meets with a peddler's booth:

> derz mit gelte widerwæge,
> der bâruc von Baldac
> vergulte niht daz drinne lac:
> als tæte der katolicô
> von Ranculât: dô Kriechen sô
> stuont daz man hort dar inne vant,
> dâ vergultez niht des keisers hant (563, 4–11)

[If its value were to be matched in money, even the Baruch of Baldac could not pay for what lay within there, nor the Katholikos of Ranculat. When Greece so stood that treasure was found there, its Emperor's hand there could not have paid for it]

Wolfram characteristically intermixes his own fiction with historical reality here. The Baruch is his own creation in Books 1 and 2, corresponding to the Caliph of Baghdad; the Katholikos is the Patriarch of the Armenian church. "Kriechen" (Greece), refers in Middle High German texts to Constantinople, and this is almost certainly an allusion to the sacking of Christian Constantinople in the spring of 1204, the notorious Fourth Crusade. Wolfram does not pass judgment here, but condemnation may be implicit. Book 11 of *Parzival* appears to have been written after 1204.

Another reference to Constantinople is significant here. *Parzival* postdates the second of Hartmann von Aue's Arthurian romances, *Iwein*, as is clear from his two allusions to the text.[7] In the Gießen manuscript of *Iwein*, Iwein attempts to surrender to Gawein, in a situation that is very reminiscent of the outcome of the battle between Parzival and Feirefiz and may well have influenced Wolfram:

> wæret ir mir der fremdest man,
> der ie ze Kriechen hûs gewan,
> ê ich iuch sô bestüende mê,
> zwâre ich sichert iu ê.[8]

> [if you were as unknown to me
> as any stranger who ever gained a castle in Greece
> rather than attack you any more,
> indeed I would have surrendered to you before.]

Perhaps this reference, too, is to be dated post-1204, given the crusaders' gains in Constantinople and the fact that "some knights and nobles from the Fourth Crusade settled in Greece and began to set up flourishing dynasties. . . ."[9] The allusion is vague, however, and cannot take us very far. Other manuscripts refer to "ze riuzen" [Russia] rather than Greece.[10]

Parzival is a work very rich in allusions to localities and to Wolfram's contemporaries (all absent in his source), so it is frustrating that we can pin down so little about its composition and patronage. Apart from the reference to "Kriechen," the other most helpful clue for dating the work is when Wolfram compares the devastation at Bearosche with that at Erfurt in 1203:

> Erffurter wîngarte giht
> von treten noch der selben nôt:
> maneg orses fuoz die slâge bôt. (379, 18–20)

> [Erfurt's vineyard still bears witness to the same extremity, caused by trampling – many a charger's hoof dealt those blows.]

In the summer of 1203 Landgrave Hermann of Thuringia had besieged the Hohenstaufen king, Philip of Swabia, in Erfurt. The civil war of 1198–1208 involved many turncoats, among whom Hermann was prominent. Hermann at this point was siding with the Welfs, under Otto IV of Brunswick and Poitou, Richard the Lionheart's favourite nephew. It is probable that Hermann was, at least for some years, Wolfram's patron.[11] In *Willehalm* Wolfram states that he has his knowledge of *Aliscans*, his Old French source, from Hermann.[12] Jeff Ashcroft has pointed to the "crusading commitment of the Thuringian Landgraves" as a possible motive for commissioning a translation of *Aliscans*.[13] Hermann himself

participated in the crusade of 1197, which was marred by the death of
Henry VI. From this point onwards a mood of disillusion with crusading
seems, however, to have set in. The Cologne Annals record the return
of Landgrave Hermann in 1198 in scathing terms: "Heinricus palati-
nus comes Reni, frater Ottonis regis, et lantgravius ac dux Brabantiae de
Iherosolimis revertuntur, infecto omni negocio apud ethnicos."[14] (Heinrich the Count Palatinate of the Rhineland, the brother of King Otto, and
the Landgrave and the Duke of Brabant [Henry the Lion] returned from
Jerusalem, all negotiations with the heathens having broken down.)[15]
The fiasco of 1204, the Children's Crusade of 1212, and the protracted
failure of the Fifth Crusade must all have had their impact.

Yet in the first two decades of the thirteenth century Walther von der
Vogelweide, Hartmann von Aue, and other poets were composing "kriu-
zliet," lyrics in the crusading cause.[16] (The slender corpus of Wolfram's own lyrics contains no crusading lyrics.) Wolfram's *Parzival* voices
criticism of Hermann's court and cites his fellow poet Walther von der
Vogelweide, who is similarly disenchanted with Thuringia (*P* 297,24–25).
Walther's stance may serve to typify the most common attitude toward
Muslims in the early thirteenth century. The most popular of Walther's
crusading lyrics, to judge from its manuscript transmission, was the *Palästinalied,* the earliest record of which is in the *Codex Buranus* of circa
1230. (The *Codex Buranus* preserves the first strophe of Walther's lyric,
together with a melody, also preserved in the Münster manuscript Z.)[17]
Walther's lyric opens with a triumphant assertion of his own arrival in the
Holy Land. It is the final strophe which is most relevant here:

> Kristen, juden unde heiden
> jehent, daz diz ir erbe sî.
> Got sol uns ze reht bescheiden
> dur die sîne namen drî.
> Al diu welt, diu strîtet her:
> wir sîn an der rehten ger.
> Reht ist, daz er uns gewer.[18]

> [Christians, Jews and heathens
> say that this is their heritage.
> God must decide in our favour, as is just,
> by virtue of His three names.
> All the world is fighting its way here:
> we are right in our desire.
> It is right that He should grant us our will.]

Wolfram's *Willehalm* shows knowledge of this lyric, paraphrasing it
in an entirely different context when he describes the Christian armies
assembled near Pitit Punt, but using identical rhymes:

al die wîle si zogeten her,
maneger slahte was ir ger.[19]

[all the time they drew near;
they had many different aims.]

Attitudes to the crusading ethic and the Orient were, however, complex, no less so than today. Neidhart von Reuental, Walther von der Vogelweide's younger contemporary, who is also referred to in *Willehalm* (312,12), sets a *Sommerlied* in the mouth of a crusader. We cannot be sure which Crusade he is criticizing, but the Fifth (Damietta) Crusade (1217–21) seems most likely. Neidhart longs to send a messenger back home to Austria, across the sea, the Mediterranean, away from the prevailing sickness, the malaria from which Henry VI had died.[20] His tone of disillusion matches that of Wolfram.

Emperor Otto IV, one of Walther von der Vogelweide's many patrons, died in May 1218, during the Fifth Crusade, in the Harzburg. He had promised to go on a crusade but failed to do so. The crusading ethos was taken very seriously at that time, and he was excommunicated by two popes. According to the chronicler Albert von Stade, on his deathbed he asked how he might atone, and he then ordered his cooks — the lowest of the low — to walk over his neck.[21]

Wolfram's source for *Willehalm*, the Old French *Aliscans,* is one of a cycle of *chansons de geste* dating from the second half of the twelfth century.[22] The attitude to the Saracens is aptly summarized by Joan M. Ferrante:

> The treatment of the Christian-pagan struggle . . . is simple and unsophisticated. . . . In their physical appearance as well as their actions, the pagans are hideous monsters, more like inhabitants of hell than human beings. The second part of *Aliscans* presents a fascinating series of such creatures: Aenre, wielding a steel hammer, has strangled and eaten untold Franks; Borrel wears animal skins and is accompanied by fourteen sons, all bearing whips; Baudus . . . is fifteen feet tall, black, with eyes like burning coals, a huge face, and carries the mast of a ship as his weapon; Haucebier, with eyes half a foot apart and red, has more force than fourteen Slavs; Agrapars is only three feet tall but broad, with red eyes, jagged teeth, a swollen mouth, a hooked nose, a hairy body and sharp nails that serve as his weapons; Walegrape, . . . fourteen feet tall, with long teeth and a tongue half of which hangs out of his mouth, wears a serpent's hide and carries a crook; Grishart . . . wields a hatchet and eats raw human flesh; his sister, Flohart, fifteen feet tall, wearing buffalo hide and armed with a scythe, emits a stinking smoke from her mouth and bites off and swallows pieces of Rainouart's hauberk.

As a group, the pagans are referred to as cowards, pigs, dogs, sons of bitches, or devils.[23]

We do not know what manuscript of *Aliscans* Wolfram was working from, but his adaptation has little room for giants, dwarves, and halitosis. Wolfram's treatment of the heathens and their beliefs is far from unsophisticated. The motif of the monstrous races does occur, but it is muted compared with *Aliscans*. In *Willehalm* Wolfram describes Gornant, one of the many kings in the Saracen forces, as hailing (like Cundrie and Malcreatiure in *Parzival*) from the vicinity of the Ganges:

> bî der *Ganjas* was des lant.
> des volc was vorn und hinden horn,
> âne menneschlîch stimme erkorn:
> der dôn von ir munde
> *gal sam* die leithunde
> oder als ein kelber muoter lüet. (35,10–17)

> [His land was by the Ganges. His people were horny back and front, lacking human voices—the sound that came out of their mouths was like that of lymers or the lowing of a calf's mother.]

These people of horny skin fight on foot with steel clubs and are extraordinarily fleet of foot. Such Gegetones or Cornuti occur frequently in medieval literature and iconography.[24] Gornant refigures in Book 7, Wolfram adding the color green to the description of his skin (351,15–18). The greenhorns appear again in Book 8 (395,18–26), as does the albino Matusalles. His wife is a Mooress from Jetakranc—a place-name derived, like many others, from *Parzival*. It follows, by dint of the same logic as obtains for Feirefiz, that his son Josweiz is of two-colored complexion (386,20).

The greenhorns excepted, the monstrous races are for the most part absent in *Willehalm;* Wolfram's heathens are palpably human. As in *Parzival,* they are fabulously wealthy. They are valorous warriors, portrayed as exact counterparts of the Christians, as knights whose fighting is often inspired by love of women, another echo of the portrayal of Feirefiz in *Parzival.*

The heathens are grouped together as "heidenschaft" (8,22), as opposed to "kristenheit" (13,1). As in Book 15 of *Parzival,* "der getoufte" is opposed to "der heiden" (8,28). The struggle between the two faiths is eternal; it will last until doomsday, "der urteilîchen zît "(402,14). The heathens are referred to as both Saracens and Moors, but they stem from a bewildering variety of countries and locations, ranging from Greenland and Scandinavia in the north to Ghana in the south, from Marseille in the west to China in the east. The geography in *Willehalm,* like that of *Parzival,* is a blend of the mythological, the fictitious, and the realistic; Jericho, Mecca, and Palestine coexist with place-names derived from the *Rolandslied* and from *Parzival.*[25] Corresponding to the geographical origins of the heathen armies is their plurilingualism, "mit der sprâche ein ander gar unkunt" (399,27; in terms of language entirely unknown to one another). Wolfram refers to seventy-two languages, of which twelve are those of the Christian world (73,7; 450,20).[26] There is something of a contradiction here, in that Willehalm escapes from the battlefield partly because of his knowledge of the heathen tongue: "in nert ouch, daz er heidnisch sprach" (105,27; He was also saved because he spoke the heathen tongue).

All these peoples are subject to Terramer, who is their emperor, the overlord of Baldac, also given the title "admirât," which may derive from the *Rolandslied*.[27] This title is also employed in Wolfram's *Titurel*, which compares the wealth of the "admirât" with that of the Holy Roman Emperor.[28] The spiritual leader of these peoples is, however, as in *Parzival*, the "bâruc" of Baldac, the Caliph of Baghdad, who corresponds to the Pope in the Christian hierarchy.

With the exception of the greenhorns, the heathens are, like Belacane, black: "manec swarzer môr, doch lieht gevar" (34,30; many a black Moor, yet bright of complexion). The tell-tale *doch* suggests there may be an echo of The Song of Songs here: "I am black but lovely."[29] Color is, for the most part, curiously unproblematic in *Willehalm*. The mixed marriage between the hero and Terramer's daughter, Giburc, is a happy and loyal one, and the issues of racial and color difference are not broached at any point.

The same cannot be said of religious issues. In *Aliscans* the Saracens, "obstinate in their mistaken beliefs . . . cannot be saved and are fit only to die."[30] The exceptions are the converts, Giburc and Rainoart. Things are far less cut-and-dried in *Willehalm*. For the most part, Wolfram adheres to orthodox crusading doctrine, such as is to be found in the crusading lyrics of his contemporaries, although, as Martin Jones has pointed out, "*Willehalm* does not, strictly speaking, qualify as an example of crusading literature, for the military expedition undertaken here at the behest of religious authorities is the work of Saracens rather than Christians."[31] The Christians are God's soldiers (19,17). They wear the cross (304,19), and if they die in battle, their souls will go to heaven (32, 6–7).

The Saracens have no such belief. As in *Parzival*, they are portrayed as polytheistic, but with the significant difference that Mohammed is named as one of their gods. Terramer appeals to "sînem liebisten got Mahmeten / und andern goten sînen" (9,8–9; his dearest god Mohammed / and other gods of his). The army in the first battle prays to Mahmet (88,18). Of the other gods who are named, one is Tervigant or Tervagant, derived from *Aliscans*, though his ultimate origin is disputed.[32] Willehalm, addressing his troops, refers to a trinity of heathen gods: Mahmet, Tervigant, and Apollo, who was one of Feirefiz's gods in *Parzival*. This is capped by Terramer's appeal to a quartet of gods, the three named by Willehalm and a fourth, Kahun, again derived from *Aliscans*, but also of uncertain ultimate origin (358,13).[33] The Saracens are also credited with belief in

Amor, "der minnen got" (25,14; the god of love), again echoing Feirefiz's belief in the gods of the classical world. In the second battle, Terramer has images of gods, decorated with gold and gems, placed high on masts in wagons, which are drawn by armor-clad oxen (352,1–9). Jesus, though, from Terramer's viewpoint, is a "zouberære," a sorcerer (357,23).

Despite the differences in beliefs that he portrays, Wolfram extends a great deal of sympathy to the heathens, a sympathy scarcely to be found in his source. He describes the great losses suffered by both sides in the first battle, and comments in his capacity as narrator:

> nû gedenke ich mir leide,
> sol ir got Tervigant
> si zer helle hân benant. (20,10–12)

[Now it grieves me to think that their god Tervigant has destined them for Hell.]

The degree of this sympathy varies, for it conflicts with crusading orthodoxy. Thus in the first battle the cross-wearing Christians suffer at the hands of "diu heidensch ungeloubic diet" (31,27; the heathen unbelievers). Yet when Arofel, King of Persia, is killed, he is praised as a "Minneritter," in words that have no parallel in *Aliscans* but are reminiscent of the death of Gahmuret: "noch solden kristenlîchiu wîp / klagen sînen ungetouften lîp" (81,21–22; Christian women still today ought to grieve over his unbaptized person).

The two main apologists for the competing religions are Terramer and his daughter, Giburc, a convert to Christianity. In Book 3 Terramer expounds his beliefs in a key speech. He acknowledges the power of the god of Christendom (107,18) in allowing a handful of knights to stand in the way of his wish to avenge the sacrilege, the "ungelouben" committed by his daughter (107,21–30). He rejects as absurd the idea of the resurrection and the concept of the Trinity; his aim is to inflict suffering upon his estranged daughter and so dishonor Jesus (108,18–22). He sees the invasion as "ein hervart ûf die kristenheit" (339,17; a crusade against Christendom).

Prior to the events in *Willehalm* Giburc, then called Arabel, was married to Tibalt of Araby. She came to love Willehalm while he was in captivity and married him, espousing the Christian faith. Like the narrator, she refers to the heathen religion as "ungelouben" (102,16). Giburc tells her Muslim kindred that they will suffer

> dises kurzen lebens ende
> und der sêle unledic gebende
> vor iuwerem gote Tervigant,
> der iuch vür tôren hât erkant. (110,27–30)

[this short life's end and the imprisoning bonds of the soul, despite your god Tervigant, who has deemed that you are fools.]

This idea of the Saracens being deceived into folly recurs in the narrator's mouth: Terramer is "vertôrt" (deluded) in his beliefs (352,14); the pagans are deceived by their gods (360,26–28).

Giburc has chosen Christ and baptism in preference to Mohammed (215,16), and regards the "Altissimus," the Christian God, as the creator, in opposition to Tervagant and other pagan gods (216,4–15). In a key passage in Book 5 she rebukes her father's folly, "tumpheit" and preaches a sermon to him, evoking the prophets, including the seers Plato and Sybil, both of whom predict the coming of Christ and the harrowing of hell in *Parzival* (465,21–30). It is entirely characteristic of the freedom with which Wolfram treats his source that the seers from the classical world are absent in *Aliscans*.

Terramer refutes Giburc's arguments, not without subtlety: "den einen möhten doch die drî / vor dem tôde haben bewart" (219,2–3; The three could surely have preserved the one from death).[34] He goes on to express little faith in Jesus generally, to doubt the harrowing of hell, and appeals to his daughter to convert back from her "ungelouben" (219,4–22).

Giburc in reply reasserts her Christian faith, her belief in the resurrection, and her loyalty to Willehalm, albeit giving elbow-room to her father's beliefs: "möhten hôher sîn nû dîne gote" (220,1; even if your gods were higher). It is Giburc who is the essential conciliatory force in the poem, although she recognizes her responsibility for the conflict, which has come about because of her desertion of Tibalt for Willehalm:

ich *schûr* sîner hantgetât,
der beide machet und*e* hât
den kristen und den heiden! (253,9–11)

[Storm that I am, falling upon the handiwork of Him who both creates and holds in His power Christian and heathen!]

Later we learn from Willehalm that Giburc's conversion and elopement were more for religious than personal reasons, and not because of his high repute (298,21–23). This may be modesty on Willehalm's part — though modesty is a rare trait in the hero of a crusading epic. More probably, these lines — not to be found in *Aliscans* — are consonant with Wolfram's desire to shift Giburc to central stage as spokeswoman for religious tolerance.

As the text progresses, compassion and tolerance play an increasingly important role. Willehalm, who killed Arofel in cold blood in Book 2 (81,11–12) when he could have accepted his surrender, goes through a change in character in the course of the work. In Book 4, Wolfram tells us:

er möht erbarmen, die halt sint
des wâren gelouben âne:
juden, heiden, publikâne. (162,28–30)

[He was capable of pity for those who are without the true faith:
Jews, heathens, publicans.]

The meaning of "publikâne" is uncertain; it may refer to heretics.[35]
Jews are again spoken of disparagingly by Willehalm's sister (180,23–25.)
Yet there are self-contradictions here. In his Agincourt-like speech to his
French troops, Willehalm refers to the atrocities wrought by the pagans,
their cutting off the breasts of baptized women, torturing their children,
slaying all their husbands, and setting them up as targets for shooting
practice (297,14–17).

Rennewart, who will later turn out to be a son of Terramer, and
therefore Giburc's brother, is a somewhat burlesque figure, with his huge
all-conquering club and outbursts of temper. Like Giburc, however, he is
a convert, or at least a would-be convert. He is assigned a speech in which
he describes his religious plight to Willehalm:

"ich bin von Meckâ,
dâ Mahmeten heilikeit
sînen lîchnamen treit
al swebende âne undersetzen."[36] (193,2–5)

[I am from Mecca, where Mohammed's sanctity carries his corpse in
the air, hovering without support.]

The belief that Mohammed's coffin hovered miraculously in the air was
widespread.[37] Rennewart, however, feels disillusioned with Mohammed,
and is turning to Christ, but in his demeaning plight as a kitchen-drudge
feels unworthy of baptism. Later, however, he asserts to his sister his belief
in the trilogy of Tervagant, Mahumet, and Apollo (291,21–23).

Giburc's celebrated speech to the council of princes has been the subject of much discussion.[38] Giburc pleads for tolerance on the grounds that
key figures in the history of Christendom were originally pagan, from Adam
onwards (307,25), before baptism parted Christians from heathendom, and
therefore she appeals to the French for tolerance in the famous line: "schônet
der gotes hantgetât!" (306,28; spare God's handiwork!). The main focus in
her speech is on "erbarmekeit" (mercy), which occurs, with its grammatical
variants, several times in her speech (307,29–30; 309,6; 309,12).

Giburc's speech is not to be viewed in isolation. Towards the end of
the unfinished epic, after the victory in the second battle, Wolfram, most
obtrusive of narrators, seems to be thinking aloud about the moral of his
reworking of *Aliscans,* and, as he points the moral, his words echo those
of Giburc:

die nie toufes künde
enpfiengen, ist daz sünde?
daz man die sluoc alsam ein vihe,
grôzer sünde ich drumbe gihe:
ez ist gar gotes hantgetât (450,15–19)

[Those who never became acquainted with baptism—is that a sin? I call it a great sin that they were slain like cattle—they are all God's handiwork].

The motif of God creating both Christians and Muslims has been moving more and more to the center of the poem. Nothing could be in starker contrast to the black-and-white crudity of *Aliscans*. The mood of *Willehalm* seems almost to anticipate the bloodless crusade, the excommunicate Frederick II's negotiations with the Arabs in 1228–29, which ended with Frederick being crowned King of Jerusalem, albeit "pelted . . . with entrails and dung" by the local, Christian, populace."[39] Wolfram probably did not live to hear of that last ignominy. He might well have shared the bewildered disillusionment of his (perhaps slightly younger) contemporary Freidank:[40]

Wâ gefuor ê keiser über mer
im banne und âne vürsten her?
und ist nu komen in cin lant
dâ got noch man nie triuwe vant.[41]

[When did an emperor ever before cross the sea,
excommunicate and without an army of princes?
And has now arrived in a land
where neither God nor man ever found fidelity.]

The Catholic Church has recently repudiated the crusades. Freidank, Neidhart, Walther von der Vogelweide, and, above all, Wolfram show that even in the early thirteenth century, attitudes to the crusades and to Islam were far from uniform. Wolfram, however, stands out alone in his tolerant treatment of Islamic peoples. The last great achievement of this most humane and original of medieval poets was to transform *Aliscans,* very much against the grain of his Old French original, into an—almost—anti-crusading epic.

Notes

[1] See the studies by Paul Kunitzsch, especially: "Die Arabica im Parzival Wolframs von Eschenbach," *Wolfram-Studien* 2 (1974): 9–35; "Quellenkritische Bemerkungen zu einigen Wolframschen Orientalia," *Wolfram-Studien* 3 (1975): 263–75; and "Der Orient in Wolframs Parzival," *ZfdA* 113 (1984): 79–111.

[2] Quotations from *Parzival* are from Karl Lachmann's sixth edition of 1926, as reprinted in Wolfram von Eschenbach, *Parzival,* Studienausgabe (Berlin: Walter de Gruyter, 1965); translations into English are from Wolfram von Eschenbach, *Parzival and Titurel,* trans. Cyril Edwards, Oxford World's Classics (Oxford: Oxford UP, 2006). Further references to this work are given in the text, using the abbreviation *P* where necessary for clarity. The numbers refer to the section and line, which are based on Lachmann's edition and apply to all the editions, both German and English.

[3] See *Wolfram von Eschenbach. Parzival: With Titurel and the Love-Lyrics,* trans. Cyril Edwards, Arthurian Studies (Cambridge: D. S. Brewer, 2004), xiii–xiv.

[4] I am indebted to the late David McLintock for discussion of this point (often over Guinness).

[5] See Heinzle's commentary on *Willehalm* 35,13. Wolfram von Eschenbach, *Willehalm: Nach der Handschrift 857 der Stiftsbibliothek St. Gallen,* ed. Joachim Heinzle, Bibliothek des Mittelalters 9 (Frankfurt am Main: Deutscher Klassiker Verlag, 1991), 858. References to *Willehalm* are to Heinzle's edition. Translations are my own.

[6] R. A. Wisbey, "Marvels of the East in the *Wiener Genesis* and in Wolfram's *Parzival,*" in *Essays in German and Dutch Literature,* ed. W. D. Robson-Scott (London: Institute of Germanic Studies, U of London, 1973), 1–41. I am indebted to Roy Wisbey for my copy of his essay. See also John Block Friedman, *The Monstrous Races in Medieval Art and Thought* (Cambridge, MA: Harvard UP, 1981), 92–99.

[7] See Hartmann von Aue, *Iwein or The Knight with the Lion,* ed. and trans. Cyril Edwards, Arthurian Archives, German Romance 3 (Cambridge: D. S. Brewer, 2007), xv–xvii.

[8] Hartmann von Aue, *Gregorius, Der arme Heinrich, Iwein,* ed. and trans. Volker Mertens, Bibliothek des Mittelalters 6 (Frankfurt am Main: Deutscher Klassiker Verlag, 2004), 7657–60.

[9] Jonathan Phillips, *The Fourth Crusade and the Sack of Constantinople* (London: Jonathan Cape, 2004), 293.

[10] See Hartmann von Aue, *Gregorius, Der arme Heinrich, Iwein,* 1047.

[11] See *Wolfram von Eschenbach, Parzival: With Titurel and the Love-Lyrics,* xiii–xvi.

[12] Wolfram von Eschenbach, *Willehalm,* 3, 8.

[13] Jeffrey Ashcroft, "'dicke Karel wart genant': Konrad's *Rolandslied* and the Transmission of Authority and Legitimacy in Wolfram's *Willehalm,*" in *Wolfram's "Willehalm": Fifteen Essays,* ed. Martin H. Jones and Timothy McFarland, Studies in German Literature, Linguistics, and Culture (Rochester, NY: Camden House, 2002), 21–41; here 33.

[14] Annales Colonienses Maximi, MGH SS 17, ed. Georg Pertz (Hanover, 1861), 808.

[15] My translation.

[16] See Ashcroft, "dicke Karel wart genant," 33; Hartmann von Aue, *Iwein*, xii–xiii.

[17] Walther von der Vogelweide, *Palästinalied*, as preserved in the Codex Buranus and Staatsarchiv Münster, MS. VII 51.

[18] Walther von der Vogelweide, *Leich, Lieder, Sangsprüche*, ed. Karl Lachmann, 14th rev. ed. by Christoph Cormeau (Berlin: Walter de Gruyter, 1996), 16,29–35. Punctuation, spelling, and translation are my own.

[19] Wolfram von Eschenbach, *Willehalm*, 323,15–16.

[20] *Die Lieder Neidharts*, ed. Edmund Wießner, revd. Paul Sappler, Altdeutsche Textbibliothek 44 (Tübingen: Niemeyer, 1984), *Sommerlied* 11.

[21] *Die Hohenstaufen: Nach zeitgenössischen Quellen*, ed. Johannes Bühler (Leipzig: Insel Verlag, 1925), 382.

[22] For the date of the text, see *Aliscans*, trans. Bernard Guidot and Jean Subrenat (Paris: Honoré Champion, 1993), 11. Joan M. Ferrante in *Guillaume d'Orange: Four Twelfth-Century Epics* (New York: Columbia UP, 1974) suggests an earlier date, "between 1160 and 1190" (16).

[23] Ferrante, *Guillaume d'Orange*, 25 and 27.

[24] See Friedman, *The Monstrous Races*, 16–17; 54–55; 96–97.

[25] See the "Namenverzeichnis" in Heinzle's edition (*Willehalm*, 1186–1328).

[26] See Heinzle's commentary on 450,23 (*Willehalm*, 1087).

[27] Heinzle, note to 432,16 (*Willehalm*, 1079).

[28] Wolfram von Eschenbach, *Titurel*, str. 93. See Wolfram von Eschenbach, *Parzival: With Titurel and the Love-Lyrics*, 275.

[29] The Song of Songs, 1:5. Quoted from *The Jerusalem Bible* (London: Darton, Longman & Todd, 1966).

[30] Ferrante, *Guillaume d'Orange*, 28.

[31] Martin H. Jones, "Cross and Crusade in Wolfram von Eschenbach's *Willehalm*," in *Literatur—Geschichte—Literaturgeschichte: Beiträge zur mediävistischen Literaturwissenschaft, Festschrift für Volker Honemann zum 60. Geburtstag*, ed. Nine Miedama and Rudolf Suntrup (Frankfurt am Main: Peter Lang, 2003), 193–207; here 193. I am indebted to Martin Jones for a copy of his essay.

[32] Heinzle, *Willehalm*, 836 (re 11,16).

[33] See Heinzle, *Willehalm*, 1045 (re 358,13).

[34] Here, exceptionally, I opt against Heinzle's edition, and have, with the majority of manuscripts, *vor* rather than *von*.

[35] See Heinzle's note to 162,30 (*Willehalm*, 952).

[36] Italics indicate letters that are unclear in the MSS.

[37] See Heinzle re 193,3–5 (*Willehalm*, 969).

[38] See, for example, the summary of recent research by Timothy McFarland in "Giburc's Dilemma: Parents and Children, Baptism and Salvation," in *Wolfram's "Willehalm": Fifteen Essays*, ed. Martin H. Jones and Timothy McFarland, Studies

in German Literature, Linguistics, and Culture (Rochester, NY: Camden House, 2002), 121–42.

[39] Steven Runciman, *A History of the Crusades* (Harmondsworth, UK: Penguin, 1965), 3:192.

[40] A page of aphorisms attributed to Freidank is interpolated in the *Codex Buranus,* but the transmission of Freidank's "Sprüche" is highly complex, dating back to the late twelfth century. See Cyril Edwards, "The German Texts in the *Codex Buranus,*" in *The Carmina Burana: Four Essays,* ed. Martin H. Jones, King's College London Medieval Studies 18 (London: King's College London Centre for Late Antique & Medieval Studies, 2000), 41–67; here 43–44.

[41] *Vridankes Bescheidenheit,* ed. Wilhelm Grimm (Göttingen: Dieterich'sche Buchhandlung, 1834), 158.

3: Perverted Spaces: Boundary Negotiations in Early-Modern *Turcica*

Silke R. Falkner

Nach dem Mittag-Essen einen Tanz durch 2. Buben (deren [die Türcken] zu ihrer Schande missbrauchen / welche verfluchte Unweiß in der Türckey sehr gemein[1]

THUS READS A REVEALING EXCERPT from Stefan Gerlach's *Tagebuch* that spans the years 1573 to 1578. In 1674 this chronicle was finally published by a grandson of the author who had traveled to Constantinople, the capital of the Ottoman Empire. In his capacity as court preacher in a German diplomatic mission, Gerlach describes the post-luncheon entertainment provided by two young male dancers. These dancers would also be expected to fulfill sexual requests — a vice that is commonly practiced in Turkey, according to Gerlach.

According to German language *turcica* published between 1453 and approximately 1700, Ottoman sexual perversion and vice was commonplace.[2] Furthermore, we repeatedly find images that link the Muslim as sexual pervert to images of him as religious fraudster, images that are in turn inseparable from the early-modern construction of the antagonistic Other. As this chapter will argue, both of these representations are directly related to the erection and defense of boundaries and space.

After the seventeenth century, a number of factors, including the West's growing military and political superiority, the Western reception of the *Arabian Nights* (with their "exotic-erotic" implications),[3] and Enlightenment concepts of religious tolerance, together engendered momentous shifts in the portrayal of Islamic cultures. This chapter, however, will explore the relationship between religion, sex, and space in *turcica* published in the time between the so-called Fall of Constantinople and the 1680s, and how the topoi produced herein interact to construct a particular picture of the Muslim as deviant / Muslim as religious fraudster. During the period under consideration, the word "Turk" was virtually synonymous with "Muslim" — *turcica* are replete with instances in which Islam is referred to as "the Turkish religion" or "Türkerey," and the phrase to "turn Turk" meant to convert to Islam.[4] A fine example of this conflation of "Turk" and

Muslim is provided by the Gerlach *Tagebuch* in a narrative about a Cypriot Christian, captured by Turks, who was taken to Constantinople, where she became a wet-nurse. She killed her own child, fathered by a Turk, so that it would not "turn Turk," after a self-administered emergency baptism: "und [sie] hat mit einem Türcken ein Kind gehabt / welches sie / so bald es gebohren / selber getaufft / darnach wieder den Boden gewor℧en / und umgebracht / daß es kein Türck werde."[5]

As Georg Simmel has already established, making the Other part of and thus a product of our own conception is the basis of sociation (Verge-sellschaftung).[6] Thus *turcica,* although purportedly concerned with the multiple threats posed by the Ottoman Turks or Muslims, are in fact far more revealing of the authorial intentions of the creators of this body of work and can be regarded as a form of inadvertent cultural self-represen-tation; to that extent they are not untypical of discourses constructing an enemy Other.

If it is true that "space" requires demarcation, definition, and limita-tion by boundaries, such boundaries must be erected and defended for the space to be perceived as such. Simmel demonstrated that space is actually merely a function of the mind, deployed to integrate unconnec-ted perceptions: "dass der Raum überhaupt nur eine Tätigkeit der Seele ist, nur die menschliche Art, an sich unverbundene Sinnesaffektionen zu einheitlichen Anschauungen zu verbinden."[7] *Turcica* reveal such a con-struction of space by displaying two distinct concepts of boundary-pen-etration: first, that the "proper" Christian belief is intermingled with the "wrong" and alien Muslim faith, thus contaminating religion and giving birth to the Koran. Second, there is the concept that Turks/Muslims are thought of and represented as sexually deviant and that their deviancy presents a threat to the boundaries of "proper," that is, Christian, sexual behavior—again, a type of contamination.

Ahead of an examination of how *turcica* enact and indeed forge links between these differing forms of boundary transgression, some historical background on the scope of this discourse will prove useful. Publishing in the early-modern age was characterized by a veritable flood of litera-ture on Turks in a range of fictional and non-fictional genres appearing in Latin or one of the European vernaculars.[8] The gargantuan corpus includes poetry, song texts, drama, novels, religious treatises and sermons, travel narratives, pamphlets, and broadsheets, both illustrated and non-illustrated. Indeed, Carl Göllner counted a thousand German imprints in the sixteenth century alone, which demonstrates its sheer size.[9] Among the factors triggering the voluminous output was a potent combination of political and technological developments. The expansionist zeal of the Ottoman Empire and the invention of the printing press with movable type sparked the publication of often fear-mongering polemics in the fif-teenth century, which then continued until well into the late 1600s. In a telling sequence of historical events, the Ottoman conquest of Constantinople on 29 May 1453 was followed in December 1454 by the publication of the so-called "Türkenkalender," arguably the oldest Gutenberg book to be preserved in its entirety.

This very "Calendar," one of the oldest printed German documents, was indeed a direct response to the Ottoman conquest of Constantinople. The nine-page anonymous masterpiece of propaganda, *Eyn manung der cristenheit widder die durken* (An Exhortation of Christianity against the Turks)[10] is a call to arms against the Ottoman armies, subdivided into twelve sections corresponding to the months of 1455. Adorned with graphic claims of past and anticipated Turkish ruthlessness, it inspired similar yet increasingly sophisticated calendars, which were issued well into the eighteenth century.[11] Anxiety about Turks and "things Turkish" eventually led to such astonishing phenomena as a biweekly newspaper solely dedicated to the "Turkish problem" and named *Turckischer Estaats- und Krieges-Bericht*. First published in 1683, it ran for 137 issues, and ultimately its collected back copies were even sold in book format in a volume entitled *Der türckische Schau-Platz*.[12]

The purpose of this discourse was twofold: it promoted moral reform in the Christian Occident (on the basis that the Turk was God's punishing tool), and it also advocated military action against the Ottoman Empire. *Turcica* served to stimulate fear and loathing of the Muslim Other, the "hereditary foe" or "arch-enemy" of Christendom, as can be seen from the titles of many works, such as Catharina Regina von Greiffenberg's *Sieges-Seule der Buße und des Glaubens, wider den Erbfeind Christliches Namen* (Victory Pillar of Penance and Faith against Christianity's Hereditary Foe, 1675), or Abraham à Sancta Clara's *Auff, auff Ihr Christen! Christliche . . . Waffen Wider Den Türckischen Bluet=Egel [und] Ottomanischen Erb-Feind* (Get Going, Christians! Christian . . . Arms Against the Turkish Leech [and] Ottoman Hereditary Foe, 1683).[13]

Returning to our central argument: one significant rhetorical strategy in *turcica* is the abundant use of sexually provocative images and language. This focus on sexuality was to be heightened and transformed by the publication of the *Arabian Nights*, a work that significantly influenced the representation of the "Orient" and the "Oriental." However, its first translation into a European vernacular—Antoine Galland's *Les mille et une nuits: Contes arabes* (1704–6)—did not appear until the early eighteenth century, and it was followed in quick succession by editions in other European languages. By that time Ottoman military power had declined sharply, and we find new forms of confrontation and engagement with the Islamic world reflected in eighteenth-century texts. When analyzing pre-eighteenth-century materials, we have to remember that while the year 1492 (when Christopher Columbus's expedition arrived in the Americas) is frequently connected to studies of the Other, 29 May 1453 (the "Fall of Constantinople") is the foundational date[14] for the birth of *turcica*. These works that focused on Turks reflect a process of Othering based on military and political inferiority, or perceived inferiority, of the writers' culture(s) that differ, therefore, from the Orientalism defined by Edward Said, which was the product of a perceived "positional superiority."[15] Gerald MacLean pointed out how "before Orientalism, there was Ottomanism," which he also calls "imperial envy"[16] and which is a notion that complicates concepts of Orientalism for the early-modern period. With the term "Ottomanism" MacLean describes "the tropes, structures, and fantasies by means of which Europeans sought to make knowable the imperial Ottoman other" (86).

However, the Other is not just a different, contrasting Other but is in many instances an evil one, an image already well-established by the sixteenth century.[17] We may want to interpret the Othering of Turks as the expression of the early-modern anxiety brought about by substantial political, economic, social, and cultural upheaval.

Stigmatization of the Other as evil may have served to cover up conflicts and contradictions within a society in flux, as well as the perceived sources of such destabilization.[18] Gaston Bachelard showed that a "house constitutes a body of images that give mankind proofs or illusions of stability."[19] Similarly, creating a geographical house or space of Christendom, by defining boundaries (walls) with respect to Islam, would generate a sense of stability. As Lynne Tatlock has suggested, when referring to books by the seventeenth-century Hamburg author Eberhard Werner Happel, *turcica* underscore the instability and chaos in the Islamic world, which may have drawn readers' attention away from the daily experience of instability and chaos in their own.[20]

Although Said's focus on Orientalism as colonial discourse might not be as useful an analytical tool for interpreting the *turcica* under scrutiny here, his socio-psychological analysis of the Other as instrumental in delineating the Self holds true. In *Orientalism* and the other publications that followed, he demonstrated the need to construct the Arab as the Other in order for the European to define a Self, given that

> the development and maintenance of every culture require the existence of another, different and competing *alter ego*. The construction of identity . . . involves the construction of opposites and "others" whose actuality is always subject to the continuous interpretation and re-interpretation of their differences from "us."[21]

Turcica do have, as Wolfgang Neuber agrees, an "immens wichtige Bedeutung . . . bei der Selbstvergewisserung und Identitätsstiftung von Gesellschaften," attesting to the immeasurable significance of the discussion about the Other for the self-assurance and identity-establishment of societies. Neuber further reminds us that we should not underestimate "den Diskurs, die Rede über etwas, als bedingende Form des Handelns und zumal als jenen Ort, wo sich soziale Übereinkunft und die Konstruktion des gesellschaftlichen Selbst vollziehen."[22]

This discourse, then, is the very site where social accord is reached and social identity constructed. Here boundaries are negotiated and "any form of self-ascertainment and the construction of identity can be found" (256). As the Turk is not thought to be so different from the Christian given the relatively comparable religious and social conventions of the two faiths/cultures, Islam is continuously portrayed as a heresy or deviation from Christianity. This, in turn, demands the erection of boundaries between those faiths, between "us" and "them," an obsession that produced an overwhelming torrent of publications and an abundance of boundary-related tropes within *turcica*.

The habitually pompous phraseology in German fifteenth- to seventeenth-century *turcica* expresses certain *topoi* fairly regularly: the Turk as arch-enemy and hereditary foe; the need for a unified Christendom as an essential prerequisite to the expulsion of Turks from Europe; the necessity of a Crusade/Holy War against Islam (which reappears again and again until as late as the second half of the seventeenth century); the Turk as the whip of God or tool of the Devil (or both);[23] the Turk as Antichrist; Turkish sexuality as deviant; and Islam as a deception or lie and the Turk as a liar (or the entire Muslim religion as fraudulent). The following discussion will focus on the latter two topoi.

Authors of *turcica* routinely refer to Islam as a "sect" and a religious hotchpotch or "mélange" to discredit the faith and demonstrate its fraudulence. The use of the word "sect" in particular constitutes an attempt to mark out a false religion. Examples can be found in Jacob Holderbusch's calendar, entitled the *Alter und Neuer Türcken-Kalender, . . . des Ottomanischen Hauses, Anfang, Aufnahm und Untergang vorzeigend* (1683; Old and New Turkish Calendar, Showing the Origins, Rise, and Fall of the Ottomans), which employs the term "Muhammedische Sect,"[24] and in Erasmus Francisci's *Die herandringende Türcken-Gefahr* (1663; The Approaching Turkish Danger) containing the similar formulation "Mahometische Secte."[25] The repeated use of this term "sect" emphasizes a secession or renunciation of a religious faith. The German term "Sect(e)" was used at this time routinely to indicate heresy or an "Irrelehre"—that is, a misguided or erroneous faith.[26]

It is important to note, then, that the Turk is not an entirely strange Other but rather a stranger in a *known* space; a deviation from the norm of the same. Wolfgang Neuber calls this phenomenon "Abtrünnigkeit vom eigenen Glauben" (apostasy), and the Ottoman Turks thus become "Fremde in einem bekannten Raum" (strangers in familiar territory).[27] This alarming closeness frequently finds expression in the idea of the "mélange" of religious doctrine (assumed to be true and factual) with "falsehoods" of varying origins. The subsequent pages will demonstrate the idea of "mélange" in several authors' writings, keeping in mind Henri Lefebvre's suggestion that abstract space inflicts and reinforces social homogeneity.[28]

In his refutation of the *Koran*, Dionysius von Rickel concludes that although the text includes some genuine truths, other content has been disproved. His refutation has the side-effect of questioning all the "truthful" portions of the *Koran* and thus its entire content. Indeed, the very title of the refutation, published in 1540, is rather revealing: *Alchoran: Das ist, des Mahometischen Gesatzbuchs, und Türkischen Aberglaubens ynhalt und ablänung* (The Koran: That is, the Content and Refutation of the Muhammedan Code and Turkish Superstition).[29] Although "Aberglaube" in contemporary usage denotes a relatively harmless superstition, like "knocking on wood" perhaps, it was used to signify far more sinister fallacies in Dionysius von Rickel's time. According to the *Grimmsches Wörterbuch*, "Aberglaube" is "was über den wahren glauben hinaus, daran neben vorbei geht" (*DW* 1:32). It is thereby that which goes beyond or passes by true faith or dogma. Given that the author cannot refute the Muslim belief in such things as Christ's miracles, he responds with the indictment that the "truth" is employed solely to cover up the "untruth":

> Ach du armer Mahomet, was misst du dir so frevel zu, das allein Christo zugehöret, dem aller Gewalt geben ist im himmel und auff erden. Wie darffstu deinen lugen mit der warheit beschönen wöllen, und etwas so der warheit änlich, under dein gedycht vermischen. . . . Item, das jüngst gericht wird über gute und böße geen, dißen zu ewiger freüd, und den anderen zu ewiger verdamnussz, ist alles war, aber deine yngemischte fantasey, on schrifft und warheit, gantz lugenhafft und erdycht.[30]

> [Oh, you poor Mohammed, how do you hold yourself up in a sacrilegious fashion, [to take] what only belongs to Christ, who has been endowed with all heavenly and earthly power. How dare you attempt to adorn your lies with the truth and mix something akin to the truth into your invention. . . . In short, the Last Judgement will be passed on the good and evil; unto the good: eternal bliss, unto the others: eternal damnation, that is all true, but your admixed fantasy, without the Bible and the truth, [is] all lies and invented.]

Given Mohammed's "blasphemy," Dionysius von Rickel's logic concludes: "The good Christian will therefore find that nothing more need be studied than the genuine and true witnesses of God's will, the Old and New Testaments. There is no need to add anything" (H, iiiᵛ). The Koran, he insists, is a mélange with ingredients from the Old and the New Testament, intermingled with fables and lies: "Er hat wol sein Alchoran gespickt, und zusammen gelesen, uß beyden Alt und Newem Testamenten, aber vil seiner fabelen und lugen darzwischen yngemischt."[31] Mohammed's Koran, according to this source, is "interlarded with and gleaned from both the Old and New Testaments," but he "admixed a lot of his fables and lies in between." In Dionysius von Rickel's opinion, then, "truth" on the one hand and "lie" or "fiction" on the other are mixed, whereby the "truth" has become contaminated or perverted. Von Rickel considers Mohammed, the mixer of this concoction, to be an impostor, because he sees the Prophet's act of merging "true" and "untrue" beliefs as an instance of deception or even perversion. The *Koran* is itself "gemischt," a textual form of mélange, exhibiting all forms of deceit, scam, superstition, and heresy: "Ja freilich zöigt es an allen betrug, beschissz, aberglaub und ketzerey."[32]

In *turcica*, the denotation of Islam as a sect, the idea of a religious mélange, and the idea of fraud go hand in hand. An example of this would be Martin Luther's rejection of Islam as "a patchwork of Jewish, Christian, and heathen beliefs" in his sermon "Vom kriege widder die Türken" (1529; On War against the Turk).[33] Luther is therefore sure that "the Turks' holiness is the very dregs of all abominations and errors."[34] In fact, the idea of Islam as a "corruption of true religion" had already been put forth by John Wycliffe in the fourteenth century,[35] and we even find it in the writings of the Humanist Erasmus, who labels Islam a "sect," and a "mélange" of Judaism, Christianity, and paganism.[36] The sixteenth-century Lutheran Justus Jonas condemns Islam as "teufflische secten, und Mahometischen yrthumb"[37] (devilish sect and Mohammedan folly), and Muslims to him are a "teuffelische rotte und secte . . . mit newer falschen lare" (a devilish gang and sect with new false teachings). For him, the Devil and the *Koran* are intricately connected, for "ertichtet der teuffel durch Mahomet ein newe lare, die alle religiones zusamen fasset" (D). Via Mohammed, insists Jonas, the Devil concocted this new doctrine that interweaves all religions—the result of which is a wickedly deceitful work: "Im Alcoran aber ist nichts dan . . . unverschampt lügen und grewlich Gottes lesterung" (E, ii). Although the "truth" of Christianity is part of the mix, Jonas denigrates the mix as a whole as a shameless falsehood and sees in the *Koran* blasphemy and indeed the work of the devil, or the "grossen grewlichen teuffels lügen."[38]

Turcica, as was stated earlier, can also take the form of songs. In one such anonymous song from circa 1683 we see Mohammed portrayed as the great and arch fraudster: "Mahomet, der groß- und Ertz-Betrieger."[39] Another song title focuses on his deceitfulness that is "dem verlogenen GOTT MAHOMET." The lyrics of that same song coin the compound noun: "Dein Lügen-Alcoran."[40] (Koran of Lies) However, it may be Abraham à Sancta Clara who with his distinctive rhetorical dexterity paints the most visually intriguing image in the 1683 *Auff/ auff Ihr*

Christen!. He eggs on his readers to wage war against the false faith by appealing to them to "streitte[n] wider den Mahometanischen Irrthum" (fight against Muslim aberration),[41] and he calls the *Koran* a crude stew, cooked by the diabolical chef Mohammed in a frying pan: a "gemischte Speiß" (3), "[vom] Teuffels=Koch [Muhammad] in einer Pfann gesotten" (131). Abraham à Sancta Clara does not stand alone with his cooking analogy; Martin Luther used the turn of phrase: "Es ist die Grundsuppe da aller grewel und yrthum" (literally: the dregs of the soup of horror and aberration) to describe Islam,[42] and Dionysius von Rickel, as noted above, employed the term "interlarded," which is today commonly used to describe bloated or inflated speech or writing style, but in his day had clear culinary connotations.

Aside from mélange and deceit, authors refer to more basic forms of apparent Islamic trickery. One example of this can be found in Salomon Schweigger's *Ein newe Reyßbeschreibung auß Teutschland Nach Konstantinopel* (1608; A New Account of a Journey from Germany to Constantinople). Like most such travel writers, Schweigger emphasizes how his observations are based his own personal experience, as can be seen from the continuation of his lengthy title.[43] Schweigger (1551–1622) was a theologian—indeed, he held the position of *Hofprediger* (court preacher)—and like Stefan Gerlach he accompanied a diplomatic party to Constantinople in 1577. Within his travel narrative, Schweigger explains to his readers what a terrible teaching Islam is; it was, after all, created by Satan himself. The fact that Satan's authorship is concealed by the text's beautiful outward appearance with its golden letters further demonstrates Islam's trickery or treachery:

> die Türckisch Lehr ist . . . ein schreckliche grewliche und abscheuliche Lehr / deren autor der alte Trach der Teuffel selbst ist / unangesehen daß sie mit gülden Buchstaben geschrieben / das ist der eusserlich schein / damit sie die Trachengestalt verstreichen / und dem grewel ein ansehen machen. (104)

In 1616 the very same Salomon Schweigger published a *Koran* refutation, entitled

> Alcoranus mahometicus, das ist: Der Türcken Alcoran, Religion und Aberglauben. Auß welchem zu vernemen / Wann unnd woher ihr falscher Prophet Machomet seinen ursprung oder anfang genommen / mit was gelegenheit derselb diß sein Fabelwerck / lächerliche und närrische Lehr gedichtet und erfunden / Auch von seinen Träumen und verführerischem Menschentand.[44]

This title, on the one hand, provides a practical example of the typical conflation of the words "Turk" and "Muslim" ("Mohammed's Koran, that is, the Koran of the Turks, their religion and superstition"). On the other hand, it presupposes that the Turks are guilty of fraud and treachery, as the "false prophet" concocted and fabricated a tempting work of fables including ridiculous and foolish teachings. Furthermore, the title refers to Mohammed's "dreams" (presumably a trivialization of his revelations) and his seductive man-made trumpery or worthless nonsense ("Menschentand").

Almost a hundred years earlier, Martin Luther even went so far as to dehumanize those who fall prey to the seductive allure of the *Koran*. In the preface to his *Koran* refutation from 1542, he states that it is important to have access to the details of Mohammed's faith in order to strengthen Christians against conversion; this is the primary rationale for publishing on matters Islamic. Here, too, he calls the text a lie and even goes to such lengths as to represent Muslims as non-humans ("unmenschen"), rocks ("Stein") and blocks ("Klotz") if they indeed believe the teachings of the *Koran:*

> Wo nu die Türcken . . . solchem Buch des Mahmets, dem Alcoran, mit Ernst gleuben, So sind sie nicht werd, das sie Menschen heissen, als die gemeiner Menschlichen vernunfft beraubt, lauter ummenschen, Stein und Klotz worden sind.[45]

Das deutsche Wörterbuch by Jacob and Wilhelm Grimm defines "Unmensch" as "counterpart" or "opposite" (gegenstück) to "mensch" (*DW*, 24:1173). This is, of course, not a historically stable idea and therefore lends itself to multiple negative meanings reflecting "[die] verschiedenheit des menschenideals in den einzelnen culturzeitaltern" (24:1173). Late-medieval and early-modern meanings of "Unmensch" include "monstrum, miszgeburt, bestia, wilder, noch nicht mensch, kannibale," as well as "zauberer, hexenmeister, hexe, satan, sodomit, päderast, Türke, gottloser, ruchloser schlechthin" (24:1173). The Grimms' example of the use of the word to refer to Turks stems from the seventeenth-century mystic Christian Hohburg: "ich lebe . . . nicht natürlich, wie Türcken und andere unmenschen, sondern geistlich."[46]

A final and powerful instance that strongly promotes the idea of Islam as a negatively hybridized faith can be found in Mathias Loncier's political book entitled *Wer da? Wer da? Der Türck / der Feind. Gebt Feur! Gebt Feur! Ha! Ha! drauff! Drauff! VICTORIA! VICTORIA! Wolmeinend ausgegeben Von einem Christlichen Erb-Feinde des Wieder-Christlichen Erb-Feindes* (1683). Mohammed has, according to Loncier, conceived of a strange religious mélange, "eine sonderliche Mängerey in der Religion ersonnen."[47] He did not do so on his own, however. His helper, presumably the Devil, infused the religious mix into Mohammed: "bließ . . . dem Mahometh / als einem bequemen Werckzeuge / die Mängerey in der Religion ein" (C1[v]). The contradiction implicit in the verbs "ersonnen" and "eingeblasen," that is between the condemnations of Mohammed as creator of Islam and as simply the Devil's tool, is overlooked by the author.

Loncier points to claims that Mohammed had additional help (beyond that of the Devil) in producing his "religious mélange" (C1ᵛ), among them a group of secretly assembled Jews who pieced together a new doctrine, which the "foolish" Arabs immediately fell for and began to honor: "Diese [Jews] stücketen und flicketen eine neue Lehr zusammen / darinn sich die törichten Araber / so fort mit Verwunderung verliebeten / und zu ehren begunten / denn die Araber sind die ersten des Mahometischen Glaubens und Antichristlichen Reichs" (C2).

The mélange ("Mängerei") blurs the perceived boundary between "true religion" and "lie." The creator of the mélange "mixes" true (that is, Christian) and untrue elements in Islam. The word "Turk" and its derivatives even came to be used when the deed was not carried out by Turks *per se*, as Brandon Beck points out: "As a verb form there was the . . . word *türcken*, to twist . . . about, or to wrap about. It meant to change or alter, usually for the worse."[48] The colloquial *türken*, incidentally, is still used today in German to express the notion "to fake" (something like a letter or document) and "to make up" (a story or report): a "getürktes Kartenspiel" would be a stacked deck of cards and "getürkte Würfel" would be loaded dice. Often, the term is employed in connection with data, such as in "die Statistik türken," meaning "to massage the figures." The discussion below will look further at how the perceived penetration of the boundaries of Christian belief and identity were associated with another transgression, this time in the sphere of sexuality. The combination of the two areas of denunciation (religious and sexual) generated a particularly powerful statement about potential cultural contamination and served to further discredit Islam in its entirety.

Although the *imago Turci* produced in texts from the fifteenth to seventeenth centuries had not been influenced by the fantastic tales of the Arabian Nights, these earlier texts were still infused with sexual connotations. In his 1529 sermon "Vom kriege widder die Türken," Luther, for instance, used terms such as "verbotten ehe" and "hunde hochzeit" to describe sexual relationships between Muslims ("Marriage," "ehe" refers here in veiled form to sexual intercourse[49]). Both these expressions highlight its illicit carnal aspects: "forbidden marriage" refers to sodomy in its broad early-modern sense, and a dog's salaciousness was proverbial.[50] Luther also called the Ottoman Empire an "öffentliche herrliche sodoma," the space where "stumme Sünden" are carried out.[51] This expression, "dumb sins," refers to all illicit and therefore sinful sexual acts, including heterosexual anal intercourse, same-sex activities, masturbation, and bestiality.[52]

Turcica regularly portray Turkish sexuality as "anti-Christian"; they constantly makes reference to polygamy, salaciousness, vice, fornication, sodomy, and repeatedly names the Turk a "dog." As in the case of religious fraudulence, derivatives of the term "Turk" came to be used metaphorically to denote sexual deviance in general, as evidenced by Luther's terms "Türkische ehe," that is forbidden, un-Christian, sexual intercourse, and "Türckische breute," signifying persons with sexual practices considered sinful by Christianity.[53] Indeed, the construction of Turkish sexual mores took on extreme forms. David Schuster, in his late seventeenth-century admonition written for the simple "German man," lest he consider converting to Islam when finding himself in an Ottoman-occupied area or when captured, insists that Muslim voluptuousness leads to multiple sexual boundary-crossings including the so-called "Turkish vice" of heterosexual anal intercourse. He ends his drawn-out list of transgressions with a most imaginative account of bestiality, extending even to fish: "Ja sie seyn so gail, daß sie auch, sonderlich die Mahometisten am rothen Meer, die jenige Fisch, so weibliche Geburts-Glieder haben, angehen."[54] Schuster's curious report of intercourse with fish is not only a rare instance where the term "Mahometisten" rather than "Türcken" denotes Muslims but, significantly for this study, also indicates the notion of another boundary crossed: that between human and animal. Of course, in this discourse, those who mix their seed with animals are the same as those who mix true and untrue religious thought.

In 1612, the travel account author Hans Jacob Breüning presents a vivid and lengthy description of bestiality in his *Orientalische Reyß* (Oriental Journey). He defames Mohammed, and thus the entire religion, by offering a tale about the Prophet's sodomitic acts with a great variety of animal species, culminating in the special treatment of a camel. Particularly interesting in this context is the use of "vermischt" in Breüning's bizarre anecdote:

> Nämblich das Machomet ihr Prophet nach dem er mit neun unnd neunzigerley generationen oder geschlechten allerhand unvernünfftigen thieren, sich vermischt, und mit denen allen zu schaffen gehabt, allhie an diesem ort ein kameel angetroffen, welches ebenmässig herhalten müssen, und weil es die hunderste zahl erfüllet, hab er darüber seinen sonderlichen segen gesprochen, dasselbige gebenedeyet und geheyliget.[55]

As the camel represented the hundredth species that had to submit to him, the Prophet is said to have spoken a "special benediction" over it, and "blessed and sanctified" the animal after "mixing his seed" with it.[56]

Breüning justifies this narrative (or rather, his telling of the story) on educational grounds: to demonstrate Mohammed's "bestialisch, viehisch, Gottloß und gantz Teuffelisch leben." The revelation of this "bestial, brutish, godless, and thoroughly devilish life" (183) is considered necessary so that the reader will grasp that Satan himself directed this prophet. Sarcastically, Breüning calls the Devil a "pure clean spirit and black angel [who] guided and led this prophet" and was responsible for his "glorious deeds and good works" which are a "great deception": "[zu zeigen] was für ein reiner sauberer Geyst, und schwartzer Engel, diesen Propheten geleitet unnd geführet, auch was seine rühmliche thaten und gute werck gewesen, und was diß für ein grosse blendtnüß sey" (183). "Glorious deeds and good works," "guiding," and "leading" are forces accepted by Christianity, and thus draw attention to a sense of usurpation by Islam, or, in Edward Said's words, a "misguided version of Christianity."[57] Islam is understood as "deception," not because it is so alien to Christianity, but precisely because it is so similar. Tropes of Islamic sexual deviancy depicting Mohammed "mixing his seed with mindless animals" parallel and reinforce metaphors of the Prophet cooking up in his frying pan a "mix" of religions, and adding fables, "false dreams," and trumpery for spice: Islam appears exposed as an essentially deviant, fraudulent, religion.

In the anonymous play *Das entsetzte Wien* (1683), Mohammed, burning with desire for this bride, Vienna, will do anything to win her:

Und Muhammed . . .,

. . .

Indem nach dieser Braut er hefftig brennt,
Läßt keine Janitzscharen,
Sie zu erobern, sparen.[58]

Vienna's relief is then celebrated with the words: "Weil sie kein Sebel mehr verletzet!"[59] In terms underwritten by two hundred years of *turcica*, Vienna is portrayed as the virgin bride, and the Ottoman Empire as the threat armed with the phallic sabre. In a similar vein, Eberhard Werner Happel, referring in 1684 to the second Turkish siege of Vienna, portrays the city as "die Vormauer der gantzen Christenheit," the wall protecting all of Christendom (in Latin *antemurale christianitatis*, "forewall" or "bulwark").[60] Vienna is effectively the hymen of Christianity: should Vienna be penetrated by Muslim force/s, the entire Christian "body"—or community—will be polluted with the semen of falsehood and deceit, that is, Islam.[61]

Happel uses similar imagery elsewhere, again employing the term "Vormauer":

Es war kaum die Bottschafft von der belagerten Stadt Wien durch Expressen denen mit Se. Käyserl. Mayst. Alliirten hohen Potentaten hinterbracht, alß ein jeder . . . bedacht war, dieser Vormauer auffs aller sondersambste und kräfftigste beyzuspringen, damit ein so beträchtlicher Orth, auß welchem halb Teutschland kan infestiret, wo nicht gar bezwungen worden, in des unglaubigen Feindes Macht verfiele.[62]

Happel explains how all (Christians) were anxious to help the besieged "forewall" because from this particular place half of Germany could be "infested" by the infidel enemy, reinforcing the above sexual analogy. The same sexual innuendo evident in the preceding quotes can be found in the depiction of Hungary after Muslim conquest offered in the anonymous pamphlet *Außführliche Relation*. It paints Hungary as a formerly noble, ancient, and Christian kingdom, and as a previous *Vormauer* against the Muslim hereditary foe, now reduced to a miserable spectacle, soaked with "precious Christian blood":

> das edle, uhralte, Christliche Königreich Ungarn, als welches bißan-hero der Christen Vor-Mauer gegen dem Erb-Feind gewesen, stehet uns billich als ein erbärmliches Spectacul vor Augen . . . mit theurem Christen-Blut befeuchtet.[63]

This interpenetration of religious, sexual, and political ideology is reminiscent of Jonathan Goldberg's 1992 discussion of a T-shirt advertisement from the magazine *Rolling Stone*. The image on the garment has the caption "America Will Not be Saddam-ized." In his introduction to *Sodometries,* Goldberg associates the image with "sodomy as the vice of Mediterranean/Islamic cultures, a recurring notion in English Renaissance texts."[64] As this chapter has demonstrated, this is also a recurring notion in historical German language *turcica*.

Both sexual deviance and the fraudulence of Islam came to be used as metaphors. And the crossing of religious and sexual boundaries was literally as well as metaphorically associated with Turks. Images of the Turk as religious fraudster and as sexual pervert are indeed inseparable in early-modern constructions of the Muslim Other, and both are linked to the erection and defense of boundaries of various forms. Such a conflation of the deviant and outlander had already been noted by Magnus Hirschfeld in 1914, and he linked the two again in his posthumously published *Racism* (1938):[65] "From the dawn of history till now it has been usual to hold specified foreigners responsible for sexual practices condemned as immoral."[66]

There is a final twist to this story: the Muslim "Others" of *turcica* have their own Others as well. This finds its expression in Stephan Gerlach's *Tagebuch,* in the continuation of the quotation that opened this chapter:

> Nach dem Mittag-Essen einen Tanz durch 2. Buben (deren sie zu ihrer Schande missbrauchen / welche verfluchte Unweiß in der Türckey sehr gemein / und daß sie von den Welschen hinein gebracht worden / auch ehrliche Türcken beklagen) halten lassen.[67]

Gerlach recounts not only that he and his company were treated to a dance after lunch by "two boys whom the Turks abuse disgracefully (that cursed practice very commonly carried out in Turkey)," but also the fact that "honest Turks" deplore this very vice, which was brought to the Ottoman Empire by the Italians in the first place. Clearly, the binary oppositions constructed in the process of identity formation are in a constant state of flux, or, as Said expressed it, ("they") are "subject to the continuous interpretation and re-interpretation of their differences from 'us.'"[68] At the same time, as Lynne Tatlock pointed out, "under different historical circumstances a different set of foreign peoples could have played these parts equally effectively."[69] The fact that this discussion about deviance in *turcica* has little to do with Turkish "nature," or genuine religious differences, but rather more with boundaries and space, or in Helmut Puff's words, a "geography of perversion,"[70] becomes particularly apparent when the source of illicit activity is not the Turks but another Other.

Notes

I gratefully acknowledge the funding received for this research from the Canadian Social Sciences and Humanities Research Council.

[1] Stephan Gerlach, *Tage-Buch/ Der von zween Glorwürdigsten Römischen Käysern / Maximiliano und Rudolpho, Beyderseits den Andern dieses Nahmens / Höchstseeligster Gedächtnüß / An die Ottomannische Pforte zu Constantinopel Abgefertigten / Und durch den Wohlgebohrnen Herrn Hn. David Ungnad / Freyherrn zu Sonnegk und Preyburg &c.... Mit würcklicher Erhalt- und Verlängerung deß Friedens/ zwischen dem Ottomannischen und Römischen Käyserthum und demselben angehörigen Landen und Köngreichen &c. Glücklichst-vollbrachter Gesandtschafft: / Auß denen Gerlachischen/ Zeit Seiner hierbey bedienten Hoff-Prediger-Ampts-Stelle / eygenhändig auffgesetzten und nachgelassenen Schrifften / Herfür gegeben durch Seinen Enckel M. Samuelem Gerlachium, Special-Superintendenten zu Gröningen/ in dem Hertzogthum Würtemberg. Mit einer Vorrede / Herrn Tobiæ Wagneri . . .* (Frankfurt am Main: Zunner, 1674), 16. Insertions in square brackets are mine, as are all translations, unless noted otherwise.

[2] *Turcica* are, for the purpose of this chapter, and following the nomenclature used in much scholarly literature after Carl Göllner's *Turcica: Die europäischen Türkendrucke des XVI. Jahrhunderts* (Bucharest: Editura Academiei, 1978), the printed materials concentrating on "Turks."

[3] See Cornelia Kleinlogel, *Exotik—Erotik: Zur Geschichte des Türkenbildes in der deutschen Literatur der frühen Neuzeit (1453–1800)* (Frankfurt am Main: Lang, 1989).

[4] While there are a few occasions when the terms "Muhammedans" or "Mahometisten" were used to refer to Muslims, the conflation of "Turk" and "Muslim" was considerably more common. See Robert Schwoebel, *The Shadow of the Crescent: The Renaissance Image of the Turk (1453–1517)* (1967; repr., New York: St. Martin's P, 1969), 226. Brandon H. Beck, *From the Rising of the Sun: English Images of the Ottoman Empire to 1715* (New York: Lang, 1987), 29. Johann Ulrich Wallich, *Religio Turcica et Mahometis Vita. Das ist: Kurtze, warhafftige, gründ- und eigendliche Beschreibung Türkischer Religion, Wie auch Leben, Wandel und Tod des Arabischen falschen Propheten Mahometis* ([No pl.]: [No publ.], 1664), 19.

[5] Gerlach, *Tage-Buch*, 54.

[6] Georg Simmel, "Das Problem der Soziologie," in *Soziologie: Untersuchungen über die Formen der Vergesellschaftung* (Berlin: Duncker & Humblot, 1908) 1–31; here 23.

[7] Georg Simmel, "Der Raum und die räumlichen Ordnungen der Gesellschaft," in *Soziologie: Untersuchungen über die Formen der Vergesellschaftung*, 460–526; here 461.

[8] Johannes Wallmann, "Reflexionen und Bemerkungen zur Frömmigkeitskrise des 17. Jahrhunderts," in *Krisen des 17. Jahrhunderts: Interdisziplinäre Perspektiven*, ed. Manfred Jakubowski-Tiessen (Gottingen: Vandenhoeck & Ruprecht, 1999) 25–42; here 35.

[9] Carl Göllner, *Die Türkenfrage in der öffentlichen Meinung Europas im 16. Jahrhundert*, vol. 3 of: *Turcica: Die europäischen Türkendrucke des XVI. Jahrhunderts* (Bucharest: Editura Academiei, 1978), 18. See also J. W. Bohnstedt, *The Infidel Scourge of God: The Turkish Menace as Seen by German Pamphleteers of the Reformation Era*, vol. 51, part 9 of Transactions of The American Philosophical Society (Philadelphia: The American Philosophical Society, 1968), 9.

[10] Anon., *Eyn manung der cristenheit widder die durken* (Mainz: Gutenberg, Dec. 1454; repr., Cologne: Gutenberg-Gesellschaft, 1928).

[11] See Ferdinand Geldner, "Bemerkungen zum Text des 'Türkenschreis' von Balthasar Mandelreiß, des 'Türkenkalenders' (1454) und der 'Ermanung . . . wider die Türken' von Niclas Wolgemut," *Gutenberg Jahrbuch* 58 (1983): 166–71; Göllner, *Die Türkenfrage*, 37; and Gustav Mori, *Der Türken-Kalender für das Jahr 1455: Eine druckhistorische Studie* (Mainz: Gutenberg-Gesellschaft, 1928).

[12] The newspaper was the *Turckischer Estaats und Krieges-Bericht*, published in Hamburg from Sept. 1683–Dec. 1684. In book form, [Eberhard Werner Happel], *Der türckische Schau-Platz: Eröfnet und fürgestelt in sehr vielen nach dem Leben gezeichneten Figuren* (Hamburg: Wiering, 1685).

[13] Catharina Regina von Greiffenberg, *Sieges-Seule der Buße und des Glaubens, wider den Erbfeind Christliches Namen* (Nürnberg: Hofmann, 1675); Abraham à Sancta Clara [= Johann Ulrich Megerle], *Auff/ auff Ihr Christen! . . . Christliche . . . Waffen Wider Den Türckischen Bluet=Egel [und] Ottomanischen Erb=Feind . . .* (Vienna: Gehlen, 1683).

[14] See Almut Höfert, *Den Feind beschreiben: "Türkengefahr" und europäisches Wissen über das osmanische Reich, 1450–1600* (Frankfurt am Main: Campus, 2003), 56–57, 314.

[15] Edward W. Said, *Orientalism* (New York: Vintage Books, 1978), 7.

[16] Gerald MacLean, "Ottomanism before Orientalism? Bishop King Praises Henry Blount, Passenger in the Levant," in *Travel Knowledge: European "Discoveries" in the Early Modern Period*, ed. Ivo Kamps and Jyotsna Singh (New York, NY: Palgrave, 2001), 85–96; here 94.

[17] Dieter Mertens, "*Claromontani passagii exemplum*: Papst Urban II. und der erste Kreuzzug in der Türkenkriegspropaganda des Renaissance-Humanismus," in *Europa und die Türken in der Renaissance*, ed. Bodo Guthmüller and Wilhelm Kühlmann (Tubingen: Niemeyer, 2000), 65–78; here 65–66.

[18] Klaus Reichert, "'Ich bin ich': Auftritt neuer Formen des Bösen in der Frühen Neuzeit," *Zeitsprünge: Forschungen zur Frühen Neuzeit* 1.2 (1997): 269–78, esp. 269.

[19] Gaston Bachelard, *The Poetics of Space,* trans. Maria Jolas (Boston: Beacon, 1969), 17.

[20] Lynne Tatlock, "Selling Turks: Eberhard Werner Happel's *Turcica* (1683–1690)," in *Colloquia Germanica* 28.3/4 (1995): 307–35; here 335.

[21] Said, "Afterword," in *Orientalism,* 329–52, here 331–32.

[22] Wolfgang Neuber, "Grade der Fremdheit: Alteritätskonstruktionen und experientia-Argumentation in deutschen Turcica der Renaissance," in Guthmüller and Kühlmann, *Europa und die Türken in der Renaissance,* 249–265; here 250.

[23] An example of this would be Martin Luther's words "Since the Turk is the rod of the wrath of the Lord our God and the servant of the raging devil," in "On War Against the Turk" (Vom kriege widder die Türcken" [1529]) in *Luther's Works: American Edition,* ed. Jaroslav Pelikan and Helmut T. Lehmann, 55 vols. (Philadelphia: Fortress P, 1955–76), 46:161–205; here 170.

[24] Jacob Holderbusch, *Alter und Neuer Türcken-Kalender, In welchem nicht allein zu finden, was in denen 4 Jahrs- und Monat-Zeiten, Gewittern und andern Zufällen zu vermuthen, Sondern auch des Ottomanischen Hauses, Anfang, Aufnahm und Untergang vorzeigend . . .* (Nuremberg: Endter, 1683), "September."

[25] [Erasmus Francisci,] *Die herandringende Türcken-Gefahr: Das ist; Wohlgemeinte, doch unvorgreiffliche Erinnerung, in was hochbesorgtem und gefährlichem Zustande, unser liebes Vatterland Teutscher Nation, und das gantze Heil. Röm. Reich jetziger Zeit stecke: auch wie diesem blutdürstigem Erb= und Ertz=Feinde fruchtbar- und ersprießlich zu begegnen wäre: Vermittelst einer Unterredung fürgestellet . . .* ([No pl.]: [no publ.], 1663), Jᵛ.

[26] See Jacob Grimm and Wilhelm Grimm, *Deutsches Wörterbuch,* 16 vols. [in 32 vols.] (Leipzig: S. Hirzel: 1854–1960), vol. 16, column 407–8. Further references to this dictionary are given using the abbreviation *DW,* the volume number, and the column number.

[27] Neuber, "Grade der Fremdheit," 255.

[28] Henri Lefebvre, *The Production of Space,* trans. Donald Nicholson-Smith (Oxford: Blackwell, 1991).

[29] Dionysius von Rickel [= Dionysius Carthusianus], *Alchoran: Das ist, des Mahometischen Gesatzbuchs, und Türkischen Aberglaubens ynnhalt und ablänung* (Strassburg: Schott, 1540).

[30] Dionysius von Rickel, *Alchoran,* H, iiv.

[31] Dionysius von Rickel, *Alchoran,* C, iv.

[32] Dionysius von Rickel, *Alchoran,* C, iv. The term "beschisz" is meant in the contemporary sense (cheat, scam, rip-off, swindle).

[33] Luther, "On War," 177. German version in *D. Martin Luthers Werke: Kritische Gesamtausgabe* (Weimar: Böhlau, 1883–2005), 30/II:107–48; here 122, 29–30. Further references to this work are given using the abbreviation WA, followed by the volume number, page, and line.

34 Luther, "On War," 184.

35 Schwoebel, *The Shadow of the Crescent*, 219.

36 Jacques Chomarat, *Grammaire et rhetorique chez Erasme*, vol. 2 (Paris: Societé d'Edition "Les Belles Lettres," 1980), 1148.

37 Justus Jonas, *Das siebend Capitel Danielis, von des Türcken Gottes lesterung und schrecklicher morderey, mit unterricht* (Wittemberg: Lufft, [1530]), "Auslegung," not paginated.

38 Jonas, E, *Das siebend Capitel Danielis*, ii; cf. also E, iii.

39 Bertrand Michael Buchmann, *Türkenlieder zu den Türkenkriegen und besonders zur zweiten Wiener Türkenbelagerung* (Vienna: Böhlau, 1983), 84.

40 Buchmann, *Türkenlieder*, 89.

41 Abraham à Sancta Clara [=Johann Ulrich Megerle], *Auff / auff Ihr Christen! Das ist: Ein bewegliche Anfrischung / Der Christlichen Waffen Wider Den Türckischen Bluet=Egel; Sambt Beygefügten Zusatz vieler herrlichen Victorien und Sieg wider solchen Ottomannischen Erb=Feind; Wie auch andere Sittlicher Lehr= und Lob=Verfassung der Martialischen Tapfferkeit; In Eyl ohne Weil / Zusammen getragen* (Vienna: Gehlen, 1683), 1.

42 WA 30/II:129, 5–6.

43 Salomon Schweigger, *Ein newe Reyßbeschreibung auß Teutschland Nach . . . Auffs fleissigst eigener Person verzeichnet und abgerissen Durch Salomon Schweigger / damal Diener am Evangelio übers dritt Jar zu Constantinopel* (Nuremberg: Lantzenberger, 1608).

44 Salomon Schweigger, *Alcoranus mahometicus* (Nuremberg: Halbmayer/Lochner, 1616).

45 Martin Luther, ed. and transl. *Verlegung des Alcoran Bruder Richardi, Prediger Ordens, Anno 1300* (Wittemberg: Lufft, 1542), T^v.

46 Christian Hohburg, *Theologia mystica* (Sultzbach: Crentz, 1730), 368.

47 Mathias Loncier [pseud.], *Wer da? Wer da? Der Türck / der Feind. Gebt Feur! Gebt Feur! Ha! Ha! drauff! Drauff! VICTORIA! VICTORIA! Wolmeinend ausgegeben Von einem Christlichen Erb-Feinde des Wieder-Christlichen Erb-Feindes* (Colberg: Campe, 1683), C, 1^v.

48 Brandon H. Beck, *From the Rising of the Sun: English Images of the Ottoman Empire to 1715* (New York: Lang, 1987), 29.

49 See *DW* 10:1642.

50 See *DW* 10:1914.

51 The expressions "verbotten ehe," "hund hochzeit," "öffentliche herrliche sodoma," and "stumme Sünden" are all in the 1592 "Vom kriege widder die Türken," in WA 30/II:107–48; here 142, 11–26. In English, *Luther's Works*, 46, 255–305; here 198.

52 See *DW* 20:395–97.

53 Luther, 1530, "An die gantze geistlichkeit zu Augsburg versamlet auff den Reichstag Anno 1530: Vermanung Martini Luther," in WA 30/II:268–356; here 337.

[54] David Schuster, *Mahomets und Türcken Greuel. das ist Kurtze, doch allgemeine Historische entwerfung des Mahometisch und Türckischen Unwesens Ursprung Krieg, Tÿranneÿ, Glaubens und Sitten* . . . : *Für den Gemeinen Teutschen Mann* (Frankfurt am Main, 1664), 374.

[55] Hans Jacob Breüning, *Orientalische Reyß Deß Edlen unnd Besten, Hanß Jacob Breüning, von und zu Buochenbach, so er selbander in der Türckey, under deß Türckischen Sultans Jurisdiction und Gebiet, so wol in Europa als Asia und Africa* . . . (Strassburg, 1612), 183.

[56] For a more in-depth analysis regarding the sexual agenda in *turcica*, see Silke R. Falkner, "'Having it off' with Fish, Camels and Lads: Sodomitic Pleasures in Turcica Discourse," *The Journal of the History of Sexuality* 13.4 (2004): 401–27.

[57] Said, *Orientalism*, 61.

[58] Anon. "Das entsetzte Wien" (1683), in *Vier dramatische Spiele über die zweite Türkenbelagerung aus den Jahren 1683–1685*, ed. Carl Glossy, Wiener Neudrucke 8 (Vienna: Konegen, 1884), 29–35; here 33.

[59] "Das entsetzte Wien," 34.

[60] Eberhard Werner Happel, *Die grausame Belagerung Der Käyserl. Residentz-Stadt Wien* . . . *Geschehen im Jahr 1683* (Hamburg: Wiering, 1684), 6.

[61] For a thorough discussion of the gendering of Christian cities and Muslim armies in *turcica*, see Silke R. Falkner, "Images of the Other: The Gender of War in *Turcica* Iconography," in *Traditions and Historical Perspectives*, ed. Attila Kiss and György Szöny, vol. 1 of *The Iconology of Gender* (Szeged, Hungary: YatePress, 2008), 127–42.

[62] Eberhard Werner Happel, *Ander Theil des Historischen Kerns, oder kurtzen Chronica Der merckwürdigsten Welt- und Wunder-Geschichte, welche in denen Jahren 1680, 81, 82, 83, 84, 85, 86, und 87 in der gantzen Welt sich zugetragen* (Hamburg: Wiering, 1688), 58.

[63] Anon. *Außführliche Relation, Welcher Gestalt Die Macht der Türckischen Pforten von verschiedenen Seculis her gewachsen; Und Wie die Christliche Königreiche, Fürstenthümer, Land und Herrschafften, Städte und Festungen nach und nach von den Türcken erobert worden. Mit Beygefügten Ursachen, warumb dem Türckischen Blut-Hund mit vereinigten Waffen zu begegnen sey* (Breslau: Jonisch, [1683]), unpag.

[64] Jonathan Goldberg, *Sodometries: Renaissance Texts, Modern Sexualities* (Stanford, CA: Stanford UP, 1992), 3.

[65] Magnus Hirschfeld, *Die Homosexualität des Mannes und des Weibes* (1914; repr., Berlin: de Gruyter, 1984), 20–22.

[66] Magnus Hirschfeld, *Racism*, trans. Eden Paul and Cedar Paul (London: Victor Gollancz, 1938), 149–56.

[67] Gerlach, *Tage-Buch*, 16.

[68] Said, "Afterword," in *Orientalism,* 329–52; here 331–32.

[69] Tatlock, "Selling Turks," 308.

[70] Helmut Puff, *Sodomy in Reformation Germany and Switzerland, 1400–1600* (Chicago: U of Chicago P, 2003), 127–139.

4: Enlightenment Encounters the Islamic and Arabic Worlds: The German "Missing Link" in Said's Orientalist Narrative (Meiners and Herder)

W. Daniel Wilson

THE CRITIQUES OF EDWARD SAID'S 1978 BOOK *Orientalism*[1] were many and varied, and some of them are addressed in the introduction to this volume. For the purposes of this chapter, the most relevant criticism is that Said did not adequately account for developments in the German-speaking lands.[2] Anticipating this criticism, Said attempted to justify his virtual neglect of the German heritage. He argued that he focused on Britain and France because they were "the pioneer nations in the Orient and in Oriental studies," and also that "these vanguard positions were held by virtue of the two greatest colonial networks in pre-twentieth-century history" (17). Further, he attests that "the sheer quality, consistency, and mass of British, French, and American writing on the Orient lifts it above the doubtless crucial work done in Germany, Italy, Russia, and elsewhere" (17). This is certainly true, though Said introduces a slight note of contradiction when he speaks of the "doubtless crucial work" in these countries and then dismisses its quality. With respect to German scholars in particular, though, the salient point is that they were armchair Orientalists—and thus

> the German Orient was almost exclusively a scholarly, or at least a classical, Orient: it was made the subject of lyrics, fantasies, and even novels, but it was never actual, the way Egypt and Syria were actual for Chateaubriand, Lane, Lamartine, Burton, Disraeli, or Nerval. There is some significance in the fact that the two most renowned German works on the Orient, Goethe's *Westöstlicher Diwan* [*sic*] and Friedrich Schlegel's *Über die Sprache und Weisheit der Inder,* were based respectively on a Rhine journey and on hours spent in Paris libraries. What German Oriental scholarship did was to refine and elaborate techniques whose application was to texts, myths, ideas, and languages almost literally gathered from the Orient by imperial Britain and France. (19)

The mention of Goethe here is somewhat gratuitous, as it is in other parts of the book. However, whenever Said mentions Goethe, he implicates him solidly in the Orientalist project; for example, in a list of twenty otherwise French and British literary writers whose work is "especially rich and makes a significant contribution to building the Orientalist discourse," Goethe's name comes first (99).

Said changed his tone quite markedly in the preface to a 2003 reprint of his book (adapted in a newspaper article widely published in that, the year of his death[3]). Here he implies that the disconnect between German scholarly and literary interest in the Middle East and an imperialist colonial presence might actually be beneficial to a view of the Orient. For Said differentiates here between "knowledge of other peoples and other times that is the result of understanding, compassion, careful study and analysis for their own sakes, and on the other hand knowledge—if that is what it is—that is part of an overall campaign of self-affirmation, belligerency and outright war" (xiv)—the latter trend not unfittingly illustrated by the American invasion of Iraq. Perhaps surprisingly, Said then praises the German classicism and humanism of Goethe and Herder for its empathetic understanding of the Islamic world, particularly in Herder's *Ideen* (1784–91) and Goethe's *West-östlicher Divan* (1819). In fact, together with the Israeli conductor Daniel Barenboim, Said sponsored an orchestra for Jewish and Arab youth called "West-Eastern Divan," which first met in 1999 in Weimar (the 250th anniversary of Goethe's birth, when Weimar was celebrated in the EU as European Capital of Culture). Barenboim explained his and Said's motivations thus: "The reason we named this orchestra is because Goethe was one of the first Germans to be really interested in other countries—he started learning Arabic when he was over 60."[4] In a measure of how "utopian" Barenboim deems the experiment and thus the heritage emanating from Goethe, he says he likes to call it "the sovereign independent republic of the West-Eastern Divan."[5]

These comments might provoke a critique of how Said buys into the common German separation of Weimar Classicism from the world of politics and, in this case, sets it against the world of conflict and war (here, the Iraq war). And perhaps more importantly, someone like Todd Kontje, author of the recent book *German Orientalisms,* would certainly take issue with Said's assertion that in their oriental studies Germans were not seeking "knowledge that is part of an overall campaign of self-affirmation"—for Kontje argues that German Orientalisms were very much part of the German search for national identity.[6] But these issues aside, the most relevant question is: Does Said present an accurate portrayal of "German encounters with Islam"? Of course, Said doesn't claim to treat such a broad topic, but he does indeed give Weimar Classicism a privileged place in his enterprise of unabashed "humanism" (xvii). It is thus perhaps appropriate to begin where Said does, with Goethe and the *West-östlicher Divan,* which, however, I will only touch on because it is treated more comprehensively elsewhere in this volume. Said cites in particular Goethe's project of understanding "Islamic literature" (xix)—but it is really Persian literature in which Goethe was interested, and in fact Islam does not come off very well in the *Divan:* such tenets as the prohibition of alcohol or of human images in art, and the Muslim notion of heaven, are roundly ridiculed, continuing a long tradition in Western literature and of course in the works of Hafis that Goethe takes as a model. Still, Goethe's view of Persian and Arabic cultures is certainly marked by the kind of attempt at empathetic understanding of an oriental culture, an understanding that Said valorizes, regardless of its limitations.

However, Said's view of German Orientalism must at least be *supplemented* by drawing attention to a less conciliatory trend in German culture, which reached its zenith at the end of the eighteenth century, and I would say that the other German writer he marshals, Johann Gottfried Herder, is implicated in this discourse, which we would have to call Orientalist. That this less conciliatory trend should be evident in the later eighteenth century at first seems strange, since this was a propitious moment for an improved understanding of Islam in the wake of the Enlightenment.[7] Earlier ages were of course infamous for their Muslim-bashing, intensified especially during the Crusades, though some chapters in this volume, among other contributions, demonstrate that the Middle Ages were hardly monolithically hostile to Islam. Later, the animosity and fear were stoked by the military threat from the Ottoman Empire, which has been called the most significant European issue in the sixteenth and seventeenth centuries aside from the Reformation. This threat culminated in the unsuccessful siege of Vienna in 1683, which led to the Treaty of Karlowitz in 1699. The danger did not suddenly end there, on the threshold to the eighteenth century, as one can often read: in the 109 years between the siege of Vienna and the treaty of Jassy in 1792, there were forty-one years of war between the Turks on the one hand and the Austrians or Russians on the other; and one of these wars, ending in 1739, resulted in territorial losses for Austria. However, by the 1760s and 1770s one can indeed say that the Turks no longer represented a serious peril for Christian Europe, and the result was a marked rapprochement between Islamic and Western European culture. The Russians did fight a further war with the Turks from 1768 to 1774, but the Ottomans were by this point so weak that they became a pawn in the conflicts among European powers and—this is crucial—entered into an alliance with Austria, which aimed to thwart Russian ambitions. In this period we find a kind of schizophrenic attitude toward Muslims (who were usually conflated with Turks): in cultural artifacts of all sorts, the image of the violent and usually lascivious Turk was still active, swinging his legendary saber and slicing up Christians; but on the other hand we find a true turcomania in Western Europe. It was in France, the country friendliest to the Ottomans for geopolitical reasons, that *turquerie* originated and blossomed, as a result of the Turkish diplomatic missions to Paris as early as 1721 and 1742. Frederick the Great aimed at a Prussian-Turkish alliance just after the Seven Years War and hosted a huge Turkish diplomatic entourage in 1763–64. The Berliners were so taken with the exotic visitors that supposedly they went around wearing turbans and eating dates. Though this German encounter with Islam hardly went beyond a sort of exotic "costume," it may have at least paved the way for a less crassly prejudiced encounter. This tradition of humanistic, enlightened openness to Islam resulted in attitudes that may have been contradictory but certainly were fundamentally different from the hostility of earlier centuries. In the eighteenth century there was even a certain pretense of seeing Orientals as superior to Europeans, in the tradition of Montesquieu's *Persian Letters* (1721). The image of the noble sultan, too, is a strange hybrid of the "noble savage" fashion, derived from North American and other peoples, and the persistent ideal of the European "enlightened" absolutist monarch.

This new turcomania fed into German classicism through the vehicle of the so-called Turkish opera.[8] In about a dozen European operas before Mozart's famous *Entführung aus dem Serail* (1782), there is a remarkably consistent plot. A Christian-European woman, after being abducted by pirates in the Mediterranean, or some such scenario, ends up as the captive of a Turkish sultan or equivalent figure; she may even become part of his harem. Her European lover or another Christian seeks to rescue her and sometimes succeeds, but usually fails because the plot is discovered. However, in the end the Muslim ruler shows a magnanimity that is often associated with Christian virtues, and he frees the woman and her would-be rescuers. The traditional negative characteristics of Muslims in Christian writings—particularly libidinal excess and a propensity to violence—are manifested at times in the sultan but are in general banished to the secondary figure, the guard of the harem or palace, usually named Osmin or Osman. From Gluck's *Die Pilgrime von Mecca* (1764) to his wildly successful *Der Kaufmann von Smyrna* (1771) and Andras Franz Holly's *Der Bassa von Tunis* (1774), from *Les époux esclaves* (1755) to *La schiava liberata* (1768), from Haydn's *L'incontro improvviso* (1775) to Joseph von Friebert's *Das Serail, oder die unvermuthete Zusammenkunft in der Sclaverey . . .* (1778), the plots show an amazing consistency that culminates in Mozart's *Entführung*. Given that this discourse was "in the air," so to speak, it is not unreasonable to see traces of it in three major works of German literature written around 1780. The most obvious is Wieland's verse epic *Oberon* (1780), which, however, generally reverts to the negative characteristics of Muslims in its abduction plot. More interesting are the permutations of the theme in more canonical literature.

In Lessing's play *Nathan der Weise* (1779) the Christian Templar with a Muslim heritage struggles to free himself from his crusading ethos, but when he hears that Nathan's supposedly Jewish daughter Recha is actually a Christian, he reverts to the Christian prejudices with which he was brought up by his Templar uncle. He says that Nathan must have stolen or bought her—a conjecture for which he has no evidence at all, but which fits the pattern of the illegitimate capture of a Christian girl by an infidel, this time of course with the interesting twist that it is a Jew rather than a Muslim from whom the Christian must be rescued. And finally, Goethe provides another variation on the theme when, in *Iphigenie auf Tauris* (prose version, 1779), he portrays Greeks—that is, men who consider themselves superior to the Eastern barbarians—who hear that a Greek priestess is held captive on the island, and likewise assume—again based only on their prejudice—that she has been bought or stolen. This play is complete with a magnanimous infidel king who graciously allows the treacherous Greeks to return home with their countrywoman, who in fact did not need rescuing. In all of these works the supposedly inferior culture turns out to be at least as enlightened as the supposedly superior culture, and often more so. In the opera *Adelheit von Veltheim*, composed by Christian Gottlob Neefe to a libretto by Gustav Friedrich Großmann, the pasha fends off the gratitude of the Christians after forgiving their treachery to him with the following words: "Alles, was ich von euch heische, ist: denkt zuweilen daran, daß ihr in der sogenannten Barbarey einen Menschen und einen Freund gefunden habt. . . . Doch, das erlaubt mir euch zu sagen, daß ich, so zu handeln, wahrlich nicht aus der Geschichte eurer Eroberungen fremder Welttheile erlernt habe."[9] Compare this with the sarcastic words of Thoas in Goethe's play, referring to the brutal history of Iphigenie's own, supposedly superior, Greek family:

> Du glaubst, es höre
> Der rohe Scythe, der Barbar, die Stimme
> Der Wahrheit und der Menschlichkeit, die Atreus,
> Der Grieche, nicht vernahm?[10]

Likewise, in Lessing's sources for *Nathan*, the noble spirit of Saladin and his tolerance of Christianity under his rule in Jerusalem contrast glaringly with the brutality of the Crusaders toward Muslims after their earlier conquest of the city. As we saw, these relatively positive portrayals of Muslims and especially Turks are full of contradictions; in particular, it is by no means a clear case of a sympathetic encounter with Islam. A good illustration of this is the requisite wine song in the operas; habitually, the Muslims complain about Mohammed's prohibition of alcohol and proceed to imbibe all they like, often getting quickly drunk because they are not used to drinking alcohol. Goethe's poetic persona in the *West-östlicher Divan* also inveighs against this prohibition (especially in the "Schenkenbuch"), and one can see not only the Persian literary heritage at work here but also the German discourse represented in the wine songs that seem to mock Islam. But the advance that these works represent over the purely negative representations of Muslims in pre-Enlightenment writings and images should not be underestimated.

Older views, however, are clearly still present among other German writers in the eighteenth century, and consideration of this continuing discourse is necessary to a balanced assessment, because it rounds out Said's rather rosy, even idealistic image of the German counter-Orientalist heritage. Among this regressive literature on Islam in the eighteenth century there are of course conservative theologians like David Friedrich Megerlin, who first translated the *Koran* into German from the original (in 1772), and who did so explicitly in order to refute this "Lügenbuch" of the "Antichrist" Mohammed; in his preface, he prays to God "diesem gewaltthätigen Reich [that is, the Ottomans], und seiner aberglaubigen [*sic*] Religion im Koran, bald ein *Ende* zu machen, daß die gedruckte [sic] *Griechen* und andere Christen, so unter seinem *Joch* seufzen, befreiet [werden] [cf. the abduction operas!], und das *Licht* des Evangelii wieder hergestellt werde; wo es durch die *Türken* nach und nach ist ausgelöschet worden"; and in case this isn't clear enough, he calls openly for a new war, in which the Turks will be defeated.[11]

More disturbing than such openly reactionary relics, however, are the explicit practitioners of Enlightenment. Most striking among these is Christoph Meiners (1747–1810).[12] A Göttingen professor of philosophy since 1772, he counted himself an adherent of Enlightenment[13] and was even one of the leading members of the secret society of Illuminati.[14] And yet, as Susanne Zantop writes, "his anticipation of nineteenth-century biological theories make[s] him a crucial link in the emergence of modern racism."[15] He is credited with being the first to divide all mankind into two races, the Caucasian and the Mongolian.[16] In dozens of essays in his journals, the *Göttingisches Historisches Magazin* (1787–91) and the *Neues Göttingisches Historisches Magazin* (1791–94), Meiners, who never left Europe, "analyzed" non-European cultures on the basis of published travelogues of others (he did write an account of his journey to Stuttgart and Strasburg,[17] so at least he counted himself among the ranks of travelers, even if not world travelers). This chapter will argue that in some of these writings Meiners anticipates the most distasteful of the French and British Orientalist discourses.[18]

The key piece is the article "Über die Natur der morgenländischen Völker," published in his journal in 1790.[19] Meiners has a sweeping definition of Orientals, ranging from the northwest African peoples to the Hindus and the Tartars. Nevertheless, he makes the brazen claim that all these people demonstrate commonality in all their cultural aspects, a uniformity that is downright "verwundernswürdig" (386). And he locates the differences between these oriental peoples and the "aufgeklärten Nationen unsers Erdtheils" squarely in their senses and nervous system ("die Organisation ihrer reitzbaren und empfindlichen Theile"; 401), from which their mental and emotional makeup and thus their behavior derive. Their senses, he claims, are "um viele Grade schärfer, und besonders gröber, als die der Europäischen Völker" (402). What he really means by this is that "die Morgenländer [sind] viel weniger empfindlich, als die Abendländer" (403). "Wenn aber auch die trefflichsten Beobachter der orientalischen Völker," Meiners writes,

> nicht so übereinstimmend in ihren Zeugnissen für die ungewöhnliche Gefühllosigkeit der Morgenländer wären, so würde man doch dieses ursprüngliche Gebrechen der Bewohner des Orients aus ihrem Betragen im Glück und Unglück, im Tode, in Martern, und bey Beleidigungen, aus ihrem ganzen äussern Benehmen und Lebensart, aus ihrer Verfassung und ihren Gesetzen, vorzüglich aber aus ihren Strafen und Züchtigungen schliessen können. (403)

It is the capacity to sustain physical punishments that interests him most. He elaborates: "Wegen ihrer geringern Empfindlichkeit ertragen sie [that is, "die Morgenländer"] die willkührlichsten Erpressungen, die schimpflichsten Mißhandlungen, die grausamsten Verstümmelungen, und Todesstrafen, die ihnen von ihren Königen und deren Dienern zugefügt werden, wie Fügungen des göttlichen Willens, oder eines unvermeidlichen Verhängnisses" (405)—and of course we see here that with "divine will," religion begins to play a part in the interpretation of the Orientals' ability to withstand punishment. However, even here Meiners insists on the primacy of the inherited character of the Orientals over their religion as a decisive factor in their constitution. He mentions that some observers attribute the supposed apathy of Orientals to Mohammed's teaching of inexorable fate. To this argument Meiners responds that many Christians, too, have such fatalist beliefs, and yet Christians behave much differently than Muslims. He claims, therefore, that "*Mahomet* schöpfte die Ergebenheit in sein Schicksal aus der Natur seines Volks; und alle seine Anhänger bestätigten seine Lehre durch ihr Leben, nicht weil er sie zuerst vorgetragen, oder so kräftig empfohlen hatte, sondern weil sie eine natürliche Folge der geringern Empfindlichkeit, der Trägheit, und Beschränktheit ihres Geistes war" (411).[20] But if it suited his purposes, Meiners could indeed marshal the influence of Islam in his explanation of the oriental character. In the course of his argument that Orientals are less tender to family members than Europeans, he mentions a possible counterargument, namely, the charitable kindness of Muslims. But Muslims' benevolence, he says, is not a result of their sympathy with the misfortune of others but rather "weil Mahomet es ihnen vorgeschrieben hat, und weil sie glauben, durch solche Stiftungen und Allmosen die Schuld der

Sünden zu tilgen, die sie durch blutige Erpressungen, und unrechtmässig erworbenes Gut auf sich geladen haben" (435). Thus, when assessing the impact of religion on cultural and racial character, or vice versa, Meiners is simply unperturbed by lack of consistency, using whatever argument he wishes in order to diminish the qualities of the oriental peoples, and specifically Orientals defined as Muslims.

Of all these qualities, it is the imperviousness to physical pain that occupies Meiners the most—he had devoted an entire article to it two years earlier,[21] reveling in lurid descriptions of the most horrid tortures and punishments to which Orientals can be exposed. He singles out the Turks for special mention for their "Geduld" when subjected to brutal torture (413). The corollary to this characteristic is the claim that Orientals themselves are so brutal that they carry out the cruelest torture without the slightest sign of abhorrence: "Die Araber können nicht nur ohne Regungen von Menschlichkeit unschuldiges Blut vergiessen, und vergiessen sehen, sondern sie finden auch ein tigerartiges Wohlgefallen an blutigen Hinrichtungen, und langsamen Martern" (440). And in this particular case Meiners asserts that this ingrained brutality does not derive from Islam, indeed is contrary to it: "Selbst *Mahomet* konnte die unauslöschliche Rachgier, die in den Herzen der Araber, wie anderer Morgenländer brennt, nicht besänftigen" (440).

The result of this line of argument soon becomes evident. Meiners cites the French travel writer Poiret to the effect that

> Der Stock und Säbel . . . sind die einzigen Mittel, wodurch man von den Arabern das Nothwendige erhalten kann. . . . Um bei den Arabern eine gewisse Achtung zu erlangen, oder sonst etwas zu erhalten, muß man sich sehr hüten, die Höflichkeit, die unter den gesitteten Völkern eingeführt ist, oder Freundlichkeit und Dankbarkeit zu erweisen. Alsdann glauben sie, daß man sie fürchtet, und sie werden nur um desto stolzer, unverschämter und hartnäckiger im Abschlagen derjenigen Dinge, warum man sie gebeten hat. Wenn man aber ein drohendes Aeussere annimmt, wenn man ihnen als unumschränkter Herr befiehlt, und sie als einen elenden Haufen von Sclaven behandelt; so werden sie nachgiebig, küssen die Hand ihres Tyrannen, und begegnen dem gemeinsten Türkischen Soldaten als ihrem Herrn. Schläge sind daher bey den Arabern ein nothwendiges Cärimoniel.[22]

Of course, Meiners is citing a French source here, so perhaps we are crediting him with too much Orientalist verve. But he clearly endorses Poiret's views and cites a Danish travel writer to clinch the point.[23] His conclusion: "Die einzigen Triebfedern der Morgenländer sind Furcht vor Strafen, und Hoffnung von persönlichen Vergnügungen oder Vortheilen" (446). And in his essay on punishments he claims that not only

German princes who rule Slavic peoples but also Europeans in the West and East Indies are "forced" to use horrible punishments on the natives.[24] Finally, he explicitly defends colonialism: while some colonial masters have abused their power over natives, he says, "es giebt doch auch mehrere Beyspiele, daß Europäer über ganze Völker, oder wenigstens über zahlreiche Pflanz-Oerter, eine unumschränkte Gewalt nicht bloß zu ihrem gegenwärtigen Vortheil, sondern auch zum Glück ihrer Unterthanen ausgeübt haben."[25]

It is thus clear that Meiners has laid the groundwork for dominating Orientals: they can be ruled if they are subjected to harsh physical force, and in fact they force their colonial masters to use such measures. And because he has pointed out throughout his essay that Orientals perversely refuse to adopt technological and scientific advances from Europeans, he even delivers—albeit implicitly—a legitimation for European domination of these lands, which Orientalist discourse viewed as a "civilizing" influence. But who is to take on this role of firm but benevolent colonizer? At the end of the essay on the nature of oriental peoples, Meiners's arguments take an unexpected turn. He speaks of the European peoples who have intermixed most with Orientals: Spaniards, Portuguese, and Italians, peoples who therefore have retained many oriental characteristics discussed in the article. Then he writes: "Unter den morgenländischen Colonien [!], die sich unvermischt erhalten haben, verdienen die Armenier, und Juden die meiste Aufmerksamkeit" (454). He devotes the rest of his remarks almost entirely to the Jews. He says that by looking at the Jews, who have lived in Europe much longer than the Armenians, one can gauge most clearly the influence of climate on the blood of entire peoples. And though the Jews have been Europeanized to a certain extent, he claims, they are still more similar to the peoples in which they have their origins: that is, they are chiefly oriental. The article then takes a strange turn. "Der gegenwärtige Aufsatz," writes Meiners, "enthält manche Data zur entscheidenden Beantwortung der Frage: ob die Fehler, die den Juden von allen Europäischen Nationen so viele Jahrhunderte lang sind vorgeworfen worden, Folgen ihrer Lage, oder Aeusserungen ihrer angestammten Natur sind"—note that he doesn't even question whether these faults exist. He not only clearly sides with the biologist interpretation but also claims that "in den letzten Zeiten der Widerwille gegen die Juden um desto allgemeiner und lebhafter geworden ist, je genauer man sie beobachtet, und ihre Wirkungen auf die Länder, wo sie bisher Schutz genossen, kennen gelernt hat" (454).

It almost seems as if Meiners turns out to have been writing an article not about Orientals in their Arabic or Muslim guise, but Jews as Orientals—but as we shall see, there is a crucial connection between Jews and Arabs or Muslims in his argumentation. Anti-Semitism, Meiners argues, is objectively justified by empirical observation; and with his remark that the

Jews have "until now" (*bisher*) enjoyed protection in Europe he suggests fairly clearly that this toleration of them ought to end. At the very end of the essay he then makes this assumption explicit.

> Ich werde in der Folge, wenn ich alles beysammen habe, was zu einer solchen Untersuchung gehört, auf die Frage zurückkommen, ob das allgemeine Beste es erfordere, oder gestatte, daß man die Juden fernerhin schütze, bis sie den Völkern, unter welchen sie wohnen, ähnlich geworden seyn, und bis sie willig und fähig seyn werden, alle Pflichten nützlicher Bürger zu erfüllen, oder ob es besser sey, ihnen zu rathen, daß sie sich in ihrem alten Vaterlande ein neues Jerusalem erbauen, und ein neues Reich errichten. Wenn die Juden so viel Muth, als die alten Griechen, oder Sachsen, oder Normänner hätten; so müsten sie schon lange daran gedacht haben, das gelobte Land den Händen der wenigen elenden Räuber zu entreissen, die in dem von ihnen verödeten Palästina übrig geblieben sind. (455)

The formal uncertainty of the first sentence of this passage is undone by the second sentence, which makes clear that Meiners favors a return of the Jews to Palestine. This is a rather bizarre turn, and it creates a complicated situation. Meiners had spoken of "colonies" of Jews and Armenians in Europe, almost as if that colonization justified a reciprocal colonization of Palestine. The colonization of Palestine will, however, be carried out by a people that is both partly Europeanized and essentially Oriental, the Jews. The envisioned colonization forestalls the assimilation of Jews, the legitimacy of which Meiners questions by asking if Europeans are even "permitted" to promote it. Thus Jews should be returned to their homeland, where they really belong. This argument, of course, was to become the familiar groundwork for Zionism, though naturally not with the underlying justification based on the supposed "faults" and biologically determined alienness of the Jews; and it was a major solution to the "Jewish question" in nationalist anti-Semitism of the nineteenth and twentieth centuries. In that guise, this notion prefigures biologically conceived anti-Semitism of the virulent modern variety, which of course also entertained the notion of sending the Jews back to Palestine because of their inborn faults.

This ideological underpinning of the colonization of Palestine must be seen as a variant of Orientalism, regardless of its unusual recourse to Jews as colonizers. For in Meiners's perspective the Jews are hybrids—they can be seen as a partly European people, but their Oriental nature provides the unique justification for this colonization, since they would be merely reclaiming their ancestral homeland. The Muslim peoples, for their part, provide legitimacy for the project because of three inborn characteristics: first, their inferiority to Europeans—meaning that the Europeanized Jews would presumably bring them cultural, technological, and scientific advances; second, they are a people easily dominated by force; and third, they are "thieves" (*Räuber*) who have stolen the Holy Land. This last is of course the granddaddy of all pretexts for colonizing Palestine, beginning with the medieval crusading ideology that was based on Muslims supposedly desecrating Christian holy sites that they illegitimately held in their power. In sum, Meiners finds Orientals lacking in "humanity" (*Menschlichkeit*),[26] so that these three justifications for dominating them can be summed up by saying that Orientals are not full human beings but a sort of subhuman—the classic modern legitimation for conquering such *Untermenschen*. And finally, in his essay on the causes of despotism, Meiners claims that enlightened peoples do not need despotic rulers and in fact tend to limit their princes' powers, but that "edlere Menschen und Völker [können] gegen Unedle eine willkührliche, zwingende, und wenn man will, widerrechtliche Gewalt zum Besten der Gezwungenen, und Unterworfenen ausüben."[27] Here, too, he explicitly marshals the argument about subhuman people: "Je thierischer Menschen sind, desto mehr muß man sie nach Art der Thiere behandeln, und je weniger moralische Bewegungs-Gründe vermögen, desto mehr muß man offenbare Gewalt zu Hülfe nehmen."[28]

Christoph Meiners, then, lays claim to being an adherent of Enlightenment, but he is clearly implicated in the worst sort of Orientalist discourse. In the larger scheme of things it would be easy to dismiss him as an exception, a racialist crackpot who had no following—and indeed, it does seem that the humanist discourse in the Turkish operas that I have described, and in Herder and Goethe, whom Said valorizes, was much more dominant in German culture. On the other hand, Meiners's influence was not insignificant. He published dozens of books,[29] and in them he recycled the arguments from his essays (though sometimes revising his views). He attracted enough attention that his journal was reviewed harshly by none other than Georg Forster, who had taken part in James Cook's three-year second voyage around the world and thus had considerably more direct experience of non-European worlds than Meiners. Forster attests that Meiners was well known—and much criticized. Meiners himself reports on the success of his writings and blames the decline of his reputation on the French Revolution with its ideas of equality, so that "man hörte nicht mehr, wenn ich bewies, daß die Neger, die Americaner, u.s.w. von Natur weit unter den Europäern stünden. Man entbrannte vor Unwillen darüber, daß ich die Rechte des Adels vertheidigte, und mich sogar gegen eine plötzliche Aufhebung der Knechtschaft der Neger erklärte. Unter den modischen Schriftstellern war keiner in seinen Angriffen auf mich heftiger und seichter, als der jüngere Forster"[30]—and with this association Meiners clearly attempts to discredit the by-then-infamous revolutionary Forster, even though Forster's critique of Meiners predates his radicalization. It seems, then, that Meiners did indeed have a following, but it seems equally clear that he was increasingly marginalized in the liberal epoch; an early, brutal review of the first issues of his new journal in the influential Jena *Allgemeine Literatur-Zeitung* seems to have more or less annihilated Meiners's reputation in the learned world.[31] Still, there is a disturbing connection to Weimar Classicism. For none other than Herder, whom Said praises for his liberal attitude toward Islam in the *Ideen,* in 1803 published a piece in his collection *Adrastea* with the title "Bekehrung der Juden," in which he also argued for the resettlement of Jews in Palestine. The Jews are, Herder says, "ein unserm Weltteil *fremdes Asiatisches* Volk." He says that the issue of whether Jews belong in European countries is no longer a religious or human rights dispute but a matter of simple policy: too many Jews in one European country can ruin it through their business activities. He then valorizes the arguments of "ein Brittischer Philosoph," who predicts that "die Juden einst in Palästina wieder werden eingeführt werden," and he ends his piece with the exclamation: "Glück also, wenn ein Messias-Bonaparte sieghaft sie dahin führt, Glück zu nach Palästina!"[32]

Herder, then, finds himself in very uncomfortable company here. Together with Megerlin and Meiners, he inveighs against the Jews as a sort of cancer on European society; like Meiners, he advocates their removal to Palestine, and he has the disadvantage vis-à-vis Meiners of not noticing the Muslim population that lived there. They seem to be invisible to him. Perhaps that is why Herder could have his relatively liberal attitude toward Muslims in the *Ideen,* his work mentioned by Said. For Herder almost certainly had no direct experience of Muslims and thus did not have to entertain the notion of living with them. Jews, by contrast, were a known quantity, the most significant minority in eighteenth-century Germany, and Herder describes this *known* Other negatively and urges its removal. Something similar could be said of Goethe, whose attitude toward Jews was at most ambivalent, and with respect to their human rights entirely negative;[33] as Said suggested in the original edition of *Orientalism,* Goethe's knowledge of Islam was abstract and, I might add, essentially literary. One might press this line of argument even further and ask whether the idolizers of Goethe in, for example, the Goethe-Gesellschaft—generally a very conservative crowd—do not simply deploy the Goethe of the *West-östlicher Divan* as a kind of political alibi, lauding his tolerant attitude toward Islam as long as it was mainly concerned with the Persian poet Hafis, while themselves generally revealing a quite different attitude toward Turkish Muslims in contemporary Germany. I think it justifiable to ask, therefore, how liberal Goethe and Herder would have been toward Muslims if they had known them, given that they were hostile to Jews in many respects. On the other hand, it would be unfair to end by faulting Goethe and Herder for attitudes toward Islam that they did not express, or faulting them for the attitudes of their admirers. It is important to point out, however, that theirs is not the only tradition in the eighteenth and early nineteenth-century discourse on Islam in Germany, and that Said's 2003 correction to his earlier implication of Germany in Orientalist discourses was one-sided. It would also seem that the Jews are in a certain sense the secret Other in these German discussions of Islam, just as Muslims are the unseen Other in the project of "resettling" Jews in Palestine; in tandem with the notion of colonizing the Muslim world went a desire to expel Jews from German society.

Notes

[1] Edward W. Said, *Orientalism*, 3rd ed. (London: Penguin, 2003), 3. Subsequent citations will be given in the text in parentheses. For a summary of some of the more important critiques, see Bill Ashcroft and Pal Ahluwalia, *Edward Said* (London: Routledge, 2001); some of them are included in *Orientalism: A Reader*, ed. Alexander Lyon Macfie (New York: New York UP, 2000).

[2] Other scholars have criticized this shortcoming. From the vantage of Africanist Islamic studies beginning in the late nineteenth century, see Roman Loimeier, "Edward Said und der deutschsprachige Orientalismus: Eine kritische Würdigung," *Stichproben: Wiener Zeitschrift für kritische Afrikastudien* 1. 2 (2001): 63–85. For the late eighteenth century, see Jan Loop, "Timelessness: Early German Orientalism and Its Concept of an Un-historical 'Orient,'" in *"Wenn die Rosenhimmel tanzen": Orientalische Motivik in der deutschsprachigen Literatur des 19. und 20. Jahrhunderts*, ed. Rüdiger Görner and Nima Mina (Munich: Iudicium, 2006), 11–25.

[3] Edward W. Said, "A Window on the World," *Guardian* (and other newspapers), 2 Aug. 2003, http://books.guardian.co.uk/review/story/0,12084,1010417,00. html (all Web sites cited in this chapter were accessed 15 Mar. 2009). David Bell evidently did not have knowledge of Said's revision of his views on Goethe when writing his paper delivered in 2004, "'Orientalizing the Orient' or 'Orientalizing Ourselves'? The Meeting of West and East in Goethe's *West-östlicher Divan*," in *"Wenn die Rosenhimmel tanzen,"* 52–66.

[4] *Time*, 25 Aug. 2002, http://www.time.com/time/magazine/article/ 0,9171,901020902–340702,00.html. See also Barenboim's obituary for Said in *Time*, 29 Sept. 2003, http://www.time.com/time/magazine/article/ 0,9171,901031006–490772,00.html.

[5] Daniel Barenboim, "Equal before Beethoven," *Guardian*, 13 Dec. 2008, http://www.guardian.co.uk/commentisfree/2008/dec/13/middle-east-classical-music (accessed 15 Mar. 2009).

[6] Todd Kontje, *German Orientalisms* (Ann Arbor: U of Michigan P, 2004).

[7] For the following, see W. Daniel Wilson, "Turks on the Eighteenth-Century Operatic Stage and European Political, Military, and Cultural History," *Eighteenth-Century Life* 9 (1985): 79–92.

[8] See W. Daniel Wilson, *Humanität und Kreuzzugsideologie um 1780: Die Türkenoper im 18. Jahrhundert und das Rettungsmotiv in Wielands "Oberon," Lessings "Nathan" und Goethes "Iphigenie"* (Bern: Lang, 1984).

[9] G. F. W. Großmann, *Adelheit von Veltheim,* ed. Otto Pniower (Postdam: Müller, 1920), 182.

[10] Lines 1936–39; cf. the prose version: "Du weißt, daß du mit einem Barbaren sprichst und traust ihm zu, daß er der Wahrheit Stimme vernimmt." Goethe, *Sämtliche Werke: Briefe, Tagebücher und Gespräche,* 40 vols. ("Frankfurter Ausgabe"), vol. I,5, ed. Dieter Borchmeyer and Peter Huber (Frankfurt am Main: Deutscher Klassiker Verlag, 1988), 612 and 192.

[11] *Die türkische Bibel, oder des Korans allererste teutsche Uebersetzung aus der Arabischen Urschrift selbst verfertiget: welcher Nothwendigkeit und Nutzbarkeit in einer besondern Ankündigung hier erwiesen von M. David Friederich Megerlin, Professor* (Frankfurt am Main: Garbe, 1772), preface, 24, 25, 29, and 30. Megerlin's reactionary viewpoint is evident in the fact that he prides himself on writing a defense of Johann Andreas Eisenmenger's infamous *Das neu entdeckte Judenthum* (*Die türkische Bibel,* 20; cf. *Entdecktes Judenthum, oder: Grundllicher und wahrhaffter Bericht, welchergestalt die verstockte Juden die hochheilige Dreyeinigkeit, Gott Vater, Sohn und Heiligen Geist, erschrecklicher Weise lästern und verunehren, die Heil. Mutter Christi verschmähen, das Neue Testament, die Evangelisten und Aposteln, die christliche Religion spottlich durchziehen, und die gantze Christenheit auf das äusserste verachten und verfluchen,* Königsberg [i.e. Berlin]: Haude, 1700–1711). In fact, Megerlin lists some benefits of reading the Koran, especially the principle of submission to God, and says: "Die *Juden* insonderheit könten manches daraus lernen, und ihren Undank gegen Gottes Wohlthaten, und Halßstarrigkeit, und *Unglauben* gegen das Evangelium *bestrafet* sehen. Ich habe deswegen auch eine besondere Schrift entworfen, gegen die *Juden,* mit dem Titel: *Mahomed* ein ernstlicher *Zeug,* wider die *Juden* und ihren Unglauben etc" (33). This book was apparently never published.

[12] On Meiners, see [Carl von] Prantl in *Allgemeine Deutsche Biographie,* ed. Historische Commission bei der Königlichen Akademie der Wissenschaften, 56 vols. (Leipzig: Duncker & Humblot, 1875–1912), 21:224–26.

[13] In the periodical's programme, Meiners says its purpose is partly "zur wahren Aufklärung . . . das Unsrige beyzutragen" (M[einers], "Vorerinnerung," *Göttingisches Historisches Magazin von C[hristoph] Meiners und L[udwig] T[imotheus] Spittler* [hereafter abbreviated as *GHM*] 1 (1787): 1–4; here 4); cf. "Ueber die Gelindigkeit, und Schärfe der Strafen unter verschiedenen Völkern," *GHM* 2 (1788): 126–42; here 128 and 129.

[14] See Wilson, *Geheimräte gegen Geheimbünde: Ein unbekanntes Kapitel der klassisch-romantischen Geschichte Weimars* (Stuttgart: Metzler, 1991), 387, and the references there.

[15] Susanne Zantop, *Colonial Fantasies: Conquest, Family, and Nation in Precolonial Germany, 1770–1870* (Durham, NC: Duke UP, 1997), 82.

[16] Sara Eigen Figal, *Heredity, Race, and the Birth of the Modern* (New York and London: Routledge, 2008), 81.

[17] Christoph Meiners, *Beschreibung einer Reise nach Stuttgart und Hebste 1801, nebst einer kurzen Geschicte der Stadt Strasburg während der Schreckenszeit* (Göttingen, Germany: Röwer, 1803).

[18] Todd Kontje, Susanne Zantop, Sara Eigen Figal, and John H. Zammito ("Policing Polygeneticism in Germany, 1775 (Kames,) Kant, and Blumenbach," in *The German Invention of Race*, ed. Sara Eigen and Mark Larrimore (Albany: State U of New York P, 2006), 35–54) have discussed Meiners's racist views, but not the relevant articles that I will be discussing.

[19] *GHM 7* (1790): 385–455. The scanned original of the entire *GHM* is available at http://www.ub.uni-bielefeld.de/diglib/aufkl/goettihistorimaga/index.htm.

[20] Meiners later counters a similar argument (of the famous travel writer Volney) that the nature of Oriental peoples could be explained from the despotism under which they suffer (416 n.).

[21] M[einers,] "Ueber die Gelindigkeit," 126–42.

[22] Meiners, "Über die Natur der morgenländischen Völker," 442–43. The reference is to Jean Marie Louis Poiret, *Voyage en Barbarie; ou lettres écrites de l'ancienne Numidie pendant les années 1785 et 1786, sur la Religion, les Coutumes & les Mœurs des Maures & des Arabes-Bédouins; avec un Essai sur l'Histoire Naturelle de ce pays*, 2 vols. (Paris: LaRochelle, 1789), 1:158–59; the book was immediately translated into German as *Reise in die Barbarey oder Briefe aus Alt-Numidien geschrieben in den Jahren 1785 und 1786 über die Religion, Sitten und Gebräuche der Mauren und Bedouin-Araber. Nebst einem Versuche über die Naturgeschichte dieses Landes. Mit Kupfern. Aus dem Französischen übersetzt, und mit Anmerkungen begleitet.* 2 vols. (Strasburg: Akademische Buchhandlung, 1789). A check reveals that Meiners was using not this translation but the French original. In 1791 an English translation was published in London.

[23] He cites Georg Høst, *Nachrichten von Marókos und Fes, im Lande selbst gesammlet, in den Jahren 1760 bis 1768: Aus dem Dänischen übersezt* (Copenhagen: Proft, 1781; the Danish original appeared in 1779).

[24] "Ueber die Gelindigkeit," 130–31; cf. M[einers], "Ueber die Ursachen des Despotismus," *GHM 2* (1788): 193–229; here 211.

[25] "Ueber die Ursachen des Despotismus," 211.

[26] Meiners claims that one can infer the "abnehmende Menschlichkeit" of a people from the increasing harshness of their punishments (*Über die Gelindigkeit*, 128). He repeats here what we saw in his essay on Oriental peoples, that the Orientals have the harshest punishments. He notes ". . . daß nirgends mildere Gesetze herrschten, und gelindere Strafen vollzogen wurden, als unter den freyen und unverdorbenen Germaniern, die Tacitus und Cäsar beschrieben" (*Über die Gelindigkeit*, 129).

[27] Meiners, "Ueber die Ursachen des Despotismus," 198.

[28] Meiners, "Ueber die Ursachen des Despotismus," 199.

[29] Especially relevant are *Grundriß der Geschichte der Menschheit* (Lemgo: Mayer, 1785), and *Allgemeine kritische Geschichte der Religionen*, 2 vols. (Hanover: Helwing, 1806–7). Meiners summarizes some of the main arguments of his article on Oriental peoples in his posthumously published *Untersuchungen über die Verschiedenheiten der Menschennaturen (die verschiedenen Menschenarten) in Asien und den Südländern, in den Ostindischen und Südseeinseln, nebst einer historischen Vergleichung der vormahligen und gegenwärtigen Bewohner dieser Continente und*

Eylande, 3 vols. (Tübingen, Germany: Cotta, 1811–15), vol. 2 (1813), 564–92. He updates his arguments with "evidence" from more recent travel writers.

³⁰ Meiners, *Untersuchungen über die Verschiedenheiten der Menschennaturen* 1 (1811), xviii–xix (Meiners's preface, quoted by the editor, his Göttingen colleague Johann Georg Heinrich Feder). On the background of the Meiners-Forster dispute, see Alexander Ihle, *Christoph Meiners und die Völkerkunde* (Göttingen: Vandenhoeck & Ruprecht, 1931), 144–45. Though Ihle's intent is to give Meiners the recognition he deserves, his conclusion is largely negative: "Viel Widersinnigem, Oberflächlichem, gewaltsam Ausgedeutetem und Wertlosem ist man begegnet" (144).

³¹ Jena, *Allgemeine Literatur-Zeitung* 1789, vol. 2, no. 136–38 (4–6 May) and 160 (28 May), cols. 273–93, 465–72. The reviewer cites numerous examples to argue that Meiners uses unreliable sources, uses them inaccurately (often in the opposite sense from the intended one), uses them uncritically, contradicts himself, piles up facts from which he draws no conclusions, makes apodictic claims without evidence, and does not order his material well or provide a synthetic view, except for his unsupportable theory of two main races of mankind (Caucasian and Mongolian).

³² Johann Gottfried Herder, "Bekehrung der Juden," first printed in *Adrastea,* vol. 4, pt. 7 (1803); repr. in *Werke in zehn Bänden,* vol. 10, ed. Günter Arnold (Frankfurt am Main: Deutscher Klassiker Verlag, 2000), 630–33.

³³ See W. Daniel Wilson, "'Humanitätssalbader': Goethe's Distaste for Jewish Emancipation, and Jewish Responses," in *Goethe in German-Jewish Culture,* ed. Klaus L. Berghahn and Jost Hermand (Rochester, NY: Camden House, 2001), 146–64.

5: Goethe, Islam, and the Orient: The Impetus for and Mode of Intercultural Encounter in the *West-östlicher Divan*

Yomb May

THE THEME OF THE "ENCOUNTER WITH ISLAM" leads us to reflect on a contemporary problem, the explosive nature of which is obvious enough. Since the 1990s, and more particularly since 11 September 2001, Samuel P. Huntington's formulation "The clash of civilizations,"[1] a phrase seldom used discriminately, has continued to haunt both political and public discourse. The polemics that flared up around Pope Benedict's address, "Glaube, Vernunft und Universität," at the University of Regensburg on 20 September 2006 have made one thing clear: anyone dealing nowadays with issues of "Orient" and "Occident," with Islam and Christianity, is skating on thin ice. For these topoi and religions are rarely communicated with any sophistication, and their continued juxtaposition only really aids in the construction of essentialized images of mutual enemies. And so, in the midst of globalization, we seem to be experiencing not a positive process of the knitting together of our world but rather an increasingly stark polarization of cultures, as well as interpretations of cultural difference that tend toward the dogmatic. The challenge confronting us in cultural studies consists, therefore, in finding alternative models for thinking about the relationship between Occident and Orient—models that are designed to promote both "understanding" and "communication" ("Verstehen und Verständigung"[2]) between these cultures.

More than most learned figures, Johann Wolfgang von Goethe, perhaps the most prominent representative of German culture and literature, was actually ahead of us in this task. This explains the unanimous view in scholarship that Goethe's engagement with the Islamic world remains groundbreaking to this day. On the one hand, Goethe's writing on the topic highlights the urgency and the volatility of the cultural-political task of reflecting on intercultural encounters.[3] On the other hand, it also exposes as absurd the assumption that encounters between cultures must necessarily lead to conflict. In this context we all think of Goethe's monumental work of 1819, the *West-östlicher Divan*.[4] Interculturally inclined literary scholarship devoted to this work in recent years has produced much of value, although a number of desiderata remain:[5] the perception of Goethe as a "Theoretiker der Interkulturalität und Alterität,"[6] in itself quite accurate, nevertheless remains far too limited by normative understandings of these two categories. And even if Goethe's efforts to promote communication between peoples remain undisputed, naturally they cannot be represented as a bequest, a "Vermächtnis," that we have to accept without question (cf. *ING*, 292). Rather, it appears to be a matter of urgent necessity to raise awareness of how, in the light of postcolonial theory, Goethe's treatment of the Orient becomes part of a process of asymmetrical intercultural encounter and represents a more complex endeavor, which cannot be absolved of contradiction and essentialism. On the contrary, given that Goethe's work aspires to represent the Middle East for German and European readers, the text has to be questioned on problematic issues such as the perception of Europe's "Other" in the age of Enlightenment. Thus Todd Kontje is absolutely right in his assertion that "[It] is time for a new look at Goethe's Orientalism particularly in the Divan, the major work of his Orientalist phase."[7]

Kontje's call is certainly justified, for Goethe's *Divan* exhibits the key characteristics of interculturally inclined literature, and it offers itself as a medium for the "Bearbeitung von kulturellen Differenzen" (*ING*, 289), differences defined from contemporary cultural perspectives.[8] For this reason, the new approach deemed so essential by Kontje in his reading of Goethe must incorporate the notion that poetically successful writing need not be seen to represent unquestionable truths. Asking questions about the limits of Goethe's poetic "Investition in Völkerverständigung" (*ING*, 289) is, therefore, a legitimate concern for any heuristic approach to the *Divan*. Scholars must not shy away from the question as to whether, living in a century marked by Europe's conviction as to the supremacy of its own civilization and its civilizing mission overseas,[9] Goethe can possibly have written about the Middle East in a mode free of colonial discursive influence. In other words, what type of discourse or rather what type of Orientalism does Goethe derive from his encounter with the cultures of this region? For as the numerous references to the *Divan* in Edward Said's groundbreaking study, *Orientalism*,[10] have already made clear, a fruitful engagement with Goethe's image of the "Orient" is only possible today if it avoids both romanticizing, antiquarian treatments of the author's life and work and also finding aspects of the present reflected back onto the historical specificity of the work. Scholarship must rather concern itself with determining to what extent Goethe's "poetische Orientreise"[11] provides an impulse for modern intercultural reflection—reflection that does not simply lead to universal conclusions about how cultures interact but also offers insight into the ambivalences that lie at the heart of such encounters.

Of course, any enquiry as to the limitations of Goethes "Investition in Völkerverständigung" might appear somewhat heretical, for it appears to cast doubts on the merits of Goethe's universal thought. But this is by no means the case. After all, as Anil Bhatti has rightly emphasized, the dialogue between cultures that Goethe placed at the heart of his universalism is "allemal besser als die gewalttätige Konfrontation."[12] Nevertheless, scholarship has to move beyond apodictic assumptions as to the exemplary nature of the dialogue between cultures in the *Divan,* particularly between "Occident" and "Orient," and examine instead the nature of that dialogue. This also infers the hypothesis that Goethe's *Divan* frequently represents an encrypted monologue, which appears on the surface to connote the "availability" of the Orient for dialogue with the Occident. Are there points at which a form of aesthetically disguised Orientalism[13] can be discerned within the *West-östlicher Divan?* Or rather, how is the *Divan* to be located within the context of those eighteenth-century receptions of the Orient that helped underwrite colonialism? In the light of this, it makes sense to test the self-conception of the particular form of European universalism to which Goethe was so committed, examining its incongruity with the self-perceptions of non-European cultures.

Postcolonially inclined xenological methodologies offer the insight that cultures never encounter each other in purely neutral terms. And similarly, for reasons of their irreducibility, there can never be wholly harmonious transitions between cultures, as is often pointed out in conventional scholarship on Goethe's *Divan.*[14] Thus a new examination of the intercultural nature of the *Divan* in East-Western terms, one focusing on both the impetus behind and the mode of Goethe's literary encounter with the Orient, should prove illuminating. Hence this chapter has two goals: it seeks to expound first on Goethe' self-conception as a mediator between East and West and, second, on how able his work is to stand up to the analytical scrutiny of our times. Leading on from this, it will test whether or not Goethe's *Divan* successfully moves beyond the shortcomings of the enlightened European view of non-European cultures, particularly of the Orient.

Despite the historical and modern controversies surrounding the dysfunctional relationship between Occident and Orient—or perhaps precisely because of these—Goethe's engagement with the themes of the cultural and religious (oppositional) differences between the Christian West and the Islamic East has received comparatively little objective, analytical treatment. It is for this reason that Katharina Mommsen's work stands out: for decades Mommsen has conducted research on Goethe's relationship to the Arabic world in a manner unparalleled in our era.[15] She not only demonstrated with diligence Goethe's remarkable interest in Islam but also contended that Goethe's vision of the Orient exerted a considerable influence on his life and work.

While those biographers of Goethe writing in the tradition of German Studies struggle to this day with the poet's passionate interest in Islam and his broadly positive stance on Islamic culture (one consequence of this being scholarly neglect of the *Divan*), scholars from the Arabic world appear to capitalize on this aspect of Goethe's work. In particular, they take a comment made by Goethe in his announcement of the *Divan* in the *Morgenblatt* in 1816, that the author "lehnt den Verdacht nicht ab, daß er selbst ein Muselmann sei" (*HA* 2:268), at face value and believe they have found in the German poet one of their own. What both of the above perspectives have in common, however, is that both attempt a particular form of ideological appropriation—one that is not guided by heuristic interests and, ultimately, leads scholarship up a blind alley.

Although Mommsen's studies have a pioneering dimension, her findings have over time come to require epistemological refinement. Such refinements are necessary because, in answering the call to engage with Goethe's intercultural thought, certain decisive aporiae in the poet's treatment of the Orient have been obscured by scholarship. Anil Bhatti offered just such a revision. His postcolonial approach represents a corrective to received readings of the *Divan,* and attempts not only to sketch out the "Grenzen der Dialogizität" exhibited by the work, but also to show how in formal terms the text strays into a realm of ambivalence (or "Zone der Ambivalenz") that cannot elude colonial discourse (*zzW,* 117). With that Bhatti breaks into new territory, his arguments further substantiated by his assertion that Goethe's engagement with the Orient was predicated upon historical presumptions that were too ideologically loaded for his work to have remained fully neutral. Thus, for Bhatti, "wird die ambivalente Stellung des deutschen Orientalismus auch am *Divan* deutlich" (*zzW,* 105). The briefest of glimpses into history serves to show how often since the crusades East-West relations had been antagonistic in nature and that it was not until the eighteenth century that positive change, however tentative and gradual, began to occur. With the consummation of the Enlightenment and its espousal of free thought, equality, and tolerance, a reevaluation of the relationship between the three great monotheistic faiths was needed. In this respect Gotthold E. Lessing's drama *Nathan der Weise* (1779) offered a shining example, in which Christianity, Islam, and Judaism are represented as religions of equal value.[16]

There can be no doubt that the new worldview of the eighteenth century exerted a powerful influence on Goethe's engagement with the East and its principle religion. Yet Mommsen has pointed out, quite rightly, that Goethe was not one to simply fall into line with fashionable attitudes of the time. In fact Goethe's interest in the Orient grew out of a particular thirst for knowledge on his part, upon which he expounded in his afterword to the *Divan*. As the heading "Noten und Abhandlungen zu besserem Verständnis des West-östlichen Divans" makes clear (*HA* 2:126–267), it was Goethe's intention to make the intellectual world of the Orient and its culture accessible to Germans. In many ways Goethe took on the role of the ethnographer here, though in one important respect he did not: his decampment to the Orient was to remain a virtual one. Yet Goethe took the opportunity to expound on the impetus underlying his engagement with the Arabic world—one that he had begun at only twenty-three years of age with his ode "Mahomets Gesang" and that, in the seventieth year of his life, heralded the final phase of his literary productivity: "denn in einer Zeit" wrote Goethe "wo so vieles aus dem Orient unserer Sprache treulich angeeignet wird, mag es verdienstlich erscheinen, wenn wir von unserer Seite die Aufmerksamkeit dorthin zu lenken suchen, woher so manches Große, Schöne und Gute seit Jahrtausenden zu uns gelangte, woher täglich mehr zu hoffen ist" (*HA* 2:128).

In order to place the implications of such comments more precisely in context, one particular, widely held misconception ought to be dispelled: namely that the huge historical shifts brought about by the Enlightenment in the form of eighteenth-century universalist thinking in Europe resulted in a process of integrating the non-European world into the historical process on an egalitarian footing. Recent studies speak to the contrary, showing the redirection of Europe's attentions to the world beyond its borders to have been a far more complex and contradictory process and validating questions such as that posed by Hans-Jürgen Lüsebrink: "Was hat die koloniale Welt mit der Aufklärung zu tun, wie ist das Phänomen des Kolonialismus, das Eroberung, Gewalt und Unterwerfung impliziert, mit dem Prozess der Aufklärung, der Freiheit, Emanzipation, Wissen und Erkenntnis meint, verknüpft?"[17]

The "Noten und Abhandlungen" themselves demonstrate that Goethe's recourse to the Middle East did not merely derive from his fascination with its poetic achievements. Goethe's project was driven by an intellectual impetus characteristic of the Enlightenment in general, namely the "Drang nach Wissen und Erkenntnis über die außereuropäische Welt."[18] But Goethe expected even more than this from his intensive studies of the Orient. Further enquiry into precisely how Goethe accessed this remote culture shows that his knowledge originated from two sources. First, there are the diverse studies of Eastern cultures he had pursed since his student days in Strasbourg. These comprised his reading of diverse translations of the Koran, such as the 1647 version produced by the French businessman André de Ruyer, and encyclopedias of the time, including the *Dictionnaire Historique* by Pierre Bayle. Other influential impulses came from historical-philosophical and philological writings of contemporaries such as Johann Gottfried Herder[19] or Friedrich Schlegel.[20] Second, there was Goethe's engagement with Persian literature, enabled largely by the Orientalist Josef von Hammer, who in 1812–13

had translated the poetry of the legendary Hafis into German. This forms
the template for the collection of poetry he began in 1814 and completed
in 1819 and entitled programmatically *West-östlicher Divan*. The fact that
this mature work of Goethe's is marked out from the start as an intercultural encounter with the Orient can be noted from a variety of poems in
the collection, although it is particularly evident in the poem that precedes the "Noten und Abhandlungen" and becomes its motto:

> Wer das Dichten will verstehen,
> Muß ins Land der Dichtung gehen;
> Wer den Dichter will verstehen,
> Muß in Dichters Land gehen. (*HA* 2:126)

This explains Goethe's explicit wish in the "Noten" "als ein Reisender
angesehen zu werden" (*HA* 2:127). What is to be undertaken, however,
is no conventional, but rather an intellectual journey, the poetic fruits of
which are to be the Divan, notable for its triadic qualities of fascination,
recognition, and contradiction.

The older Goethe begins by emphasizing that his oriental encounter
is to proceed "vom Standpunkt der Poesie," which can be explained in
terms of Goethe's acceptance of Herder's view that literature contains
"ein gewisser Kern der Nation immer in seinem Charakter" (*HA* 2:134).
This fits in with our modern conception of culture as text,[21] and it is
in this sense that Goethe is ultimately to be understood when he writes
that Persian poems in general and those of Hafis in particular are to be
valued as "Dokumente einer bedeutenden Weltausbildung" (*HA* 2:152),
the genesis of which is to be traced back to oral traditions: "Wenn wir
uns nun zu einem friedlichen, gesitteten Volke, den Persern, wenden, so
müssen wir, da ihre Dichtungen eigentlich diese Arbeit veranlassten, in
die früheste Zeit zurückgehen, damit uns dadurch die neuere verständlich
werde" (*HA* 2:134).

In the context of the "cultural turn" in literary studies this way forward appears quite up-to-date,[22] though considering the "Noten und
Abhandlungen" a question mark must be placed over Goethe's comments, given that he derived his notion of the Persian oral tradition from
written documents conditioned by the then prevailing reception and perception of the Orient. As he was unable to access the original sources, the
"Noten" do not provide empirical and ethnographic but rather mediated,
second-hand insights. Thus describing the discursive form of Goethe's
writing as a form of "imaginativer Orientalismus" appears justified.[23]
How aware Goethe was of this situation during his writing is difficult to
prove. One thing remains certain, however: that Islam and the Prophet
Mohammed are met with particular admiration.

Not least through his aforementioned studies, Goethe was clearly
aware of the importance of Islam for interpreting and understanding

oriental cultures. Indeed: "Eine so zarte Religion, gegründet auf die Allgegenwart Gottes in seinen Werken der Sinnenwelt, muß einen eignen Einfluß auf die Sitten ausüben" (*HA* 2:136). For this reason alone Islam finds in German literature one of its most important poetic articulations in the *Divan:*

> Wofür ich Allah höchlich danke?
> Daß er Leiden und Wissen getrennt.
> Verzweifeln müßte jeder Kranke
> Das Übel kennend, wie der Arzt es kennt.
> Närrisch, daß jeder in seinem Falle
> Seine besondere Meinung preist!
> Wenn Islam Gott ergeben heißt,
> Im Islam leben und sterben wir alle. (*HA* 2:56)

Naturally, the monument Goethe is erecting to Islam here still places Goethe scholarship in Germany in a quandary, as it has in the past. Given that the poet's praise of the faith might potentially cause disquiet in the Christian world, a balanced or rather reflexive understanding of Goethe's relationship to Islam is seldom sought. In this way, precisely the creative distance that Goethe maintains in dealing with Islam is ignored or overlooked:

> Wenn man auch nach Mekka triebe
> Christus' Esel, würd' er nicht
> Dadurch besser abgericht,
> Sondern stets ein Esel bliebe. (*HA* 2:57)

Katharina Mommsen is quite right in this connection in asserting that Goethe saw in Islam an alternative to "den Dogmen der Kirche, die seinem religiösen Empfinden entgegenkam."[24] It should be added, however, that Goethe by no means saw this "alternative" in terms of the repudiation of the Christian worldview but viewed it rather in terms of its renewal and enrichment. The linguistic images painted by Goethe also clearly show that his encounter with Islam exhibits both admiration and contradiction, and that, above all, he never adopted an apodictic stance toward the religion.

The nuanced vision of the Orient and of Islam, which Goethe still demands today from his readers, can be traced back to his lectures on works in Arabic and Persian, held early in 1815 at the court of Weimar. Goethe conceived the lectures as a forum within which cultivated society of the Weimar court could become familiar with the Orient. One of the most prominent participants was Charlotte von Stein, who wrote on 22 February to Knebel: "Goethes Umgang mit dem Orient ist uns recht erfreulich; denn er lehrt uns diese wunderliche Welt kennen . . .

Wir wollen auch aus dem Koran etwas hören. Die Herzogin freut sich dieser Lektüre sehr und wir alle nicht weniger."[25]

The manner in which, even during the writing of the *Divan,* Goethe was trying to attune his audience to the world of the Orient is testimony to the difficulties he faced at that time in establishing an intercultural dialogue with that region and its cultures. Apparently Goethe—and he was himself aware of the fact—required an ingenious strategy to legitimize what was, for the era, a highly unusual project. It can be presumed that Goethe recognized or at least sensed in some way "dass pädagogische Informationsarbeit notwendig ist, um Geschmack am fremden Essen zu erwecken."[26] And what better means to achieve this goal than lectures at the court of Weimar?

Yet this strategy, which does have something of an elitist character, appears not to have come off, for on 26 September 1818 Goethe wrote to Boisserée: "Der *Divan* ist abgedruckt wird aber noch zurückgehalten, weil Erläuterungen und Aufklärungen anzufügen sind. Denn ich hatte an meinen bisherigen Hörern und Lesern, (alle höchst gebildete Personen,) gar sehr zu bemerken, daß der Orient ihnen völlig unbekannt sei; weshalb ich denn, den augenblicklichen Genuß zu befördern, die nötigen Vorkehrungen treffe."[27] The second sign of the strategy's failure can be found in the "Vorkehrungen," which Goethe substantiated in the prose section of the *Divan.* The "Noten und Abhandlungen," constitute an explanatory text, one with which Goethe intended to continue the "pädagogische . . . Informationsarbeit" begun in his oriental lectures and that he designed to compensate for something he had found to be lacking in Hammer-Purgstall's translation of Hafis. Although Hammer's *Fundgruben des Orients* and his Hafis translation offered an indispensable basis for the *Divan,* Goethe criticized Hammer's work for its failure to offer a more general cultural context—a failure that Goethe wished to put right (cf. *zzW,* 114).

Goethe hoped of his *Divan* "daß ein unmittelbares Verständnis Lesern daraus erwachse, die mit dem Orient wenig oder nicht bekannt sind" (*HA* 2:126). In attempting to make "foreign" oriental cultures comprehensible, Goethe came to the view that these elude the European grasp "wenn man sie nach einem Maßstabe mißt, den man niemals bei ihnen anschlagen sollte" (*HA* 2:183). In writing this Goethe implies what Bhatti finds to be a defining factor of the *Divan,* namely its "Hermeneutik vom Eigenen und Fremden" (*zzW,* 111). Yet the question of which yardstick Goethe used in trying to map out the Orient, and of whether or not he remained objective in assessing both his own and his "other" culture, has thus far remained unanswered. The fact alone that, in compiling his work and in engaging with Islam, Goethe relied entirely upon materials from the European reception of the Orient means that his work already comes with a eurocentric bias that cannot simply be excised from the *Divan*. For it is wrong to assume that Goethe's criticism of these sources make him automatically an expert on the Orient.

Of course, Goethe placed his efforts on matters oriental within the context of the "Prozeß der Vermehrung von geistigen Einsichten"[28] instigated by the Enlightenment, and the superiority of his knowledge of the Orient vis-à-vis his "Weimarer Weltbewohner[n]"[29] is undeniable. Yet, similarly undeniable is the discrepancy between Goethe's claims for his work and its ability to offer objective insights into oriental cultures. Goethe did appear to be aware of the limitations of the mediating role he adopted between East and West—he attempts to excuse himself in advance, thus: "Man entschuldigt ihn [den Reisenden, Y.M.], wenn es ihm auch nur bis auf einen gewissen Grad gelingt, wenn er immer noch an einem eigenen Akzent, an einer unbezwinglichen Unbiegsamkeit seiner Landsmannschaft als Fremdling bleibt" (*HA* 2:127). Goethe's awareness of the limits to which the foreign can be assimilated can also be discerned in his reflections on the various forms of translation. In this Goethe anticipated a key discovery, the implications of which would only later be recognized, after the crisis in ethnography, in the form of "thick description."[30]

There is also the fact that Goethe did not address his public as an Orientalist, as a scholar researching Middle Eastern culture, but rather did so explicitly as a poet. As a traveler or on occasion as a "Handelsmann," as he dubbed himself metaphorically, he openly displayed his "Waren," which he "auf mancherlei Weise angenehm zu machen sucht" (*HA* 2:127). This mode of mediating a foreign culture poses the question of the extent to which any "goods" thus transformed take any account at all of the self-conception of the Orient. Ultimately, of course, Goethe had "keinen Zugang zu den Originalquellen über das Leben des Propheten. Er war angewiesen auf das, was ihm durch die Tradition, gebrochen durch die Perspektive der europäischen Berichterstatter, an Informationen übermittelt wurde."[31]

We can, therefore, concede that the selected products brought home by the "traveling" poet offer only limited insights into the complexity of the culture visited. Nevertheless, the principle idea underlying the *West-östlicher Divan* remains at the heart of Goethe's multifarious efforts to extend the eurocentric perspective eastward and thus set in motion an intercultural hermeneutic process. The poet views the Orient both as the means to lead him beyond the European horizon and the occidental Enlightenment, and the medium within which that development will take place.

Gottes ist der Orient!
Gottes ist der Occident!
Nord-und südliches Gelände
Ruht im Frieden seiner Hände. (*HA* 2:10)

Nowhere is Goethe's attempt to distance himself from an essentialized battle between Christianity and Islam more in evidence than in this quatrain—the kind of battle Voltaire had represented in his drama *Le fanatisme ou Mahomet le prophète* (1741). Instead Goethe favors an approach that represents the all-encompassing unity of God. This idea of unity in diversity appears to be the foundation upon which Goethe builds his encounter with the Orient—one in which the conceptual roots for his model of *Weltliteratur* are to be found. It is for these reasons that Goethe is of the opinion "daß keine Grenze zwischen dem, was in unserm Sinne lobenswürdig und tadelhaft heißen möchte, gezogen werden könne, weil ihre Tugenden ganz eigentlich die Blüten ihrer Fehler sind. Wollen wir an diesen Produktionen der herrlichsten Geister teilnehmen, so müssen wir uns orientalisieren, der Orient wird nicht zu uns herüberkommen" (*HA* 2:181). Viewed from a culturally chauvinistic position, Goethe's appeal to Europeans to orientalize themselves, "so müssen wir uns orientalisieren," does come across as irritating—it belongs to that form of ambivalent (rhetorical) device that can easily be misinterpreted if taken too literally. For nothing would be more misleading and misconceived than to read Goethe as denigrating European culture in favor of the oriental. It is more the case that Goethe was suggesting in the *Divan* that engagement with the Orient meant allowing a long-overdue opening, transformation, and renewal of the West. The concept of renewal is to be understood here as a broadening of cultural horizons by transcending conventional prejudices about the Orient. Goethe is seeking here to enlighten further his own culture, an aspiration that makes Goethe of relevance not only in cultural and religious terms but also in matters poetological, aesthetic, and anthropological. It is thus no coincidence that he preludes the *Divan* with the following poem:

> Nord und West und Süd zersplittern,
> Throne bersten, Reiche zittern,
> Flüchte du, im reinen Osten
> Patriarchenluft zu kosten,
> Unter Lieben, Trinken, Singen
> Soll dich Chisers Quell verjüngen. (*HA* 2:7)

Nowhere is the creative accretion of meaning and knowledge (*Sinnzuwachs*) achieved by Goethe more visible than in this central motif depicting the rejuvenation of the Occident at the wellspring of the Orient. However, one should beware of making snap judgments on this "positive" representation of the Orient, for traces of Orientalist practice are discernible here, too. Formulations such as "im reinen Osten" conjure an image of the Orient that has been rightly identified by Kontje as belonging to late-eighteenth-century Orientalist discourse, for the East is identified with an essentialized topos of simplicity that functions as a contrast to the West.[32]

If the *West-östlicher Divan,* a collection and knitting together of intellectual products of Western and Eastern origin, seems initially to recognize the autonomy of the Orient, or put differently, "das Recht auf kulturelle Differenz" (*ING,* 288), then Goethe's notion of writing as hovering "zwischen zwei Welten" implies that he is attempting to distance himself from the nationalistic tendencies of role models of his time. What is striking in all of this is not only Goethe's flight to the East, undertaken to escape the political turmoil of the Napoleonic wars, but also his distance from Classicism, as still represented by Schiller's position:

Zugemeßne Rhythmen reizen freilich,
Das Talent erfreut sich wohl darin;
Doch wie schnelle widern sie abscheulich,
Hohle Masken ohne Blut und Sinn.
Selbst der Geist erscheint sich nicht erfreulich,
Wenn er nicht, auf neue Form bedacht,
Jener toten Form ein Ende macht. (*HA* 2:24)

A further example is offered by the poem "Lied und Gebilde" from the "Buch des Sängers":

Mag der Grieche seinen Ton
Zu Gestalten drücken,
An der eignen Hände Sohn
Steigern sein Entzücken;

Aber uns ist wonnereich
In den Euphrat greifen,
Und im flüss'gen Element
Hin und wider schweifen. (*HA* 2:16)

Whereas Goethe had adhered to Classicism up until Schiller's death in 1805, vaunting the completeness of poetic form, he now found in the lyrical poetry of the Middle East a new formal principle for his art, one that found expression in the boundlessness of poetic language. The last stanza of the poem "Derb und Tüchtig" runs thus:

Wenn des Dichters Mühle geht,
Halte sie nicht ein:
Denn wer einmal uns versteht,
Wird uns auch verzeihn. (*HA* 2:17)

Similarly programmatic is the poem entitled "Unbegrenzt":

Daß du nicht enden kannst, das macht dich groß,
Und daß du nie beginnst, das ist dein Los.
Dein Lied ist drehend wie das Sterngewölbe,

Anfang und Ende immerfort dasselbe
Und was die Mitte bringt, ist offenbar,
Das was zu Ende bleibt und anfangs war. (*HA* 2:23)

The fact that Goethe was drawing on the poetry of the Middle East in order to renew or perhaps further develop Germany's poetry, a poetry that still appealed to antiquity, has lead to the hypothesis in scholarship that Goethe looked upon the Persian poet Hafis, from whom he borrowed the term "Divan," as a role model. This hypothesis can easily be dismissed, however, given that the concept of "role model" ("Vorbild") is shown up to be wholly inapplicable both by the title of the *West-östlicher Divan* itself and by individual texts. A good example of this can be found in the penultimate stanza of the poem cited above:

Und mag die ganze Welt versinken
Hafis, mit dir, mit dir allein
Will ich wetteifern! Lust und Pein
Sein uns, den Zwillingen, gemein! (*HA* 2:23)

Two inferences can be made from this use of the metaphor of the twins ("Zwillinge"): first, of course, Goethe is putting forward the notion that Occident and Orient are relatives of a sort. Goethe based his view on the fact that the literature of the two cultures articulated a common human experience. Second, the metaphor makes it clear that the poet's symbolic self-dissolution, his act of positioning himself between two worlds, is driven by the idea of liberation from eternals, imperatives, and laws. The lyrical "I," identifiable here with Goethe himself, and Hafis, poet of the Orient, are conceived as equals, a conception that suggests the possibility of dialogue conducted on equal terms. Precisely for this reason Hafis cannot in anyway be dubbed as Goethe's role model in the traditional sense. Goethe does, though, see in Hafis the premise of an intercultural paradigm:

Herrlich ist der Orient
Übers Mittelmeer gedrungen;
Nur wer Hafis liebt und kennt
Weiß, was Calderon gesungen. (*HA* 2:57)

One of the finest responses from the East, one that can be cited as a counterpart to Goethe's viewpoint, was formulated by Muhammad Iqbal in a poem in praise of Goethe:

Des Westens Meister, jener deutsche Dichter,
Verzauberter der persischen Gesichter,
Er formt das der reizend Kecken, Schlanken
Und bracht dem Osten einen Gruß der Franken.

Des "Ostens Botschaft" ist die Antwort mein —
Auf Ostens Abend goß ich Mondenschein.
Seitdem ich ihn erkannt, nie pries ich mich
Dir sage ich, wer er ist, und wer ich![33]

From this poetic echo we can see that Goethe's Western-Eastern interculturalism did not remain a monological one-way street. Iqbal's response appears to alleviate any suspicion that Goethe's encounter with the Orient arose from colonial aspirations of some "mission civilisatrice." Rather, the response directs attention to a highly developed awareness of intercultural competency, which Goethe himself formulated so poetically:

Wer sich selbst und andere kennt,
Wird auch hier erkennen:
Orient und Okzident
Sind nicht mehr zu trennen
Sinnig zwischen beiden Welten
Sich zu wiegen, lass' ich gelten;
Also zwischen Ost und Westen
Sich bewegen sei zum Besten! (*HA* 2:121)

Here Goethe is informing both his era and our own about his understanding of how cultures merge into each other. There is, however, a discrepancy between the views he takes in the "Noten" and his poetic execution of them—one that becomes apparent when he attempts a comparison between the four great religions, Judaism, Islam, Christianity, and Buddhism, in the "Noten und Abhandlungen" and that marks not inconsiderable ambivalences in his discourse on the Orient:

Die jüdische Religion wird immer einen gewissen starren Eigensinn, dabei aber auch freien Klugsinn und lebendige Tätigkeit verbreiten; die mahometanische läßt ihren Bekenner nicht aus einer dumpfen Beschränktheit heraus, indem sie, keine schweren Pflichten fordernd, ihm innerhalb derselben alles Wünschenswerte verleiht und zugleich durch Aussicht auf die Zukunft Tapferkeit und Religionspatriotismus einflößt und erhält.

Die indische Lehre taugte von Haus aus nichts, so wie denn gegenwärtig ihre vielen tausend Götter, und zwar nicht etwa untergeordnete, sondern alle gleich unbedingt mächtige Götter, die Zufälligkeiten des Lebens nur noch mehr verwirren, den Unsinn jeder Leidenschaft fördern und die Verrücktheit des Lasters als die höchste Stufe der Heiligkeit und Seligkeit begünstigen. . . . Dagegen gebührt der christlichen das höchste Lob, deren reiner, edler Ursprung sich immerfort dadurch bestätigt, daß nach den größten Verirrungen, in welche sie der dunkle Mensch hineinzog, eh man sich's versieht, sie sich in ihrer ersten lieblichen Eigentümlichkeit, als Mission, als Hausgenossen- und Brüderschaft, zur Erquickung des sittlichen Menschenbedürfnisses, immer wieder hervortut. (*HA* 2:149)

In these comments Goethe effectively rescinds the notion of the equality of religions for which Lessing appealed in *Nathan der Weise*. For one thing, this confirms that the Enlightenment as a movement did not hold one consistent view on the relationship between the religions. However, the starkly contrasting manner in which particularly Islam and Buddhism are devalued by the poet clearly derives from hierarchical intellectual impulses underlying the wider colonialist project and its approach to religion.[34]

Goethe's comments on the relationship between Christianity and the other faiths reveal a colonialist approach to religion on his part, not a conception of religious equality. Particularly disconcerting is the fact that the positive image of Islam cast in the excerpt from the poem is at best downplayed—though not actually reversed—in the "Noten." This material in itself highlights a disparity between the poetic content of the *Divan* and Goethe's notes, a disparity that has hitherto gone unnoticed. On the other hand, Bhatti is right to point out that the "Noten" have an ethnographic predisposition, because they do construct the Orient as an "Erkenntnisgegenstand" (*zzW,* 118); that is, the Orient is made accessible in the "Noten und Abhandlungen" in such a way that the melding of East and West in the poetry is accompanied by an emphasis on cultural difference elsewhere, and one that displays shockingly essentialist characteristics. "Was aber dem Westländer niemals eingehen kann," writes Goethe in the section entitled "Despotie" in the "Noten," "ist die geistige und körperliche Unterwürfigkeit unter seinen Herren und Oberen, die sich von uralten Zeiten herschreibt, indem Könige zuerst an die Stelle Gottes traten" (*HA* 2:169). Crucial here is, for one thing, the fact that Goethe appears as representative of the "Westländer," whom he distinguishes from Orientals in terms of their "geistige und körperliche Unterwürfigkeit."

Naturally, Goethe's rejection of these characteristics could have been intended as a critique of European absolutism (*zzW,* 119), though the mechanism he chose to do this simultaneously undermined the Oriental as an equal partner in dialogue, "weil der Orient der europäischen Imagination ein entdeckbares passives Anderes war" (*zzW,* 108). In fact, the *West-östlicher Divan* ultimately documents a Western monologue delivered at a passive Orient. Thus Goethe's veneration of the holy scriptures of the *Koran,* together with his connection with Islam in general, is highly problematic. What existed was rather a cultural divide, and one that created a colonialist distance between the poet and his object of interest. Not even his enthusiasm for the achievements of oriental cultures, clearly discernible in certain of the poems, is consistently maintained: "Die persische Dichtung aber und was ihr ähnlich ist, wird von dem Westländer niemals ganz rein, mit vollem Behagen aufgenommen werden" (*HA* 2:169).

When we look at it this way, there appears to be a rift in the affinity with Hafis that Goethe announced in the *Divan* poems. While Buddhism and Islam are devalued, so, conversely, the status of Christianity—the religion that will be the salvation of the "dunkele[r] Mensch"—is raised. Noteworthy material when considering Goethe's implicitly hierarchical approach can also be found in his letter to Reimer of 25 May 1816, in which he wrote: "Die eilf Bände *Asiatic Researches* sind ein Abgrund in den man sich nicht ungestraft hineinstürzt.—Verbleiben Sie in den griechischen Regionen, man hat's nirgend besser; diese Nation hat verstanden aus tausend Rosen ein Fläschchen Rosenöl auszuziehen."[35] Thus Bhatti's notion of Goethe as a thinker ". . . zwischen zwei Kulturen schwebend . . ." appears in need of some revision. Bhatti ascribes to Goethe an impartiality to which the poet himself may have aspired, though it is one that, given the imperialist characteristics of his Enlightenment context, he could not wholly maintain.[36] Finally, the "Noten und Abhandlungen" effect a unilateral transfer of knowledge—running from East to West—that at times diverges from the dialogue lyrically presented in the poetry. Even the "Buch Suleika," still regarded today as one of the most beautiful in the *Divan,* is evidence that Goethe's engagement with the Orient was not a selfless one. There the poet uses the oriental figures of Hatem and Suleika to encrypt his love affair with Marianne von Willemer.

Nonetheless, the "weltbürgerliche Offenheit gegenüber allen menschlichen Kulturen"[37] practiced by Goethe can be seen to offer a framework for intercultural encounters, which both raises awareness about cultural difference and aspires toward intercultural capability. On 20 July 1827 he wrote to the Scottish author and thinker Thomas Carlyle, stating that the literature of foreign cultures could only succeed "wenn man das Besondere der einzelnen Menschen und Völkerschaften auf sich beruhen läßt, bei der Überzeugung jedoch festhält, daß das wahrhaft Verdienstliche sich dadurch auszeichnet, daß es der ganzen Menschheit angehört" (*HA* 12:353).

Whether or not this process succeeds depends not least upon the ability of individual cultures to take Goethe's theoretical insights and translate them critically into practice. Only then can the scenario of clashing civilizations be superseded by one of peaceful co-existence, mutual understanding and bilateral communication. The metaphor of the *Divan* (meaning "collection" or "gathering") stretches beyond the mere idea of a synthesis of Occident and Orient, anticipating the cosmopolitan thinking that later in 1827 Goethe crystallized into his oft-cited concept of

"Weltliteratur." It is precisely this central concept of the *Divan* phase of Goethe's writing that shows us that we must read Goethe's engagement with the Orient as *pars pro toto* for his universal thinking. This universalism, not free of contradictions, is predicated on a call for mutual recognition between cultures and for the overcoming of the intellectual paralysis exhibited by national literatures concerned only with themselves.

Here, perhaps, one thing ought to become obvious: given the blind alley into which the contemporary relationship between "East" and "West" is leading, one might think Goethe had already moved beyond our limited horizons. Even if we believe that much progress has been made since Goethe's era, we can still only gain from engaging with his conceptual models as we face the challenges of globalization. Such engagement cannot be limited to simplistic interpretations of the poet's own theories of the intercultural as a well-intentioned, value-neutral "Aufforderung zum Aufbruch in andere Länder."[38] However, we might follow Bhatti in his assertion that dialogue is "die Grundlage für die Regelung menschlicher und gesellschaftlicher Beziehungen" (zzW, 104) and so, in our age of increasing cultural conflict, Goethe seems quite right in his central call and we can take the *Divan,* together with his concept of *Weltliteratur,* as the poet's most informative response to an increasingly globalized world.

The merits of Goethe's project must not become a tool to be used indiscriminately, however. Subjected to postcolonial scrutiny, the concepts underlying Goethe's "poetische Reise" come under fire for their sacrosanct claims. Although his discourse did not yet show the signs of the imperialist excesses exhibited by the literal oriental journeys of the nineteenth and twentieth centuries, Goethe's approach is at least partly a function of that form of European Universalism that, fuelled by curiosity, a thirst for knowledge, and a drive toward progress, marked the beginning of European colonization. In this context, the figure of the traveler plays a central role. Although Goethe only traversed the Orient in a "poetic" mode, he presented himself as a mouthpiece for oriental cultures—a claim rightfully exposed as colonialist by postcolonial criticism. Thus Goethe's writing on these topics bears testimony to the often underestimated ambivalences of the European Enlightenment and its relationship to the non-European world. Our task involves not merely acknowledging Goethe's *Divan* and concept of "Weltliteratur" as historical achievements but also providing the necessary correctives to its non-critical reception. Does Goethe not have Suleika give voice to the thought that ought to guide our reading of the *Divan* (*HA* 2:87): "Süßes Dichten, lautre Wahrheit"?

—*Translated from German by James Hodkinson*

Notes

[1] Samuel P. Huntington: *The Clash of Civilizations and the Remaking of the World Order* (New York: Simon & Schuster, 1998).

[2] Konstantinos P. Romanós, "Verstehen und Verständigung zwischen Christentum und Islam: Das gemeinsame griechische Kulturerbe als Vermittlung," in *Verstehen und Verständigung: Ethnologie, Xenologie, Interkulturelle Philosophie*, ed. Wolfdiedrich Schmied-Kowarzik (Würzburg: Königshausen & Neumann, 2002), 337–42.

[3] Joachim Sartorius, "Im Namen Goethes: Zu den ideellen Fundamenten der auswärtigen Kulturpolitik heute," in *Im Namen Goethes! Erfundenes, Erinnertes und Grundsätzliches zum 250. Geburtstag Johann Wolfgang von Goethes*, ed. Markus Hänsel-Hohenhausen (Frankfurt am Main: Verlag der Goethe-Gesellschaft Frankfurt, 1999), 283–93. Further references to this work are given in the text using the abbreviation *ING* and the page number.

[4] Johann Wolfgang von Goethe, *Werke, Hamburger Ausgabe*, 14 vols., 15th ed. (Munich: DTV, 1994); vol. 2: "Gedichte und Epen 2," ed. Erich Trunz. Quotations from Goethe's *Divan* are taken exclusively from this edition. Further references to this work are given in the text using the abbreviation *HA* and the volume and page numbers.

[5] Michael Hofmann, *Interkulturelle Literaturwissenschaft: Eine Einführung* (Stuttgart: UTB, 2006), particularly the chapter "Goethes Auseinandersetzung mit dem Orient im *West-östlichen Divan*" (71–85).

[6] Cf. Peter Matussek, *Goethe zur Einführung* (Hamburg: Junius, 1998), 164–67.

[7] Todd Kontje, *German Orientalisms* (Ann Arbor: U of Michigan P, 2004), 119.

[8] On this see particularly Homi K. Bhabha, *Die Verortung der Kultur* (Tübingen: Stauffenburg Verlag, 2000).

[9] Hans-Jürgen Lüsebrink, "Von der Faszination zur Wissenssystematisierung: Die koloniale Welt im Diskurs der europäischen Aufklärung," in *Das Europa der Aufklärung und die außereuropäische koloniale Welt*, ed. Hans-Jürgen Lüsebrink (Göttingen, Germany: Wallstein Verlag, 2006), 9–18, esp. 16.

[10] Edward Said, *Orientalism* (New York: Vintage Books, 1979), esp. 167–68.

[11] Anne Bohnenkamp, "Goethes poetische Orientreise," in *Goethe-Jahrbuch* 120 (2003): 144–56.

[12] Anil Bhatti: "' . . . zwischen zwei Welten schwebend. . . .' Zu Goethes Fremdheitsexperiment im *West-östlichen* Divan," in *Goethe: Neue Ansichten—Neue Einsichten*, ed. Jans-Jörg Knoblock and Helmut Koopmann (Würzburg: Königshausen & Neumann, 2007), 103–21, esp. 110. Further references to this work are given in the text using the abbreviation *zzW* and the page number.

[13] Cf. Mirjam Weber, *Der "wahre Poesie-Orient": Eine Untersuchung zur Orientalismus-Theorie Edward Saids am Beispiel von Goethes "West-östlichem Divan" und der Lyrik Heines* (Wiesbaden: Harrassowitz Verlag, 2001).

[14] As Erich Trunz writes in the afterword to the *Hamburger Ausgabe*: "Bei dem allen ist der *Divan* zugleich ein Buch der Begegnung, er ist *west-östlich*. Zwei Literaturen, zwei Kulturen begegnen einander" (*HA* 2:564).

[15] Katharina Mommsen, *Goethe und der Islam,* ed. Peter Anton von Arnim (Frankfurt am Main: Insel, 2001).

[16] Gotthold Ephraim Lessing: *Nathan der Weise: Text und Materialien,* ed. Ingrid Haaser (Berlin: Cornelsen, 1997). Further reading can be found in Wilfried Barner, Gunter E. Grimm, Helmut Kiesel, and Martin Kramer, eds., *Lessing: Epoche—Werk—Wirkung* (Munich: C. H. Beck, 1998).

[17] Lüsebrink, "Von der Faszination zur Wissenssystematisierung," 9.

[18] Lüsebrink, "Von der Faszination zur Wissenssystematisierung," 10.

[19] Johann Gottfried Herder, *Ideen zur Philosophie der Geschichte der Menschheit,* ed. Martin Bollacher (Frankfurt am Main: Deutscher Klassiker Verlag, 1989). Of interest here is the nineteenth book.

[20] See Harald Wiese, *Eine Zeitreise zu den Ursprüngen unserer Sprache: Wie die Indogermanistik unsere Wörter erklärt* (Berlin: Logos Verlag, 2007).

[21] Cf. Doris Bachmann-Medick, ed., *Kultur als Text: Die anthropologische Wende in der Literaturwissenschaft* (Frankfurt am Main: Fischer, 1996).

[22] Cf. Jürgen Pieters, "Literature and the Anamnesis of History," in *Methods for the Study of Literature as Cultural Memory,* ed. Raymon Vervliet and Annemarie Estor (Amsterdam: Rodopi, 2000), 45–56.

[23] Hendrik Birus, *Goethes imaginativer Orientalismus,* Jahrbuch des Freien Deutschen Hochstifts 1992: 106–28.

[24] Mommsen, *Goethe und der Islam,* 48.

[25] *Briefe von Schillers Gattin an einen vertrauten Freund.* ed. Heinrich Dünker (Leipzig: F. A. Brockaus, 1856), 181–82.

[26] Bhatti, "zwischen zwei Welten schwebend," 113. Unfortunately Bhatti limits this fascinating insight to the "Noten und Abhandlungen" of the *Divan* and does not discuss Goethe's attempts to prepare his audience for the work.

[27] Johann Wolfgang Goethe, *West-östlicher Divan: Studienausgabe* (Stuttgart: Reclam, 2005), 602. See also *HA* 2:126.

[28] See Peter-André Alt, *Aufklärung* (Stuttgart: Metzler, 1996), 3.

[29] Cf. Manfred Koch. *Weimarer Weltbewohner: Zur Genese von Goethes Begriff "Weltliteratur"* (Tübingen: Niemeyer, 2002), 266.

[30] Cf. Clifford Geertz, *Dichte Beschreibungen: Beiträge zum Verstehen kultureller Systeme* (Frankfurt am Main: Suhrkamp, 1983), especially the chapter "Dichte Beschreibungen: Bemerkungen zu einer deutenden Theorie von Kultur" (7–43).

[31] Mommsen: *Goethe und der Islam,* 251.

[32] Cf. Kontje, *German Orientalisms,* 122.

[33] Sir Muhammad Iqbal, *Botschaft des Ostens (Als Antwort auf Goethes West-östlichen Divan),* trans. from Persian and commentated by Annemarie Schimmel (Wiesbaden: Harrassowitz, 1963), 9.

[34] Cf. Jürgen Osterhammel, "Welten des Kolonialismus im Zeitalter der Aufklärung," in *Das Europa der Aufklärung und die außereuropäische koloniale Welt,* ed. Hans-Jürgen Lüsebrink (Göttingen: Wallstein, 2006), 19–36.

[35] Johann Wolfgang von Goethe, *Briefe der Jahre 1814–1832,* vol. 21 of the Gedenkausgabe, 2nd ed. (Zürich and Stuttgart: Artemis Verlag, 1965), 307.

[36] Cf. Suzanne Zantop, "Dialectics and Colonialism: The Underside of the Enlightenment," in *Impure Reason: Dialectic of Enlightenment in Germany,* ed. Daniel Wilson and Robert Holub (Detroit, MI: Wayne State UP, 1993), 301–21.

[37] Thomas Zabka, "Humanität," in *Goethe Handbuch: Personen, Sachen, Begriffe,* vol. 4/1, ed. Bernd Witte, Theo Buck, Hans-Dietrich Dahnke, Regine Otto, and Peter Schmidt (Stuttgart: Metzler, 1998), 498–501, esp. 499.

[38] Bohnenkamp, *Goethes poetische Orientreise,* 145.

6: Moving beyond the Binary? Christian-Islamic Encounters and Gender in the Thought and Literature of German Romanticism

James Hodkinson

MANY OF THE CONTRIBUTIONS IN THIS VOLUME demonstrate a tension between those texts that present the encounter between Islam and Christianity as an insurmountable clash of cultural and religious binary opposites and those texts that resist that tendency. This chapter seeks to explore how that tension manifests itself in the thought and writing of the Romantic period, which we will we consider to have begun around 1796 and to have ended by the late 1820s.[1] What forms did the Romantic encounter with Islam take? Although the German-speaking territories did in the eighteenth and nineteenth centuries produce a range of itinerant Orientalist anthropologists and travel writers, some of whom ventured into Islamic territories and wrote about their experiences, the German Romantic encounter with Islam was not predicated upon the "real" encounters that were facilitated by travel—indeed, travel was far more common and more widely documented in the context of the colonial expansion of other European nations.[2] Like previous generations of Germans, the Romantics approached Islam through bookish learning in libraries and lecture halls and artists' work in ateliers and galleries: the encounter was with a geographically remote Other religion and those nations and peoples it had ostensibly shaped.

The Romantic treatment of Islam has been traditionally identified with the wider European project of constructing a fantasy of the Orient, as defined in Said's *Orientalism*.[3] While Said has much to say about Romanticism in general and about Islam (as understood within the Orientalist tradition) and does, on odd occasions, mention German cultural contributions to these fields, he rarely connects the three. Said emphasizes, for instance, a vaguely Romantic predilection for the Orient as "exotic locale" (*O,* 118) or deals with Herder's attempts in his *Ideen zur Philosophie der Menschheit* (1784–91) to establish a kinship between Christianity and Islam founded on his idealistic model of transcending prejudice through a form of cross-cultural empathy (*O*, 118). Friedrich Schlegel, the one *bona fide* German Romantic he deals with in any depth, is discussed in terms of his own peculiar ethnic-linguistic definition of the Orient as the location for the highest ideals of Romanticism (*O*, 98). Todd Kontje's later study is, however, more subtle and closes some of the gaps in Said's discussion. As shown earlier in this volume, Kontje's study gives a wide-ranging critical discussion of how German forms of Orientalist writing have fulfilled diverse functions within the process of constructing a sense of European and later specifically German identity from the Middle Ages to the present.[4] Kontje examines Romantic constructions of the Orient in terms of a literary compensation for Germany's "absence of Empire" in what was becoming an imperialist age for other European nations. He produces an interesting reading of Novalis, whom he rightly sees as both a political radical and a conservative — a writer who lays out a blueprint for a non-exclusive German Empire, characterized by a "gentler German cosmopolitanism that will reawaken the pre-national spirit of European unity and reconnect Europe to the East" (99). While Kontje's contribution on Romanticism does not deal specifically with Islam, this chapter will test whether his concepts of acceptance and communication also apply to representations of specifically German-Islamic relationships, both within Novalis's novel and elsewhere.

While there is a systematic survey of the specifically Islamic in English Romanticism,[5] the same appears not to be true for the German tradition, so even taking Kontje into account a fuller discussion of Islam in German Romanticism is required. Much German Romantic writing is marked by a set of key philosophical and aesthetic developments vis-à-vis the Enlightenment, many of which could have a bearing on *how* writers and thinkers represented this particular encounter. There is, for one, the fascinating intersection between aesthetics and the philosophy of identity; there are the theories of language and communication; and also what many regard to be the modern birth of a Christian thinking which recognizes the validity of other faiths. This chapter will ask whether or not Romanticism, despite apparently being "exterior to what it describes" and exerting a "kind of intellectual authority" over its object of study (*O*, 17–20), also marks an attempt to restructure the power relationships thought to be unavoidably bound up with the European encounter with Islam: does German Romantic writing configure instances of dialogue with an articulate Islamic subject, one predicated on an ethically driven sense of mutual recognition—even if this occurs within the written worlds of literary fiction and scholarship? The chapter will ask, furthermore, to what extent Romantic texts represent Islam by drawing on a catalogue of specific binary stereotypes, with Islam as an "Other" religion segregated from the West by crudely defined notions of linguistic difference; with the (Christian) West cast as "rational" vis-à-vis the "irrational" world of Islam; with

Muslims depicted as religious fanatics with aspirations to militaristic expansion in contrast to "righteous" and "wronged" Christians; or, conversely, with Islam as a weaker, passive, on occasion feminized Other buckling under the military and cultural potency of resurgent Christendom. The study will also consider how these processes of representing Islam interact with other hierarchical systems of representing identity, such as Romantic discourses on ethnic and gender difference, and examine whether or not this interaction promotes or undermines the view of Islam and Christianity as irreconcilably different and mutually alienated.[6]

Throughout, the chapter will aim to read Romanticism in terms of its own theoretical aspirations, testing how it can be seen as a critical response to reductive traditions of representing Islam that have been exposed and problematized by contemporary theorists such as Said. The discussion will proceed in two parts, with the first reconstructing some of the key aspects of Romantic theories of identity and communication and showing how these are reflected in the prose fiction of Romanticism. Do Romantics such as Friedrich Schleiermacher and Friedrich Schlegel manage in their theoretical writings to cease presenting the encounter as a clash or meeting of binary opposites. The second part of the chapter focuses the questions outlined above on two literary texts, an episode from Novalis's novel *Heinrich von Ofterdingen* (1801) and E. T. A. Hoffmann's short story *Das Sanctus* (1819), which represent Christian-Islamic encounters located in recognizable and characteristically fraught historical contexts. Both texts allow for close examination of how Romantic models of language and communicative agency succeed or fail in realizing ideals of communication across perceived lines of religious and cultural difference and also frame the encounter in terms of the problematic of gender issues around 1800.

The theoretical basis of Early German Romanticism grew for the most part from a critique of the idealist philosophy of Johann Gottlieb Fichte, as laid down in his *Wissenschaftslehre* (1794–95): this is as true of Novalis as of the brothers Schlegel, Friedrich and August Wilhelm, and the theology of F. E. D. Schleiermacher. The Romantics sought to shed new light on Fichte's central proposition that the subject constituted its own identity, effectively calling itself into self-conscious existence through a creative act, a fusion of willpower and productive imagination. For Fichte, this act of "self-positing" simultaneously distinguished the subject from the object, the "self" from that which was "not self," or what he designates "Nicht-Ich," or "non-ego."[7] For the Romantics, the subject's act of self-positing is not an absolute ontological truth, whereby the self simply becomes, but rather one of linguistic or semiotic equivalence. Novalis wrote: "Das Wesen der Identität läßt sich nur in einem Scheinsatz aufstellen. Wir verlassen das Identische um es darzustellen."[8] It is this quality of self-reflexive relativity, born of the notion that all phenomena are transcendental in essence and therefore mediated through language, that characterizes Early Romantic thinking and writing. All human understanding, be it in the realm of self-insight, scientific knowledge, or religious speculation, is a self-consciously artifical representation of a higher, inaccessible truth. As a fiction, identity is itself a changeable structure, and it is this very changeability that forms the basis of a new understanding of religion, which has consequences for the Romantic view of Islam.

It was Friedrich Ernst Daniel Schleiermacher (1768–1834) who applied the core aspects of Romantic thinking to the most sustained examination of religion. As Richard Crouter notes, Schleiermacher remained a dedicated Christian in the tradition of Calvin, who nevertheless developed a philosophical stance on the nature of God and religion, and a view of society founded upon a tolerant secularism and inter-confessional understanding of religion.[9] Central to Schleiermacher's apparent tolerance of and respect for other faiths is a notion of religiosity that appears to stretch beyond the structures of scriptural dogma and organized religion.[10] Romantic thought acknowledged the impossibility of knowing any one thing absolutely and this, of course, applied no less to the absolute itself. God, as this absolute, cannot be known rationally but can be experienced through the individual's participation in what Schleiermacher terms God-consciousness.[11] Moving beyond wholly rational thought, the subject experiences the divine as the absolute within him or herself, as something that hovers at the edge of consciousness or experience. When the subject experiences the divine, a feeling that Schleiermacher calls "absolute dependence," "das schlechthinige Abhängigkeitsgefühl,"[12] is engendered within him. Albert Houranni notes that, for Schleiermacher, experience of God is "anterior to knowing or doing" and therefore not wholly expressed through organized religions and their scripturally derived doctrines.[13] It is in this context, says Houranni, that Schleiermacher approaches the three great monotheistic religions in his key text *Der christliche Glaube*.

For Schleiermacher, Judaism is dying out, though Christianity and Islam are seen as still contending for mastery of the human race.[14] So for all of his relativism, the theologian reverts to a model of historically grounded, polarized opposition between the Christian and Muslim worlds, even if this is offered as an ostensibly objective diagnosis. In looking at this apparent "contest," Schleiermacher writes as a Christian who undoubtedly believes his faith is superior. In §8 of *Der christliche Glaube*, Islam is presented as a self-consciously monotheistic religion that nevertheless emphasized the action of the sensual world upon the emotions, thus bringing it closer to pagan polytheism: "Der Islam verrät durch seinen leidenschaftlichen Charakter und den starken sinnlichen Gehalt seiner Vorstellungen ohnerachtet des streng gehaltenen Monotheismus doch einen starken Einfluß jener Gewalt des Sinnlichen auf die Ausprägung der frommen Erregungen, welche sonst den Menschen auf der Stufe der Vielgötterei festhält."[15]

Christianity, in contrast, represents the purest form of monotheism, occupying a "higher" stage of development in the history of religions, as "die vollkommenste unter den am meisten entwickelten Religionsformen."[16] However, to this he added the typically Romantic idea that all that is finite, mortal, and subjective needs some structure or mediator in order for it to be brought into communion with God. So, given that organized religions merely connect us with divinity rather than containing or expressing it in any absolute sense, no one religion has a monopoly on truth, and all religions must contain an element of corruption, even religion in its highest form: Christianity. Schleiermacher sees this as unavoidable, when the infinite descends into the sphere of time and submits to the influence of finite minds. Of Schleiermacher, Hourani says succinctly, "No man or community possesses the whole of religion, but all have something of truth in them."[17]

Schleiermacher serves as an interesting case in hand for this discussion. While the theoretical framework of his model of religion might on one level appear to relinquish the religious and cultural supremacy of Christianity, he nevertheless colonizes and re-codifies Islam in a manner to suit his argument: he sacrifices little of his German-Christian "authority" over Islam. He demonstrates the way in which Romantic theory can seem to open out interesting possibilities for rethinking the dualistic and antagonistic relationship between Christianity and Islam but can fail to progress beyond precisely such an established position when dealing explicitly with the issue.

Theology was not the only Romanticized discipline to deal with Islam: the anthropological and historical lectures and essays of Friedrich Schlegel (1772–1829) provide another rich source of commentary. There is a wealth of differences between the younger and the older Schlegel. His disillusionment with revolutionary ideals, already nascent in his distaste for the political Revolution and the Great Terror of 1790s France, became more pronounced in later life. In 1809 he took up a post as secretary in the court and state chancellery in Vienna and in the same year accompanied Archduke Charles to war, issuing fiery proclamations against Napoleon and editing the army newspaper, marking an obvious shift in his political mentality. While scholarship no longer attaches quite so much importance to this change, or indeed draws quite such sharp divisions between the works of Schlegel prior to 1808 and his writings of the next two decades,[18] this later work undeniably propounds more conservative views of nation and culture. This was no longer Schlegel the Romantic ironist, who had reveled in the intellectual freedom offered by the Romantic view of the fickleness of truth and meaning and the possibility of their provocative manipulation through language, but Schlegel the essentialist, who engaged in a project of writing and lecturing on political, religious, and literary history and sought to represent what he believed to be the "essential character" of peoples, nations, religions, and cultures.[19] Perhaps unfortunately for Romanticism's reputation, it was the older Schlegel who wrote on Islam, chiefly in lecture series held between 1811 and 1829.

In her essay on Schlegel's writings on China, Lucie Bernier makes a comment that seems equally true of his approach to Islam in these later lectures, namely that "Christianity is used to measure and construct non-European peoples and cultures within the Western perception of the philosophy of history. Christianity is given supreme value, and related religions are considered to be corrupted in varying degrees, with non-theistic cultures bringing up the very rear."[20] It is the twelfth lecture in the 1829 series *Philosophie der Geschichte*, on the "Charakterschilderung des Mahomet und seiner Religion, so wie der arabischen Weltherrschaft: Neue Gestaltung des europäischen Abendlandes und Wiederherstellung des christlichen Kaisertums,"[21] in which Schlegel gives Islam his fullest treatment. As the title promises, Schlegel's reading of Islam is rooted in his view of the essential ethnic "character" of the Arabic people and in a view of the historical figure of Mohammed as an individualized expression of that character. The Arabs, he notes, were to be characterized by their fierce independence ("Selbstgefuhl"), a well-defined sense of moral conviction (a "moralische Kraft des Willens"), but also by their tendency to divide and squabble among themselves (*KFS* I,10:275–76). Schlegel describes Mohammed himself as an example of many of these great qualities but also as arrogant, fanatical, and a militant enforcer of his own view of Islam's superiority over Christianity and Judaism. Schlegel also attacks Islam theologically. He criticizes Mohammed's insistence on the absolute unity of God and his own non-divine status, and his consequent failure to perform miracles, commenting, too, on what he sees as Islam's failure to mirror the Christian doctrine of forgiving one's enemy, writing of: "Ein Prophet ohne Wunder, eine Religion ohne Geheimnis und eine Moral ohne Liebe, welche den Blutdurst befördert, und mit der entschiedensten Sinnlichkeit anfing und endigte" (*KFS* I,10:276). The lecture is particularly scathing in its critique of Islam as a "sensual" religion, with its vision of heaven lacking in the divine mystery of a Christian God, comprising nothing more than a infinite harem of virgins and beautiful gardens stretching as far as the eye could see. This sensualism, together with the unyielding zeal and overt emotionality characterizing Islam, is identified as the remnants of heathenism, which are further indicated by its adherents' idolatrous journeying to and worship of the black stone of the Kaaba in Mecca, referred to as a "Götzenstein."

It is quite obvious that, for all of the apparent awe with which he speaks of the strength of purpose underlying the empire building of the so-called Mohammedans, Schlegel regards Islam as an antagonistic Other. In a moment of great irony, though not self-conscious Romantic irony, Schlegel, having delivered this most divisive of lectures, places the blame for divisions between Christianity and Islam firmly on Muslim shoulders. The Islamic prohibition of alcohol is read by Schlegel not so much as a moral directive but more as an insidious attempt to discredit the Christian drinking of wine at holy communion and thus to erect insurmountable barriers between the faiths:

> So zeigt sich in vielem auch wieder eine feindliche Absicht gegen das Christentum. Vielleicht war selbst das Verbot des Weins nicht so sehr bloß als eine moralische Vorschrift gemeint, die als solche eben nicht so streng beobachtet sein dürfte, als in der religiösen Absicht gegeben, um durch diese ausgesprochene Verwerfung über den Wein, als den einen wesentlichen Bestandteil des christlichen Dankopfers, dieses mit anzugreifen und dadurch eine unübersteigliche Scheidewand zwischen seiner Lehre und dem Christentum zu ziehen. (*KFS* I,10:276)

And how did Schlegel see the future of relations between the two faiths? In the thirteenth lecture of his 1827 series *Philiosophie des Lebens,* entitled "Von dem Geiste der Wahrheit des Lebens, in seiner Anwendung auf die öffentlichen Verhältnisse; oder von der christlichen Staatsverfassung und dem christlichen Rechtsbegriff," the only hope for reconciliation between Christianity and Islam is shown to depend upon the Islamic world's adoption of certain "christliche Sitten," particularly the Christian "Friedens-Prinzip," which he sees as the model for international tolerance between states and as a corrective for the irrational fanaticism abounding among Muslims (*KFS* I,10:264–67). For all their sophistication, the two Romantics writing *theoretically* on Islam find themselves complicit in the tradition of representing the faith in a unidirectional mode. Whether or not individual writers and thinkers were conscious of the fact, this tradition effectively seeks to shore up a model of Christian Europe by presenting Islam as an antipodal religion, crudely sensuous, violent, and expansionist, and, needless to say, no real dialogue is sought with the other faith.

Does the literary prose of Romanticism offer a different vision of Islam? There already appear to be concrete links between the fourth chapter of Novalis's *Heinrich von Ofterdingen* and Hoffmann's *Das Sanctus.* Both seek to represent an encounter with Islam by embodying Islam in the form of a woman. For Novalis this is "Zulima," for Hoffmann the almost identically named "Zulema." Both appear to be variations on a linguistic root common to Semitic languages: derived from an Aramaic word, "Shlama," translated as "Salaam" in Arabic and "Shalom" in Hebrew, both Zulima and Zulema are female forms of a name meaning "well-being," or in some cases "peace" or "peaceful one."[22] Ironically for the women, they both find themselves on conflict lines between pre-Enlightened Christian Europe and the Islamic world, though their fates and functions appear quite different in their respective texts. On a theoretical level Novalis appeared to have a potentially quite liberal notion of organized religion. Applying his post-Fichtean thought to religion, he wrote that as God (or the absolute) was absent from the finite structures of human reflection and culture, organized religions were of relatively limited value: of course humanity needed an aesthetic means to commune with God, a "mediator" as he called it, but the choice of that mediator was to be free:

> Nichts ist zur wahren Religiosität unentbehrlicher als ein Mittelglied—das uns mit der Gottheit verbindet. Unmittelbar kann der Mensch schlechterdings nicht mit derselben in Verhältniß stehn. In der Wahl dieses Mittelglieds muß der Mensch durchaus frey seyn. . . . Es ist ein Götzendienst im weitern Sinn, wenn ich diesen Mittler für Gott selbst ansehe. . . . Wahre Religion ist, die jenen Mittler als Mittler annimmt . . . (SFH 2:440–42, 73)

However, does Novalis succeed in converting this theory into explicit statements about the value of other religions, their rituals and practices?[23] The answer lies elsewhere in his work, for where theoretical reflection ends, the incomplete novel *Heinrich von Ofterdingen* begins to explore the polyvalent approach to religions in terms of a Christian-Islamic encounter.

Ofterdingen is a Romantic work in a medieval setting: specifically scholars have contended this to be the mid-twelfth century, during the Crusade under Friederich II von Hohenstaufen, which eventually led to the Christian occupation of Jerusalem (1228–29) (SFH 1:628,231). In the fourth chapter the male protagonist, the fledgling poet Heinrich, comes upon a castle, in which he encounters a group of Christian crusaders freshly returned from an expedition in the Holy Land with stories to tell, songs to sing, and various spoils of war. Drinking with them, Heinrich appears entranced by the tales of exotic lands and demonic foes: "Heinrich hörte mit großer Aufmerksamkeit den neuen Erzählungen zu" (SFH 1:230). The words of their song depict the Muslims currently as "occupying" Jerusalem, referring to them as "wilde Heyden," defiling Christ's grave (SFH 1:231). The first strophe of their song, in fact, personifies the grave as an individual possessed of its own voice, though one all but drowned out in its cries for help by the mocking voices of the heathens: "Es klagt heraus mit dumpfer Stimme: Wer rettet mich von diesem Grimme!" (SFH 1:231). Part of the crusaders' quest, then, has been to free that voice — but also, in the process, to silence others: Zulima, the female Muslim slave held captive outside the castle, is effectively one of the spoils of war, and her voice has no place at the feasting table. However, Heinrich's attitude toward and encounter with Zulima and consequently with Islam turns out very differently.

There are a number of significant forces shaping Novalis's treatment of this encounter. First, the poet's source for the figure of Zulima is cited as the eponymous figure from Johann Georg Jacobi's *Nessir und Zulima: Eine Erzählung nach Raphael* (1782).[24] Here Zulima is the daughter of a Zoroastrian priest banished with her father from their Persian homeland for their tolerance of other religions, constantly fleeing persecution by members of the other monotheistic religions, and captured and sold into slavery on several occasions before finding some degree of solace when freed by and married to a "reformed" Muslim nobleman, who was formerly her master. In writing a tale about a Zulima figure Novalis appears to be connecting with a post-Enlightenment tradition calling for peaceful coexistence of all faiths based on mutual understanding and communication.[25] Moreover, Novalis introduces this material into a novel with an underlying theoretical ideal of communication. In his encyclopedic writings Novalis sought to move beyond a monological, subject-centered model of discourse in which the Other is reduced to a mute inverse of the self. Engaging critically with Fichte once more, Novalis rejected the model of the "Nicht-Ich," proposing rather "Statt Nicht-Ich: Du" (*SFH* 111:429–30). This formula can be used as the basis for a wholly new reading of how Novalis treats the relationship between the individual (often male) subject and its (often, though not exclusively, female) Others.[26] First, the formula represents a moment of recognition in which the self recognizes its Other as distinct from itself but also as an equivalent center of moral and communicative agency: in short *another self.* From this recognition grows a necessarily ethical dimension to the relationship between "Ich" and "Du": they must cooperate with each other. This cooperation necessitates a mutual consensus on the sharing of communicative rights and, ultimately, the reorganization of any one-sided power relationship.

From the crusader's perspective Zulima is an object that has been mastered, a thing to be sung about, not a woman who can sing. In the same way that she is literally her captor's physical possession, so too her identity remains an object of their cultural authority. However, Heinrich withdraws from the company of the knights, an act that betrays something of his desire to move beyond their songs, behavior, and politics. He is drawn out of the castle's confines by the evening outside, feeling "von der goldenen Ferne gelockt" (*SFH* 1:233). There are several similar instances of Heinrich's feeling drawn away from an experience or a setting to which he has become accustomed, drawn toward something else that is alluring in its otherness. It is in this context that Zulima is presented, possibly as the very embodiment of that otherness. She is, at first, disembodied song:

> Er schweifte durch das wilde Gebüsch und kletterte über bemooste Felsenstücke, als auf einmal aus einer nahen Tiefe ein zarter eindringender Gesang einer weiblichen Stimme von wunderbaren Tönen begleitet, erwachte. Es war ihm gewiß, daß es eine Laute sey; er blieb verwunderungsvoll stehen, und hörte in gebrochner deutscher Aussprache folgendes Lied (*SFH* 1:234)

Zulima's song has the quality of wondrousness associated with all poetry, but it is also described as being sung in broken German. This combination of her locus in the text as an apparent antipode to the crusaders, singing her song that tells of her exotic homeland where myrtle trees grow and crystal-clear springs flow, all married to her linguistic otherness, have led critics like Kamakshi Murti to refer to Zulima explicitly as an "Exotin," a potent if static mixture of gendered and Orientalist fantasies.[27] Kontje acknowledges such readings, highlighting the differences between Zulima on the one hand and Heinrich as a representative of a dynamic, progressive and "male" Europe on the other. Yet he also points to a certain redemption of Zulima, through her representation as a reflective and philosophically informed member of another culture: given that Heinrich is destined for androgynous transformations in Novalis's posthumously published notes on the novel's completion and also that Zulima is destined to return at that point in the text in various guises, Kontje feels that this unconventional treatment of gender mirrors a similarly new model of the relationship between Europe and the East. This is founded on mutual recognition and reconciliation and simultaneously represents a new gentler form of German nationalism and appeals to a pre-national sense of European identity.[28] Yet does Zulima appear as a specifically Islamic subject, independent and articulate in her own right?

In bidding Heinrich to come closer, reducing the physical space between them, Zulima actually begins to dismantle one of the major factors contributing to binary perceptions of opposition between cultures, namely that of perceived physical otherness and its articulation in language.[29] In Heinrich's face she sees qualities that remind her of her own brother:

> Euer Gesicht dünkt mir bekannt, laßt mich besinnen — Mein Gedächtnis ist schwach geworden, aber Euer Anblick erweckt in mir eine sonderbare Erinnerung aus frohen Zeiten. O! mir ist, als glicht ihr einem meiner Brüder, der vor unsrem Unglück von uns schied, und nach Persien zu einem berühmten Dichter zog. (*SFH* 1:236)

This physical similarity undermines the notion of an essential ethnic division between the occidental and the so-called oriental peoples, and in suggesting this Novalis also begins to imply that there is no ethnically or doctrinally derived fundamental division between the Christian and Islamic faiths. Zulima develops this idea, complicating the relationship between the two faiths in a productive way by discoursing on the specifics of both the common ground and the divisions between them. In describing the Crusades, she criticizes the Christian West, but only on the grounds that it fails to accept Islam as a valid religion in its own right, a "Du" rather than a "Nicht-Ich," while Islam appears capable of doing this in respect of Christianity:

> Wie ruhig hätten die Christen das heilige Grab besuchen können, ohne nöthig zu haben, einen fürchterlichen, unnützen Krieg anzufangen der . . . auf immer das Morgenland von Europa getrennt hat. . . . Unsere Fürsten ehrten andachtsvoll das Grab eures Heiligen, den auch wir für einen göttlichen Profeten halten. (*SFH* 1:237)

Her faith is conceived of as pluralist in its acceptance of various religious prophets; Islam, in contrast to the Crusaders' Christianity, accepts not only Mohammed but also Christ, the prophet of its *apparent* enemy, as its other mediator. From his encounter with Zulima Heinrich not only hears another song, different from those he has heard hitherto, but learns again that poets in general must listen to and allow space for others' voices: in leaving the castle, withdrawing from the crusader's songs, Heinrich offers Zulima the space to use hers. In returning to the castle, he experiences the strange need to become in some way her savior, though he is unsure of how he is to achieve this: "Er suchte die sinkende Hoffnung seiner Begleiterinn, ihr Vaterland dereinst wieder zu sehn, zu beleben, indem er innerlich einen heftigen Beruf fühlte, ihr Retter zu seyn, ohne zu wissen, auf welche Art es geschehen könne" (*SFH* 1:238). It seems that Heinrich is embracing more passionately a belief in allowing others the space for self-representation, and this is again reflected in the portrayal of his parting from Zulima. In approaching her for the first time Heinrich had wished that he had his own lute. In parting, though, Heinrich will not accept hers, which she offers as a gift, insisting that she keep the means to produce her song.

What happens to Zulima as the text progresses, however? Does her encounter with Heinrich remain part of his experience and does Islam merely serve to enrich a Christian journey of self-discovery, only to be forgotten again, without attaining again its own voice or presence? The novel was traditionally thought to have something of the character of a *Bildungsroman* about it, apparently presenting the personal development of one distinct, often male, subject, along the course of linear time such as a career or a lifetime. This might lead to expectations that *Ofterdingen* does indeed only have a passing encounter with Islam, serving only to aid the German poet. However, even in its unfinished state, the novel comes with several bundles of handwritten manuscripts containing plans for its continuation. Novalis planned for the novel's second part to dispense with realistic portrayals of a journey through linear time and geographical space and replace it with an increasingly metaphorical journey. This ideal fictional mode is a representation of what Novalis called the "geistige Gegenwart," in which those figures apparently left behind by the narrative in favor of Heinrich's individual progress are in fact reintroduced and remain present in this imagined, higher reality. Among these is Zulima, who enters into a series of bizarre metamorphoses, exchanging identities with other women and even Heinrich himself (*WWWN*, 228–38). Although the encounter between religions is not thematized explicitly at this point, it is clear that, in his ideal realm of poetry, Novalis represents authorship not as an activity engaged in by isolated, egocentric individuals but as a collaborative, "intersubjective" enterprise—one, that is, that requires the subject to recognize that it does not enjoy absolute freedom of expression if that freedom effectively limits the expressive powers of another. Thus the ideal of *Poësie* appears to make provision for a collective of many voices, which upholds the communicative rights of all characters regardless of gender, ethnicity, and faith.

Judged from a contemporary standpoint, Novalis's Zulima might not appear quite so radical a figure: as well as an exotic cultural Other, she has also been read as a female mouthpiece for male authorial ideas (*WWWN*, 185–87). Why did Novalis choose a woman to represent Islam? He might, wittingly or unwittingly, be seeking to underline divisions between Christian and Muslim by gendering cultural difference, continuing a tendency in much Enlightenment thought and writing of feminizing the Islamic and the Oriental (*O*, 207–8). Yet, as the Zulima episode in the novel also shows, by the standards of the unreconstructed late-eighteenth century Novalis had begun undermining binary models of gender that reduced women to silent muses and had begun to posit a creative, expressive female subject in their place. In her brief appearance in the text, Zulima refers to the Romantic hermeneutics involved in decoding the hieroglyphs on ancient pre-Muslim monuments, puts forward a pluralistic (and hence poetic) model of religion, and even begins to refer to how poetry can lead to an aesthetic process of reinventing the self in diverse ways (*SFH* 1:236–37)—an act tantamount to genius, in Novalis's thinking.[30] As a poet and philosopher who thinks and discourses on theology and intercultural politics, she thus debunks a series of eighteenth-century stereotypes about both women and Muslims as irrational and non-intellectual. So if issues such as gender stereotyping and the traditional power relationships and ethics of self-expression pertaining historically to both genders were already the object of conscious experimentation in Novalis's theoretical and literary writing, then the representation of Christianity and Islam by gendered figures need not serve to reinforce stereotypes of either faith, nor need it imply an irreconcilable opposition between the two.

E. T. A. Hoffmann was not a philosophically driven theorist in the sense that earlier Romantics were, yet theoretical reflections on the nature of art and language are in abundance in his work. A recent study by Magdolna Orosz discerns two theories of art and poetry in operation in Hoffmann's thinking, one of which she describes as mimetic, concerned with "reiner Nachahmung der Natur" a simple attempt to reproduce what the senses supply to the conscious mind.[31] This is set against a non-mimetic notion, in which art's object is envisaged in the artist's imagination—a vision that the artist subsequently seeks to transfer to the page or the canvas. Orosz points usefully to one way in which these theories related to Hoffmann's work: they seem to engender the idea that the representational act is a difficult struggle, one that involves the artist's trying to avoid lapsing either into a practice superficially and mechanically representing visual reality or into wholly imagined solipsism, whereby the text or image loses its connection to material reality.[32] This later Romantic theory, fascinating though it is, presents art as a problematic struggle and does not contain the same optimistic model for unambiguous communication through mutual recognition between subjects that we found in Novalis. It is perhaps, then, with more pessimism that the historically informed reader approaches the Christian-Islamic encounter in the short story *Das Sanctus*.

Das Sanctus tells, among other things, the story of Zulema, which is set during the conflict between the Christian Spanish and the Moors in Granada in the 1490s. Again, Zulema is a captive of war, taken prisoner after a rout of the Moorish forces. She is given the chance to convert to Christianity, enters a convent, and is baptized and renamed Julia. At times the narrative emphasizes her cultural and religious otherness: her first period in the monastery is marked by her grief at separation from her original culture and her singing of Moorish "Romanzen," which Hoffmann characterizes strongly from the European standpoint in terms of their otherness, even its discordance with the Christian musical context: "Sonderbarerweise klangen jetzt die Zithertöne . . . auch hoch und recht widrig, beinahe wie das grellende Gepfeife der kleinen mohrischen Flöten."[33] Similarly, although Zulema initially accepts Christianity, her devotional singing still appears indelibly colored by the ethnic traditions of her own song, reminding us of her origins: "ein seltsamer Gesang, halb mohrisches Lied, halb christlicher Kirchengesang" (156). When her captor Aguillar and her former lover and mentor the Muslim Hichem fight a dual, Hichem curses Christianity for having converted her into a bride of what he sees as a pagan deity, while Aguillar, in his opposing quest to retain cultural possession over this newly Christianized woman, metaphorically splits Zulema/ Julia down the middle: "Nennst du Zulema deine Geliebte, so sei Julia, die zum Glauben bekehrte, die Dame meiner Gedanken, und sie im Herzen . . . will ich gegen dich bestehn im wackeren Kampf" (157).

These conflicts are destructive for Zulema in a number of ways. First, she loses her singing voice. The fact that she has lost this prized quality means, as Birgit Röder has shown, that she is as already as good as dead for Hichem.[34] Aguillar also only loves one aspect of Zulema, namely Julia, his own Christianized, Romantic ideal of her (*SMNH*, 144–45). Both men appear to labor under a negatively reductive image of each other's religions—Hichem refers, for instance, to Christianity as heathen in its use of a "blutig dornengekröntes Götzenbild"; Aguillar refers disparagingly to Islam as "Mahoms schnödem Dienst"[35]—yet, arguably, the two rival men are not wholly motivated by religious zeal but by a desire to possess and rule differing aspects of Zulema's identity and to do so without recognizing her as a person in her own right. Thus she appears to be positioned upon intersecting fault lines, one running between two mutually antagonistic men and one between the two faiths of Christianity and Islam that are locked in mutually exclusive opposition. How is Zulema's fate resolved, however? Following a Moorish uprising, in which the insurgents are locked into in a burning house, her voice is heard singing the "Sanctus": the doors are opened and she leads her countrymen into the cathedral during the marriage of Ferdinand and Isabella, where she sings a perfect rendition of the Christian liturgy, ending with the Latin phrase "*Dona nobis pacem*" ("Give us peace") before sinking dead into the queen's arms. Subsequently the surviving Moors, full of wonderment at the Christian music, convert to Christianity. Yet, if we wish to speak of a "victory" of Catholic Christianity over Islam in Hoffmann's text, we cannot explain that victory in terms of the superiority of the former over the latter. In fact Röder has shown the conversion of the Moors to be a matter of inevitability as they are hopelessly overpowered and wish to save their own skins (*SMNH*, 145–46). Their enthusiasm may well have more to do with their wonderment at the beauty of Christian church music than with any doctrinal conviction on their part. Furthermore, there is a line of argument that deems other issues more important than religious conflict.

It is obvious that the text complicates the Christian-Islamic relationship via the theme of gender. In the clash of Christian and Muslim patriarchs, for instance, Hichem is the physically weaker, more passive figure, perhaps feminized in the way Said felt typical of the Orient in Western discourse (*O*, 207–8). In that way the text can also be seen to echo Enlightenment discourses on gender, which constructed an active "masculinity" and "passive" femininity and used gendered stereotypes to reinforce dualistic differences between Christianity and Islam.

However, the gender issues run deeper still in the text. Both religions wish to possess and (re)indoctrinate Zulema, and to exploit her singing voice to express their own cultural and religious identity (*SMNH,* 144), which makes the story as much about the ultimately fruitless struggle for expressive agency by a female artist. Moreover, Zulema's tale occurs within an inset narrative, itself located in a vitally important outer frame. There, three figures, the *Enthusiast,* the typically Hoffmannesque "Kapellmeister," and a medical doctor, muse over how to restore the lost singing voice of a talented German soprano Bettina. She, too, has apparently lost her voice, though in her case this is after leaving church during the "Sanctus" of Haydn's Mass in D Minor, the Enthusiast having warned her that she would be "cursed" if she did. By way of a therapy intended for Bettina, whom he believes to be suffering from a solely psychological trauma, the Enthusiast relates the story of Zulema, in the awareness that Bettina is, although hidden, secretly listening to his words from behind a door. The effect of this therapeutic story is, of course, that Bettina regains her voice. It is the psychological trauma of the threat of the curse, a threat made by a man, that robs Bettina of her voice. The Kapellmeister, mirroring Hichem's thoughts on Zulema in the inner story, thinks Bettina would be better dead than living without her singing voice. Although we might not take his histrionics seriously (*SMNH,* 147), we can see how Bettina's "problem" is both caused and, in a perverse sense, "solved" by men, passed back and forth and between the doctor with his medical wisdom and the *Kapellmeister* with his personal aesthetic crises, and overseen by the Enthusiast.

Das Sanctus, then, shows how women across history have struggled to establish their identity as individuals and their autonomy as artists when caught between networks of patriarchal power, be they military, religious, cultural, or psychological. Arguably Hoffmann expresses the struggle between Christianity and Islam in terms of a woman's fate, but he undermines the purely religious focus of that struggle by personifying the two faiths as two male figures with personal, ultimately nonreligious motives for controlling Zulema. Zulema, in turn, is identified with Bettina in the outer frame: having "recovered" from the trauma of the "curse," Bettina ends the text as an artist able once more to perform, and yet she has been shown to be the victim of a series of acts of male power, the man's "curse" having taken away her voice and a man's therapeutic story having "restored" it. So while the issue of male power in the outer narrative is framed initially within a discourse of Christian punishment and forgiveness, this part of the story might be read as a demonstration of how apparently gender-neutral conflicts are in fact about gender after all, though they may be disguised. Yet is *Das Sanctus* more a story about male-female conflict, one in which the Christian-Islamic encounter is rendered subordinate to issues of gender, indeed rendered largely meaningless? In fact another issue needs to be considered, namely the religious encounter inherent in the relationship between the framework and the inset narratives.

The story of Zulema is being retold in a nineteenth-century patriarchal setting, though this does not occur in a religious vacuum: the story is narrated in a European setting in which Christianity is the dominant religion. From this perspective the German figures take the story of Zulema and use it for their own purposes, appropriating her identity and ascribing to her memory their own significance. In a sense, Zulema might be thought to die two deaths. She dies, literally, in the fifteenth century, a victim of patriarchal conflict, but she dies figuratively a second time as her death is narrated for a purpose. While Bettina-as-artist may be trapped as an object of male power, lacking in autonomy, the means by which Zulema's performative faculties are restored is itself predicated upon a further form of exploitation, namely the erasure of an individual's identity as a Muslim. In this way Western culture, in the form of the singer specializing in Christian devotional music, is shown to perpetuate itself at the expense of Islam. Of course Islam no more had an absolute claim over Zulema than did Christianity, and she was no conventional Muslim by the end of her story, yet any *trace* of Zulema's original Muslim identity not yet erased in the course of the inset narrative is finally lost at its end: the climactic point of her death. The song she sings before death can be read as her enactment of a Romantic ideal of pure song (*SMNH*, 146) yet, significantly, her song of choice is also part of the Christian culture and her choice of it underlines the loss of her Islamic identity. In the course of the tale she moves from being a Muslim into a state of fascinating hybridity between the two faiths and in death is not represented as a conventional Christian martyr. Her legacy, however, can be read as that of a woman whose last words bear testimony to the power exerted over her by the Christian religion.

Furthermore, when Bettina's singing voice is restored in the outer narrative, she exercises her recovered gift by again singing a particular piece of music in a specific context:

> Als drei Monate darauf der reisende Enthusiast der gesundeten Bettina, die mit herlicher Glocken-Stimme Pergoleses Stabat mater (jedoch nicht in der Kirche, sondern im mäßig großen Zimmer) gesungen hatte, voll Freude und andächtigen Entzückens die Hand küßte, sprach sie: "Ein Hexenmeister sind Sie gerade nicht, aber zuweilen etwas widerhaarigter Natur," "wie alle Enthusiasten" setzte der Kapellmeister hinzu.[36]

The restoration of Bettina's singing has been read in a number of ways. The involvement of male figures in the process is of course testimony to the importance of the theme of gender: while she dispels any notion of his having any literal supernatural power over her (he is no "Hexenmeister"), Bettina acknowledges the enthusiast's uncanny ability to elicit voice from her.[37] Alternatively, Ulrich Schönherr sees this point in the story as Hoffman's attempt to relocate the sublimity of religious music in a secular context, concluding that the outer frame depicts the restoration of Bettina's voice as "an aesthetic conversion which leaves the context of religion altogether":[38] Hoffmann does indeed emphasize that Bettina's comeback is in an overtly secular location rather than a church. Nevertheless, it is Christian music that Bettina sings. Specifically, the piece is Giovanni Battista Pergolesi's famous 1736 setting of the "Stabat mater"—a piece of Roman Catholic liturgy in which the first line "*Stabat mater dolorosa*" ('The mother stood full of sorrow") refers to the Virgin Mary's suffering at Christ's crucifixion.[39] However, Bettina's rendition of her piece serves as a direct contrast to Zulema's rendition of "Dona nobis pacem" in the inset tale: despite her artistic susceptibility to male influences, Bettina regains her voice by hearing of the death of Zulema, though she is spared the earlier woman's fate and may go on performing. In this subtle sense, *Das Sanctus* is also a story about the restoration of a Christian woman's voice at the expense of that of a once-Muslim woman. Complicated as it is by other themes, at times exposed as a façade for deeper-seated gender conflict, at others interwoven with lofty Romantic aesthetic debates, the Christian-Islamic encounter nevertheless continues to haunt Hoffmann's text until its end. It is a text, though, that appears to offer little scope or hope for reimagining how Christianity and Islam might rethink their relationship as anything but a power struggle, in which one side is bound to be dominated by the other.

This chapter has sought to demonstrate how, in reading Romantic texts, we can begin to move beyond the view that the eighteenth- and nineteenth-century cultural canon offers nothing but fantasies of Islam represented in opposition to Christianity, for we find instances in which that stereotyping is broken down and replaced by representations of Christians and Muslims engaging in acts of mutual recognition, relinquishing cultural authority, and willingly engaging in dialogue. While the external trappings of many figures in the prose fiction of this time might appear to be touched by stereotypical dualisms of self and Other, Christian and Muslim, and masculine and feminine, texts from this period also begin to undermine those dualisms in a range of subtle ways. The discussion also serves as a warning, however, not, in our enthusiasm, to reconstruct Romanticism as a wholly misunderstood epoch free of limited binary thinking about relationships between religions—that tendency is more than virulent in the period. In their treatment of the Christian-Islamic encounter, then, it seems the German Romantics are as diverse and rich in ambiguities as they are on so many other issues.

Notes

[1] There exists a long-running debate on the "integrity" of the Romantic epoch in Germany, with some scholars seeing divisions between an earlier, more revolutionary Jena Romanticism and the later, more diffuse and politically reactionary Romanticism after 1806, while others trace lines of continuity between authors in terms of literary technique and aesthetic experimentality. For a brief overview see James Hodkinson, *Novalis, Women and Writing: Transformation beyond Measure?* (Rochester, NY: Camden House, 2007), 24 and 51–52. It is not, however, my intention here to reconstruct this debate or map out discussions of representations of Islam substantially in terms of these epochal distinctions.

[2] Cf. Edward Said, *Orientalism*, 3rd ed. (London: Penguin, 2003). Further references to this work are given in the text using the abbreviation *O* and the page number. Said points to the fact that the German experience of Islam/ the Orient was non-colonial and more often than not geographically remote: bound to bookish scholarship and libraries, it was a based on a more refined scholarship of British- and French-gathered source material. This of course does not preclude the existence of a tradition of travel writing on Islamic culture by German speakers, and works of this nature were indeed produced, often written by women, such as Ida Hahn-Hahn (1782–1857), whose *Orientalische Briefe* (1844) are of interest, and the Austrian Ida Pfeiffer (1797–1858), known for her extensive Asian and Pacific travel writing and particularly *Eine Frauen-fahrt um die Welt* (1850); of particular interest in connection with Pfeiffer was the ambiguous view of Islam offered in *Reise in das Heilige Land* (1842).

[3] For a full and critical reconstruction of Said's methodology and findings, see the introduction to this volume, 2 and 11–13.

[4] See introduction to this volume, 11–13.

[5] See Mohammed Sharafuddin, *Islam and Romantic Orientalism: Literary Encounters with the Orient* (London and New York: Tauris, 1994).

[6] Karoline von Günderrode's play *Mahomed, der Prophet von Mekka* is fascinating on gender and Islam: the author portrays a potent male figure from history, dramatizing the period from the prophet's revelations to his return to Mekka. As the play raises issues different from those dealt with here, I shall treat this text in future publications. See *Karoline von Günderrode, Sämtliche Werke und ausgewählte Studien,* ed. Walter Morgenthaler, Karin Obermaier, and Marianne Graf, 3 vols. (Basel and Frankfurt am Main: Stroemfeld, 1990–91), vol. 1, 110–200.

[7] See §2 of the *Grundlage der gesamten Wissenschaftslehre,* in Johann Gottlieb Fichte, *Sämmtliche Werke* (Berlin: Veit & Comp, 1845), 1:101–5.

[8] See *Novalis. Schriften. Die Werke Friedrich von Hardenbergs,* ed. Paul Kluckhohn, Richard Samuel, Heinz Ritter, Hans-Joachim Mähl, and Gerhard Schulz, 3rd ed., 6 vols. (Stuttgart: Kohlhammer, 1977–), 2:104,1. Further references to Novalis's works are given in the text using the abbreviation *SFH* followed by the volume, page, and fragment/entry.

[9] Richard Crouter, *Friedrich Schleiermacher: Between Enlightenment and Romanticism* (Cambridge: Cambridge UP, 2005), 3 and 123–39.

[10] On Schleiermacher in an interfaith context, see Thomas E. Reynolds, "Rethinking Schleiermacher and the Problem of Religious Diversity: Toward a Dialectical Pluralism," *Journal of the American Academy of Religion* 73.1 (Mar. 2005): 151–181.

[11] Friedrich Ernst Daniel Schleiermacher, *Der christliche Glaube nach den Grundsätzen der evangelischen Kirche*, 7th ed., ed. Martin Redeker, 2 vols. (Berlin: Walter de Gruyter, 1960).

[12] See Friedrich Schleiermacher, *Der christliche Glaube*, 1:31. Further references to this work are given in the text using the abbreviation *DcG* and the page number.

[13] Albert Hourani, *Islam in European Thought* (Cambridge: Cambridge UP, 1991), 23–24.

[14] Hourani, *Islam in European Thought*, 24.

[15] Schleiermacher, *Der christliche Glaube*, 56.

[16] Schleiermacher, *Der christliche Glaube*, 56.

[17] Hourani, *Islam in European Thought*, 24.

[18] On the differences between the older and the younger Schlegel see Klaus Behrens, *Friedrich Schlegels Geschichtsphilosophie, 1794–1808* (Tübingen: Niemeyer, 1984), 247–74. See also 171–84 on the scope and intellectual dynamics of Schlegel's historiographical writing.

[19] Behrens, *Friedrich Schlegels Geschichtsphilosophie*, 160–84.

[20] See Lucie Bernier, "Christianity and the Other: Friedrich Schlegel's and F. W. J. Schelling's Interpretation of China," *The International Journal of Asian Studies* (2005): 2:265–73.

[21] Friedrich Schlegel, *Kritische-Friedrich-Schlegel-Ausgabe*, ed. Jean-Jacques Anstett, Ernst Behler, and Hans Eichner, 35 vols. (Paderborn, Vienna, and Zurich: Schöningh, 1958–). Further references to this work are given in the text using the abbreviation *KFS* followed by the section, volume, and page numbers. Here: "Zwölfte Vorlesung: Charakterschilderung des Mahomet und seiner Religion, so wie der arabischen Weltherrschaft: Neue Gestaltung des europäischen Abendlandes und Wiederherstellung des christlichen Kaisertums" (*KFS* I, 9:269–90).

[22] See Annemarie Schimmel, *Von Aliz bis Zahra: Namen und Namenvergebung in der islamischen Welt* (Munich: Eugen Diederichs Verlag, 1989), 22.

[23] There are points in his work as a whole at which Novalis might seem to privilege Christianity. William O'Brien's reading of the *Hymnen an die Nacht* points to an example. In the fifth hymn, which O'Brien sees as an allegorical representation of the history of world religions, the advent of Christianity is shown in a particularly positive light. This is not to say that Hardenberg makes Christ the only mediator of Romantic religion; he is the most important however, because he reveals mediators for what they are: representatives of divinity which are not identical to that higher power. William A. O'Brien, *Novalis: Signs of Revolution* (Durham, NC, and London: Duke UP, 1996), 268–69.

[24] Novalis's editors make multiple references to the poet's having read Jacobi's text (*SFH* 4:694) and draw our attention to his reference to the text and obvious interest in its message of interfaith tolerance (*SFH* 3:913,280).

[25] The brief spells of peace and freedom enjoyed by Nessir and Zulima occur during periods of cohabitation with enlightened members of other religions, during which all parties come to respect each other's faiths via exchanges of knowledge through dialogue.

[26] Much of the thesis of my publication *Women and Writing in the Works of Novalis: Transformation beyond Measure?* is based on the premise that Novalis attempts with some success to rework the self-Other dualism in his literary texts. See, in particular, chapters 4 and 5, 134–243. Further references to this work will be given using the abbreviation *WWWN* and the page number.

[27] See Kamakshi P. Murti's entry on the "Exotin" in *The Feminist Encyclopedia of German Literature*, ed. Friederike Ursula Eigler and Susanne Kord (Westport, CT: Greenwood, 1997), 133–35.

[28] See Kontje, *German Orientalisms* (Ann Arbor: U of Michigan P, 2004), 99. For a reading of Zulima as a poetically capable, self-expressive, poetically active female subject see Hodkinson, *WWWN*, 185–87 and 221–22.

[29] The issue of how skin color became a fetishistic function of white European discourse, which used physically perceived ethnic difference as a means to fix and limit the image of the non-European, was most powerfully discussed by the psychoanalyst and critic Frantz Fanon in his essay *Peau noire, masques blancs* (1952). See Frantz Fanon, *Black Skin, White Masks*, trans. Charles Lam Markmann (New York: Grove P, 1967).

[30] See again Hodkinson (*WWWN*, 185–87 and 221–22). On the "genius" of female figures in Novalis see also James Hodkinson, "Genius beyond Gender: Novalis, Women and the Art of Shapeshifting," *Modern Language Review* 96 (Jan 2001): 103–15.

[31] Cited in Magdolna Orosz, *Identität, Differenz, Ambivalenz: Erzählstrukturen und Erzählstrategien bei ETA Hoffmann* (Frankfurt am Main: Lang, 2001), 50–51.

[32] Orosz, *Identität, Differenz, Ambivalenz*, 49–54.

[33] E. T. A. Hoffmann, *Das Sanctus*, in *Sämmtliche Werke in sechs Bändern*, 6 vols., ed. Wulf Segebrecht, Hartmut Steinecke, Gerhard Allroggen, and Ursula Segebrecht (Frankfurt am Main: Deutscher Klassiker Verlag, 1985), 3:141–160; here 153.

[34] Birgit Röder, *A Study of the Major Novellas of E. T. A. Hoffmann* (Rochester, NY: Camden House, 2003). Further references to this work are given in the text using the abbreviation *SMNH* and the page number.

[35] Hoffmann, *Das Sanctus*, 157.

[36] Hoffmann, *Das Sanctus*, 160.

[37] On this see Jürgen Barkhoff: "Inszenierung—Narration—his story: Zur Wissenspoetik im Mesmerismus und in E. T. A. Hoffmanns 'Das Sanctus,'" in *Romantische Wissenspoetik: Die Künste und die Wissenschaften*, ed. Gabriele Brandstetter and Gerhard Neumann (Würzburg: Königshausen & Neumann, 2004), 122.

[38] On this see Ulrich Schönherr: "Social Differentiation and Romantic Art: E. T. A. Hoffmann's *The Sanctus* and the Problem of Aesthetic Positioning in Modernity," *New German Critique* 66, Special Issue on the Nineteenth Century (Autumn 1995): 3–16.

[39] See http://campus.udayton.edu/mary/resources/poetry/stbmat.html (accessed 29 Apr. 2009).

7: Forms of Encounter with Islam around 1800: The Cases of Johann Hermann von Riedesel and Johann Ludwig Burckhardt

Jeff Morrison

IN THE CONTEXT OF A VOLUME CONCERNED WITH German encounters with Islamic culture it may seem bizarre to deal with two authors who write of or publish their travels in a language other than German. Clearly, many highly interesting authors have reported on their experience and interpretation of Islamic culture in German and might appear to be of more obvious interest to German scholars. However, the case will be made in this chapter that the two authors under discussion, namely the German travelogue writer Johann Hermann von Riedesel (1740–85) and the Swiss adventurer Johann Ludwig Burckhardt (1784–1817), are particularly revealing of a period of German/Swiss cultural development and that their travel accounts provide, alongside overt discussion of foreign cultures, testimony of the fragility of their own cultural positions. The discussion will begin with Riedesel's travel report, the *Remarques d'un voyageur moderne au Levant* of 1773, which appeared in translation as *Bemerkungen auf einer Reise nach der der Levante* in 1774 and in a new translation in 1940 as *Randbemerkungen über eine Reise nach der Levante, 1768*.[1] The perceived significance of the text is reflected in the fact of its double translation—and indeed in the speed of the first translation—although this is rather at odds with the progressive downgrading of Riedesel's observations from a "modern traveler's notes" in the French edition to mere notes and then marginalia in the German versions.[2] The second text was produced by Johann Ludwig Burckhardt (as John Lewis Burckhardt) on behalf of the African Association (or, more fully, The Association for Promoting the Discovery of the Interior Parts of Africa) in England and entitled *Travels in Nubia* (posthumous: London, 1819).[3]

These texts are interesting not least because of the authors' decisions to publish in French and English respectively. However, the linguistic issue is not the only interesting one—although it is one to which this chapter returns later. In the case of each author there is above all a clear impetus to engage with alien cultures to an unusual degree, reflected not least in the itineraries of their journeys, which extend beyond the conventional "Grand Tour." Both of them are then, by the standards of their age, adventurous travelers, although they clearly differ in the extent of their appetite for that adventure. Riedesel was in many respects a typical eighteenth-century "Grand Tourist,"[4] but even when working his way through the conventional itinerary he adopted a more serious approach than many of his contemporaries, who prioritized visits to the brothels of Naples over the study of art in Rome; furthermore Riedesel's journey went beyond the normal destinations of Rome and the less accessible Athens to reach Constantinople.[5] Turkish territory was beyond the remit of many of the standard guidebooks available to him and certainly less familiar in its cultural and societal manifestations than any of the more conventional destinations. Burckhardt, for his part, operates on a wholly different scale of adventure. He learned Arabic and traveled extensively in Africa and the Middle East, reporting for the African Association. His work had genuine novelty value for his British employers and readers, particularly his "re-discovery" of Petra after a very short visit and his work would have been still more striking to his more limited German/Swiss readership, since they had less exposure to the tradition of exploration and the implied enterprise of colonialism of which his work is representative. The two texts are then, in their subject matter alone, interesting enough to bear examination here. The question of authorial language and the associated issues of cultural self-identification and the perceived relative authority of the different languages cannot, however, be sidestepped; it would be inappropriate to concentrate solely upon the respective itineraries and the outward evidence of the encounter with Islam that is shown in the texts. That encounter is in each case predicated upon a choice of language that may shape the nature of the response to the alien culture and indeed determine the nature of the reception of any report.

It is clearly not an insignificant act to write in a language other than one's native tongue.[6] The reasons may, of course, be purely pragmatic. The author may simply have found a foreign publisher, have secured foreign funding, or wish to target a new audience. There may also be more to it than that. In the case of our two authors, the decision to publish in French or English is a crucial act of public cultural self-identification or cultural alignment; it is simultaneously an act of commentary upon the perceived status of the home, German/Swiss, culture. It is self-explanatory that any instance of encounter with an alien culture leads not only to an awareness of that culture (to whatever degree) but also to a renewed awareness of the home culture. Travel in that sense does not merely offer a lens through which to observe other cultures but also operates as a looking-glass in which the traveler may observe himself and the culture he represents. Of course, this act of self-reflection need not be a complex process. There are many instances of travelers who, in observing the apparent absurdities of an alien culture, find righteous confirmation of the superiority of their home culture. One might think here of the multitude of patronizing accounts of African and South American culture produced in Europe until well into the twentieth century that are wholly unencumbered by any critical self-reflection.[7] Even eighteenth-century German accounts of Italy, the great store of classical antiquities and Renaissance art that every traveler wished to see, constantly criticize the state of modern Italy (and often the perceived excesses of Catholicism) on the basis of the assumed superiority of an ordered, northern, often Protestant home-place.[8] Thankfully, neither of our authors is routinely as crude as this in his judgments; where they are crude, we can identify ambivalence in their attitudes or begin to understand the reason for the heavy-handed, judgmental attitudes, since where they appear they can often be understood as compensatory in nature, that is as a reflection of the insecurity the author experiences as a representative of home culture(s) rather than as a calculated or even aggressive response to the unfamiliar. The noun "culture" is here consciously offered in its plural form. Riedesel, in writing in French, clearly identifies himself with a culture other than his obvious home culture. Likewise Burckhardt positions himself culturally by his use of English. But these are not simple acknowledgements of debt to another culture.

To be a German/Swiss intellectual in the late-eighteenth or early-nineteenth century was to find oneself in a complex situation. Place of birth or residence could operate as only the crudest indicator of cultural location in the broader sense. Even the briefest glance at the broad cultural coordinates of Riedesel's life makes this clear. As a minor German aristocrat Riedesel felt more comfortable speaking and writing French than German. His class identified itself culturally with the equivalent class in France but could be seen as more broadly representative of a trans-European class system left over from medieval times. His education was probably classical, and to that extent many of his preferences in art and literature and much of his understanding of history or politics will have been focused upon Rome and Athens, cultures whose hold upon Northern Europe have been seen as "tyrannical."[9] In Riedesel's case the hold was certainly firm and was reinforced by his exposure to Johann Joachim Winckelmann, the most powerful advocate of the supremacy of ancient Greek culture of his generation.[10] Winckelmann saw the imitation of Greek art by German artists as the perfect means of German cultural renaissance. To copy the best ancient Greeks was, according to Winckelmann's rather tangled argumentation, a patriotic act and not the act of cultural submission that it might seem. However, he favored writing in German rather than French, and Riedesel's Winckelmannian patriotism is reflected in his German-language travelogue on Sicily (which predates the volume on the Levantine), the writing of which must have been very arduous.[11] In this volume there is no sense of the ironic position represented by the "forced" production of a text in German that implicity laments the demise of German artistic culture in comparison with the splendour of ancient Greece. In the more private sphere, if he read contemporary German literature, then he read a literature largely under the spell of foreign literature, particularly French. As if this web of cultural influences were not enough, it is clear that Riedesel did not seek inspiration only from Romance cultures. As a man with commercial and, above all, political interests, Riedesel looked to Britain.[12] Even on the basis of this crude survey of the cultural configuration of Riedesel's life, it is difficult to arrive at any sense of what it was for Riedesel to be German. His German identity could reasonably be seen as provisional, as awaiting the arrival of a more stable sense of German identity. On that basis one might expect that any encounter with a more obviously alien culture (Turkish or Moorish Islamic in Riedesel's case) might also be complex or equivocal, as indeed is often the case. His text can, however, also be crude in its judgments in a manner that is, as was suggested above, compensatory. The crude dismissal of the Islamic in some instances appears to allow the writer brief moments of clarity about where he comes from, of self-definition of a kind that must have been difficult for him much of the time. In dismissing aspects of Islamic culture he positions himself clearly as (for example) non-Muslim, non-Eastern, and so on. One function of an encounter with Islamic culture is then to enable the author to establish a reassuringly clear sense of who he is (and is not)—even when that clarity is entirely at odds with the realities of his multi-faceted home culture(s). The encounter with Islam may then serve to simplify (or perhaps travesty) the negotiation between cultures where we might expect more layered and sophisticated interaction.

The choice of language of our two authors is then the first sign for readers of the difficulties that lie ahead in their reading of these texts. And any sense of this difficulty simultaneously alerts readers to the problem that they will have in placing these authors within the linear patterns of the discourse on Orientalism as established by Said and outlined in the introduction to this volume.[13] It is surely reasonable to imagine readers seeking to place the texts in this context since, after all, Said's persuasive treatment of the phenomenon of Orientalism provides the intellectual starting-point for most modern readers who might be interested in materials such as these. While Said includes relatively little German material in his discussion, the clear suggestion is that German intellectual and literary life is rooted in and so reflective of the wider Orientalist discourses prevailing, particularly in France and Britain, throughout the eighteenth and nineteenth centuries. It is equally apparent that some figures from the German literary scene fit less well into Said's broad scheme. One might argue that, should one wish to accommodate them, Riedesel and

Burckhardt would fit very uneasily. While they may indeed embrace or at least embody positions that are typical of the Orientalist, they are also in turn products of cultures that are themselves dominated by influences from neighboring and earlier cultures, as suggested earlier in connection with Riedesel. To that extent they could be seen as agents of Orientalist discourse and so implicated in a colonial enterprise of the kind laid bare by Said, and simultaneously as products of a broad and sometimes subtle cultural imperialism. In discursive terms they are the colonizing and colonized and so caught in a cultural double bind. The kind of conundrum represented by the cases of Riedesel and Burckhardt is, of course, precisely the kind of thing that Said needed to avoid in establishing the broad case for Orientalism; it is also exactly the kind of difficulty that must engage the next generation of scholars.

For all that they can both be seen as representative of a particular phase in the development of German/Swiss culture and German/Swiss cultural relations with Islam, the texts under discussion here nonetheless have highly divergent properties. One might say that Riedesel's text, despite his destinations, is rooted in the familiar, in the familiar opinions and outlooks of the age. In Riedesel's text it is interesting to observe what happens when the focus of the traveler's attention shifts from familiar objects—in this case the high-status relics of classical antiquity—to less familiar materials, particularly the art and culture of the Islamic world. Burckhardt is a very different figure. His life appears to be determined by a desire to embrace novel experiences. The fact that he was Swiss hardly appears as an issue except insofar as he manages to pass off Swiss-German dialect as rough Indian dialect and so manage a safe passage in Africa, traveling as an Indian Muslim pilgrim.[14] He was educated substantially in Germany and subsequently in England, where he developed his knowledge of Arabic at Cambridge University. Aware of the direction in which his travels would take him, he also studied the Koran (particularly in Syria).[15] He seems, then, a man likely to have—by the standards of the age—an open mind toward new cultural experiences, in stark contrast to Riedesel. The intellectual baggage being carried by our two travelers appears to be very different; and yet each in his own way struggles with that baggage.

It is interesting, however, that given the very different starting-points of our two writers they nonetheless both end up producing rather frustrating books that offer less evidence of engagement—whether positive or negative—with the new target culture(s) than one might expect from a modern perspective; it is particularly disappointing when we consider how much trouble the authors went to in order to engineer the encounters in the first place. The introduction to this chapter has suggested some important reasons why this may be the case, over and above the general competence of the authors. Furthermore, both authors were subject to generic constraints that may have limited the scope of their work; neither volume belongs to a genre that would encourage presentation of intimate personal or profound intellectual reflection upon the encounter with Islam—though it need not exclude it. We are then confronted with texts that are likely to be extremely elusive for all sorts of reasons. They are not willfully elusive but elusive because of the highly unstable cultural and literary positions that the authors embrace. It is important to investigate how those positions emerge in the texts themselves.

Johann Hermann von Riedesel was a minor nobleman from Hesse who had the typical advantages of someone of his status. Of particular significance was his ability to embark on a Grand Tour and, as mentioned earlier, to get to know Winckelmann in Rome. Following Winckelmann's lead, and building upon his own education, which enabled him to cite classical literature at every turn, Riedesel saw the primary purpose of his travels as confirmation of the superiority of the culture of the ancients.[16] This perspective extends to his criticism of modern Italian and Greek culture, which he sees as decadent when compared to its former heights. His benchmarks are very rigid. We see this in his first publication, a report on his travels to Sicily and Magna Graecia, in which he acts as Winckelmann's eyes, checking certain sites on his behalf. As he travels, his report is shaped by his recording of the extent to which the culture he encounters deviates from the benchmark culture. This approach extends from the fine arts and architecture to his observations on the economy, civic society, physical appearance of citizens and even climate of "modern" Sicily. In almost every aspect Sicily is a disappointment, and only the occasional reminder of former greatness—in the form of the ruins of a great temple or of an individual with the assumed ideal proportions of the ancients—maintains his enthusiasm for the project. Clearly the wisdom borrowed from Winckelmann acts as a crude filter for Riedesel, preventing him from achieving any kind of unmediated response. This is most tellingly revealed in a little absence in his publication. One of the more important aspects of the architectural landscape in Sicily is the influence of Moorish settlement. Riedesel barely records it; as one editor pointed out he is "ein bedeutender Meister im Übersehen" (R, 10). If things can be placed on his scale of aesthetic, political, or geographical qualities, then he is in a position to write about them. If they explode the category they must be damned or ignored. This method may seem crude, but he would have felt it justified by a whole tradition of European thinking about Islamic culture and the tacit presence of Winckelmann. He could perhaps hardly be expected to expand the critical categories of his age, least of all within the generic constraints of the travelogue.

It is interesting to see how the blocking mechanism operates when Riedesel extends his travels toward Constantinople. We might fear the worst when we read, for example, the preamble to his description of Constantinople, which takes the form of a brief history lesson:

Konstantinopel, einst die Residenz der griechischen Kaiser und die Hauptstadt ihres Reiches, jedoch auch, wie man hinzufügen könnte, die der Unwissenheit, des Fanatismus und des Vorurteils, ist heute die des Ottomanischen Reiches. Sie ist noch der Sitz der Barbarei; aber das Volk, das sie heute besitzt, hat, wenn auch die gleichen geistigen Mängel, so doch nicht dieselben Laster des Herzens, wie sie die Griechen des sinkenden Römischen Reiches aufwiesen. (*R, 123*)

It is not possible to construe this as a positive perspective; indeed, it is tainted by an awful arrogance in assuming insight into the hearts and minds of the Turks and, still worse, in assuming moral superiority over them. However, Islamic culture is not simply dismissed; it makes it onto the scale of culture and is not simply excluded from it as we might have expected and as would have been the case in many texts of the period. Riedesel performs a bizarre balancing act in his reception of the Islamic world. On the one hand, he rushes to judgment; on the other he moderates his views — Constantinople, we have heard, is barbaric, but not *the most* barbaric. His judgment is also tempered by its historical perspective; we are shown that Constantinople is subject to historical processes, just like the Roman Empire, which he cites in evidence. On that basis the — albeit decadent — state of Constantinople is understandable in specific historical terms and not simply damnable. Elsewhere we hear, for example, that Constantinople is filthy and often ugly, and yet in the most backhanded of compliments Riedesel also tells us: "Trotzdem finden sich einige Schönheiten in diesem Misthaufen" (*R*, 124). He appears utterly unaware of how drastic this formulation is. Beauty is, according to his and his teacher's understanding, the surest indicator of divinity; one need not look further than Winckelmann's descriptions of a statue of Hercules for confirmation of this certainty.[17] To locate the divine in the dungheap is at once offensive and heretical; furthermore the observation shows the limitations of an author who cannot comfortably understand beauty unless it is a sanitized or textbook beauty. The criteria that Riedesel normally applies to any given object no longer work; a generous reading suggests that he finds the living — economic, sanitary — conditions in Turkey unbearable and hence calls the place a "Misthaufen." On this basis (and in line with contemporary understanding of the preconditions for artistic production) it should be impossible for this particular Islamic society to produce beautiful art.[18] In direct contradiction of the theory, beauty is present; Riedesel's drastic formulation reflects his own sense of impotence in explaining this "impossibility," he finds himself in an intellectual impasse. Elsewhere views are described as "bezaubernd," individual objects as "schön" or "groß" (to choose epithets at random) and yet they are all tainted by an assumed barbarity. Clearly Riedesel is not unique in being stuck between a rock and a hard place in his response to Islamic culture. He is burdened by the common prejudices of his generation and a specific set of prejudices associated with his classical and classicizing education. Even when he manages to cast these off and achieve a degree of appreciation of the unfamiliar culture, he has yet to develop the tools to articulate his appreciation. Two further simple references to the quality of the local art make this clear. Riedesel notes the lack of representation of animals or men in religious buildings. It is explained thus:

> Die Türken dürfen ja Abbilder von Menschen oder Tieren nicht machen; ein Gebot Mohammeds verbietet ihnen dies, um sie von Götzendienst abzuhallten. Eine allzu üppige Fantasie, die die Morgenländer immer dazu treibt, die eingebildeten Dinge als wirklich erscheinen zu lassen. (*R*, 125)

The degree of certainty is frightening to the modern reader; apparently all Turks take all images literally. Riedesel would have justified his position on the rich imagination of Asians by reference to Winckelmann, who deployed a bizarre brand of what one might call geographical psychology.[19] Temperament is, according to this method, a product of climate. Hot climates produce fiery temperaments, hot heads, and wild imaginations. When Riedesel does not have this or some other brand of absolutizing cultural theory to enable his judgment of the alien culture, he struggles to articulate his position. Hence when he finds, against the odds, that he likes the decor in a castle, he does not have the language to express this. If the "edle Einfalt und stille Größe" identified by Winckelmann is not present in the architecture, then Riedesel is left only with rather limp formulae. And so the ornate local decor is "in recht annehmbarem Stil."[20] The attractive artistic products of Islamic culture cannot be described using a critical language designed for a different purpose—in Riedesel's case the idealization of Greek culture—and instead their positive properties are acknowledged in unhelpful, neutral terms that must leave the reader rather puzzled; Riedesel himself is often reduced to merely listing features of buildings without any significant critical input.

We have no reason to believe that Riedesel was trying to be evasive in his formulations or that he was damning the products of Islamic culture with faint praise. It seems more likely that his rather unfulfilling response to the alien culture is a product of his own lack of self-confidence or his inability to establish his own criteria for the assessment of something new that could not be accommodated within the value schemes he had inherited; Islamic culture makes his aesthetic criteria, his religious terms of reference, and his understanding of social, economic, and political structures redundant. Our overwhelming impression of Riedesel is of a kind of cultural incompetence comprising on the one hand willingness to experience new things and on the other the inability to articulate that experience or to draw from it in any productive way. To that extent he provides fine evidence of the limitations of his value schemes. Germans such as Riedesel would presumably have drawn confidence from the fact that they were in many respects typical Europeans of their age and class. Given the rather precarious cultural, economic, and political climate in the Germany of the time, it must have been reassuring to have the certainty of attitudes shared with one's European peers, whether toward art, industry, or society. And yet when confronted with Islamic culture the complex construct of attitudes that is the eighteenth-century German traveler is revealed as a house of cards—full of holes and without solid foundations. Inherited attitudes prove disabling rather than enabling in the manner one might expect. The encounter with Islam serves to tell us very little about Islam in this case; it tells us rather more about the fragility of the value schemes according to which Riedesel was trying to operate. Perhaps the single passage cited below concerning Turkish customs indicates better than any other the kind of bind in which Riedesel finds himself:

> Non in depravatis, sed in his, quae bene fecundum naturam se habent, considerandum est, quid sit naturale Arist. Polit.

> Über die Türken, ihre Sitten und Gebräuche ein endgültiges Urteil fällen zu wollen, ist ein Irrtum, in den verschiedene Schriftsteller verfallen sind. Voreingenommen gegen diese Ungläubigen, die ohne Gnade von der christlichen Bescheidenheit verdammt warden, haben einige alles an ihnen schlecht gefunden und sie zum Teufel geschickt. Andere, im gleichen Maße für sie eingenommen, haben alles an ihnen bewundert und sie auf die romantischste Weise beschrieben. Wenige brachten es fertig, ein gesundes Urteil zu fällen, zu dem sie berechtigt sind durch einen langen Aufenthalt im Lande, die genügende Kenntnis der Sprache und die Urteilsbildung, die durch Handlungen einerseits und die Gründe hiefür andererseits, zwischen Ursache und Wirkung hervorgerufen wird. Denn wie der menschliche Geist und Verstand dazu neigt, verschiedene Richtungen zu nehmen und verschiedene Urteile über dieselben Dinge zu fällen, je nach dem Klima, der Religion, den Erziehungsgrundsätzen, nach dem Gesichtswinkel, von dem aus man eine Sache betrachtet, kurz gesagt nach hunderttausend nebensächlichen Gründen, können wir manche Handlungen der Türken übel auslegen oder ihnen ganz andere als die wahren Gründe für ihr Handeln unterschieben. Denn schließlich hat noch niemand jene Gleichgültigkeit oder vielmehr Verachtung, die die Türken gegen die Christen hegen, die sie unnahbar, schweigsam und ungesellig macht, überwinden können. Ohne Bildung, ohne Bücher, ohne Schrifttum, kümmern sie sich nicht um das Warum der Dinge; gestützt einerseits durch die Gewohnheit, andererseits durch den Glauben an das unentrinnbare Schicksal, lassen sie alles gehen, wie es will, und bleiben gelassen. Nach alledem müssen wir zugeben, daß ein Urteil über die Türken schwer und unsicher ist. (R, 143)

This passage posits a new way of seeing Islam in its Turkish manifestation. This manner of seeing embraces old (Aristotle) and new, enlightened impulses. The aim is balanced assessment and not hasty judgment of the alien culture; the passage acknowledges the context in which Turkish customs developed and the Western perspective from which they are being viewed. The signs are hopeful and yet the discursive product is a series of tired old assertions about Turks concerning their dislike of Christianity, their shallowness, their acceptance of fate. Their implied—and implausible—counterparts are Western Christians who accept other faiths, constantly question their own actions, and shape their own fates. The last sentence of the passage cited should be the crucial one—yes, indeed, it is a tricky business to understand the Turks; we should indeed be careful in our judgments. Sadly, this sentence seems deeply ironic appearing, as it does, in the wake of direct statement of prejudice. The enlightened perspective can be seen to deconstruct itself before our very eyes.

John Lewis Burckhardt clearly attempted a much more profound degree of engagement with Islam. The anecdotal evidence of his preparatory work is clear and positive.[21] One might expect that this would enable a reasonably unmediated experience of Islam—in stark contrast to Riedesel. Certainly, in his five major publications, the *Travels in Nubia, Travels in Syria and the Holy Land, Travels in Arabia,* the *Arabic Proverbs,* and the *Notes on the Bedouins and Wahábys* (all published posthumously) there is a much greater sense of proximity to the new culture, a first impulse to see the unfamiliar as interesting.[22] There is, however, some biographical evidence that may serve to qualify our high expectations of Burckhardt as an open-minded traveler. We know that Burckhardt witnessed the influence of the Republican French in Basel and so saw the threat to his nation and his family. His subsequent moves to Germany and Britain are then not neutral acts. His identification with Britain and in particular with the British colonial enterprise could be seen in this light as a specific response to his experience of French political and military outreach. Ultimately his position is that of a man suspended between cultures—not just because he was a representative of the multicultural and multilingual Swiss nation, born in French-speaking Lausanne to an old Basel family—and to that extent, while it differs in its specifics, it is not unlike the position of Riedesel reported above.

The first factor that impacts upon the quality of Burckhardt's reports themselves is the novelty factor. While he was clearly not the first explorer of Africa and the Middle East, his role was very much that of rediscoverer. In fact, this seems to be not an uncommon aspect of the literary reprocessing of Islam. The tradition of encounter with Islam was long-established, as the earlier contributions to this volume make clear. However, each generation appears to have to rediscover Islam for itself and on its own terms. This would certainly apply to Burckhardt, who was visiting places long forgotten—and off established trade routes—and it has a clear impact upon the quality of his reports. A primary characteristic of his first publication, *Travels in Nubia,* is the listing of new experiences, from the local dress, dialect, or religious practice to the amount of litter on the streets. Furthermore Burckhardt is obliged to cover agriculture, transport, trade, and industry. The need to provide a comprehensive sense of what is available for his sponsors, the need to act as their eyes and ears, can lead to a prioritization of quantity of material over quality of response. Many observations are recorded without commentary as if to acknowledge the function of the African Association at home as interpreter of the material. In this connection we are, of course, reminded of the function of the African Association, not merely as an academic operation but rather as representative of colonial tendencies in the political sphere of British society.[23] Exploration was not a politically neutral activity in the nineteenth century.

Even if we manage to block out contextual political issues and generic considerations such as those mentioned above and concentrate upon the aspects of the travel report that show the particular qualifications of Burckhardt as traveler—his untypical knowledge of language and religion—we can still come away from the text a little confused; Burckhardt can at times seem clumsily judgmental. For example, he often found himself rather disappointed by the degree of adherence to religious tradition he observed among Muslims, as in this example from early in *Travels in Nubia:*

> But in this part of their religious rites, as well as in the performance of their daily prayers, I observed much indifference amongst the plurality of the Turks I saw here, as well as of those with whom I travelled afterwards from Suedieh to Aleppo. Amongst the latter were many who, during eight days, did not pray once: even two Hadjis, who had performed the Mekka pilgrimage, were of that number. Some would pray once, others twice a day, before sun rise, and after sun set; only three or four of the caravan were strict in regularly chaunting the three daily prayers, to which number the Koran limits the duty of travelers; but I did not find that more respect or deference was paid to them than to the others.

It is rather difficult to judge the tone here. Are we meant to take from this the fact that Muslims are superficial in their religious observance and not even able to maintain the reduced level of prayer required of travelers? Perhaps we are meant to be reassured at the lack of fanaticism or the fact that respect is not blindly associated with religious devotion? Elsewhere he can be disappointed by the degree of knowledge that the local people have of their own culture and language. We hear in a report from Aleppo, for example:

I am now so far advanced in the knowledge of Arabic, that I understand almost every thing that is said in common conversation, and am able to make myself understood on most subjects, although sometimes with difficulty. I have made acquaintance with some Shikhs, and some of the first literati amongst the Turks of Aleppo, who from time to time visit me. I owe this favour principally to Mr. Wilkins's Arabic and Persian Dictionary. The common manuscript dictionaries, or Kamus, being generally very defective, the learned Turks are often very glad to consult Wilkins, and never do it without exclaiming "How wonderful that a Frank should know more of our language than our first Ulemas." Learning at Aleppo is in a very low state; no science, the Turkish law excepted, is properly cultivated; not even that of Arabic grammar, which is so necessary to the interpretation of the Koran. I am assured by the best authority, that there are now in this town only three men (two Turks and a Christian) who know this language grammatically. The chief quality of a literary man is that of getting by heart a great number of verses made upon different occasions, and of knowing the proper opportunity of reciting them; to this must be added, a knowledge of the different learned significations of one and the same word, and of the words which express the same idea.

It is difficult to miss the rather arrogant tone of this passage. Burckhardt places himself at the center of this scene. The locals come to him for knowledge of what is theirs and he provides it by proxy through Wilkins's book. The locals lack the intellectual skills—interpretation, rationalization, composition. They even lack what are in Burckhardt's narrow terms the "literary" skills that do not seem to amount to much more than rote learning. The tools of scholarship are, of course, in this instance provided by the West. He strikes a similar tone in a later passage about Fakirs:

I have more than once mentioned the Fakirs, or religious men. They are likewise known by the appellation of Fakih (فقيه), i.e. a man learned in the law. There are few respectable families who have not a son or relation that dedicates his youth to the study of the law. At the age of twelve or fourteen he is sent to some of the neighbouring schools, of which those of Damer, on the road to Shendy, of Mograt, and of the Sheygya are at present the most celebrated. There they are taught to read and write, and to learn by heart as much of the Koran and of some other prayer books, as their memory can retain. They are taught the secret of writing amulets or charms; and at the age of twenty they return to their homes, where they live, affecting great uprightness of conduct and strictness of morals, which amount however to little more than not to smoke tobacco, or drink Bouza in public, and not to frequent the resorts of debauchery.

We become slightly suspicious when we are referred to those things which "their memory can retain." Perhaps it is a rather unfair reading, but surely we are being invited to believe that their minds will not retain much. Any skepticism seems founded when we then hear that these young men merely "affect" uprightness while actually only avoiding public misbehavior.

In other places he seems to acknowledge religious devotion to a greater degree — but again with a sour undertone:

> Amongst others, I saw a copy of the Koran worth at least four hundred piasters, and a complete copy of Bochari's Commentaries upon the Koran, worth double that sum, at the Cairo book-market. These books are brought from Cairo by the young Fakys of Damer themselves, many of whom go to study there in the mosque El Azher, or in the great mosque at Mekka, where they remain for three or four years, living during that time principally upon alms and stipends. In the schools at Damer they teach the true reading of the Koran, and deliver lectures on the Tefsyr (explanations of the Koran), and on the Touhyd, or the nature of God, and his divine attributes. They have a large well built mosque, but without a minaret; it rests upon arches built of bricks, and the floor is covered with fine sand. This is the coolest spot in Damer, and much resorted to by strangers to pass a few hours in sleep after the mid-day prayers. Around an open place adjoining the mosque are a number of school-rooms. Many Fakys have small chapels near their own houses, but the Friday's prayers are always performed in the great mosque. The chief Fakys live with great ostentation of sanctity, and the Faky el Kebír leads the life of a hermit; he occupies a small building in the midst of a large square in the town. One part of this building is a chapel, and the other a room about twelve feet square, in which he constantly resides day and night, without any attendants, and separated from his own family. He lives upon what his friends or disciples send him for breakfast and supper. About three o'clock in the afternoon he quits his chamber, after having been shut up all the morning, occupied in reading, and takes his seat upon a large stone bench before the building. He is here joined by all his fraternity, and business is then transacted until long after sun-set. I went once to kiss his hands, and found him a venerable figure, entirely wrapped up in a white cloke. He asked me from whence I came, in what school I had learnt to read, and what books I had read; and he seemed satisfied with my answers. Near him sat a Moggrebyn Shikh, a native of Mekinéz, who had come from Mekka, to serve as his scribe, and who transacted all the public business. I was told that this person had found means to amass a large sum of money.

One cannot fail to notice that it is the frame of this anecdote that gives it its force. It begins with discussion of the high price of books sold by religious and ends with talk of the private wealth of those charged with doing the public business of the religious. One can only hope that he also cast a similarly calculating eye upon the practices of the established churches in his various other homelands. Even the hajj is not spared a rather cynical treatment. Religion and trade apparently operated hand in hand, and if trade was threatened then religious devotion necessarily also waned:

> The hopes of re-establishing the pilgrim caravan to Mekka is entertained only by those fanatic Turks, who, from the discontinuance of it, prognosticate the fall of the empire. The important English coffee trade, opened within the last twelve months, between Malta and the Levant, considerably lessens the desire of the Hadj in the minds of all those who were in the habit of performing the pilgrimage merely in order to buy up Mocha coffee at Mekka, which they sold with great profits at Damascus, Aleppo, and Constantinople. The greater half of the pilgrims were merchants of coffee and India goods. At present American coffee has entirely supplanted that of Yemen all over Syria and the Syrian desert.

Burckhardt does not always maintain this tone. Elsewhere we certainly see great respect for scholarship, religious devotion, trading skills, and indeed the general humanity of Muslims, but negative value judgments are never far from the surface. The value judgments have a different basis than do those we saw in Riedesel. While Riedesel tries to grasp Islamic culture from the position of an outsider, Burckhardt styles himself at times as an insider. Burckhardt claims a kind of ownership of Islamic culture, whereas Riedesel tries hard not to reject it out of hand. Burckhardt apparently sees nothing ironic in his adoption of this perspective; he certainly never reflects upon his own status as a product of an unstable culture, acting by proxy for a dominant colonial power. He appears unaware that he is performing a brand of cultural gymnastics while all the while asserting that his feet are firmly on the ground.

The above treatment could easily appear hard on both of the authors; my intention was quite the opposite. We must, of course, remember that both men—and particularly Burckhardt—went to enormous lengths to encounter Islam and that their reports were very important for contemporary audiences. They made great efforts and they took their work seriously but they were clearly at times hampered either by generic constraints, publishers expectations, their own inability to cast off deeply embedded and simultaneously highly inappropriate value schemes, or the arrogant assumption of a wholly fallacious insider-position in an alien culture. We should not, however, rush to judge those who sometimes themselves rush to judge. Clearly neither of our authors has even arrived at this stage of their careers at a firm sense of their own identity (if such a thing is possible). Is Riedesel the German-writing aesthete, the man more at home writing in French on travel or English on economic matters, or perhaps the later statesman; is Burckhardt Swiss, German, British—or Muslim, as many felt he had become? On the unstable basis of confused expectations, novel experiences, and developing personality we should perhaps not expect too rounded a view of Islamic culture. Perhaps it is safer to see the work of our authors as reflective in the first instance of a particularly unstable period of German/Swiss cultural development; above all our texts provide evidence of self-encounter under the guise of the encounter with Islam. The two volumes are, at the very least, cautionary tales, albeit not in the conventional sense; they caution the reader against any reading of the encounter with Islam in simple terms. Encounter is, whether in Riedesel's or Burckhardt's terms, not a simple meeting between opposing cultures.

Notes

[1] In the body of the text all references will come from the 1940 German edition of the text, namely Riedesel, *Randbemerkungen über eine Reise nach der Levante*, trans. L. M. Schultheis, ed. E. E. Becker (Darmstadt: Gesellschaft Hessicher Bücherfreunde, 1940) and will be given in the text using the abbreviation *R* and the page number.

[2] Another view of Riedesel's travels is allowed by the elaborately titled composite volume *Reisen des Freiherrn Johann Hermann Riedesel zu Eisenbach durch Sizilien, Großgriechenland, den Archipelagus nach Constantinopel und durch Großbritannien in den Jahren 1767, 1768 und 1770 in Briefen an den Freund Winckelmann, seine Schwester die Gräfin Degenfeld geb. Riedesel zu Eisenbach und seinen Vetter Diede zum Fürstenstein* (Jena: Frommann, 1830). These materials are evaluated by Becker in the introduction to our chosen translation and provide a much thinner resource for the parts of his travels that detail the encounter with Islam.

[3] John Lewis Burckhardt, *Travels in Nubia* (London: John Murray, 1819). In the body of this chapter all references are taken from the electronic version of the text uploaded by the University of Adelaide and available at http://etext.library. adelaide.edu.au/b/burckhardt/john_lewis//nubia/ (accessed 4 Dec. 2008). This electronic edition has no conventional pagination but quotations are easily located by using the Find function of a computer and typing in a phrase. Given the rarity of the original text this inconvenience would seem acceptable.

[4] The best biographical treatments of Riedesel are provided in the introductions to his two major publications: see notes 1 and 8.

[5] A compact treatment of the patterns of motivation for travel to Italy in the eighteenth century is available in Jeffrey Morrison, *Winckelmann and the Notion of Aesthetic Education* (Oxford: Clarendon, 1996), 1–19. For the specifics of Riedesel's journeys see 69–168.

[6] One might, of course, refer here to the "mother tongue." As this term suggests, one's first language is often seen as having a fundamental, formative role; the

acquisition or subsequent abandonment of that language is thus a critical issue affecting identity formation. The question has, inevitably, been approached from a number of angles. R. E. Keller sees, for example, the adoption of French in eighteenth-century Germany as an unproblematic historical product of the cultural ascendancy of France. Keller, *The German Language* (London: Faber & Faber, 1978), 486–87. More common is discussion of the implications of language choice for the sociolinguistic identity of the individual, particularly in the (often critical) wake of Lev Vygotskii's *Language and Thought*, ed. and trans. E. Hanfmann and G. Vakar (London: Wiley, 1974). Educationalists, in particular, find themselves constantly confronted with the problematic interface of language and identity. See David Block, *Second Language Identities* (London: Continuum, 2007). This is the case even where postmodern theoretical impulses might cause us to doubt the possibility of any stable notion of "identity." See Arnd Witte, "Communicamus, ergo sum: Interkulturelles Fremdsprachenlernen und seine Implikationen für Identitätskonstrukte," in *Acta Germanica: German Studies in Africa*, Jahrbuch des Germanistenverbandes im südlichen Afrika 35 / 2007, ed. Anette Horn (Frankfurt am Main: Peter Lang, 2008), 129–41.

[7] There are, of course, too many such texts to mention. It would indeed be more difficult to find texts that display a more tolerant attitude to the Other.

[8] Riedesel is here often as guilty as many of his contemporaries, as we can see *passim* in his first publication the *Reise durch Sicilien und Großgriechenland* (Zurich: Orell, Geßner, Füßli & Co., 1771) (republished *as Johann Hermann Riedesels Freiherrn zu Eisenbach Sendschreiben über seine Reise nach Sizilien und Großgriechenland,* ed. Kasimir Edschmid (Darmstadt: Gesellschaft Hessischer Bücherfreunde, 1939)).

[9] The most extreme formulation of this position is provided by E. M. Butler in *The Tyranny of Greece over Germany* (Beacon Hill, MA: Beacon P, 1958). Her account of the German propensity to succumb to influence is colored by her fresh memory of perceived German submission to Hitler.

[10] Johann Joachim Winckelmann (1717–68) was one of the most powerful contemporary advocates of neoclassical aesthetics and an important innovator in art historical and archaeological theory and practice. The most compact formulation of his positions can be found in his first publication, *Gedanken über die Nachahmung der griechischen Werke in der Malerei und Bildhauerkunst* (Dresden: Walther, 1755) available with a number of his other small treatises in Johann Joachim Winckelmann, *Kleine Schriften, Vorreden, Entwürfe,* ed. Walther Rehm (Berlin: de Gruyter, 1968). It is also available in a shorter form in *Gedanken über die Nachahmung der griechischen Werke in der Malerei und Bildhauerkunst—Sendschreiben—Erläuterung* (Stuttgart: Philipp Reclam Jun., 1969). Riedesel spent a good deal of time with Winckelmann and maintained a correspondence with him. See Johann Joachim Winckelmann, *Briefe,* ed. Walther Rehm, 4 vols. (Berlin: de Gruyter, 1968).

[11] See note 8 above.

[12] See note 2 above. The reports from Britain have a wholly different emphasis when compared with those from Italy or Greece. Perhaps this can be traced to the fact that they were written after the death of Winckelmann in 1768 and in the

period before Riedesel's emergence as a statesman. See Becker's introduction to the *Randbemerkungen*.

[13] See introduction.

[14] See the letter of 22 May 2009 contained in the online version of the text.

[15] For a fuller if more romantic biographical treatment see Katherine Sim, *Desert Traveller: The Life of Jean Louis Burckhardt* (London: Victor Gollancz, 1969). Note the use of the French version of his name, which he apparently (and ironically) preferred. Burckhardt spoke and wrote French despite his reservations about the French and his English employment and later English-language publication.

[16] The exact nature of Riedesel's education is unclear, since detailed documentary evidence is missing. Becker makes some suggestions in his introduction to the *Randbemerkungen* about where Riedesel might have developed his interest in classical antiquity. It did not happen at the University of Erlangen, where there was at that time no tuition in Greek.

[17] See Winckelmann, *Kleine Schriften*, 169–73.

[18] See Morrison, *Winckelmann*, 20–23, for a brief treatment of contemporary theories of the production of art.

[19] Winckelmann's *Geschichte der Kunst des Altertums* (Dresden: Walther, 1764) depends very heavily upon such assumptions.

[20] The Winckelmannian formula can be found at Johann Joachim Winckelmann, *Gedanken*, 20. The Riedesel quotation is from Riedesel, *Randbemerkungen*, 131.

[21] An alternative source of biographical information is contained in the introduction to *Travels in Nubia* and in the letters published in that volume, which predate his journey.

[22] The Burckhardt volumes not discussed here are *Travels in Syria and the Holy Land* (London: John Murray, 1822); *Travels in Arabia: Comprehending an Account of Those Territories in Hedjaz Which the Mohammedans Regard as Sacred* (London: Colburn, 1829); *Arabic Proverbs or the Manners and Customs of the Modern Egyptians* (London: John Murray, 1830); and *Notes on the Bedouins and Wahábys: Collected during his Travels in the East* (London: Colburn & Bentley, 1831).

[23] The association was founded only in 1788 and operated on the basis of subscription from members to fund its research. Burckhardt was following in the footsteps of other sponsored travelers such as John Ledyard, Simon Lucas, and Mungo Park, whose *Travels from the River Gambia to the Niger, in the Years 1796–7* (London: The African Association, 1798) had been hugely popular. While the attitudes of the association's writers varied, and indeed were sometimes liberal by the standards of the age (for example, with regard to slavery), they all reflect the political status and aspirations of contemporary Britain.

8: Displacing Orientalism: Ottoman *Jihad*, German Imperialism, and the Armenian Genocide

Rachel MagShamhráin

THIS CHAPTER EXAMINES VARIOUS DISCOURSES involved in German-Turkish relations from the 1890s until the end of the First World War, arguing that they are evidence of a more multidirectional Orientalism than is suggested by Edward Said's idea of a hegemonic West representing and therefore controlling an essentialized East.[1] Orientalism, these discourses reveal, does not occur along the single trajectory suggested by its name. It is not simply a nonreversible, monodirectional phenomenon radiating out from the West onto a passive Eastern object, but rather, as Sheldon Pollock among others has argued, something that can also emanate from the East, be applied by the East to itself, and even be applied by the West to the West.[2] In short, the dialectics of Orientalism are infinitely more conflicted, complex, decentered, and displaced than Said's approach indicates.

The image of the "sick old man of Europe" as a passive Eastern pawn in Western imperialist power games is a case in point, failing to do justice to the extent to which the Ottoman Empire was an active participant in the major power plays of the period, all the while serving its own political agendas, which included a hegemonic national project based on ideas of "ethnic-national homogeneity," or, as John Morrow puts it, "historians have long credited the German government with manipulating the Ottoman government into the war to foster German aims of an empire from Berlin to Baghdad. . . . More recently [however, they] have recognized that the . . . Young Turks had their own aims, and . . . manipulated the Germans."[3] Only a paradigm that departs quite radically from Saidean Orientalism[4] can adequately account for the intricacies of the relationship between Wihelmine Germany and Turkey, which cut across traditional East-West cultural cleavages in the service of political and economic interests on both sides, and which required at times that even the most dominant cultural tropes determining difference and affinity be treated in an intriguingly casual fashion. This meant, for instance, that while a traditional and uncritical association of the Orient with Islam still doubtlessly prevailed at the time (an association with which, incidentally, even post-Saidean scholarship is still struggling),[5] religious divides that served the purposes of Othering the Orient were convolutedly downplayed.

Jennifer Jenkins has recently argued for more attention to be paid to "the centrality of the Ottoman Empire, and its border with Europe, [and] to the various forms taken by German Orientalism," and sees the need for a timely "reminder of the profound and long-standing relationship between Germany and the Ottoman Empire—wiping away the historical amnesia that surrounds this topic, at least on the German side," especially in the context of Turkey's wish to accede to the EU and the opposition this has encountered in various quarters.[6] The historical amnesia, which has allowed Angela Merkel, for instance, to argue that the potential accession of Turkey to the EU would be a "Katastrophe für die politische Union Europas,"[7] primarily on the basis of Turkey's human-rights record, has been facilitated to a certain extent by Said's exemption of Germany from the worst excesses of European Orientalism in his landmark work of 1978. In the first two-thirds of the nineteenth century, he writes, Germany had no "protracted sustained national interest in the Orient," and thus did not engage in Orientalism in the same sense that France and Britain did. Said therefore considers the German Orient to be "almost exclusively a scholarly, or at least a classical, Orient: it was made the subject of lyrics, fantasies, and even novels, but it was never actual, the way Egypt and Syria were actual for Chateaubriand, Lane, Lamartine, Burton, Disraeli, or Nerval."[8]

While Said's argument largely holds true for most of the nineteenth century, by the reign of Wilhelm II Germany's interest in the Orient was by no means purely scholarly, and the attitude to the Orient, encapsulated in Bismarck's famous 1878 statement that the Balkans were not worth "die Knochen eines einzigen pommerschen Grenadiers," simply no longer pertained.[9] In fact, what remained of the Ottoman Empire would soon become what was effectively "a Turkish client state beholden to [Germany] financially, technically . . . , and militarily."[10] In a sense, it was a colony in all but name, and Germany's political and economic activity nothing less than an *actio in distans* colonialism. In the words of the Protestant theologian Friedrich Naumann, founder of the Christian socialist *Nationalsozialer Verein* party and part of Wilhelm II's entourage on his second Orient trip of 1898, the plan for Turkey was "das Land wirtschaftlich von uns abhängig machen, um es später politisch kontrollieren zu können."[11]

One slightly bizarre manifestation of Germany's increasingly "actual" interest in the Orient was Kaiser Wilhelm's declaration during that selfsame trip of an everlasting friendship between the German emperor and "His Majesty the Sultan and the three hundred millions of Moslems who, in whatever corner of the globe they may live, revere in him their

Khalif."[12] In this speech, given as he stood at the tomb of Saladin in Damascus, he also took the opportunity to chastise Protestantism for its comparative lack of unity and appealed to his German subjects to strive to impress Muslims by their acts of charity, thereby awakening in them a respect for and love of Christianity. Although the German foreign ministry encouraged the belief that the Kaiser was merely visiting the region to make a pilgrimage to the Holy Land, he was actually actively cultivating an alliance between Germany and the Ottoman Empire, for, as he put it to "dear cousin Nikki" in August 1897, "the Mahometans [would be] a tremendous card in our game in case you or I were suddenly confronted by a war with the certain meddlesome Power," that power being none other, of course, than Britain.[13]

A second, perhaps equally peculiar, manifestation of Germany's growing imperialist intentions toward the Orient was the Ottoman Empire's declaration of *jihad* on the Entente powers in November 1914. A note written by the Kaiser in late July of that year makes it quite clear that this idea of an anti-British *jihad* was German rather than Turkish in origin: "Unsere Consuln in Türkei und Indien, Agenten etc. müssen die ganze Mohamedanische Welt gegen dieses verhaßte, verlogene, gewissenlose Krämervolk [i.e. the English] zum wilden Aufstand entflammen; denn wenn wir uns verbluten sollen, dann soll England wenigstens Indien verlieren."[14] Thus, perhaps unsurprisingly, in the proclamation of *jihad* by the Sheikh-ul-Islam, the enemies identified are not infidels in general, as one might expect, but rather, coincidentally, the enemies of Germany:

> Oh, Moslems! Ye who are smitten with happiness and are on the verge of sacrificing your life and your good for the cause of right, and of braving perils, gather now around the Imperial throne, obey the commands of the Almighty, who, in the Koran, promises us bliss in this and in the next world; embrace ye the foot of the Caliph's throne and know ye that the state is at war with Russia, England, France, and their Allies, and that these are the enemies of Islam. The Chief of the believers, the Caliph, invites you all as Moslems to join in the Holy War.[15]

Despite the call to arms, Henry Morgenthau, the American ambassador to the Ottoman Empire at the time, noted, albeit with the benefit of hindsight and in the patronizing manner of his day and culture, that the entire project was doomed to failure from the start because "the Mohammedans of such countries as India, Egypt, Algiers, and Morocco knew that they were getting far better treatment than they could obtain under any other conceivable conditions" (*AMS*, 116). And so Morgenthau (evidently oblivious to the irony inherent in his position) saw the declaration of Holy War as little more than "evidence of the fundamental German clumsiness and real ignorance of racial psychology" (*AMS*, 116).

The *New York Times* of 7 July 1918 agreed with Morgenthau's assessment, reiterating his remark that a *jihad* of this kind was impossible, for one thing because "simple minded Mohammedans could not understand why they should prosecute a holy war against Christians with Christian nations, such as Germany and Austria, as their partners."[16] However, the idea that "230,000,000[17] Mohammedans [might] have risen as one man and precipitated upon the world the most horrible riot of destruction and massacre that the world has ever recorded" was not initially considered to be quite so unlikely a prospect, if only because the bizarre alliance between Turkey and Germany made such strange things seem perfectly possible. And so "the world for a brief period stood aghast at the possibility of what might occur [if] the Mohammedans met the expectations of the Kaiser and the Caliph and responded as they should have responded according to the tenets of their faith."[18]

Notoriously anti-British, Kaiser Wilhelm II had long entertained the idea that the British Empire might be undermined by manipulating the forces of burgeoning pan-Islamism, seemingly unaware that the concerns of pan-Islamism might not precisely coincide with those of Germany. For although the *Kaiserreich* had initially been alarmed by the rapid spread of Islam in the late nineteenth century, particularly in Africa, where it had colonies, the diplomat, archeologist, and Orientalist Max von Oppenheim managed to foster the belief that Islam, which he claimed was by its very nature militant, could readily be harnessed as an effective weapon by the Germans and directed against Britain.

As Kris Manjapra has pointed out, by 1908 "Germany had the second-largest shipping traffic with India, after Great Britain,"[19] giving rise to an intense trade rivalry between the two nations with regard to the subcontinent, not to mention other British overseas possessions. The importance of the Indian Empire to Germany's economy played a part in the development of Oppenheim's bafflingly simplistic plan to turn Islam against the British. There were 94 million Muslims in the British Empire,[20] more than half of whom lived in India,[21] and if they could be made to rise up *en masse* at the declaration of *jihad* and crush the infidel British (while sparing the infidel Germans), this would render Britain less of a competitor in the struggle for imperialist influence. The rhetorical arsenal for this project was readily provided by the ethnological discourses of the period, which tended to ascribe mentalities and motives to entire peoples.[22] In the specific case of Islam, since the Crusade of 1096 when the worlds of Christianity and Islam first came into contact in a significant sense, Muslims had been associated in the European imagination with war and the warrior spirit, as in the *chansons de geste,* where the Saracens were depicted as "worthy of respect, a good enemy, [and] difficult to conquer."[23] And this was a view that Oppenheim certainly shared, characterizing the Muslims, whom he hoped to incite to insurrection, as, among other things, bellicose by nature.[24]

Despite a "zwanzigjährige[r] Aufenthalt im Orient,"[25] Oppenheim had, somewhat bafflingly, failed to recognize, however, that it was in the main Indian Hindus, not Muslims, who were inclined to engage in subversive activity against the British Empire. Moreover, he failed to consider that the declaration of Holy War by an Ottoman Sheikh-ul-Islam might not speak to Muslims worldwide, many of whom simply did not recognize his authority and right to declare *jihad* in the first place.

Oppenheim's ignorance is all the more baffling when contrasted with the insights of his contemporary, the famous Dutch Orientalist Christiaan Snouck Hurgronje, whose intimate knowledge of Islam had helped the Dutch defeat the native Indonesians in the so-called Aceh War. As Hurgronje pointed out in a publication of 1915, the fragmentation of the Muslim population over different states posed a major, if not insurmountable, impediment to a Holy War of the kind Germany hoped to unleash: "The *jihad*-program assumes that the Mohammedans, just as at their first appearance in the world, continuously form a compact unity under one man's leadership." But this, he notes, had long since ceased to be the case, and "by this disintegration the continuance of the world conquest, as it was started in the first century of Islam, is made impossible."[26] He also noted that the tendency to view the Caliphate as a kind of Muslim papacy was misguided and a dangerous European projection onto the East that doomed projects such as Oppenheim's to failure: "Certain European writers sometimes have felt induced to represent [the Caliphate] as a kind of religious princes [*sic*] of Islâm, who voluntarily or not had transferred their secular power to the many territorial princes in the wide dominion of Islâm . . . a sort of Mohammedan papacy. . . .]Here, as elsewhere, the multitude preferred legend to fact."[27]

Despite the fact that Oppenheim's assumptions were so fundamentally flawed and at variance with the insights of such established Islamists as Hurgronje, the British in India took the precaution of getting the Nizam of Hyderabad to declare that, although the Sultan of Turkey was nominally head of Islam worldwide, the First World War was a political rather than a religious conflict, and therefore the call to Holy War was invalid and would be ignored by him.[28]

While Oppenheim's essentializing notions about Islam are pure Orientalism in the sense that Said meant it (a hegemonic discursive act performed by the West on the East, albeit, in this case, with Great Britain as the indirect target), at the time of the so-called "unholy" German-Turkish alliance[29] the Turks were themselves engaging in Orientalism of another kind—an "eastern Orientalism," to borrow Sheldon Pollock's term (*DO*, 96). Pollock uses the expression to indicate that "the movement of Orientalist knowledge may be multidirectional. We usually imagine its vector as directed outward—toward the colonization and domination of Asia; . . . we might [however] conceive of it as potentially directed inward—toward the colonization and domination of Europe itself" (*DO*, 76–77). In this analysis the expression will be used to indicate that while the Ottoman Empire was no doubt the object and victim of Western Orientalist discourses and policies, it also both encouraged the Western gaze and cultural projections for its own purposes (Turkey was, for example, the passive instigator of the Turko-German alliance of 2 August 1914)[30] and, all importantly, was engaged in inwardly directed hegemonic discourses of its own, of which more later. This Eastern Orientalism, or Orientalism in, of, and for the East, is not to be confused with the interpellation of the colonized by the colonizer. In other words, although Turkey was certainly to some extent what Kiossev calls a "self-colonizing culture,"[31] that is to say one that, due to a sense of lack or inadequacy, "willingly" imports and adopts outside values, its participation in hegemonic discourses cannot be reduced to the simple internalization of Western ideas. If Orientalism is simply "a discourse of power that divides the world into 'betters and lessers' [facilitating] the domination (or 'orientalization' or 'colonization') of any group" (*DO*, 77), indigenous discourses of power in the Ottoman Empire of the period were themselves independently Orientalist. If we fail to recognize this, we find ourselves automatically engaging in the crass form of essentializing Orientalism found in the *New York Times* article above, reducing German involvement in the Near East in the late eighteen and early nineteen hundreds to a West-to-East Orientalism, whereby dastardly Germans used their financial clout and rhetorical cunning to bamboozle poor "simpleminded" Ottomans into doing their bidding, including declaring Holy War on the enemies of the *Vaterland*.

In other words, Turkish-German relations of the period cannot for a variety of reasons simply be regarded as what Homi K. Bhabha saw as a necessarily symbiotic relationship or interdependency between European colonial conqueror and Oriental conquered.[32] When talking about the relationship between Orient and Occident in the case of Wilhelmine Germany and the Ottoman Empire, it is essential to recognize that there are also "Orientalist discourses within nation-states [both East and West] that operate internally and objectify, stigmatize and essentialize a particular geography, ethnicity and culture."[33] To call the discursive battlefield "Orientalism" at all, then, is in a way misleading, because focusing on the East-West divide elides the Orientalism that occurs in all cultures vis-à-vis both other cultures and elements within themselves. A good case in point would be the "dhimmitude" of Shari'a states,[34] or, relatedly, the Tehcir Law of the Ottoman Empire and the ensuing Armenian genocide in which perhaps as many as 1.8 million Armenians were killed in a brutal and systematic campaign of eradication. However, Orientalism, misleading or not, is such a fixed category of modern critical thought that any discussion of Turkish-German relations cannot just ignore it. But if it cannot be dismissed it must be revalorized so that Eastern acts of "Orientalism" such as the Armenian *Aghed* are not forgotten in postcolonialism's blame game.

To return to German-Ottoman inter-involvement in the Wilhelmine period, another curious by-product of the relationship was "a tradition of German anti-Armenian propaganda that emerged in response to German foreign-policy needs after the 1880s."[35] Despite the fact that the persecuted Armenians, like the Germans, were Christians (notwithstanding the Dvin Council), and despite the deep Christian-Islamic fault line that Oppenheim had hoped to exploit in a *jihad*, Germany took an anti-Armenian stance during the Turkish suppression of what was cast as Armenian sedition and secessionism. For one thing, Germany needed to ingratiate itself with the Ottomans, upon whom it was now parasitically dependent, and for another, Germany was deeply concerned by pro-Russian Armenian feeling and the risk of growing Russian influence in the Balkans. As a result of its vested interest in Anatolia, a particularly distorted and negative image of "the Armenian" developed in Germany at around this time, an exemplary instance of which can be found in Karl May's 1897 travelogue *Auf fremden Pfaden*. His description of an encounter with what he sees as a typical Armenian begins comparatively moderately with a depiction of the man's long, angular, haggard body and narrow forehead but soon gains momentum when it reaches the bloodless lips, "stark gebogene, breitflügelige" hawk nose and "listige," hooded eyes, basing arguments about the (moral) character of the Armenian people as a whole on these caricatural physiognomic observations:

> Die stark entwickelten Kauwerkzeuge und das breit vortretende Kinn liessen auf Egoismus, Rücksichtslosigkeit und überwiegend tierische Affekte schliessen, während die obere Hälfte des Gesichts eine bedeutende, absichtlich verborgene Verschlagenheit verriet. Wenn dieser Mann nicht ein Armenier war, so gab es überhaupt keine Armenier! Ein Jude überlistet zehn Christen; ein Yankee betrügt fünfzig Juden, ein Armenier aber ist hundert Yankees gewachsen; so sagt man, und ich habe gefunden, dass dies zwar übertrieben ausgedrückt ist, aber doch auf Wahrheit beruht. Man bereise den Orient mit offenen Augen, so wird man mir recht geben. Wo irgendeine Heimtücke, eine Verräterei geplant wird, da ist sicher die Habichtsnase eines Armeniers im Spiel.[36]

This stereotype is eminently recognizable, of course, as an ethnographic *Wandertopos,* applied at other historical junctures *mutatis mutandis* to both Jesuits and Jews. We should, however, note that the image of the cunning Armenian was not entirely a late-nineteenth-century German invention, although it certainly served the country's political purposes to revive the topos at that time. It is a more widespread and older trope, used, for instance, in 1826 by the English travel writer and social reformer J. S. Buckingham in a description that, while certainly less negative, also ascribes a fundamental shrewdness to the Armenians, who "dispersed all over Asia . . . exert their natural genius for trade, principally in speculations as money-changers. . . . They are naturally formed for commerce—cunning among those they know, reserved with strangers, temperate from economy or avarice, and humble and accommodating for the sake of interest."[37]

It may seem extraordinary that Germany would not object in any meaningful way to the persecution of fellow Christians by Muslim Turks, especially in light of Article 61 of the Congress of Berlin of 1878, in which the European powers pledged to support the Ottoman Armenians. But a passage by the German Orientalist Paul Rohrbach, who began to explore and write about the Ottoman Empire in the late nineteenth century, leaves us in no doubt about Germany's real priorities: "Der Besitzer Armeniens beherrscht unmittelbar sowohl das Östliche als auch das obere Mesopotamien. . . . Soll also die Türkei erhalten bleiben, so muss auch Armenien türkisch bleiben, und weil wir die Türkei stützen müssen, so lange eine Möglichkeit dazu besteht, kann nicht zugelassen werden, dass Armenien in die Hände Russlands fällt."[38]

The change in foreign policy that saw Christian Germany taking the part of Muslim Turkey against the "cunning and treacherous" Christian Armenians was brought about, like so many changes of the day, by the railway. When the Deutsche Bank was granted a concession by the Ottoman Caliphate in 1888 to build a railway line between the Bosporus at Constantinople and Angora, the first leg of a planned line all the way to Baghdad, Germany suddenly became aware of the potential that the Ottoman Empire held as an extraterritorial economic sphere of influence. Previously the *Kaiserreich* had seen the crumbling Turkish Empire only as a tub thrown to a whale, a means of distracting France, England, and Russia, thus minimizing their threat to real German interests in Central and Eastern Europe. But with the completion of Baron von Hirsch's Oriental Railway in 1888, Berlin was now directly linked to Istanbul by rail and would soon be linked to Konya in central Anatolia, and eventually to Baghdad, and with these rail links came economic ties. Germany realized that the collapse of the Ottoman Empire would immediately result in its being carved up by the main European powers, whose involvement would inevitably obstruct Germany's spreading influence in the region. Ironically, Germany needed to keep the Ottoman Empire intact for as long as possible since it could profit from it more *in toto* than in part.

Rosa Luxemburg's so-called *Junius Pamphlet* of 1915 demonstrates just how far-reaching, and in her view damaging, German involvement was in the Near East on the eve of the First World War, calling Turkey the "most important field of operations of German imperialism."[39] In the course of work on the Baghdad railway, a scheme that R. I. Money saw as restoring prosperity to a central Anatolia that had "degenerated" after the breakup of the Seljuk state,[40] Lake Karaviran and the Plain of Konya were drained and irrigated respectively, developments that Luxemburg refuses to see as Western gifts to a primitive Anatolia, arguing instead that:

> The reverse of this wonderful work of "peaceful culture" is the "peaceful" and wholesale ruin of the farming population of Asia Minor. The cost of this tremendous undertaking was advanced, of course, by the Deutsche Bank on the security of a widely diversified system of public indebtedness. Turkey will be, to all eternity, the debtor of Messrs. Siemens, Gwinner, Helfferich, etc. . . .
>
> Thus a twofold purpose is accomplished. The farming population of Asia Minor becomes the object of a well organized process of exploitation in the interest of European, in this case German, financial and industrial capital. This again promotes the growth of the German sphere of interest in Turkey and lays the foundation for Turkey's "political protection." At the same time the instrument that carries out the exploitation of the farming population, the Turkish Government, becomes the willing tool and vassal of Germany's foreign policies.[41]

Naturally, Germans rarely stated the nature of their interest in the Ottoman Empire as baldly as this, so as not to alienate the Ottomans or draw too much English, French, and Russian attention to the "actual" nature of Germany's involvement. Sanitizing, palliating discourses were used instead to make Germany's intervention both less perturbing to the other Great Powers and more palatable to itself. And so German activity in the region was frequently portrayed in terms of a *mission civilisatrice,* a concept that had long since provided the French and the English with justification for their colonial activities, casting these foreign incursions as a high-minded attempt to share the benefits of European civilization with less fortunate parts and peoples.

One such account of German inroads into Anatolia comes from the editor of the *Deutsche Rundschau* and author of various oriental travelogues, Paul Lindenberg. In an often quoted passage from his *Auf deutschen Pfaden im Orient* of 1902 he traces German participation in the affairs of the Near East back to the Third Crusade, when the Holy Roman Emperor, Barbarossa, led an army across Anatolia in an attempt to take back the Holy Land from Saladin, the selfsame Saladin at whose tomb Wilhelm II had declared his undying loyalty to "three million" Muslims. The passage is worth quoting in full because of the stark counterpoint it offers to Luxemburg's completely unromantic portrayal of Germany's real interests and their impact on the Anatolian landscape.

Zu Ostern 1190 war es, als Kaiser Barbarossa, glaubensmutig und
thatenfroh, an der Spitze seines erlesenen Kreuzfahrerheeres hier ent-
langzog, um nach Klein-Asien hinüberzusetzen und, dasselbe durch-
querend, gen Jerusalem vorzudringen, ohne daß er das ersehnte Ziel
erreichen sollte!

Jahrhundert um Jahrhundert verstrich, in Vergessenheit schie-
nen die endlosen Gebiete versunken zu sein, die einst die deutschen Gewappneten auf schweren Rossen durchzogen, hin und
wieder, wenn der starke Holzpflug des türkischen Bauern die Erde
aufwühlte, kamen die bleichen Überreste eines der heldenmütigen
Genossen des Rotbart-Hohenstaufen zum Vorschein, oder ein ver-
wittertes steinernes Kreuz zeigte die Ruhestätte eines mannhaften
Ritters an, der unter heißer Sonne zusammengebrochen oder den
Feinden erlegen war. . . .

Und eines Tages hielten die Deutschen selbst ihren Einzug in Ana-
tolien, auf denselben Pfaden, welche die Kreuzritter gezogen, aber
nicht wie jene mit trutzigen Waffen und hoch zu Roß mit wehenden
Bannern: Werkzeuge und Maschinen aller Art führten sie mit sich
und in ihrem Gefolge ein Heer von emsigen Arbeitern, gegraben
wurde und gebaut, schwindelnde Abhänge und reißende Ströme
wurden überbrückt, Berge durchbohrt und Sümpfe ausgetrocknet,
wo bisher auf hindernisreichen Wegen lange Kamel-Karawanen ent-
langgestapft, da dehnten sich gleißende Schienenstränge aus, auf
welchen am Anfang der 90er Jahre pustend und schnaubend die
ersten Lokomotiven—"Landdampfer" nannten sie die türkischen
Bauern—einherrollten, Leben, Bewegung, Kultur in jene halbver-
gessenen Gebiete bringend, . . . die nun wieder von Jahr zu Jahr in
wirtschaftlicher wie politischer Beziehung ganz erstaunlich an Wich-
tigkeit gewinnen.

So kämpfen die neuen Deutschen in Klein-Asien, ihr Sieg aber
heißt die Anatolische Eisenbahn, mit deutschem Geld von deutschen
Ingenieuren erbaut und unter musterhafter deutscher Verwaltung
stehend.[42]

Lindenberg's text casts German involvement in the Ottoman
Empire as a modern, more civilized version of the Crusades, suggesting that, because of the Crusades, the Germans have a kind of prior
and natural claim on the territory involved, if not exactly a god-given
right to be there. German financial benefits are portrayed as unintended
but welcome by-products of what is primarily a crusade to bring Asia
Minor, the birthplace of civilization but a place that time has since forgotten, forward in technological, political, and economic terms.[43] The
financial-cum-cultural mission has taken over from the religious one,
but the two are nevertheless clearly seen by Lindenberg as forming a
logical continuum. It is also interesting that Lindenberg should cast a
backward glance at Germany's participation in a Christian Holy War of

the twelfth century, when some 800 years later Germany was master-minding an Islamic Holy War against Christendom.

In fact, it is remarkable that Lindenberg's in-many-ways-convention-ally-Orientalist description of German involvement in Anatolia makes any mention whatsoever of the Crusades with their suggestion of inelidable religious differences between "East" and "West," especially when Kaiser Wilhelm had been so careful to avoid the subject in Damascus, despite the fact that he was speaking at the tomb of the great Salah-ad-Din, nemesis of the Crusaders. After all, while similarities between the Crusading and imperialist spirits were certainly not lost on the Ottomans themselves,[44] German courtship of Turkey around 1900 required the active downplay-ing of some longstanding if problematic ideas of Self and Other in West-ern thought, particularly those that were by-products of what Mary Anne Perkins refers to as the "Christendom narrative,"[45] the totalizing grand narrative generated by Christian culture that allowed Europeans to take so many liberties abroad.

This downplaying of dominant narratives in the service of foreign investment was by no means an easy business. The German position on the Armenian question, perhaps even more than Oppenheim's strange idea of a German-Christian-inspired Muslim-Ottoman *jihad* against the Christian Entente states, posed particular problems, and it demonstrates the logical and rhetorical contortions required by Germany in this period to escape the clutches of the pervasive and now counterproductive Chris-tendom narrative. Pastor Friedrich Naumann, who saw Germany's role in the Near East as divinely ordained, made an admirable attempt at squar-ing the circle, advocating that Christian Germans ignore the pogroms against Christian Armenian because "unser Volk auch dem Christentum am besten dient, wenn es sich selber im Völkerkampfe stark erhält."[46] In other words, as the diplomat Alfons Mumm von Schwarzenstein put it in 1896, it was "nicht die Aufgabe der deutschen Politik . . . sich um die Christen in der ganzen Welt zu kümmern und einen europäischen Kreuz-zug gegen den Halbmond ins Leben zu rufen."[47] Even though Germany was endeavoring by remarkable feats of logic to negate a religious divide that might jeopardize its involvement in Anatolia, it is important to note here and elsewhere the insistent if unwelcome spectral presence of reli-gious difference in various legitimizing discourses used by Germany to establish and preserve its hegemonic power in the territories of the Otto-man Empire. While Naumann, Schwarzenstein, and Lindenberg all dis-tance themselves from the traditional Christian-Muslim antagonism that inspired the Crusades, this antagonism remains something of an elephant in the room, recurring almost involuntarily in even the most turcophile discourses of the period. Religion was, after all, one of the legitimizing discourses underpinning European imperialism itself, and an important part of the colonial apparatus.[48] Since it was impossible to avoid the issue of religion altogether, therefore, Germany's cultivation of Turkish friendship required a cunning restating of religious difference and playing down of the colonial uses to which Christianity had been and was still being put. Consequently, while Christianity and its evangelizing mission are not altogether ignored—they cannot be, since for centuries the world had been "haunted by the religious imagination of colonial Christendom"[49]—they are made subordinate either to questions of national interest (Schwarzenheim and Naumann) or incorporated into the idea of German imperialism as a modernizing and civilizing force (Lindenberg). (It should not be forgotten, of course, that there was simultaneously a return of this repressed religious division, often in grotesque and pointed form. An 1898 political cartoon from the Genevan weekly *Le Carillon,* for instance, shows Abdul Hamid asking the Kaiser, "Gestattet dir dein Christus, dich für Mohammed zu schlagen?" to which the Kaiser replies "Mein Gott ist mein Säbel!" On the ground at their feet lie the Bible and the Koran.[50])

Turkey's persecution and murder of its Christian Armenian population not only elicited positively byzantine legitimizing discourses from a Germany that wanted to defend its involvement in and with the Ottoman Empire. It also provides evidence of both the omnipresence and omnidirectionality of Orientalism. The genocide happened in two major waves, the first taking place in the 1890s under Sultan Abdülhamid II and coinciding with Germany's Ottoman railway projects and the concomitant declaration of eternal "friendship" between the *Kaiserreich* and the *Sublime Porte*.[51] The second, more brutal, wave took place in 1915 under the so-called Three Pashas and coincided with the Gallipoli campaign of the First World War,[52] likely taking place at precisely this juncture because the state of war lent itself both to the committing and disguising of these atrocities.[53] In any case, there can be no doubt that the Ottoman Empire was convinced that it could get away with this large-scale ethnic cleansing, or, as it was then portrayed, eradication of a dangerous fifth column, and that it was encouraged in this belief by the fact that it has an ally as powerful as Germany. As Baron Calice, the Austro-Hungarian Ambassador to the Ottoman Empire, put it, the Sultan could feel "unter dem schützenden Schild Deutschlands, dem er schon soviel verdankt, mehr denn je frei und sicher."[54]

In a perfect example of "Eastern Orientalism," Enver Pasha, the *de facto* dictator of the Ottoman Empire from 1913, described the Armenians to the concerned American ambassador in precisely the same "orientalizing" way that Oppenheim had depicted "the Muslims," namely as a homogenous cultural-cum-religious group that reacts *en masse* and is a potential source of separatism, fanaticism, and rebellion. (Of course, while Oppenheim had seen this as a good thing, to be exploited in Germany's interests, Pasha, ironically, felt that any populace with such traits needed to be eradicated for the good of the state.) Whether or not Enver

Pasha's characterization was a matter of conviction or merely served the purpose of vindicating his anti-Armenian policies to the United States is irrelevant. The discourse engages in the same "Othering" that is at play when Oppenheim describes Muslims, or the "fanatische Heerscharen des Orients" as he calls them,[55] as "kriegerisch" and "von Hass beseelt." Like Oppenheim's Muslims, Pasha's Armenians are seen as having a religious-cum-racial loyalty that transcends their loyalty to the state to which they belong, preventing them from becoming a "real part of our nation," and making it likely that they would "attack us [the Ottoman Turks] in the back." They are, in Pasha's words, a people with a "revolutionary pro-gramme" (*AMS*, 236), a sentiment echoed by his Minister of the Interior, Talaat Bey, who, in a wonderfully convoluted piece of logic, goes on to express surprise at the US ambassador's worries about the genocide, saying, "You [Morgenthau] are a Jew; these people are Christians. The Mohammedans and the Jews always get on harmoniously. We are treating the Jews here all right. What have you to complain of? Why can't you let us do with these Christians as we please?" (*AMS*, 208). Perhaps even more so than Pasha's straightforward essentializing and demonizing description of the Armenians, the uneasy bedfellows in Talaat Bey's statement neatly demonstrate Pollock's point that Orientalism does not occur along a neat West-to-East axis but twists and turns and makes quantum and improbable leaps over and back across the seemingly most entrenched divides.

Even Ambassador Morgenthau's classification of the Turks slightly later in his memoirs as "dull-witted and lazy" (*AMS*, 231), which Rachel Kirby sees as proof positive of a "proclivity toward linguistic distillation of ethnic types in the writings of [Western] diplomats" in the Ottoman Empire,[56] and which thus seems to fit the Saidean paradigm perfectly, turns out to be more complicated. It was, in fact, an attempt by Morgenthau to demonstrate to Talaat Bey, in an *argumentum ad absurdum*, the insulting implications for the Turkish "national character" of Bey's own argument that the Armenians' business acumen was allowing them to "enrich themselves at the expense of the Turks." This Western reiteration of what turns out to be a preexisting intra-oriental Orientalism reveals again that Saidean Orientalism is too simple a paradigm to account for any of the articulations, to borrow Laclau and Mouffe's concept, involved in the multilateral struggle for discursive hegemony in the Ottoman Empire of the First World War period.

Yet another instance of a multi- rather than uni-directional "Orientalism" is provided by Hans Barth's notorious anti-Armenian, pro-Turkish diatribe *Türke, wehre Dich!* of 1898. An extremely Turcophile and anti-Catholic journalist, Barth played on modern German anti-religious sentiment in his criticism of Western efforts to garner support for the Armenians during the pogroms of the late nineteenth century, calling these efforts an eighth Crusade (meant here in an emphatically pejorative sense), casting those supporting Armenia's cause as interfering, pro-clerical, and outmodedly religious busybodies and portraying the Turks as the only gentlemen of the Orient. A large part of his work takes direct issue with the efforts of the Pietist missionary Johannes Lepsius to draw the German public's attention to the plight of the Armenians, for instance in his bestselling *Armenien und Europa: Eine Anklageschrift wider die christlichen Großmächte und ein Aufruf an das christliche Deutschland* of 1896. What is interesting about Barth's anti-Armenian, anti-Lepsian diatribe is that it adopts Lepsius's arguments practically wholesale, not demolishing them so much as reproducing them and then inverting or negating them. They survive almost intact in Barth's work in the form of long quotations that cannot always readily be distinguished from the author's own text. Barth then merely adds a "not true" to each carefully preserved point, unwittingly demonstrating a strange rhetorical reversibility in this discursive field, where the selfsame arguments serve seemingly diametrically opposed purposes. This phenomenon of reversibility, the bidirectionality of which is at odds with the West-to-East discursive trajectory that Said's Orientalism implies, can be observed, for instance, when Barth accuses Lepsius of failing to differentiate sufficiently between Kurds and Turks, indiscriminately calling them both Muhammedaner.[57] Barth promptly goes on to perform the selfsame maneuver himself, lumping all Armenians into the category of "Reichsfeind, . . . Revolutionär und Anarchisten" (40).

Another dimension of the multidirectionality of Orientalism becomes clear when Barth starts to juggle all the "Others" of his argument at once. He begins by arguing that many of the outrages committed against the Armenians were perpetrated not by Turks *proper* but by Kurds, who, while they are also Muslims, are *only* Muslim in the sense that the Armenians are Christians (that is, not; presumably, in the case of the latter, because of the schism). Moreover, he continues, the Turks themselves have had to suffer from Kurdish barbarity. However (he then claims, coming full circle now), the perpetrators of the recent violence (presumably both against Armenians and Turks) may not even be Kurdish nomads at all but rather radical Armenian revolutionaries in disguise:

> Gewiss hatten ja die tiefer im Innern wohnenden Armenier vielfach unter der Willkür kurdischer Nomaden zu leiden, die das friedfertig-gesetzliche Expropriations-Prinzip ihrer armenisch-indogermanischen Vettern in ihre drastischere Weise, das wucherische Rupfen ins derbe Plündern übersetzten—aber teilten sie dies Schicksal nicht mit der festansässigen türkischen Bevölkerung? Auch der Türke hatte sich ja von jeher mit den Nachkommen der raublustigen alten "Gordyäer" herumzuschlagen, deren "Islam" (viele von ihnen sind überhaupt Christen) kaum mehr wert ist als das "Christentum" der Armenier. . . . Angesichts des grundverschiedenen Charakters von Osmanli

und Kurden ist darum auch hundert gegen eins zu wetten, dass—wo wirklich Grausamkeiten vorkamen—sie das Werk kurdischer Nomaden oder . . . armenischer Revolutionäre waren. (36–37)

Because it has to negotiate a path for its new prejudices through such a dense and rooted jungle of old ones, the philoturkic, anti-Armenian German Orientalism of this period requires a convoluted logic that can make an Armenian of a Kurd, if need be. Accordingly, our German author defends the Muslim Ottoman Turks to his primarily Western audience by first "Othering" or orientalizing the Muslim Ottoman Kurds, using this orientalizing device as a stepping stone to the Othering or foreignizing of Christian Armenians, whose very Christianity is used to defamiliarize and exoticize them. And while Barth cannot ever fully collapse the religious distinction between Christian Europeans and Muslim Turks, he can claim that Christianity is irrelevant in modern-day, progressive Europe, adding for good measure that Armenian Christianity is not Christianity proper anyhow. Similarly, while he cannot deny that Armenian property has been stolen by the "wrong kind" of Muslim (that is, Kurds not Turks), he de-exoticizes the crimes and the perpetrators by implying that these acts were merely a more open, honest, Islamic version of Armenians' pernicious, if peaceful and lawful, "theft" of (presumably Turkish) property by means of the financial cunning innate to that people.

In short, Barth's discourse involves three degrees and directions of orientalization or defamiliarization. He orientalizes the Kurds, using this exoticism (their nomadic, barbaric "Islam") to set them apart from civilized Muslims, here the Turks, who, by contrast, are automatically familiarized. He then orientalizes or "Others" the Armenians by distinguishing their Christianity (a potentially familiarizing element) from that of Christian Europe and by implying that the un-Turkish excesses of the barbaric Kurds were in fact the deeds of sly Armenians in disguise. Finally, he exoticizes Lepsius, and other pro-Armenian German or European Christians, casting their philo-Armenian attitude as "unchristliche Wut" (21).

What this demonstrates, aside from the labyrinthine rhetorical tactics required by the German-Turkish alliance in the period of the Armenian massacre, is that Orientalism, in other words the discourses used to legitimize hegemonic behavior, is far more convoluted than suggested by Said's idea of "[Western] knowledge and power creating 'the Oriental.'"[58] Contrary to its name, the mechanism called Orientalism is at work in any strategic projections of difference or familiarity as a means to specific ends. It is a discursive missile that can be directed as easily at and by a German and a Christian as at and by a Turk and a Muslim.

As scholars such as David Kopf, Bernard Lewis, and Richard G. Fox have suggested,[59] the West-to-East Orientalism identified by Said is problematic for several reasons. Most critically, perhaps, it fails to recognize its own orientalizing moment (and concomitant shortcomings as a meta-discourse). It also fails sufficiently to take into account the fact that not all European discourse about the Orient involves essentializing Western projections onto the East in the service of hegemony, and that Orientalism (inasmuch as the concept has any value) has at times had a preservative function, for instance when it *qua* discipline has preserved aspects of another culture for that culture. And, as Pollock noted, a further blindspot of Said's Orientalism is that it fails to recognize that the West-East cultural axis has no monopoly on exoticizing and marginalizing discourses and, if the term Orientalism is to have any currency, it has to be forced to take account of and "include discursively similar phenomena" (*DO, 77*). So, while not denying the reality of colonialist Orientalism, we must recognize the same processes of Othering at work in say National Socialism, the Indian caste system, or the Armenian genocide.

Aspects of the Ottoman-German relationship at the turn of the nineteenth century highlight the inadequacy of the category of Orientalism in its early Saidean form, which still insists on an innate difference between Orient and Occident albeit while critiquing it, and ascribes to Orientalism a strict West-to-East trajectory. To transpose Michael Davidson's idea slightly, a more appropriate way of representing the complex ways in which hegemony works would seem to be "not . . . the usual East-West trajectory, but tendrils sent out from multiple sites."[60] And, if first-degree (original pre-Saidean) Orientalism results in a "partial view of Islam"[61] in every sense, and the second-degree (corrective) Orientalism of Said merely replicates the same problems albeit at a critical remove and couched in postcolonial terminology, this third-degree rhizomic recasting of Orientalism hopes that recognizing the Othering or foreignizing role of the concepts of Orient, Occident, Christianity, and Islam in discursive practices of both East and West will allow a fuller picture to emerge.

Notes

[1] This basic idea is perhaps most succinctly expressed in his often quoted passage that defines Orientalism as "a western style for dominating, restructuring, and having authority over the Orient." Edward Said, *Orientalism* [1978] (London: Penguin, 1984), 3.

[2] See Sheldon Pollock, "Deep Orientalism? Notes on Sanskrit and Power beyond the Raj," in *Orientalism and the Postcolonial Predicament: Perspectives on South Asia*, ed. Carol Appadurai Breckenridge and Peter van der Veer (Philadelphia: U of Pennsylvania P, 1993), 76–133. Further references to this work are given in the text using the abbreviation *DO* and the page number. Of course, the idea of "internal colonialism" dates back much further than this. It was employed by Lenin in *The Development of Capitalism in Russia* and Gramsci in *The Southern*

Question to describe the exploitation of subgroups within a society, and further developed in the 1960s and 1970s, for example by Michael Hechter.

[3] For the first quotation see: Donald Bloxham, *The Great Game of Genocide: Imperialism, Nationalism, and the Destruction of the Ottoman Armenians* (Oxford; Oxford UP, 2005), 14. For the Morrow quotation see: John Howard Morrow, *The Great War: An Imperial History* (London: Routlegde, 2003), 52.

[4] The term "Saidean Orientalism" may seem to conflate the critic of Orientalist knowledge and the hegemonic knowledge he was critiquing. However, the term is used here quite deliberately, because Said's critique is itself still Orientalist, its deconstructions notwithstanding, preserving the spurious central distinction that also underpinned the discourses he is attacking.

[5] For Said this blanket association of Islam with the Orient is valid inasmuch as it was "only the Arab and Islamic Orient [that] presented Europe with an unresolved challenge on the political, intellectual, and for a time, economic levels." Said, *Orientalism*, 74–75.

[6] Jennifer Jenkins, "German Orientalism: Introduction," *Comparative Studies of South Asia, Africa and the Middle East* 24.2 (2004): 97–100; here 99.

[7] Angela Merkel, Speech to the Bundestag, 16 Dec. 2004.

[8] Said, *Orientalism*, 19.

[9] Quoted in Mustafa Gencer, *Bildungspolitik, Modernisierung und kulturelle Interaktion: Deutsch-türkische Beziehungen (1908–1918)* (Münster: LIT Verlag, 2002), 237.

[10] Isabel V. Hull, *Absolute Destruction: Military Culture and Practices of War in Imperial Germany* (Ithaca, NY: Cornell UP, 2006), 268.

[11] Friedrich Naumann, *Asia: Eine Orientreise über Athen, Konstantinopel, Baalbek, Nazareth, Jerusalem, Kairo, Neapel* (Berlin-Schöneberg: Buchverlag der Hilfe, 1913), 164.

[12] Quoted in Donald M. McKale, *War by Revolution: Germany and Great Britain in the Middle East in the Era of World War I* (Kent, OH: Kent State UP, 1998), 9.

[13] Isaac Don Levine, *The Kaiser's Letters to the Tsar: Copied from the Government Archives in Petrograd* (London: Hodder & Stoughton, 1920), 57.

[14] Quoted in "'Gemeines Krämergesindel': Wilhelm II. über die Engländer," *Der Spiegel*, 11 Mar. 1964: 62.

[15] Quoted in Henry Morgenthau, *Ambassador Morgenthau's Story* (Detroit, MI: Wayne State UP, 2003), 112. Further references to this work are given in the text using the abbreviation *AMS* and the page number.

[16] "Morgenthau in Turkey," *New York Times*, 7 Jul. 1918, sec. Editorial, 24.

[17] The total Muslim population of the world was estimated at 232,966,170 in 1906. S. M. Zwemer, E. M. Wherry, and James L Barton, eds., *The Mohammedan World of Today* (New York: Young People's Missionary Movement, 1906), 289.

[18] James L. Barton, "Kaiser and Sultan: Germany's Long Cultivation of the Turks for the Present Unholy Alliance," *New York Times* 14 Jul. 1918, sec. Special Articles, 41.

[19] Kris K. Manjapra, "The Illusions of Encounter: Muslim 'Minds' and Hindu Revolutionaries in First World War Germany and After," *Journal of Global History* 1 (2006): 363–82; here 366.

[20] Ronald Hyam, "The British Empire in the Edwardian Era," in *The Oxford History of the British Empire: The Twentieth Century,* ed. Judith Brown and William Roger Louis (Oxford: Oxford UP, 1999), 47–63; here 48.

[21] According to the 1881 census there were 50 million Muslims in India, making up approximately one-fifth of the subcontinent's total population. See David Lelyveld, *Aligarh's First Generation: Muslim Solidarity in British India* (Oxford: Oxford UP, 1996), 14. By the time of the 1911 census the number had risen to 66,647,299. See *Statistical Abstract relating to British India from 1903–04 to 1912–13* (London: His Majesty's Stationary Office, 1915), http://dsal.uchicago.edu/statistics/1903_excel/1903.007.XLS (accessed 27 Mar. 2007).

[22] For a discussion of the part played by German ethnological discourses in the idea of an anti-British *jihad* see Manjapra, "The Illusions of Encounter."

[23] See John McManners, *The Oxford History of Christianity* (Oxford: Oxford UP, 2002), 199.

[24] Max von Oppenheim, "Die Revolutionierung der islamischen Gebiete unserer Feinde," quoted in Wolfgang G. Schwanitz, "Max von Oppenheim und der Heilige Krieg: Zwei Denkschriften zur Revolutionierung islamischer Gebiete 1914 und 1940," *Sozial.Geschichte* 19.3 (2004): 28–59; here 48.

[25] Schwanitz, "Max von Oppenheim und der Heilige Krieg," 54.

[26] Christiaan Snouck Hurgronje, *"The Holy War": Made in Germany,* trans. Joseph E. Gillet (New York: Knickerbocker P, 1915), 7–8.

[27] Hurgronje, *"The Holy War,"* 16–17.

[28] McManners, *The Oxford History of the British Empire,* 231.

[29] The expression "unholy alliance" was used by James L. Barton in his article for the *New York Times* to describe the strange bedfellows of the Turkish-German alliance. See note 18 above.

[30] For details of how Enver Pasha used two English-built Ottoman battleships to lure Germany into the alliance, see Philip Mansel, *Constantinople: City of the World's Desire, 1453–1924* (London: Penguin, 1995), 370.

[31] Alexander Kiossev, "Megjegyzések az önkolonizáló kultúrákról," *Magyar Lettre Internationale* 37 (2000): 7–10.

[32] Homi K. Bhabha, *The Location of Culture* (London: Routledge, 1994), 36–39.

[33] Welat Zeydanioglu, "'The White Turkish Man's Burden': Orientalism, Kemalism and the Kurds in Turkey," in *Neo-Colonial Mentalities in Contemporary Europe? Language and Discourse in the Construction of Identities,* ed. Guido Rings and Anne Ife (Newcastle upon Tyne: Cambridge Scholars Publishing, 2008), 155–74; here 156.

[34] The term "dhimmitude" was coined by Bat Ye'or to describe the special laws governing Christians and Jews (*dhimmi*) in Islamic states. Bat Ye'or, *Islam and Dhimmitude: Where Civilizations Collide* (Cranbury, NJ: Fairleigh Dickinson UP, 2001).

[35] Hilmar Kaiser, *Imperialism, Racism, and Development Theories: The Construction of a Dominant Paradigm on Ottoman Armenians* (Princeton, NJ: Gomidas Institute, 1997), 2.

[36] Karl May, "Der Händler von Serdescht" in *Auf fremden Pfaden* (1897; repr., Bamberg: Karl-May Verlag, 1952) 199.

[37] James Silk Buckingham, "Unpublished Manuscripts of a Traveller in the East," *The Oriental Herald and Journal of General Literature*, 34.11:91–103; here 94.

[38] Quoted in Artem Ohandjanian, *Armenien: Der verschwiegne Völkermord* (Vienna: Böhlau Verlag, 1989), 208.

[39] Karl Liebknecht, Rosa Luxemburg, and Franz Mehring, *The Crisis in the [sic] German Social-Democracy: The "Junius" Pamphlet* (New York: The Socialist Publication Society, 1991), 41–43.

[40] R. I. Money, "The Irrigation of the Konia Plain," *The Geographical Journal* 54.5 (1919): 298–303; here 298.

[41] Liebknecht, Luxemburg, and Mehring, *The Crisis in the German Social-Democracy*, 41–43.

[42] Paul Lindenberg, *Auf deutschen Pfaden im Orient* (Berlin: Dümmler, 1902), 175–76. Quoted in Malte Fuhrmann, "Denn Orient deutsch machen: Imperiale Diskurse des Kaiserreiches über das Osmanische Reich," http://kakanien.ac.at/beitr/fallstudie/MFuhrmann1.pdf (accessed 27 Mar. 2007).

[43] See also Friedrich Dernburg, *Auf deutscher Bahn in Kleinasien: Eine Herbstfahrt* (Berlin: Julius Springer, 1892), 2.

[44] The Ottomans of the late nineteenth century also saw latter-day European incursions into their territory under whatever guise in terms of the Crusades. "In der politischen und intellektuellen Führungsschicht des Osmanischen Reiches wurde es in den letzten Jahren des 19. Jahrhunderts üblich, die damalige Politik Europas gegenüber dem Islam im allgemeinen und der Türkei im besonderen in einer historischen Parallele zu den Kreuzzügen zu sehen. Sultan Abdülhamid II. äußerte wiederholt die Ansicht, Europa führe gegen ihn und sein Reich einen Kreuzzug im Gewande der Politik—eine Vorstellung, die so ganz abwegig nicht erscheint, wenn man sich jenen Teil der europäischen Publizistik und Literatur des 19. Jahrhunderts vor Augen führt, in dem der Kreuzzugs-Gedanke in modern-kolonialistischem Zusammenhang belebt und gepredigt wurde." Werner Ende, "Wer ist ein Glaubensheld, wer ist ein Ketzer? Konkurrierende Geschichtsbilder in der modernen Literatur islamischer Länder," *Die Welt des Islams* 23.1 (1984): 70–94; here 81.

[45] Perkins has noted that while progress has been made in the last two centuries in terms of Europe's irrational fear of "heathens" and "barbarians," there are two images of Otherness that have proved particularly persistent. The most enduring Others of Europe, she claims, have been Russia and Islam. It is against these that "the Christendom narrative has traditionally sought to define European civilization." Mary Anne

Perkins, *Christendom and European Identity: The Legacy of a Grand Narrative since 1789* (Berlin: de Gruyter, 2004), 255.

[46] Naumann, *Asia,* 141.

[47] Quoted in Norbert Saupp, "Das Deutsche Reich und die Armenische Frage, 1878–1914" (PhD diss., Cologne University, 1990), 112.

[48] Kamakshi Murti has recently noted the need for more attention to be paid to the role played by German missionaries "in actively fostering the . . . colonial agenda." Kamakshi P. Murti, *India: The Seductive and Seduced "other" of German Orientalism* (Westport, CT: Greenwood Publishing Group, 2000), 8.

[49] Henry Goldschmidt, "Introduction: 'Heathens' and 'Jews' in the Colonial Imagination," in *Race, Nation, and Religion in the Americas,* ed. Henry Goldschmidt and Elizabeth McAlister (Oxford: Oxford UP, 2004), 33–34; here 34.

[50] See Thomas Hartmut Benner, *Die Strahlen der Krone: Die religiöse Dimension des Kaisertums unter Wilhelm II vor dem Hintergrund der Orientreise, 1898* (Marburg, Germany: Tectum, 2001), 230.

[51] Coincidentally or not, just at this time the use of Armenian labor on the railway project was considered. See Paul Müller-Simonis, *Durch Armenien, Kurdistan und Mesopotamien: Vom Kaukasus zum persischen Meerbusen* (Mainz: Franz Kirchheim, 1897), 168. At any rate, during later waves of persecution, the Baghdad Bahn project afforded its Armenian laborers some measure of protection. The railway company resisted the attempts of the German officer, Böttrich, head of the railway section of the Ottoman general staff, to deport its Armenian workers for ultimate eradication. See Richard G. Hovannisian, *Remembrance and Denial: The Case of the Armenian Genocide* (Detroit, MI: Wayne State UP, 1999), 92.

[52] Robert Manne has argued somewhat controversially that the two events are not merely contemporaneous but related. He argues that the Ottoman government would not have decided upon the systematic eradication of Ottoman Armenians had they not felt that the tide of war was turning against them. It felt that the empire could not withstand internal dissent at such a critical time, and decided to exterminate what it saw as a dangerous subversive minority. Robert Manne, "A Turkish Tale: Gallipoli and the Armenian Genocide," *The Monthly* 20 (2007): 20–28.

[53] This was certainly part of Nazim Bey's argument in favour of the genocide in early 1915: "It is absolutely necessary to eliminate the Armenian people in its entirety, so that there is no further Armenian on this earth and the very concept of Armenia is extinguished. We are now at war. We shall never have a more suitable opportunity than this." Quoted in G. S. Graber, *Caravans to Oblivion: The Armenian Genocide, 1915* (New York: Wiley, 1996), 87–88.

[54] Quoted in Artem Ohandjian, *Österreich-Armenien, 1872–1936: Faksimilesammlung diplomatischer Aktenstücke,* 12 vols. (Vienna: Ohandjian Eigenverlag, 1995), 4:2710.

[55] Oppenheim, quoted in Wolfgang G. Schwanitz, "Max von Oppenheim und der Heilige Krieg," 43–57.

[56] Rachel Kirby, *The Culturally Complex Individual: Franz Werfel's Reflections on Minority Identity and Historical Depiction in "The Forty Days of Musa Dagh,"* (Lewisburg, PA: Bucknell UP, 1999), 121.

[57] Hans Barth, *Türke, wehre dich!* (Leipzig: Rengersche Buchhandlung, 1898), 37.

[58] Said, *Orientalism*, 27.

[59] David Kopf, "Hermeneutics versus History," *The Journal of Asian Studies* 39.3 (1980): 495–506; Bernard Lewis, "The Question of Orientalism," *The New York Review of Books*, 24 Jun. 1982: 49–56; and Richard G. Fox, "East of Said," in *Edward Said: A Critical Reader*, ed. Michael Sprinker (Oxford: Blackwell, 1992), 144–46.

[60] Michael Davidson, *Guys Like Us: Citing Masculinity in Cold War Poetics* (Chicago: Chicago UP, 2003), 78.

[61] Alexander Macfie, *Orientalism* (London: Longman, 2002), 4.

9: German-Islamic Literary Interperceptions in Works by Emily Ruete and Emine Sevgi Özdamar

Kate Roy

I N THIS CHAPTER I WILL CONSIDER the encounter with Islam through the medium of language in literary texts by the contemporary Turkish-German writer Emine Sevgi Özdamar and the late nineteenth-century Arab-German writer Emily Ruete.[1] The contexts in which the two women write are of course vastly different. Özdamar's short story "Großvater Zunge" and her novel *Das Leben ist eine Karawanserei hat zwei Türen aus einer kam ich rein aus der anderen ging ich raus*[2]—her texts that engage most directly with Islam—were published in 1990 and 1992 respectively, at which time Turks and other ethnic minorities were already a substantial presence in Germany. In contrast Emily Ruete's *Memoiren einer arabischen Prinzessin* (now titled *Leben im Sultanspalast*)[3] was published in 1886, while her text *Briefe nach der Heimat,* probably written in the 1880s,[4] came to light after her death in 1924 but was first published in German only in 1999: she belongs far more to the European era of colonization, Orientalism, and the scramble for Africa. And yet Özdamar and Ruete share much in the critical "Islamic" encounters with German and Germany that they produce. This is demonstrated not least by the fact that there was support for publication of Ruete's *Briefe* in 1999 and that her *Sultanspalast* has recently been republished.[5] As Fedwa Malti-Douglas observes, "her textual journey is more than simply a set of memoiristic . . . flourishes that keep the reader's feet firmly planted in the nineteenth century."[6]

It is significant that both writers have chosen German as the language of their literary expression, even if they use it very differently. Ruete, the first known Arab woman to publish an autobiography[7]—the *Memoiren*—is considered to have pared down language in comparison with other memoir writers of her time, while Özdamar's creative use of language has often been a focus of reviewers' comments. Some, for example, refer to the "ungewohnte, verzaubernde" language in *Karawanserei.*[8] However, Özdamar's language could be considered to be "overloaded" in a Deleuzian sense, where the grammatical constants of the major language are repeated and varied, sometimes under the influence of other languages, to the extent that their dynamics create a multitude of voices that deterritorialize German.[9] Though a century apart, Ruete's and Özdamar's literary responses to Islamic culture in a German setting both complicate the dynamics of intercultural communication.

Emine Sevgi Özdamar (1946–), as a well-established Turkish-born author who has lived in Germany for more than thirty years, needs little introduction. She first traveled to Germany at the age of nineteen, spending two years in Berlin as a guest worker, then trained as an actress in Turkey, then returned to make her career in theatre in Europe. She later began to write, while continuing to act, direct, and appear in films. Sayidda Salme (1844–1924), who became Emily Ruete, was born in Zanzibar, the daughter of Said bin Sultan, the Sultan of Oman and Zanzibar. She left Zanzibar in 1866 after her relationship with the German trader Heinrich Ruete and her pregnancy were discovered. She traveled first to Aden where, joined by Heinrich Ruete some months later, she converted to Christianity, taking the name Emily. They married, before setting out for Hamburg in 1867. Three more children were born to the couple (the first had died soon after birth), but Heinrich Ruete later died in an accident, leaving Emily, who had only recently attained a degree of fluency in German, to raise the children alone. She decided to remain in Germany in the belief that her husband would have wished their children to be "richtige Deutsche."[10] Later in life Ruete became "a pawn in the German East Africa policy"[11] when she decided to visit Zanzibar in 1885, seeking to claim her inheritance.[12] Bismarck used her situation as a premise for an attempt to secure Zanzibar for Germany. He saw Ruete's son as a potential German heir to the throne, and furthermore as someone with whom he could outmaneuver the English, who were, for their part, close to Sultan Barghash, Ruete's brother. While this strategy proved unsuccessful and Ruete herself no longer useful to German colonial aspirations, it ultimately led to the Heligoland-Zanzibar Treaty of 1890, whereby Tanganyika became a German colony and Zanzibar a British protectorate.[13]

Ruete wrote about her return to Zanzibar for the first time in nineteen years in the following terms: "Der Mensch ist zu einem großen Teile nur das, was Leben, Erfahrung und die gebietenden Verhältnisse aus ihm machen: ich verließ meine Heimat als vollkommene Araberin und als gute Muhamedanerin, und was bin ich heute? Eine schlechte Christin und etwas mehr als eine halbe Deutsche!" (S, 252). E. van Donzel notes that the last sentence of this passage—on which the editor of the Briefe, Heinz Schneppen, places such weight[14]—is crossed out in what was intended to become Ruete's revised edition of Sultanspalast.[15]

My exploration of how Islam is encountered in these texts will cover two related aspects: how, through language, Islamic identities come into being and are juxtaposed in the text, and how encounters are effected within language. Özdamar mixes the sacred and the profane through language in which Sufism, *ghazals*,[16] and Koranic verses all come together, and the Arabic script itself is rendered through descriptions of its form in the German language. These techniques demonstrate how multiple Islamic voices are always already part of German, and how German is reterritorialized in them. In contrast, Ruete's texts are overtly pedagogical, writing back in response to the discourses of the time, and armed with their terminology. She does not dispute the vocabulary of Orientalist discourse (speaking of "uns Orientalen," for example (*BH*, 126)), but the context in which she deploys it is telling. Schneppen has argued that in *Sultanspalast* she speaks as a "Christian," however this interpretation seems questionable.[17] It is true that Ruete positions herself more ambiguously in *Briefe*, however in *Sultanspalast* she uses the pronoun "wir" when referring to Muslims positively, and similarly positions herself as an "Orientalin" when critiquing German behavior.

Özdamar's "Großvater Zunge" and Ruete's *Briefe* both play out in Germany. The backdrop for "Großvater Zunge" is that of a still-divided Berlin; for the *Briefe* it is first Hamburg, then Dresden, Rudolstadt, Berlin, Cologne, and again Berlin, the only German city in which Ruete claims to have felt somewhat at home (*BH*, 130). As literary works there are differences to account for: "Großvater Zunge" is clearly a fictional text, whereas Ruete's letters are (apparently) autobiographical. However, Ruete's text is fictionalized by its very presentation as letters, a fiction that is enhanced in the German edition of 1999, where inserted titles break the text into short segments, each with a heading (such as "Neue fremde Welt" (*BH*, 17)). This insertion of titles at once isolates them as individual letters and reveals how they have been positioned by the editor. In fact Ruete's original text is continuous, written in three notebooks with the text ending abruptly.[18]

Uncertainty surrounds the identity of the addressee of Ruete's letters, positioned as a friend in Zanzibar. Schneppen writes: "Wenn sie in ihren *Memoiren* über Sansibar schreibt, denkt sie an Deutschland. Schreibt sie in ihren *Briefen* über Deutschland, ist Sansibar der Bezug. Beide Texte leben vom Vergleich. Beide gehören zusammen."[19] In fact both texts have Germany as their object. While apparently addressed to an Arabic speaker in Zanzibar,[20] the letters are written in German. Their point of reference is Germany, and the fiction of the (unidentified) addressee in Zanzibar allows Ruete to speak her mind.

Both authors re-place[21] the German language to control it as a means of communication—but in different ways. Ruete's text can be seen as didactic, in that she takes up the language in a manner that Annegret

Nippa, an editor of Ruete's memoirs, has described as almost ethnographic in its prolific narration of the details of everyday life, turning this "knowledge" back on Germany in the *Briefe*.[22] Like the protagonist of Jean Rhys's *Wide Sargasso Sea*, a writing-back narrative that reshaped our understanding of *Jane Eyre*, Ruete refers to Europe as a dream (*BH*, 10, 17), already implying the unthinking of the power dynamics that create and then oppose the center (Europe) and the margins. In this sense, the mere fact of writing in German is the challenge Ruete presents to an Orientalist discourse and particularly to a discourse of knowledge of the Other. Nippa writes that it was the "schnörkellose Sprache" of Ruete's memoirs that caused the public of the time, more used to "leichte Memoirenliteratur," to be somewhat taken aback.[23] Ruete's placement of herself as "unkultiviert" in relation to German society and her simultaneous subversion of this notion through the context of her statements produce a similar effect in her letters. For example, when describing her first visit to a church in Germany, Ruete declares that she finds it arrogant of people not to bow down before God, then comments: "Auch empfand mein nach abendländischen Anschauungen völlig unkultiviertes Gemüt es gar zu entweihend, als ich sah, daß mitten im Gebet um Geld gebettelt wurde" (*BH*, 42). Here she constructs herself as uncivilized, yet immediately *de*constructs this notion with clear ideas of what civilized behavior should be.

In her writing Ruete plays with the terms "Orient" and "West," terms that Edward Said has demonstrated to be made of human effort, "partly affirmation, partly identification of the Other."[24] In so doing, she enters into an already structured debate of "the absolute demarcation between East and West, which . . . had been years, even centuries, in the making."[25] Yet it is within this debate that she challenges power structures by engaging in parodic mimicry in Bhabha's sense, as "double articulation . . . which 'appropriates' the Other as it visualizes power," while repeating a difference that "poses an immanent threat to both 'normalized' knowledges and disciplinary powers."[26] The mechanisms of the discourse provide in themselves the means for subverting it. In mimicking the discourse, and thereby challenging Europe's belief in its knowledge of the Orient,[27] and the power that this implies, she undercuts the hierarchical relationship between the supposed norm and supposed Other.

For Özdamar, a hundred years later, re-placing language becomes a re-positioning, in which German is infused with plural Islamic voices. In her use of apparently "flowery" language, we could question whether she is also playing with Orientalist discourse. Praise for the exotic charm of the foreignness of her language in reviews was meant to be a positive celebration of her innovative use of language, but it is also patronizing, in terms of the ethnicization it implies, as well as in the assumption that this innovation had sprung from the "immigrant" author's supposed lack of command of German.[28] We could however read Özdamar in a very different way. In overloading language she blows apart the categories of "West" and "Orient" in this text. As Deleuzian scholar Christian Jäger describes, "Variation, die sich bis Überfrachtung steigert" multiplies the constants (or norms) of a language to the extent that they lose their power through sheer accumulation.[29] Özdamar's re-placement, or de- and reterritorialization of German in the Deleuzian sense, produces affect, where features in the text assault readers and "[disrupt] the everyday and opinionated links we make between words and experience."[30] This disruption is mediated through the poetic to help us to recognize what is already present in German and in Germany. Thus for both writers it is through texts written in the German language that they transform German encounters with Islam.

Ruete's Germany was, she states, not particularly plural in comparison to Britain and France: she notes that there are not many "exotische Menschen" and feels that she is "beständig beobachtet" when she goes out to a concert or to the theatre (*BH*, 27). Yet, despite this apparent curiosity, she also encounters people's lack of willingness to acknowledge their own ignorance and their belief that they already "know" about her:

> [Man hatte] schon die tollsten Geschichten von der Araberin zu erzählen gewußt. Unter anderm, ich sei so dick wie ein Faß, obgleich ich zu jener Zeit eher einer Bohnenstange ähnlich sah. Ich hätte die Haare und Gesichtsfarbe einer Negerin. Meine Füße sollten so klein sein wie die Füße einer Chinesin. (*BH*, 28)

This context of "ignorant knowledge" vis-à-vis Arabs and Islam is perpetuated, Ruete believes, by the travel writers she despises. In *Sultanspalast* she attacks their descriptions of the situation of women:

> Ich bin überzeugt, man wird mich als geborene Orientalin für parteiisch halten und es wird mir doch nicht gelingen, die schiefen und falschen Ansichten, welche in Europa und besonders in Deutschland über die Stellung einer arabischen Frau gegenüber ihrem Manne im Schwunge sind, gründlich auszurotten. Der Orient ist eben trotz der erleichterten Verbindungen noch viel zu sehr das alte Fabelland, und über ihn darf man ungestraft erzählen, was man will. Da geht ein Tourist auf einige Wochen nach Konstantinopel, nach Syrien, Ägypten, Tunis oder Marokko und schreibt dann ein dickleibiges Buch über Leben, Sitten und Gebräuche im Orient. (*S*, 131)

Ruete demonstrates that she is aware that it is the question of knowledge that is at stake and the notion that those who "know" may not believe her version of events. She cites an Arab proverb: "Wer dich nicht kennt, kann dich auch nicht bewerten" (*BH*, 94). It is with this notion that she formulates a critique of the central Orientalist assumption of knowledge.

Ruete had also to contend with published accounts of her life, for example, the biographical portrait of her in the *Illustrierte Zeitung,* which came out in 1885, a year before her *Memoiren.* We encounter here a kind of Christian fable-style rewriting of her story, of "die wunderbare Umwandlung einer arabischen Prinzessin in eine ehrsame deutsche Dame," woven into a romanticized account of the circumstances surrounding her journey to Germany:

> Sie wurde Christin und folgte dem ihr angetrauten Gatten in dessen ferne Heimat. Hier wurde die Afrikanerin Schritt für Schritt in das Wissen der modernen europäischen Zivilisation eingeführt. . . . Als scharfdenkende Orientalin erkannte sie jetzt, daß, so verwandt sich auch die Moral der Lehre Mohammeds mit der christlichen Lehre zeigt, in der engen Begrenzung des Islams doch ein Hindernis für die geistige Entwicklung der Bekenner derselben enthalten ist, während sich den Christen die Aussicht bietet, durch das Streben nach einem idealen Vorbilde den denkbar höchsten Grad der Vollkommenheit zu erringen.[31]

Ruete writes against the "fairytale," as Nippa has identified: "Gegen diese Reduktion, dieser rein literarischen Existenz als Märchenfigur wehrte sie sich, zuerst indem sie schwieg, später indem sie schrieb."[32] Importantly, her writing challenges not just what Germans believed they knew about her, and the implied erasure of her own story but also the implied notion that an Arabian princess is not "ehrsam," and, crucially, the reading of Islam, here presented as a barrier to self-improvement.

In response, within a section of the letters that Schneppen has provocatively titled "Zwischen Islam und Christentum,"[33] she deconstructs the "geistige Entwicklung" supposedly open to her now she is freed from the "constraints" of Islam:

> Dem Pastor genügte es offenbar, zu allem, was er mir sagte in einer mir völlig unverständlichen Sprache bei der Taufe und darauf folgenden Trauung, mich das "Yes" aussprechen zu hören, denn weiter war ja nichts mehr nötig. Von da an war ich für das Christentum gewonnen, mit dem Übrigen sollte ich jedenfalls allein fertig werden. (*BH,* 15)

Interest in her conversion is limited to the superficial. She relates her disappointment that Christians were not keen to guide her spiritually: "Ich kam mir selbst so verächtlich falsch vor, eine Christin zu heißen und doch keine klare Idee zu besitzen, *was* das Christentum überhaupt bedeutet. Ich wußte davon nur so viel, wie gerade im Koran steht, weiter aber nichts" (*BH,* 16). Guidance comes in a different sense. Ruete balances her "ungebildeter Geschmack" for theatre with her discomfort at seeing priests mocked in a play in a manner she sees as "unehrerbietig." She relates her neighbor's response: "Als meine Nachbarin meinen Unmut darüber merkte, sagte sie mir ganz lakonisch: 'Aber Sie sind doch eine Protestantin, und was gehen Sie die katholischen Priester an?'" (*BH*, 35). Again, the viewpoint of those who are supposedly "ehrsam" and have cultured tastes is deconstructed by the juxtaposition of notions of "Ehre." The Arabian princess, whom the *Illustrierte Zeitung* had effectively suggested was not "ehrsam," and who constructs herself here as having an "ungebildeter Geschmack," resists the "unehrerbietig" treatment of the priests. She strengthens her position by stressing her adopted role as the convert from Islam: "Es war mein für das Christentum unreifer Geist so wenig ermutigt von dem, was ich gesehen und gehört hatte, daß ich mehr bekümmert als erfreut nach Hause ging" (*BH*, 35).

Nippa relates how Ruete's memoirs were not quite what the public of the time were expecting, providing them with more than the "Nacherzählen vordergründig faszinierender Ereignisse."[34] In the case of the *Briefe* Ruete's children wavered over their publication, deeming them potentially "viel zu traurig und zu intim," and finally entrusting them to the Leiden Orientalist Christiaan Snouck Hurgronje with instructions that they should not be published without family approval until after 1940.[35] Yet rather than being too sad and intimate, they were perhaps a little too uncomfortable for the reading public of the time, unused to the Orient writing back. As has been argued about postcolonial literatures, Ruete's writing abrogates "the constraining power" and appropriates "language and writing for new and distinctive usages."[36]

Özdamar's writing has a different contextual setting, with a Muslim community now established in German and Germany. "Großvater Zunge" is firmly situated in Berlin. As it opens, the narrator has crossed into West Berlin and stands outside Ibni Abdullah's door in Wilmersdorf. Having had her first Arabic lesson with him, she then takes her first five Arabic letters to a park in East Berlin near the *Berliner Ensemble,* a pattern that is repeated. When Ibni Abdullah travels to Saudi Arabia, the love-sick narrator goes to the Kurfürstendamm to count Arabs. After her lessons begin again, Ibni Abdullah confines her to his room for forty days. When the narrator subsequently leaves the room, she returns to the Ku'damm to count the Arabs backward to zero (*GZ*, 45). The journey into Arabic and back is seen as a journey back to the Turkish past as a means to go forward, and all the words she re-gathers through the Arabic lessons acquire at the same time their German translations.

By Özdamar's time Germany is visibly ethnically plural. Far from the lack of "exotische Menschen"—as Ruete terms it in Orientalist-style vocabulary—we can cite the Berlin info magazine *Zitty*'s poster marketing campaign of the early 2000s entitled "Die Stadt bin ich," which displayed close-up portraits of the faces of Berliners of "all colors, lifestyles, ages, and sexes," a strategy that, as Ruth Mandel identifies, simultaneously commodified otherness and gave these Others "a stake in the very city that often marginalized and 'foreignized' them."[37] In "Großvater Zunge" the narrator is able to count Arabs on the Ku'damm and, later, to count back down from sixty-six (*GZ*, 45):

> Ich ging zum Kudamm, stand da, zählte alle arabischen Männer, die da vorbeikommen, ich setzte mich in ein arabisches Restaurant, schickte den Kellner sechsmal Wasser holen, damit ich sechsmal Araber zähle. Ich ging den arabischen Frauen mit Kopftüchern hinterher, ihre schwangeren Töchter neben ihnen, ich will unter ihre Röcke gehen, ganz klein sein, ich will ihre Tochter sein in Neukölln. Turmstraße. (*GZ*, 21–22)

The Muslim presence sparks the narrator's apparent desire to adopt an Arab/Islamic identity, a desire that is later tempered. In "Großvater Zunge" the German language is made to bear more than one "Islamic" language, and in so doing the text's creative engagement with social forces that stratify and territorialize identity around static notions such as "East" and "West"—notions played with and subverted, but nonetheless adhered to, by Ruete—is effected. For this reason my focus in this chapter is not on what the text *says* as such,[38] but on what it *does* through the move from the didactic to the poetic. Thus, rather than attempting to categorize its content, I advocate a way of reading the text for how it "works," for the transformative forces inherent in it, in the cramped conditions of political constriction, forced intimacy, and language contact and contamination, the space from which minor literature emerges. Metaphors of the Arabo-Islamic literary past are evoked through the language of the text, and, in their new context, open up the narrative, so that a relationship with the Arabic script, and perhaps more significantly for my argument, the presence of, and dialogue between, different Islamic "languages" are mediated through German. Here the German language is not an entity that is different from these languages; indeed, it is no longer even distinct from them.

The connotations of the Arabic lessons are fused with the notion of the Koran as the first book published in Arabic, and the language as "directly dispensing Allah's word and law."[39] Its bond with the script is religious and iconic, especially for non-Arabic speakers of Islamic origins.[40] In Özdamar's text, however, the poetic treatment of the script—the connection to the script as a visual entity—produces something different from its symbolic meaning. Here the protagonist, and by implication the reader, find themselves at a distance from the meaning of the words but simultaneously able to recognize their physicality, their power as objects to express. Reclaiming the words-as-script in a different way serves to distance the texts from the content of the Koran, creating something impenetrable, but at the same time taking control of the image. The language's permanent status either as

"Arabic" or as a language with religious connotations is lost, and the protagonist enters into a different relationship with the language:

> Es kamen aus meinem Mund die Buchstaben raus. Manche sahen aus wie ein Vogel, manche wie ein Herz, auf dem ein Pfeil steckt, manche wie eine Karawane, manche wie schlafende Kamele, manche wie ein Fluß, manche wie im Wind auseinanderfliegende Bäume, manche wie laufende Schlangen, manche wie unter Regen und Wind frierende Granatapfelbäume, manche wie böse geschreckte Augenbrauen, manche wie auf dem Fluß fahrendes Holz, manche wie in einem türkischen Bad auf einem heißen Stein sitzender dicker Frauenarsch, manche wie nicht schlafen könnende Augen. (*GZ,* 18)

The words, personified through German, become more than the language they apparently convey. They function "exotically," in that they are rendered strange and their "otherness is manufactured" through perception.[41] The protagonist's response to the letters divorces the words from their linguistic meaning and creates in the reader the same feeling of estrangement experienced by the narrator in reading and relating to the Koranic text, just as the narrator's desire to approach and grasp the *ghazal* imagery—a principal focus of this chapter—later in the text is her alternative to the discipline of learning Arabic through the Koran.[42]

Brigid Haines and Margaret Littler discuss the interweaving Koranic quotations juxtaposing Allah's "judgmental wrath" (in the text recited by Ibni Abdullah's students) with his "creative goodness" (the narrator's "inner voice") and the interplay of Koranic quotations speaking of "the endless damnation of sinners" and a Turkish folksong speaking of "the endlessness of desire."[43] Their suggestion that this represents the juxtaposition of Sunni Islam and a resistant, heterodox "Turkish" Islam could be developed further by considering the text as intertextually related to a classical Arabic literary form known as *mu'āradah,* "according to which one person will write a poem and another will retaliate by writing along the same lines, but reversing the meaning."[44] My reading of this text through *mu'āradah* and the imagery of the *ghazal,* as will be discussed below, is doubly transformative and productive in the context of "Großvater Zunge." Apparently orientalizing language in fact functions as strategic exoticism[45] to disrupt binaries of "East" and "West" by transforming German to carry the resistance or confrontation between two Islamic languages. Crucially, it functions to reterritorialize different Islamic languages in German. German is hereby involved in a multiple becoming-Islamic. It is becoming other than itself—intense—and is then re-grounded in aspects of semantics and vocabulary.

The narrator's resistance to Ibni Abdullah's constant invocation of the more austere passages from the Koran is related through imagery from Sufi love poetry: it is the intense divine love of Sufism that serves as a model for all the forms of love found in *ghazal* poetry. The narrator's words effect a German reterritorialization of the *ghazal*, for example in the following passage: "Weingebender, bring mir Wein, nimm meinen Verstand mit Wein weg . . . Knabe, bist du aus einer Huri geboren . . . deine Wimpern sind Pfeile, die mein Blut tranken, deine saubere Stirn ist ein verfluchtes Meer" (*GZ*, 28). The cup-bearer, or *saki*, a young man who serves wine to the assembly, is one of the standard symbols of the *ghazal*, who unites religion and human love.[46] He is often a metaphor for God, or for God's message, "which inspires . . . as wine inspires the drinker" (*HL*, 160). A *huri* is a nymph who serves the needs of the faithful in paradise (*HL*, 308). The *ghazal* passages immediately follow a description of a meal setting in "Großvater Zunge" and do not form a part of the conversation between Ibni Abdullah and the narrator. Instead they appear freely in the text, unconstrained by speech marks, as a sort of extra-subjective monologue. The lines link to Ibni Abdullah's prosaic comment "Du trinkst mit demselben Tempo wie ich, sehr schön" (*GZ*, 28), and are apparently addressed to him, as the *saki*, both the giver of wine and (through the Arabic lessons) of religion, and as the human object of the narrator's love.

It is also through the coordinates of the *ghazal* that the narrator is identified as both lover and beloved: "Ich sprach wie die Nachtigall, blaß geworden wie die Rosen" (*GZ*, 32). The nightingale symbolizes the lover, who sings to his unfeeling, beautiful beloved, the rose (*HL*, 310–11). Again feelings are not rooted in the subjectivity of the character of the narrator but rather conveyed by the external textual features—in this case *ghazal* references. Both nightingale and rose appear throughout "Großvater Zunge," and it is significant that when the narrator first meets Ibni Abdullah "seine Hand roch nach Rosen" (*GZ*, 15).[47] Like the rose he proves unresponsive (wanting a pure love) and will ultimately become the object of an unfulfilled love.

It is with examples such as these that "Großvater Zunge" functions with both *mu'āradah* and *ghazal*, which contribute importantly, reterritorialized into two distinct languages that battle it out through the German text. Here, in becoming other than itself, the German language is freed from its origins in particular identities and histories, its surface detail becoming instead a vehicle for the *creation* of identities. The overloading of language has transformative potential. The notion of a non-uniform and mobile identity, created through a disruptive use of language,[48] points to how Özdamar's writing could be considered to be disruptive of hierarchies rather than merely subverting them. Disrupting German, as here, is what Deleuze and Guattari term a "deterritorialization of the mouth, the tongue and the teeth,"[49] where it undergoes a multiple becoming-Islamic through *ghazal* and Koranic imagery.

In the years between the writing of Ruete's *Briefe* and Özdamar's "Großvater Zunge" Germany has acknowledged itself as a country of immigration and has branded itself a "world-open," cosmopolitan society.[50] Seemingly, much has changed. Yet it would be appropriate to question whether the changes have been less fundamental than one might suppose, given the renewed popularity of Ruete's texts which, though challenging the supremacy of the "West," reproduce a clear "East"-"West" divide. Here, we could juxtapose Germany's aborted colonial aspirations (as encapsulated in Ruete's case and writings) with what Özdamar describes as the creation of colonies "on [its] home territory," following the migrant worker agreements of the 1960s.[51] Indeed, Ruth Mandel sees Germany's world-openness as a "selective cosmopolitanism," marginalizing the experience of migrants such as Turkish-Germans who, despite having "now penetrated nearly every stratum of German society," are still perceived as *Ausländer* by virtue of "an increasingly essentialist vision of culture—'Islamic vs. Christian,'" through which they are now "more likely to be seen as Muslims in an unwelcoming environment."[52]

The two texts that provide the main focus of this chapter were written a hundred years apart but were not published a hundred years apart—in fact the publication of Özdamar's text predates that of Ruete's. Despite how she has been read or edited, Ruete's insertion of herself into Orientalist discourse with critical intent can now be read as a writing back in the postcolonial manner. Malti-Douglas's review of 1996 has argued that Ruete's writing, with its "sharp comparisons between Europe and the Orient . . . should be required reading for all those interested in the Middle East, in Muslims in the West," and, furthermore, that it has "the ability to insert itself into many of the contemporary debates on the Muslim world both in the East and the West."[53] Özdamar's writing, on the other hand, while it can also be seen as self-orientalizing, renders that dualist thinking obsolete—she is more fundamentally disruptive of binaries in her use of language. Furnishing us on the one hand with a new perspective on an old confrontation, and on the other with a poetics that insists on its transformation, ultimately both texts can be read as critical interventions in the German encounter with Islam.

Notes

[1] I have opted to call Sayidda Salme/Emily Ruete only Emily Ruete in this chapter. This is in the interests of consistency, as her texts were published under the name "Emily Ruete, geb. Prinzessin Salme von Oman und Sansibar." There does not appear to be a consensus on naming conventions among editors and commentators: while Nippa and Freeman-Grenville opt for "Salme," Schneppen calls her "Salme" when talking about her life pre-baptism and "Emily Ruete" afterwards, van Donzel calls her "Emily Ruete," and Julius Waldschmidt alternates and also invents the appellation "Salme-Emily." See, for example, Annegret Nippa, "Nachwort von Annegret Nippa," in Emily Ruete, *Leben im Sultanspalast,*

ed. Annegret Nippa (Hamburg: Die Hanse, 2007), 269–88; G. S. P. Freeman-Grenville, "Introduction," in Emily Said-Ruete, *Memoirs of an Arabian Princess,* ed. G. S. P. Freeman-Grenville (London: East-West Publications, 1994), vii–xiii; Heinz Schneppen, "Einleitung" and "Nachwort," in Emily Ruete, *Briefe nach der Heimat,* ed. Heinz Schneppen (Berlin: Philo, 1999), 7–8 and 145–96; E. van Donzel, "Introduction," in Sayyida Salme/Emily Ruete, *An Arabian Princess between Two Worlds: Memoirs, Letters Home, Sequels to the Memoirs, Syrian Customs and Usages,* ed. and intro. E. van Donzel (Leiden: E. J. Brill, 1993), 1–134; and Julius Waldschmidt *Kaiser, Kanzler und Prinzessin: Ein Frauenschicksal zwischen Orient und Okzident* (Berlin: trafo verlag, 2005).

[2] Emine Sevgi Özdamar, "Großvater Zunge," in *Mutterzunge: Erzählungen* (Cologne: Kiepenheuer & Witsch, 1998), 15–48; Emine Sevgi Özdamar, *Das Leben ist eine Karawanserei hat zwei Türen aus einer kam ich rein aus der anderen ging ich raus* (Cologne: Kiepenheuer & Witsch, 1992). Further references to "Großvater Zunge" will be interpolated in the text, where it will be referred to as *GZ.*

[3] Emily Ruete, *Leben im Sultanspalast.* Further references will be interpolated in the text, where *Sultanspalast* will be referred to as *S.*

[4] Emily Ruete, *Briefe nach der Heimat,* ed. Heinz Schneppen (Berlin: Philo, 1999). Further references will be interpolated in the text, where the *Briefe* will be referred to as *BH.* E. van Donzel argues that there is some evidence that early sections of the letters were based on notes made on Ruete's voyage out from Zanzibar in 1866. See Van Donzel's footnote 2 to his English translation of the letters in *An Arabian Princess between Two Worlds,* 408.

[5] *Leben im Sultanspalast* was reissued in German in September 2007 (see bibliographical references above), and in English in March 2008: Emily Said-Ruete, *Memoirs of an Arabian Princess of Oman and Zanzibar: The Extraordinary Life of a Muslim Princess between East and West* (Coventry: Trotamundas P, 2008).

[6] Fedwa Malti-Douglas, *"An Arabian Princess between Two Worlds: Memoirs, Letters Home, Sequels to the Memoirs, Syrian Customs and Usages,* by Sayyida Salme/Emily Ruete." *Journal of the American Oriental Society* 116.4 (1996): 794.

[7] Freeman-Grenville, "Introduction," vii.

[8] This example, from the *Braunschweiger Zeitung,* is cited in Nilüfer Kuruyazıcı, "Emine Sevgi Özdamars *Das Leben ist eine Karawanserei* im Prozeß der interkulturellen Kommunikation," in *Interkulturelle Konfigurationen: Zur deutschsprachigen Erzählliteratur von Autoren nichtdeutscher Herkunft,* ed. Mary Howard (Munich: iudicium, 1997), 179–88; here 183.

[9] Deleuze and Guattari define overloading as a process leading to the disempowerment of the majority language (here, German) not through a metaphoric use of language but through its proliferation, creating a "mobile paraphrase bearing witness to the unlocalized presence of an indirect discourse at the heart of every statement." Gilles Deleuze and Félix Guattari, *A Thousand Plateaus: Capitalism and Schizophrenia,* trans. Brian Massumi (London and New York: Continuum, 2004), 115.

[10] Nippa, "Nachwort," 281.

[11] Van Donzel, "Introduction," 81.

[12] In fact, as a Christian convert Ruete was no longer entitled to her inheritance under Muslim law. See Van Donzel, "Introduction," 79.

[13] See, for example, Van Donzel and Waldschmidt for a further discussion of Ruete in the context of German East Africa.

[14] Schneppen, "Nachwort," 172.

[15] Van Donzel, "Introduction," 32.

[16] The name given to one tradition of Arabic love poetry: Roger Allen, *An Introduction to Arabic Literature* (Cambridge: Cambridge UP, 2000), 172–73.

[17] Schneppen, "Nachwort," 171.

[18] For a format that is closer to the original see E. van Donzel's English translation: Ruete, *An Arabian Princess between Two Worlds,* 407–510.

[19] Schneppen, "Nachwort," 162–63.

[20] Van Donzel, "Introduction," 4–5; Ruete, *Briefe,* 130.

[21] The "re-placement" of the postcolonial text is centered on "an attempt to control the processes of writing," and to "[restructure] European 'realities.'" Replacing discourse by asserting control over it effects a "writing back," a challenge to the worldview that shapes center and periphery. Bill Ashcroft, Gareth Griffiths, and Helen Tiffin, *The Empire Writes Back: Theory and Practice in Post-Colonial Literatures* (London and New York: Routledge, 2002), 32 and 77.

[22] Nippa, "Nachwort," 280.

[23] Nippa, "Nachwort," 280. Both texts are written in quite a different style from the translation of her letter in Arabic to her brother (given in Van Donzel, "Introduction," 49–63). In German, Ruete seems intentionally to avoid linguistic exoticism.

[24] Edward W. Said, *Orientalism* (London and New York: Penguin Books, 2003), xii.

[25] Said, *Orientalism,* 39.

[26] Homi K. Bhabha, "Of Mimicry and Man: The Ambivalence of Colonial Discourse," in *The Location of Culture* (London and New York: Routledge, 1994), 121–31; here 122–23.

[27] Said, *Orientalism,* 39–40.

[28] As discussed in Moray McGowan, "'Sie kucken beide an Milch Topf': Goethe's *Bürgergeneral* in Double Refraction," in *Language—Text—Bildung: Essays in Honour of Beate Dreike,* ed. Andreas Stuhlmann and Patrick Studer in cooperation with Gert Hofmann (Frankfurt am Main: Peter Lang, 2005), 79–88; here 85–86. Additionally, Tom Cheesman outlines how Turkish-German intellectuals such as Şenocak and Göktürk "saw Özdamar's work as relaying an exotically picturesque Orient by occluding the diverse traditions of modern Turkish literary and intellectual culture and thereby reinforcing the view, commonplace among European intellectuals, that Turkey is a backward, peasant society with little or no developed, modern culture." Tom Cheesman, *Novels of Turkish German Settlement: Cosmopolite Fictions* (Rochester, NY: Camden House, 2007), 73.

[29] Christian Jäger, *Minoritäre Literatur: Das Konzept der kleinen Literatur am Beispiel prager- und sudetendeutscher Werke* (Berlin: Deutscher Universitätsverlag, 2005), 32.

[30] Claire Colebrook, *Gilles Deleuze* (London and New York: Routledge, 2002), 23.

[31] Cited in Schneppen, "Nachwort," 172–73.

[32] Nippa, "Nachwort," 275–76.

[33] See Ruete, *Briefe*, 15. While arguably indicative of Ruete's personal position post-baptism, Schneppen's invocation of the "clash of civilizations" here is profoundly discomforting in its contribution to the "manufacturing" of this notion, which Said describes as ongoing in our time. See Said, *Orientalism*, xxii.

[34] Nippa, "Nachwort," 280.

[35] Schneppen, "Einleitung," 7, "Nachwort," 191.

[36] Ashcroft et al., *The Empire Writes Back*, 6.

[37] Ruth Mandel, *Cosmopolitan Anxieties: Turkish Challenges to Citizenship and Belonging in Germany* (Durham, NC, and London: Duke UP, 2008), 314.

[38] This has been well covered in the critical literature. See, for example, Bettina Brandt, "Collecting Childhood Memories of the Future: Arabic as Mediator Between Turkish and German in Emine Sevgi Özdamar's *Mutterzunge*," *Germanic Review* 79.4 (Fall 2004): 295–315; and Brigid Haines and Margaret Littler, "Emine Sevgi Özdamar, 'Mutter Zunge' and 'Großvater Zunge' (1990)," in *Contemporary Women's Writing in German: Changing the Subject* (Oxford and New York: Oxford UP, 2004), 118–38.

[39] John A. Morrow, "Arabic Instruction in France: Pedagogy or Politics?" *International Journal of the Humanities* 4.6 (2007): 17–24; here 17–18. Morrow further cites "the saturation of spirituality into the Arabic language that took place via the Qur'an and the Sunnah with the arrival of Islam" (17).

[40] Morrow, "Arabic Instruction in France," 18.

[41] Graham Huggan, *The Postcolonial Exotic: Marketing the Margins* (London: Routledge, 2001), 13.

[42] Haines and Littler similarly argue that the relationship with the script itself represents the narrator's preferred alternative to the disciplined instruction of Arabic through the Koran ("Emine Sevgi Özdamar," 125).

[43] Haines and Littler, "Emine Sevgi Özdamar," 135–36.

[44] As outlined by Barbara Harlow, "*Mu'āradah* [has] the literal meaning of confrontation, opposition, or resistance." Barbara Harlow, *Resistance Literature* (New York and London: Methuen, 1987), 24.

[45] Huggan, *The Postcolonial Exotic*, 32.

[46] Ralph Russell, *Hidden in the Lute: An Anthology of Two Centuries of Urdu Literature* (Manchester: Carcanet, 1995), 143. Further references will be interpolated in the text, where this work will be referred to as *HL*.

[47] Haines and Littler provide an alternative reading of the significance of this phrase as evoking the Turkish proverb "roses bloom where the master strikes" ("Emine Sevgi Özdamar," 131).

[48] This notion is put forward by Elizabeth Boa, in "Sprachenverkehr: Hybrides Schreiben in Werken von Özdamar, Özakin und Demirkan," in *Interkulturelle Konfigurationen: Zur deutschsprachigen Erzählliteratur von Autoren nichtdeutscher Herkunft*, 115–38; here 135.

[49] Gilles Deleuze and Félix Guattari, *Kafka: Toward a Minor Literature*, trans. D. Polan (Minneapolis: U of Minnesota P, 1986), 19.

[50] Mandel, *Cosmopolitan Anxieties*, 14.

[51] Cited in David Horrocks and Eva Kolinsky, "Living and Writing in Germany: Emine Sevgi Özdamar in Conversation with David Horrocks and Eva Kolinsky," in *Turkish Culture in German Society Today*, ed. David Horrocks and Eva Kolinsky (Oxford: Berghahn, 1996), 46–54; here 52–53.

[52] Mandel, *Cosmopolitan Anxieties*, 12–14.

[53] Malti-Douglas, "*An Arabian Princess between Two Worlds*, by Sayyida Salme/ Emily Ruete," 794.

10: Dialogues with Islam in the Writing of (Turkish-)German Intellectuals: A Historical Turn?

Karin E. Yeşilada

WITH THE TERRORIST BOMBINGS of Istanbul 2003, Madrid 2004, and London 2005, Islamist terrorism finally reached European cities in the aftermath of the US bombings of 11 September 2001. In 2006 bombings were averted in Germany, but it was clear that Germany was not safe from Al-Qaida aggression.[1] Discussions of a "tödliche Toleranz" toward Muslims in Germany followed.[2] Federal anti-terror measures even reached the universities. In early 2007 the Bavarian Office for the Protection of the Constitution (*Verfassungsschutz*) published a demand addressed to the academic staff of Bavarian universities for more intense surveillance of unconstitutional Islamist activities in and outside Bavaria. The demand asked staff to report any instances of remarks indicating radical Islamic tendencies, Islamist activities, or indeed anything hinting at sudden changes in lifestyle on the part of either students or teaching staff.[3] With Muslims accounting for 4% of Germany's population,[4] the German educational system is faced with a growing number of German and migrant-German students with a Muslim background. And yet Islam still is a subject dealt with only by the media and, sadly, has almost no place on the academic curriculum. This seems particularly strange when many intellectuals of the second immigrant generation, who have grown up and been educated in Germany, come from a cultural background combining the *Koran* and Goethe's *West-östlicher Divan*.[5] This is true for authors such as the Turkish-German Zafer Şenocak (born 1961) or the Persian-German Navid Kermani (born 1967), who both grew up in Muslim families, went to German schools, and graduated from German universities. Is their personal history as migrants quite so linear, and is their occupation with Islam and the *Koran* suspicious, after all? And what about German converts? Are Muslim intellectuals in Germany to be considered a threat to the system or as partners in dialogue? Encountering Islam in contemporary German literature means looking more closely and in a more differentiated manner at how German-Muslim writers respond to the ongoing debate on Islam in Germany.

Among the many Muslim-German intellectuals Zafer Şenocak will receive most attention here, as he is one of the most prominent Turkish-German Muslim intellectuals working in contemporary German literature. In his new collection of essays, *Das Land hinter den Buchstaben* (2006),[6] he examines current Islamic positions both in and outside Germany. With a nod to the "other side," Christoph Peters's novel *Ein Zimmer im Haus des Krieges* (2006)[7] will be discussed, as it is about a German convert who has turned into an Islamistic terrorist. These examples provide interesting internal and external perspectives on Islam in Germany, as well as presenting their authors' views on the subject.

The debate on Islam in Germany changed radically after 9/11, when it became clear that the leading terrorists involved in the attack had previously lived unnoticed in Germany. The emergence of so-called Islamic undercover-agents or "sleepers" suddenly put all Muslims in Germany, and especially those of Arabic or Turkish background, under suspicion.[8] In this light, Turkish migration to Germany was now considered not only a failure but also a danger, as Günther Lachman argues in *Tödliche Toleranz*.[9] With a generation of supposedly failed, non-integrated, underdog migrants turning into radicals, Europe faced what he calls the danger of the return of totalitarianism in the form of neo-Islamism. One of the effects of this ongoing debate was that many intellectuals with a Muslim background found themselves on the defensive because of their religious identities.

Being "Muslim" has in fact become a central marker of identity in the aftermath of the 2001 terror attacks, not least because Samuel Huntington's powerful if harsh thesis of the cultural clash between the Western and Islamic worlds seemed to have been proved right.[10] In his critique of Huntington, Amartya Sen centers his argument on the idea of a diversity of identities and biographical outlines.[11] Accordingly, the notion of a singular identity is an illusion, for a person is subject to a wide range of influences that simultaneously help to constitute his or her identity, including nationality, geographical location, gender, race, class, or even private matters such as nutritional habits or taste in music. Sen warns that reducing this complexity to just one aspect of cultural identity, or defining a person merely through religion, leads to dangerous antagonisms between supposed singularities, fomenting potential conflicts worldwide.[12] To reduce Muslims to their Islamic identity is also to ignore the diversity of Islam: Turkish Muslims, for example, may be entirely different from Saudi Arabian Muslims. Moreover, as Sen points out, strong beliefs do not necessarily exclude liberal thinking. Western notions of the tolerance of Muslims are based on the misunderstanding that religious tolerance and political tolerance are one and the same. For Sen, "fundamental" belief does not stand in opposition to democratic thinking.[13]

Unaffected by Sen's differentiated ideas, today's public discourse in Germany positions writers who had previously been perceived as migrant-German writers in a new role as public Muslims, and it no longer asks about their fictional or poetic writing but rather about their Islamic upbringing and attitudes. More or less involuntarily representing their new (or rather: newly discovered) Muslim identity, many of these intellectuals, who (or whose parents or grandparents) come from oriental countries, draw on their inside knowledge.[14] Iranian-German writers such as Navid Kermani or SAID, who both grew up with Islam, give account of their personal experience with Islamic culture. In a collection of essays and interviews, former president of the German PEN-club SAID (born 1947) reacted to the debate by defining his own position outside Islam. The title of his book, *ich und der islam* (2005)[15] is thus possibly rather misleading, for SAID actually insists upon his intellectual distance from religion. His younger fellow-countryman Navid Kermani, a graduate in Oriental Studies, approaches Islam through his publications and studies on Islam and Muslim intellectuals.[16] In a forthcoming publication he gives an account of (his) Muslim identity and explores Muslim life in Germany in particular.[17] However, the rhetorical title *Wer ist wir?* indicates that Kermani, like many other Muslim intellectuals, feels uncomfortable at being crudely labeled a Muslim. In contrast, Turkish-German author Feridun Zaimoğlu makes a clear point of being a "German Muslim."[18] In his literary and theatrical work he creates Muslim figures and repeatedly refers to Islam as part of Turkish migrant identity, as well as claiming ownership of a brand of "German Islam" as part of his own identity. One of his latest theatrical works puts Islamic figures and themes on stage, while his presence at the national "Islam Konferenz" drew attention to his views on Islam and Kemalism.[19]

Within this chorus of Muslim intellectual voices Zafer Şenocak represents a differentiated position of his own. Born in Turkey, he came to Germany at the age of nine, starting his literary career as a poet and translator of Turkish and Osmanic poetry in the early 1980s. Emerging as an essayist from the early 1990s onward, Şenocak has been the most important Turkish-German commentator on the relations between Turks and Germans, Turkey and the West, and matters that can be described broadly as oriental-occidental. While his literary prose and poetry attract less critical attention (although he will get an entry in the forthcoming edition of the *Kindler Lexikon der Weltliteratur*), his essayistic work has gained him the reputation of a public intellectual.[20] As Leslie A. Adelson rightly states, Şenocak's role as commentator started in a decade that "began not only with German unification but also with the Persian Gulf War."[21] While the former historic event brought about a distinction between Germans and non-Germans, the latter created divisions between Muslims and the West. German Turks, Adelson argues, were confined to the role of the Muslim "Other" in both cases.

Islam, though immanently present from the beginning, had never been at the center of Şenocak's writing until September 2001. After 9/11 Şenocak began to comment on Islamic perspectives, responding to the new demand for supposed experts on Islam ("Islamexperten") in the media. During the 1990s Şenocak analyzed the complex modern situation of Turks in Germany in the light of the historical relationship between the German Reich and the Ottoman Empire, exploring an epoch of shared German-Turkish history. He also reminds German readers of the specific fate of Islam under Kemalism in Turkey: following the new state ideology of Mustafa Kemal Atatürk, religion was reduced (or rather, banned) to the private realm and therefore lost its formerly powerful political role.[22]

This latter aspect is at the heart of his latest essays; the Turkish-Islamic cultural heritage seems to be what is hinted at by the title of *Das Land hinter den Buchstaben,* his fourth essay collection. The subtitle *Deutschland und der Islam im Umbruch* suggests major changes in both Germany and Islam. The forty-five essays date from September 2003 to August 2006 and are grouped into five chapters: while the eponymous first section (9–25) has three biographical essays, the main section, "Zwischen Koran und Sex Pistols" (27–111), explores Islam generally in twenty essays, which are followed by five essays on specific aspects of Islam in the third section, "Warnung vor heiligen Stätten" (113–36). The fourth section takes the focus back to Germany and its Muslim immigrants ("Deutschland: Standortübungsplatz," 139–53), whereas the last section places the focus on the self-reflexive aspect of his writing, entitled as it is "Dichter gibt Auskunft" (189–215). How then does Şenocak position himself as a (Muslim) writer in the current discourse on Islam?

In the very first essay, "Mein Vater, ein türkischer Lebenslauf" (*LHB,* 11–18), Şenocak tells his father's life story. This is a biography marked by the clash produced by the cultural revolution of 1923. Kemaleddin Şenocak, born in 1926, a typical child of the republic ("Republikkind"), grew up in the years of the cultural revolution, yet despite the general trend toward modernization he still stuck to "his Islam." His biography combines the influences of Turkish modernity on the one hand and Islamic fanaticism on the other. Şenocak senior remained skeptical of modernity and pleaded for a greater emphasis on religion in this new Turkish secular state. He started editing an Islamic journal in the 1950s and later went to Germany ("weil es ein freies Land war"), distancing himself from the people who were later to become the leading figures in Turkey's Islamic movement (such as Necmettin Erbakan, whom Şenocak senior openly criticized).

Zafer Şenocak discusses the pros and cons of the Turkish revolution as regards the effects on Islam and the Turkish Muslims. He describes how his father's initial activism on behalf of Islam slowly developed into a sort of fanaticism. There is constant debate on this subject between father and son, the latter criticizing the former for his double standards. In fact, Şenocak senior's demands for greater freedom were meant only to serve his own narrow purpose, and his aims cannot be read as a manifesto for universal freedom of speech. Zafer Şenocak, however, draws a parallel with the broader Turkish context when he remarks that freedom is the freedom to think differently or independently ("die Freiheit des Andersdenkenden"; *LHB*, 16)—something that had to be learned the hard way in Turkey.

Şenocak also reflects on this in the context of the current situation in Germany. By telling his father's life story, he presents not only a personal story but also Turkish history and its complex implications for a heterogeneous Turkish society. In doing so he thus undermines the German monolithic, stereotypical notion of Turkey and the Turks. In accordance with Amartya Sen's ideas, Şenocak presents Turkey as a multifaceted culture, as a dialogue partner with manifold cultural aspects and historical backgrounds. Şenocak demands a dialogue with Turkey and its new Islamist government, insisting that this offers Germany a historical opportunity that should not be missed. He concludes with a note about his father and how he helped him to see things differently:

> Die widersprüchliche Gestalt meines Vaters hat mir geholfen, vermeintliche Gegensätze nicht immer in scharz-weiße Bilder zu gießen. Die Grautöne sind immer da und aussagekräftig für den, der sie wahrnehmen will. "Orient" und "Okzident" mögen nach wie vor die Denkschablonen von Kulturalisten und Nationalisten aufrechterhalten. Sie existieren in unserer kommunikativen Welt aber nur noch als irrationale Fiktionen. Sie sind falsche, gefährliche Zeugen. (*LHB*, 18)[23]

This nod to Edward Said's critique of Orientalism is what Leslie A. Adelson calls the "poststructuralist mode of thought and orientation" in Şenocak's writing.[24] Never dutifully indebted to any school of thought, Şenocak has pleaded elsewhere for a "negative Hermeneutik," a method that allows him to think well-known patterns anew and question them thoroughly.[25] This negative hermeneutic produces a heterogeneous, hybrid picture of Islam, of Turkey, of Turks, and of Turkish culture. Writing, as Matthias Konzett puts it, "against the grain" of stereotypes, Şenocak does not remind only Germans to reflect; Turks must also consider their positions.

To a greater extent than in his previous work in the essay genre, *Das Land hinter den Buchstaben* offers a topography of Zafer Şenocak's intellectual development from childhood onward. In a kind of continuation of his father's story, the third essay, "Das Geheimnis der Nachmittage" (*LHB*, 21–25), describes his Turkish childhood between Islam and Kemalism.

The first-person narrator's (and probably Şenocak's) Muslim father and his Kemalist, secularist mother lived together on the basis of a mutual contract that strictly regulated the coexistence of the worldly and the religious, as well as the education of their child: "Obwohl Gott zwischen ihnen stand . . . , hielt ihre Ehe, weil sie einen Vertrag gemacht hatten, an den sie sich strengstens hielten" (24). Obviously this could be read simply as an autobiographical comment by the Turkish author. Yet on another level the story of the nuptial contract serves as a parable of the coexistence of Islam and laicism in a democracy. And it is a parable meant for Germany and Turkey alike, for both countries have ongoing debates on how Islam is to be integrated into society.

This story is also about how Şenocak, as a young boy, was left to wonder about what was going on in the locked room, where his father assembled every Friday with his Muslim friends, while his mother left to go shopping with her women friends. The locked room with its secret society sparks the little boy's imagination: he imagines that there might be aeroplanes in there, or perhaps men kissing one another in secret.[26] In this essay, the "Geheimnis der Nachmittage" stands for the alluring mystery of Islam and for the impact of the mysterious on Şenocak's own writing, as the narrator concludes from his contemporary point of view: "So blieb mir die Welt der Freitagnachmittage verschlossen. Ich sollte dankbar dafür sein, denn diese verborgene Welt hat lange Zeit meine Phantasie angeregt. Das verschlossene Zimmer wurde zu einem Hinterzimmer meiner Gedanken" (*LHB*, 23).

In an earlier essay Şenocak described how his writing myth (*Schreibmythos*) arose in an atmosphere of rationalism and of mysticism, a contradictory tension that characterized his parents' home.[27] In *Das Land hinter den Buchstaben* he dedicates the whole first chapter to the mystic side of Islam, a realm that stimulates the author's fantasy. Naming it the *Country Behind the Letters,* he once again looks beyond the alleged literal-mindedness of orthodox Islam and opens an entirely different horizon instead, the undefined, the contradictory, the unnamed realm of an in-between space that begins where orthodoxy ends: a realm "behind the letters." This coincides with Homi K. Bhabha's notion of the Third Space,[28] and with what Şenocak often depicts as a position neither here nor there, but *beyond* ("jenseits"), and as the center of his writing.[29] Şenocak's scepticism of binary oppositions is shared by other writers of Muslim origin.[30]

The second chapter of Şenocak's essay collection, called "Zwischen Koran und Sexpistols," explores the clash between Muslim culture and modernity, traditionalist religion and Western culture. Twenty essays form the very heart of the reflections on this complex matter. The title essay, "Zwischen Koran und Sexpistols" (29–33), starts with the assertion of the necessity of a dialogue between Muslims and Christians. Yet Şenocak also demands dialogue within the Muslim community itself:

"Nicht der Dialog der Religionen, sondern ein Dialog unter den Muslimen ist erforderlich. Wo aber findet er statt? Von wem wird er geführt?" (29). Even though every terrorist attack nowadays produces the same ritualized reactions of media attention, the posing of questions as to "why" and "how," the call for dialogue between religions and so on, no real discussion seems to take place, for one fundamental question remains unasked: "Die Muslime nämlich müssten sich die Frage stellen, warum die Attentäter ausgerechnet aus ihren Kreisen kommen? Woher der Hass kommt, der so weit geht, nicht nur andere sondern auch sich selbst zu zerstören?" (29). By addressing the Muslims and referring this central question back to them, Şenocak makes his own critical position clear. He demands of today's Muslims self-exploration and a readiness for skepticism and self-critique.[31]

For Şenocak personally, literature became the crucial link between modernity and Islam. Mystical literature, particularly the poems of the Turkish medieval Sufi poet Yunus Emre, which Şenocak translated in the late 1980s,[32] was of enormous help in his effort to bring together separate worlds, as he points out: "Ohne die Arbeit an Emres Werk hätte eine harte Grenze meine Innen- und Außenwelt getrennt, wäre ich zwischen Koran und Sexpistols ein Opfer unvereinbarer Gegensätze geworden" (*LHB*, 31–32). This breaking down of boundaries was clearly vital to his own creative work. He states also: "Für meine kreative Arbeit, letztlich für meine Existenz schlechthin wurde die Durchlässigkeit dieser Grenzziehung zur Voraussetzung" (32). It may well have been the skepticism and humility typical of Sufi poetry that shaped Şenocak's dialectical attitude. All questions are reflected back onto the self rather than projected onto the Other. This approach is skeptical rather than apodictic. Şenocak resumes his primary question of dialogue in the essay, pointing out the necessity for self-understanding. In the dialogue with Islam, the West therefore needs to be more thoughtful in terms of asking the questions: "Die Fragen, die wir an den Anderen stellen, auch an uns selbst zu richten. Einen Dialog im Inneren führen, bevor wir das Wort an den Anderen richten" (33). Reflection, he concludes, is a primary condition for any dialogue.

Şenocak opens a new field by bringing up the idea of Islamic renaissance. He does so out of the conviction that contemporary Islam desperately needs role models of tolerant figures from its own history in order to take the attention away from a Sharia-centered fanaticism. In so arguing, Şenocak adopts the role of a cultural mediator, a "Kulturvermittler." This comes naturally to the artist who believes in the power of art and philosophy: Islam, he argues, needs role models who can do better than merely repeat the rules of the Sharia. What are needed are artistic interpreters with a love for the arts and philosophy (*LHB*, 39).[33] An example of this would be the last Ottoman Kalif Abdülmecid, who was a talented painter of nudes—something unthinkable by contemporary Islamic standards.[34] Here Şenocak refers to his earlier criticism (in 1994) of the new fundamentalist movement, which was led only by engineers and technicians, who had no understanding of diversity, contradiction, or skepticism, and who preferred black-and-white thinking to the more complicated hermeneutics of the in-between.[35] A decade later, and in the wake of the new Islamic terrorism, Şenocak deliberately enlarges on this matter, presenting many examples from an epoch of Islamic Renaissance, when critical thinking and creative belief were still highly valued. What he demands is an overcoming of "das mentale Ghetto," as he calls it, and a critical attitude toward tradition ("Islam übersetzen"; *LHB*, 54), but he also calls for a rewriting of Western curricula, which generally tend to ignore Muslim philosophers totally (53). And Şenocak enters a religious-philosophical argument when he justifies this demand for critical thinking: truth, he says, lies with God and not with the believer. The latter is just searching for the truth and is thus skeptical and humble (57) and certainly nothing like the apodictic, self-righteous fundamentalists, whom he constantly denounces.

In his strong criticism of Islamic fundamentalism Şenocak still exhibits a dialectical approach toward Islamic and non-Islamic views. Using the example of the Mohammed cartoons controversy, which had led to violent protests all over the Muslim world in 2006,[36] Şenocak first criticizes the Danish newspaper, the *Jyllands Posten*, and its editor, whose attitude, according to Şenocak, aimed at provoking the Muslim fanatics rather than discussing Islam and its theological principles. "Is this really what is left of European critical, progressive thinking?" he asks (*LHB*, 43), wondering if the distorted image of Islam current in so many editors' minds still reflects the European Enlightenment. However, Şenocak also attacks Muslim fanatics sharply for their violent reactions and for not knowing better than to reproduce and live up to the European cliché of the Muslim radical. In this way, he argues, reality proved the cartoons right in the way that they depicted the Muslim as a terrorist, as a migrant who cannot be integrated, as a potential danger to an open Western society (44).

Şenocak explores the impact of the subsequent debate ("Karikaturenstreit") upon European societies in terms of the rising disillusionment with multiculturalism. Quoting the chief editor of the *Jyllands-Posten*, who considered the integration of cultures an impossible project (as Şenocak quotes him: the "gulf between Western culture and the Muslim world" was "bigger than the Grand Canyon"), the Turkish-German author reminds his readers of the fact that metropolitan cities such as Berlin, London, or Paris are actually located precisely in that "Grand Canyon." He warns against Europe's clinging to "homogenisierende Kulturphantasien" (*LHB*, 44) and consequently resembling the Muslim world to a greater and greater extent; in doing so he questions the theory of a clash of civilizations in general. Furthermore, the author refers to a contextual shift; Islamophobia is replacing anti-Semitism in right-wing propaganda, and a slogan like "Kauft euer Gemüse nicht bei Muslimen" (44) certainly rings a bell for him.

While the theoretical discourse inherent to the cartoon controversy was mainly focused on the binary oppositions of freedom of speech versus censorship, and of Muslim Aniconism (Bilderverbot) versus blasphemy, it also brought up the aspect of the counter-Enlightenment of Muslim society in general.[37] Şenocak, on the other hand (and many other Muslim intellectuals with him), is more interested in the tradition of Islamic Enlightenment, which he traces back to earlier centuries. Following his Iranian-German colleague SAID in this respect, Şenocak reminds his readers that there had been dialogue and interaction between Muslim, Christian, and Jewish cultures for hundreds of years, in places like Al-Andalus.[38] Seeing in this a model for an Islamic renaissance, Şenocak demands a new era of coexistence of different cultures. He therefore calls on his fellow Muslims to rediscover the rich tradition of Islamic philosophy, a tradition that, having been erased from European curricula, has also vanished from the Muslim collective memory, leaving the field open for fanaticism and fundamentalism. Trying to show examples of how that could work, Şenocak emphasizes the need for translations of existing Islamic literature and philosophy and the need for contemporary Muslim philosophers who could help transform Islam into a modern religion, as well as stressing the importance of a new form of language to enable controversial thinking.[39]

Analyzing the structural problems of Islam, Şenocak suggests a need to decipher its inner logic, distinguishing between Samuel Huntington's notion of a clash between different cultures and what he sees as a cultural clash within Islamic culture itself (*LHB*, 47). With the traditional feeling of the superiority of the Muslim world toward other cultures comes the tendency to ignore the challenges of the modern world—the "Denkfaulheit" for which his father had reproached his fellow Muslims (15). Consequently, Zafer Şenocak urgently demands an honest and thorough analysis of the real reasons behind the vicious circle of terror and violence, and therefore a discussion of the culturally immanent problems of Islam. Still far removed from such a discussion, contemporary radical Islam appears to Şenocak to be suffering from a "lebensbedrohliche Fieberattacke in der Modernisierungskrise." However, any dialogue with Islam has to be based on differentiation and ambiguity, as Şenocak explains in two central essays that explore the structures of a possible dialogue with Islam. These essays, published under the programmatic title "Spielräume für Mehrdeutigkeit I" and "II" (45–52), address Western and Muslim readers alike. Şenocak reminds them of a fatal misunderstanding between Western and Muslim societies, which manifests itself in the former ignoring the constituent violence in the latter. Any dialogue with Islam is doomed from the beginning if the West acts rationally and skeptically in a dialogue while Muslims act as representatives of a traditional religion with an absolute claim to truth (49). As long as this mismatch exists, the dialogue will not work—a view shared by scholars, too.[40]

The dialogue between Islam and Christianity, as Şenocak repeatedly points out, was once facilitated by shared heritage. Authors as recent as Johann Wolfgang von Goethe or Alphonse de Lamartine could still fall back on knowledge about Islam and its principles. How can it be, Şenocak ponders, that this knowledge has vanished from collective European memory? The positive "scope of ambiguity," as he calls it, thus emerges from an absence, from the void in European consciousness that has replaced the memory of cultural coexistence in former epochs. Likewise, the achievements of Islam have been obliterated from the Muslim heritage, turning, as Şenocak complains, Muslims into "Analphabeten ihres eigenen kulturellen Erbes" (*LHB*, 51). In order to take up the dialogue where it once was interrupted by so-called "holy wars," both sides need to meet as equals and open themselves up to self-criticism. Şenocak argues that at the center of any debate that is meant to be constructive there has to be self-criticism, and that criticism of the other can only be launched from a self-reflective attitude. This is the foundation of a "Gespräch mit Spielräumen für Mehrdeutigkeit" (51), of a dialogue with scope for ambiguity. For the poet Şenocak this ambiguity is echoed in Islamic mysticism, and he affirms that it still can be traced in his recent poetic work.[41]

Being anything but an advocate of simple arguments, Şenocak deploys his principle of skepticism and dialectical thinking throughout his entire literary work. In his fictional prose he uses irony as a means to undermine fixed identities, and he often leads his figures into labyrinths in order to deprive them of any orientation. Indeterminacy becomes a major principle in narratives where "gender, text, nation and origin" often enough dissolve, as Moray McGowan has pointed out in an essay on Şenocak's male prose figures.[42] Though not obviously or avowedly Muslim, these protagonists (as, for example in his third prose book *Der Erottomane*, 1999) represent the Turkish-German man. But while they might be expecting a Muslim prototype, the German reading audience never get what they expect, for "Şenocak's Turkish-German man," explains McGowan, "is postmodern, polymorphous, sometimes indeed androgynous, affirming and exploring the dissolution of boundaries"[43]—in short, a complete nightmare to any ordinary Muslim radical. In this respect Şenocak's routine deployment of pornographic language and images, as seen in *Der Mann im Unterhemd* as well as in *Der Erottomane*,[44] goes against the rigid notion of cleanliness and purity of a Sharia-focused, radical Islam.

As a prose author, Şenocak deliberately writes against the grain of Muslim conformity, transferring the skepticism of earlier Muslim philosophy to his fiction. The topographies of his erotic narration stand for what he calls "Die Vermessung des dunklen Kontinents" (as the essay is called; *LHB*, 59–62). Şenocak's essays on Islam, as well as his literary prose, create a realm of ambiguity, a metaphorical topography behind the letters, and mark what Leslie A. Adelson calls the "Turkish Turn" in contemporary German literature.[45]

Moving now toward German literature and its encounters with Islam: the dialogue between Islam and the West appears at the center of Christoph Peters's *Ein Zimmer im Haus des Krieges,* which was published in August 2006 to great acclaim. It featured at the 2006 Frankfurt Book Fair, alongside John Updike's *Terrorist* and Kiran Nagarkar's *Gottes kleiner Krieger,* two novels on similar themes that were published in German translation that same year.[46] At a time when suitcase bombings had been averted only by luck in Germany, the German reading audience was presented with three new novels, all featuring a Muslim terrorist as protagonist. Though not too unexpected in the global context of the September 2001 attacks and the wave of terror that has spread out over Europe since then, the figure of an Islamic radical is exceptional in contemporary German literature, since very few contemporary German (that is, German-born) writers have created Muslim protagonists.[47] The Muslim generally does not yet have a role or a voice of his own in contemporary German literature.

In this respect Christoph Peters (born 1966)[48] provides the readers of his novel *Ein Zimmer im Haus des Krieges* with a surprise, as the hero Abdullah is neither of Muslim nor of foreign origin. Abdullah's real name is Jochen Sawatzky, and he is a German convert to Islam. Given that a growing number of Germans have converted to Islam over the past years, Peters' hero reflects a historical development as well as offering the possibility for identification, since he is of the same cultural background as most of his German readers. The novel is set in Egypt in 1993 and is divided into two narratives. The first part (*ZHK*, 9–82) follows a group of Muslim terrorists on their way from a secret camp in the mountains of the Egyptian desert to the temple area of Luxor, which they plan to bomb. They are, however, ambushed and overwhelmed by the Egyptian military. Six of the nine terrorists are killed in action; three, among them the protagonist, are wounded and imprisoned. The narrative reports the events of one day (14 November 1993) in a highly dramatic way. Suspense is created as the first-person narrator, Jochen Sawatzky, alias Abdullah, slowly prepares himself for the forthcoming raid, only to face death some few hours later. The second part of the novel finds Sawatzky in solitary confinement in an Egyptian prison. The German ambassador to Egypt, Claus Cismar, who is introduced as the second protagonist, deploys all diplomatic means to save the German convict from the probable death penalty. Their three meetings in prison result in dialogues, in the course of which the diplomat tries to understand the terrorist's motivation for his actions, but without any success. Alongside these scenes we are offered episodes from Cismar's private life in Egypt—he is unhappily married to a German theatre critic and starts an affair with a colleague from the French embassy. In the end Cismar collapses with an acute stomach ulcer and symptoms of stress and has to leave Cairo in a hurry before the Sawatzky case is resolved. Apparently the German terrorist is sentenced to death and hanged. The second part of the narrative covers the period from 15 November to 14 March and the greater part of the novel.

This text is technically interesting, using various voices—first or third-person, inner monologue, administrative report, and scriptural quotation. The action can thus be viewed from a personal, political, theological, or administrative perspective. The various perspectives are maintained in order to thwart any simple understanding of events. The failed terrorist attack comes as a surprise to both terrorists and readers at the end of part 1, and the result of Cismar's unsuccessful efforts to get the convict out of prison is only revealed at the end of the novel. A second line of suspense is created through Sawatzky's and Cismar's confrontation during their meetings in prison; here the novel develops the idea that the protagonists are themselves conflicting personalities. Two very different men, who at the same time are very much alike, negotiate their points of view. Cismar had once favoured leftist radicalism and now enjoys a bourgeois life in a leading position as the representative of the German state. Sawatzky got deeply involved in a version of Islam, turned into a terrorist, was convicted, and now faces the death penalty, but he is not willing to compromise. Diplomacy meets real radicalism; existential ennui meets existential wrath. With the dialogue with Islam being staged literally, the novel centers around the key question of why somebody would become so fanatical as to kill for an ideology. In this way Peters echoes public discourse after the September 2001 attacks.

The protagonist's profile is established retrospectively. Jochen Sawatzky suffered from the typical unsettled childhood with an absent father, an American GI, and a mentally unstable, equally absent(-minded) mother.[49] Because of his interrupted schooling, drug experiences, and petty crimes, the youngster gradually became alienated from society, until he hit rock bottom. Redemption then came through Islam, specifically through a group of young Muslim radicals and through an Arab woman. Having fallen in love with the beautiful Arua, Jochen not only wanted to convert to Islam but at the same time developed an ambition to make amends and to give her proof of his courage. Thoroughly detesting the system that failed him, he now wants to fight it. Sawatzky's mission is a strange mixture of romanticism (he imagines how Arua will cry at the news of his heroic death; 25), determination, and despair: "Wer seine Wunschvorstellungen dem Kampf auf Gottes Weg vorzieht, endet als Kleinbürger" (25), he says, repeating a slogan common to any revolutionary commitment. His commitment is, however, to God, as he constantly recites *suras* from the *Koran,* affirming the Holy Book's revelatory impact on him:

> Man will flüchten, sich an einem geheimen Ort verstecken, für alle Zeit unauffindbar sein. Aber das Buch ist stärker. Es hält einen fest, bricht den Widerstand. . . . So ist es gewesen. . . . Ich habe auf meiner Unvoreingenommenheit beharrt, und doch ist passiert, wovon die Gläubigen rund um den Erdball berichten. . . . Ich redete mir ein: Es ist nur eine Übersetzung, sie kann keine Wirkung haben. Trotzdem: Zum ersten Mal, seit mein Gedächtnis etwas vermerkt, herrschte Ruhe. Und sie kehrte wieder, immer wenn ich las. (32–33)[50]

The account of his personal revelation shows that the former outcast from German society has now become part of the *umma,* the worldwide community of believers who share his personal experience of being overwhelmed by a spiritual feeling. His complete submission to the authority of the divine brings him the spiritual peace for which he always wished. What he experiences is the well-known experience of personal salvation through spirituality, which can happen in any religion. But he also gives proof of what Şenocak criticizes as the unreflected claim to truth of an Islamism that is merely focused on the orthodox repetition of the *Koran* instead of its interpretation.[51] In this way, the convert's new name, Abdulla, hints at his new role as a "servant of Allah" (its literal meaning).

Sawatzky comes to embrace terrorism via the political activity of his new peer group of Islamists in Germany, led by the Egyptian student Karim, through whom the German convert gets involved in the political context of the radical Islamist movement in the Arab world.[52] Peters depicts the political environment in Egypt with reference to the Middle East conflict, the 9/11 attacks, and the ensuing war in Afghanistan, and also evokes the issue of European tourism to Egypt. Islamist terrorism is pointedly aimed at Western tourists in order to damage the Egyptian government by restricting its most important source of foreign exchange. By bombing the classic tourist sites, such as the temple of Luxor, they hope to force the government into giving up its pro-Western policy and its rigid suppression of Islamist activities.[53]

Peters elaborates on the different aspects of Islamist politics and their context by presenting the official reaction of the Egyptian government (mirrored in the diplomatic notes), as well as voices from the Egyptian general public (for example, Cismar's chauffeur, who supports Islamism). While the panic of the European tourists is anticipated by the terrorists, the German diplomatic community acts rather indifferently to the ongoing conflict. Cismar's own German wife is more frightened than his French lover, who displays a more critical attitude. The European community is heterogeneous in itself, yet distinct from the Egyptians.

In trying to liberate the German terrorist from prison, Claus Cismar thus represents an isolated position.

The reason behind this is explained in terms of his own political background. The son of an East-German baron who was a National Socialist official, Cismar grew up in a Catholic family in the East-German countryside. He was a law student in 1968 and was politically influenced by this epoch. Though different from the less privileged Sawatzky, the young Cismar, too, had tended toward radicalism and sympathized with the German radical Rote Armee Fraktion (RAF), partly because he was ashamed of his father's political heritage: "Er schämte sich" (155). But the more radical the RAF became, the more he distanced himself from the political escalation, believing in gradual change through institutions rather than through killings:

> Man konnte Einzelpersonen töten, gegen Strukturen halfen auch Bomben nicht. Was blieb, war "der lange Marsch durch die Institutionen" . . . Die Entscheidung war ein Opfer. Sie bedeutete den Abschied von Helden und Taten, die mit ihrer Entschlossenheit und Kraft alles zum Guten wenden konnten. Statt dessen wurde er Teil des Systems. (155)

Like Sawatzky, Cismar, too, "converts," but his conversion is not a glorious one, as he is merely converted into a member of the bourgeoisie. This enables him, nevertheless to make his way through the system, taking on the representative role of ambassador; subsequently he consolidates his position through marriage to a bourgeois woman who is completely ignorant of his political past.[54] Cismar now uses his position to make contact with the young German radical. Even though he is confronted with difficulties during their meetings, he is determined to keep up the dialogue, in order to get to know as much as possible about the convict for the sake of freeing him (*ZHK*, 195). Their discussion touches on general evaluations of the two different political movements. To Cismar they are very much alike in their propagandistic aspect: the Islamists phrases do not differ much from those of the German terrorists of the 1970s, except for the fact that "Gott spielte damals keine Rolle" (132). Yet Sawatzky fiercely rebukes the post-1968 movement for its "materialism," for merely being concerned with power and property, without touching the "heart." When he starts reciting from the *Koran* instead, Cismar feels that the discussion gets out of control (138–43) and later admits that there is no time for "politische Grundsatzdebatten" (195) within their short meetings. Peters indicates that the time limit is not the only reason for his aversion to a deeper discussion: in the history of the RAF, too, certain questions of principle (notably the "Gewaltfrage") remained unanswered (160). In this way, Cismar's discussions with Sawatzky seem to serve as a continuation of former RAF-related debates. The figure of Cismar is presented as an alternative model; in contrast to the young Muslim activist he abandoned radical ideas for the sake of an alternative (the long march through institutions). Consequently, the dialogue fails, as do both characters; Cismar loses his position, and Sawatzky is eventually hanged. Still, there has been a subtle development in their relationship, especially in the way the elder ambassador succeeds in establishing a protective father role for the young prisoner (305), and despite the situation and their confrontation, personal affection develops.[55] At this point the dialogue takes place between two generations, with the elder one handing down advice to the younger. On the whole, the "dialogue between Islam and democracy," as it could be called, does not arrive at any concrete solution or any answer.

Critics who have compared Peters's novel to similar subjects in the novels of Nagarkar and Updike were disappointed with the German novel, as it did not satisfy their expectations.[56] Most critics would have liked to know more about the various reasons for Sawatzky's conversion, calling for a literary depiction of what Şenocak has called the "scope of ambiguity." This all the more astonishing in that the author himself describes the writing process, which took a full decade, as having been inspired by a German convert and Hizbullah activist who had been arrested in Israel in 1997. In September 2001, with the novel still underway, his initial intention of presenting the protagonist as plausibly as possible, up to the point that the Western reader begins to question himself, was thrown into question.[57] Nonetheless, Peters does succeed in doing this. In fact, the Westerner figure in his text has to struggle hard to prove the Muslim radical's arguments wrong, and starts to question himself, something that in turn has consequences for the reader, who gets the chance to reflect on the arguments made by both sides rather than just stick to one singular (Western) point of view.[58]

In a time of intense debate on Islam, the two writers, Peters, the German Christian, and Şenocak, the German-Turkish Muslim, engage in dialogue with Islam from differing points of view. Christoph Peters staged the debate between the religious and the secular from the position of a Western novelist without personal insight into Islam. Still, describing himself as having been a Catholic fundamentalist first and later a sympathizer with left-wing extremism,[59] Peters claims personal insights into both political and spiritual fundamentalism, as well as claiming to introduce a historical dimension to the debate on radicalism. He therefore imagines what Islamic fundamentalism could be like and tries to explore this through his treatment of the theme of political fanaticism. The end of his novel shows that dialogue fails under restrictions of time and political pressure, and that it fails as soon as terrorism is involved.[60]

Zafer Şenocak in his essays in *Das Land hinter den Buchstaben,* on the other hand, suggests a new interpretation of the *Koran* and a new skepticism toward the holy word as the basic principle of communication.

Coming from a family background that included the secular as well as the religious, he is well acquainted with having to negotiate between different positions. By his understanding, a "fatal speechlessness" characterizes the Muslim community today, resulting in massive frustration, which then again erupts in fanaticism and violence. Merely equipped with the *Koran,* Şenocak argues, today's Muslims are lost in the world, homeless in the present time, prisoners of their self-built mental ghetto and reductive ideology. Following his own negative hermeneutic, the author explores the unspoken, uncanny realms of religion and poetry, the "land behind the letters." This also links him to the culture of the Ottoman period, or to the epoch of Al-Andalus, when Islamic culture offered a wider range of theological and artistic freedom. With contemporary Islam facing huge transformations, it seems essential to create a link to this forgotten Islamic tradition, he argues. But there is no communication between the generations as yet.[61]

In Şenocak's case the "turn" to history means reconnection with the Islamic renaissance, emphasizing the role of translators who can transfer messages from the past into the complicated present. However, this task must be performed by both Muslims and the West. The West, too, should be aware of its own contradictory process of cultural transformation, in order to expect a similarly contradictory culture from Islam. He notes, "Wer heute das Gespräch mit Muslimen sucht, sollte sich an die Geschichte erinnern und nicht so tun, als sei das christliche Erbe Europas identisch mit den Werten der Aufklärung. Das christliche Abendland hat ähnlich wie das muslimische Morgenland eine in sich widersprüchliche Kultur hervorgebracht" (*LHB,* 100). Cismar, in Peters's novel, enters the debate with a Muslim radical, confronting him with newer German history. What if he had argued with the tradition of the Islamic Renaissance instead? Şenocak underlines the necessity for referring to the liberal tradition in Islamic heritage when entering a dialogue. "Wie töricht ist es heute, angesichts dieser Komplexität, den Islam jenen Kräften zu überlassen, deren kultureller Analphabetismus und arrogante Ignoranz Gewalt und Barbarei produzieren" (100). In this way both authors argue with respect to history, thus introducing a "historical turn" into the contemporary dialogue with Islam — however differently they depict it.

Notes

[1] In July 2006 two suitcase-bombs were found in (and safely removed from) regional trains in Dortmund and Koblenz, both of them set by Islamist terrorists. In September 2007 police averted several bombings aimed at Frankfurt airport, a NATO-airbase in Ramstein, and several US facilities by arresting three suspects. They all belonged to a so-called Islamist "Dschihad-Union."

[2] See Alice Schwarzer, ed., *Die Gotteskrieger und die falsche Toleranz* (Cologne: Kiepenheuer & Witsch, 2002); Günther Lachmann, *Tödliche Toleranz: Die Muslime und unsere offene Gesellschaft* (Munich: Piper, 2005).

[3] In German: "Besondere Verhaltensweisen wie z. B. einen Bruch im Lebenswandel, radikal-verbale Äußerungen oder Beschäftigung mit einschlägiger Literatur." See two articles in the German newspaper *Süddeutsche Zeitung:* Martin Thurau, "Schläfer-Suche an der Universität," 14 Mar. 2007; and Steffen Heinzelmann, and Martin Thurau, "Universitäten sollen Islamisten melden," 15 Mar. 2007. With the dread of Islamist terror attacks in Germany becoming more and more concrete, the Bavarian Minister of the Interior, Günther Beckstein (who became Bavarian Minister-President in 2007), saw a "highly abstract danger." Criticism came from most of the Bavarian universities' chancellors, who pointed out the fatal effect on the reputation of German universities abroad.

[4] The standard publication on Muslims in Germany is Ursula Spuler-Stegemann, *Muslime in Deutschland: Positionen und Klärungen,* 3rd ed. (Freiburg: Herder, 2002) (new edition forthcoming Sept. 2009). See also Faruk Şen and Hayrettin Aydin, *Islam in Deutschland* (Munich: C. H. Beck, 2002).

[5] Recent studies on migrants of the second generation place the focus on religion: see Klaus Kreitmeir, *Allahs deutsche Kinder: Muslime zwischen Fundamentalismus und Integration* (Munich: Pattloch, 2002); and Gabriele Swietlik, "'Als ob man zwei verschiedene Köpfe in einem hätte . . .' —Religiöse Sozialisation zwischen Islam und Christentum," in *Alltag und Lebenswelten von Migrantenjugendlichen,* ed. Iman Attia and Helga Marburger (Frankfurt am Main: IKO, 2000), 139–56. Until recently there has been little interest in the academic discussion of Islam in contemporary German literature. For earlier discussions, see Walter Dostal, Helmut A. Niederle, and Karl R. Wernhart, eds., *Wir und die Anderen: Islam, Literatur und Migration,* Wiener Beiträge zur Ethnologie 9 (Vienna: WUV Univ. Verlag, 1999).

[6] Zafer Şenocak, *Das Land hinter den Buchstaben: Deutschland und der Islam im Umbruch* (Munich: Babel, 2006). Further references to this work are given in the text using the abbreviation *LHB* (where necessary for clarity) and the page number. All translations are my own unless indicated otherwise.

[7] Christoph Peters, *Ein Zimmer im Haus des Krieges* (Berlin: btb, 2006). Further references to this work are given in the text using the abbreviation *ZHK* (where necessary for clarity) and the page number.

[8] See Werner Schiffauer, *Die Gottesmänner: Türkische Islamisten in Deutschland* (Frankfurt am Main: Suhrkamp 2000).

[9] See Günther Lachmann, *Tödliche Toleranz.*

[10] See Samuel Huntington, *The Clash of Civilizations and the Remaking of World Order* (New York: Simon & Schuster, 1996).

[11] Amartya Sen: *Identity and Violence. The Illusion of Destiny.* New York (Penguin) 2006. Quote from "Muslims and Intellectual Diversity," 14–16.

[12] See Amartya Sen, *Identity and Violence,* 7–9, and chapter 1, esp. 13.

[13] See Amartya Sen, "Muslims and Cultural Diversity," in *Identity and Violence,* 14–16. This is echoed by a recent study on European Muslim elites, who apparently

tend to the political left wing while at the same time defining themselves as "very religious." See also Jytte Klausen, *Europas muslimische Eliten: Wer sie sind und was sie wollen* (Frankfurt am Main: Campus, 2006), 37.

[14] In this respect most of these authors differ from the many authors of books *on* Islam, who write in a pseudo-expert manner from an outside position. See Ursula Spuler-Stegemann's critical chapter on books on Islam in her *Muslime in Deutschland*, 28–31.

[15] SAID, *ich und der islam* (Munich: C. H. Beck, 2005). The following quotations refer to the essay of the same title, "ich und der islam," 7–27.

[16] Alongside these studies and reports about Iran and the Middle East, such as *Der Schrecken Gottes: Attar, Hiob und die metaphysische Revolte* (Munich: C. H. Beck, 2005); *Schöner neuer Orient: Berichte von Städten und Kriegen* (Munich: C. H. Beck, 2003); *Iran—Die Revolution der Kinder* (Munich: C. H. Beck, 2000); and *Gott ist schön: Das ästhetische Erleben des Koran* (Munich: C. H. Beck, 1999), Kermani also writes literary fiction. See more on his Web site, http://www.navidkermani.de.

[17] See Navid Kermani, *Wer ist wir? Deutschland und seine Muslime* (Munich: C. H. Beck, 2009).

[18] See interviews with Zaimoğlu in the context of the first Islam Konferenz, particularly: Daniel-Dylan Böhmer, "Ja, es gibt einen deutschen Islam," *Frankfurter Allgemeine Sonntagszeitung*, 1 Oct. 2006.

[19] See the following interviews: "'Die Polemik vergiftet das soziale Klima': Gespräch mit dem Regisseur Neco Çelik und dem Schriftsteller Feridun Zaimoğlu über ihr Stück *Schwarze Jungfrauen*," *Islamische Zeitung*, 6 Apr. 2006; and "Guten Morgen, Deutschland!" *Islamische Zeitung*, 28 Sept. 2006. For further discussion see my article on Feridun Zaimoğlu in *Kritisches Lexikon zur deutschsprachigen Gegenwartsliteratur (KLG)*, ed. Heinz Ludwig Arnold (Munich: edition text + kritik, 2007), 86. Nlg. 08/07 (86th supplement, Aug. 2007), 1–20, A–M. See also Margaret Littler's contribution in this volume. For those who are not familiar with Turkish history, "Kemalism" is the (founding) state ideology of the new secular Turkish Republic founded by Mustafa Kemal Atatürk in 1923.

[20] See Matthias Konzett, "Writing against the Grain: Zafer Şenocak as Public Intellectual and Writer," in *Zafer Şenocak*, ed. Tom Cheesman and Karin E. Yeşilada (Cardiff: U of Wales P, 2003), 43–60. For a detailed discussion of Şenocak's writing, see also James Jordan in that volume, "Zafer Şenocak's Essays and Early Prose Fiction: From Collective Multiculturalism to Fragmented Cultural Identities," 91–105; see also my entry "Zafer Şenocak" in the *Kritisches Lexikon zur deutschsprachigen Gegenwartsliteratur (KLG)*, ed. Heinz Ludwig Arnold (Munich: edition text + kritik, 2006), 84. Nlg. 10/06 (84th supplement, Oct. 2006), 1–15, A-G. Leslie A. Adelson provides an American translation of central essays in Şenocak's *Atlas des tropischen Deutschland*, as well as an analytical introduction to his essayistic work in her introductory article, "Coordinates of Orientation: An Introduction," in her book *Zafer Şenocak: Atlas of a Tropical Germany: Essays on Politics and Culture, 1990–1998* (Lincoln, NE and London: U of Nebraska P, 2000), xi–xxxvii. The title refers to Şenocak's essay collection *Atlas des tropischen Deutschland* (Berlin: Babel, 1992).

[21] Adelson, "Coordinates of Orientation," xxii.

[22] See Şenocak's novel *Gefährliche Verwandtschaft* (Munich: Babel, 1998) as well as the following novels, which appeared in Istanbul, Turkey: *Alman Terbiyesi* (Istanbul: Alef, 2007) and *Köşk* (Istanbul: Alef, 2008). See Leslie Adelson, *The Turkish Turn in Contemporary German Literature: Toward a New Critical Grammar of Migration* (New York: Palgrave Macmillan, 2005); and Tom Cheesman, *Cosmopolite Fictions: Novels of Turkish German Settlement* (Rochester, NY: Camden House, 2007) for a closer analysis of Şenocak's central novel, *Gefährliche Verwandtschaft*. See Karin Yeşilada, "Die klassische Migration gibt es nicht mehr: Interview mit Zafer Şenocak," at http://www.migration-boell.de/web/integration/47_2005.asp (Mar. 2009) for discussion of his Turkish work.

[23] Adelson identifies Said's postcolonialist critique of Orientalist discourses as a key motif in Şenocak's essayistic prose. Adelson, "Coordinates of Orientation," xxviii.

[24] Adelson, "Coordinates of Orientation," xxvii–xxviii.

[25] See Şenocak, "Der Dichter und die Deserteure," in *War Hitler Araber? Irre-Führungen an den Rand Europas* (Berlin: Babel 1994), 21–28, esp. 28. For an English translation and a commentary, see Şenocak, *Atlas of a Tropical Germany*, 37–42, esp. 42, and Adelson, "Coordinates of Orientation," xxix–xxx.

[26] For a discussion of spatial metaphors (such as the locked room mentioned here), see Leslie A. Adelson, "Against Between: A Manifesto" in Cheesman and Yeşilada, *Zafer Şenocak*, 130–43, esp. 138–41.

[27] See Şenocak, *Atlas of a Tropical Germany*, 80.

[28] Homi K. Bhabha, *The Location of Culture* (London: Routledge, 1994).

[29] See Zafer Şenocak, "Jenseits der Landessprache," in his *Zungenentfernung: Bericht aus der Quarantänestation* (Munich: Babel, 2001).

[30] German-Iranian author SAID, for example, also experienced an atmosphere of tolerance in his childhood. Born and raised in Tehran, capital of a Muslim country, he describes the "convivencia," the harmonious coexistence of his strictly religious grandmother, his Westernized cousin, and his religious, though non-practicing, Muslim father in a typical Persian family of that time. Although he later never practiced religion himself, he, like Şenocak, was deeply influenced by the intriguing atmosphere of Muslim culture. In his essay, "ich und der islam" (see note 15), he writes, "dennoch, soziologisch bin ich muslim. denn es ist nicht entscheidend, was der erwachsene später räsoniert, sondern was das kind gesehen, gerochen und gehört hat" (9). SAID also alerts us to the great eras and topographies of Muslim, Jewish, and Christian "convivencia" in places like Andalusia, Baghdad, or Bosnia. The cultural peaks of those symbiotic epochs are echoed in the cultural mosaics of modern metropolitan centers like Berlin, Paris, London, or New York. In the aftermath of 9/11 SAID reminds us of the fragility of that harmony. See SAID: "Nachwort," in *Das Wunder von al-Andalus: Die schönsten Gedichte aus dem maurischen Spanien*. ed. and trans. from Arabic and Hebrew, with commentary by Georg Bossong (Munich: C. H. Beck, 2005), 273–76.

[31] SAID, who fled Iran twice and chose to remain in German exile and write using a pen name, is similarly critical of the totalitarian structures in Iran. Still, he refuses

to put the blame exclusively on the Islamist radicals, and he analyzes this growing radicalization of Islam in a dialectical manner instead, considering global as well as regional aspects. His personal remoteness from Islam saved him from being disappointed by the Islamic revolution and its ongoing terror. "Wieviel kraft müssen diese muslime aufbringen, um an ihrer religion festzuhalten—trotz der verheerenden auswüchse ihrer politik?" he asks in SAID, *ich und der islam*, 8–10.

[32] Yunus Emre, *Das Kummerrad / Dertli Dolap: Gedichte*, trans. and postscript by Zafer Şenocak (Frankfurt am Main: Dağyeli, 1986). Şenocak's translation (which preceded Annemarie Schimmel's later German version) was praised as "congenial" by critics.

[33] The original says: "Der Islam braucht geistige Leitfiguren, die etwas anderes schaffen als die Regeln der Scharia nachzubeten. Er braucht musische, den Künsten und der Philosophie zugeneigte Interpreten" (39).

[34] See the second essay in this chapter, "Ein Kalif, der Aktbilder malt," 35–40.

[35] See his essay "Ingenieure des Glaubens" in *War Hitler Araber*, 9–20. "Der Islam der Ingenieure," he argues there, "ist eine mit mathematischer Präzision ausgeübte religiöse Engstirnigkeit"(17).

[36] "Karikaturen des Glaubens—Europa wird der islamischen Welt immer ähnlicher" (*land*, 41–44). The article refers to the Mohammed cartoons controversy (in German referred to as "Karikaturenstreit"), which was triggered by twelve cartoons of the prophet Mohammed, first published on 30 Sept. 2005 in the Danish newspaper the *Jyllands-Posten* (under the title *Muhammeds ansigt*—The Face of Mohammed). Meant to criticize (self-)censorship and radical Islam, the cartoons, some of which showed Mohammed as a terrorist with a bomb in a turban or as the guard of paradise ("Stop! We ran out of virgins!"), were republished on 17 Oct. 2005 by the Egyptian newspaper *El Fagr*. The violent protests against them did not start until Jan. 2006, then spread out over the Muslim world, leading to arson attacks on Scandinavian embassies, consumer boycotts in Middle East countries, lawsuits, and, above all, to the death of 140 people (mostly killed by the police during protests). For a survey of European press, cf. http://signandsight. com/features/590.html (Jun. 2009), as well as http://en.wikipedia.org/wiki/ Jyllands_Posten_Muhammad_cartoons_controversy (Jun. 2009) for an overview article. See also Silvia Naef, *Bilder und Bilderverbot im Islam vom Koran bis zum Karikaturenstreit* (Munich: C. H. Beck, 2007); and Siegfried Jäger, *Der Karikaturenstreit im "Rechts-Mitte-Links"-Diskurs deutscher Printmedien*, in *Mediale Barrieren: Rassismus als Integrationshindernis*, ed. Siegfried Jäger and Dirk Halm (Münster: Unrast, 2007).

[37] See the German-English publication by Bernhard Debatin, ed., *Der Karikaturenstreit und die Pressefreiheit: Wert- und Normenkonflikte in der globalen Medienkultur / The Cartoon Debate and the Freedom of the Press* (Berlin and Münster, Germany: Lit, 2007). See also Ursula Baatz, Hans Belting, and Navid Kermani, eds., *Bilderstreit 2006: Pressefreiheit? Blasphemie? Globale Politik?* (Vienna: Picus, 2006).

[38] The first collection of poetry from al-Andalus in the German language, *Das Wunder von al-Andalus*, was published as part of a series entitled "Neue Orientalische Bibliothek" at C. H. Beck publishers (see note 30 above). The series presents major

titles of classical and modern Persian and Arab literature in bibliophilic volumes. See http://www.chbeck.de (*Neue Orientalische Bibliothek* Series).

[39] Şenocak, "eine Sprache, die zum kontroversen Denken anregt," in "Islam übersetzen" (*LHB*, 55).

[40] Ursula Spuler-Stegemann constantly denounces the naive tolerance of Protestant church officials in particular towards radical Muslims, who do not necessarily consider themselves loyal to the constitution. See Ursula Spuler-Stegemann, ed., *Feindbild Christentum im Islam: Eine Bestandsaufnahme,* 3rd ed. (Freiburg: Herder, 2004). In Christoph Peters's fictional depiction of such a constellation, the dialogue indeed goes wrong.

[41] Asked about the influence of Islamic poetry on his work in an interview, Şenocak replied, "Es gibt ja weiterhin noch oder immer wieder Spuren islamischer Mystik in meiner Poesie. Die kritische Beschäftigung mit der islamischen Religion spielt ja auch in meiner essayistischen Arbeit eine wichtige Rolle." See the whole interview as part of an online special on migrational literature on the Web site of the Heinrich-Böll-Stiftung, "Die klassische Migration gibt es nicht mehr: Interview mit Zafer Şenocak" http://www.migration-boell.de/web/integration/4/_2005.asp.

[42] Moray McGowan, "Odysseus on the Ottoman, or 'The Man in Skirts': Exploratory Masculinities in the Prose Texts of Zafer Şenocak," in Cheesman and Yeşilada, *Zafer Şenocak,* 61–79.

[43] See McGowan, "Odysseus," 64.

[44] Zafer Şenocak, *Der Mann im Unterhemd* (Berlin: Babel, 1995); *Der Erottomane: Ein Findelbuch* (Munich: Babel 1999).

[45] See Adelson, *The Turkish Turn in Contemporary German Literature* and "Against Between: A Manifesto" on this matter.

[46] John Updike, *Terrorist,* trans. Angela Praesent (Reinbek: Rowohlt, 2006); Kiran Nagarkar, *Gottes kleiner Krieger,* trans. Giovani and Ditte Bandini (Munich: A1, 2006).

[47] Sten Nadolny's *Selim oder Die Gabe der Rede* (Munich: Piper, 1992), and Thorsten Becker's *Sieger nach Punkten* (Reinbek: Rowohlt, 2004), are some of the rare exceptions.

[48] Christoph Peters studied painting before becoming a writer. He has won several prizes for his writing.

[49] There is no further hint in the novel about Sawatzky's possible feelings of embarrassment or even shame at being the illegitimate child of an American GI, nor about the fact that his later wrath is directed against his own origins. Peters leaves this ironic aspect open to speculation.

[50] Sawatzky repeats this experience in the conversation with Cismar, blaming Western society for his breakdown, which, he insists, would have never happened to him in an Islamic country (184–86).

[51] Şenocak describes today's Muslims in an essay as "Gefangene des eigenen Hauses" (*LHB*, 69–72). Further: "Heute stehen die Muslime mit dem Koran in der Hand und verloren auf der Welt da" (71).

[52] For detailed information on the Muslim Brotherhood, see Johannes Grundmann, *Islamische Internationalisten: Strukturen und Aktivitäten der Muslimbruderschaft und der islamischen Weltliga* (Wiesbaden: Reichert, 2005).

[53] The terrorist's strategy resembles that of the 9/11 attacks in hoping to achieve maximum media impact: "Diesen Krieg entscheiden Bilder, nicht die Zahl der Opfer" (*ZHK*, 47).

[54] Ines is in fact only interested in 1970s fashion, not politics, and uses terms such as "radicalism" only to describe the arts (*ZHK*, 156 and 159).

[55] See *ZHK*, 305–6: When Cismar tells Sawatzky about his sudden and involuntary return to Germany, Sawatzky is really sorry. Cismar in return rewards him with the present of an expensive fountain pen.

[56] According to some, the author did little more than present commonplace arguments, failing to illuminate the young radical's motivation to become a terrorist; other critics were disturbed by an excess of clichés. In contrast to this, Kiran Nagarkar's novel about his protagonist Zia Khan gradually turning into a radical Muslim terrorist was received with more appreciation. It seems, then, that Peters's novel was seen in the light of the other two existing novels.

[57] See Peters in the interview with Julia Encke: "Es ist der Versuch, die islamistische Position argumentativ so aufzurüsten, daß wir als Westler unsere ganze Energie aufbringen müssen, um sie zu widerlegen," in "'Ich war ein katholischer Fundamentalist': Interview mit Christoph Peters," *Frankfurter Allgemeine Zeitung*, 17 Feb. 2006, 46. (Still available at www.faznet.de.)

[58] Staging this dialogue as a battle of positions in a debate, Peters goes further than, for example, Feridun Zaimoğlu, whose radical Islamists, the "Yücel" figure in *Kanak Sprak* (1995), or the "Gotteskrieger" in *Zwölf Gramm Glück* (2004), (full bibliography in note 60) address their phrase-mongering about Islam to an anonymous, unreplying readership. Whenever these phrases meet a critical interlocutor, though, they become more fragile and open to contradiction (as the Muslim girls' positions in the two intertwined "Gottesanrufung" stories show).

[59] See Julia Encke's interview, note 57 above.

[60] It would be interesting to compare the Sawatzky figure to similar figures in German literature. Feridun Zaimoğlu depicted the figure of the radical Islamistic German Turk twice: The Islamist "Yücel" in his early prose *Kanak Sprak: 24 Mißtöne vom Rande der Gesellschaft* (Hamburg: Rotbuch, 1995), 137–41, and the figure of the "Gottes Krieger" in his short-story collection *Zwölf Gramm Glück: Erzählungen* (Cologne: Kiepenheuer & Witsch, 2004), 122–56. While "Yücel" expresses his radical views only in words, that is through verbal expression, the "Gottes Krieger" has been called to action by the leader of his sect. The story relates the emancipation of the former sect member from his radical Islamist sect: he leaves the sect because, first, he disapproves of the sect leader's double moral standards, and, second, because he starts a sexual relationship with a woman twice his age. Particularly the figure of the "Herzprediger," that is sect leader, recalls the Islamist terrorists of Al-Qaida. The radical Islamists in the story "Gottes Krieger" clearly reflect characteristics of the Islamist terrorists of Al-Qaida.

61 Jewish-German literature and thinking are significant for the subtext of Şenocak's essays, and consequently he draws some parallels between Judaism and Islam as regards the historical transformation process. He bases his argumentation on his reading of Elie Wiesel and Franz Kafka (see "Ungeschriebene Briefe an die Väter" [*LHB*, 79–83], and "Postscriptum" [*LHB*, 85–86]). At a time when Judaism lost touch with some fundamental values at the end of the nineteenth century, writers like Sigmund Freud and Franz Kafka expressed the huge process of transformation of assimilating Jews into the European bourgeoisie. With contemporary Islam in a similar situation at the outset of the twenty-first century, parallel writer-figures are missing, thus leaving Muslims without any contextualization of the huge cultural clash that is going to divide generations, Şenocak argues. While Kafka could, for example, ask his father about Jewishness (or rather blame him for no longer upholding it), Muslim sons and fathers remain silent. In this respect the young radical Jochen Sawatzky in Christoph Peters's novel *Ein Zimmer im Haus des Krieges* represents the silence between the generations, between sons and fathers, as he grew up fatherless. Peters links his radicalism to an epoch of German radicalism in the 1970s, showing the parallels between the two movements.

11: Michaela Mihriban Özelsel's Pilgrimage to Mecca: A Journey to Her Inner Self

Edwin Wieringa

THE MOST INTIMATE FORM OF ENCOUNTER with Islam is to embrace it and become a Muslim. In the present-day atmosphere of fear of Islam and Islamism, however, Western converts tend to be viewed by their compatriots with suspicion, if not downright hostility. Is conversion to Islam not a motivating factor in becoming a terrorist? In March 2007, in a Saturday issue of the *Frankfurter Allgemeine Zeitung* (*FAZ*), its third page was completely devoted to what was called a "drastic" increase in the number of German converts to Islam. The news was announced on the first page under the sensationalist heading of "Himmel oder Hölle," stating that "Die Einladung zum Islam wird als Ausbruch aus der Mehrheitsgesellschaft gerne angenommen" and this polarizing tone was also adopted in the article itself which appeared, rather revealingly, under the category of "Politics," and not under "Religion" or "Society."[1]

The term "Mehrheitsgesellschaft" in the *FAZ* article may perhaps sound neutral and objective, but in fact it functions as an alternative for the highly politicized word "Leitkultur" which can be translated as "guiding culture" or "leading culture." The suggestion made by right-wing politicians belonging to the conservative Christian Democratic Union that German culture—whatever that may be—should be the "defining culture" for the country's immigrants and foreign workers became a national political issue in 2000 as part of heated debates about multiculturalism and national core values. The specific word "Leitkultur" was quickly labeled politically incorrect, some criticizers hearing echoes of the Nazi lexicon in expressions of national pride.[2]

The idea of a deep dichotomy between two opposing worlds, namely the "West" and "Islam," is perhaps nowhere more pronounced than in popular German discourse with such revealing terms as "Leitkultur" and the much-feared conception of an Islamic "Parallelgesellschaft." The latter term is primarily targeted at the troublesome issue of the "integration-resistant" ethnic minority group of the estimated 2.7 million Turks, mostly living in their own separate Turkish-speaking Islamic communities.

Nowadays the recurring theme of immigration as a problem in Western European countries is primarily concentrated upon Muslims. Discussing the present-day anti-Islamic public debate with regard to immigrants in the Netherlands, the Islamicist Rudolph Peters speaks of an "Islamization of migration," that is, a xenophobic line of reasoning that attributes problems connected with immigration to Islam.[3] Since the early 1990s, Peters argues, the "migrants' culture was more and more equated with Islam and problems connected with migration were blamed on Islam."[4] In the Dutch national press an image is conjured up of Muslim migrants whose entire lives are dominated by Islam, and this "Islam is represented as uniform, monolithic and unchangeable and embodying the opposite of what are considered as the Dutch or European identity and core values."[5]

This is not very different from the situation in Germany, but in the German media there is an added expression of a deep-seated angst about a widening gap between an ever increasing number of Muslims amidst a shrinking and graying autochthonous population. Scaremongers like to paint a nightmarish picture of an imminent "Eurabia," pointing to the existence of complete neighborhoods in major cities that have already turned into places "where there's little hint of Western culture," and in which "Islam and the Islamic way of life dominate."[6] In an interview at Princeton University on 28 July 2004 with the conservative Hamburg-based daily *Die Welt,* the famed veteran Islamicist Bernard Lewis—the same scholar who in a 1990 article titled "The Roots of Muslim Rage" coined the infelicitous expression "clash of civilizations"—gloomily predicted that "Europe will be a part of the Arabic West, of the Maghreb," and added that Europe would have Islamic majorities by the end of this century "at the very latest." Referring to Lewis's alarmist remark, the conservative Dutch politician Frits Bolkestein, then the outgoing European Union competition commissioner, supported this doomsday scenario regarding the bleak future of Europe in an address at the University of Leiden on 6 September 2004. "Current trends only allow one conclusion," Bolkestein pronounced apodictically, "the USA will remain the only superpower. China is becoming an economic giant. Europe is being Islamicized."[7] It should come as no surprise that a few weeks later, in a speech at the Humboldt University in Berlin, he fervently defended what he called the necessity of a "Leitkultur": "eine Leitkultur [ist] notwendig, um zu verhindern, dass sich eine parallelle islamistische [*sic*] Gesellschaft entwickelt, in der wesentliche europäische Werte nicht gelten."[8]

The idea that the German "Leitkultur" may in the near future be eroded by the looming threat of an expanding Islamic "Parallelgesellschaft" is receiving daily reinforcement from the news media. The mistrustful question of whether today's converts to Islam could be tomorrow's terrorists became most acute when, in September 2007, the police arrested Fritz G. and Daniel S., two young militant German converts, for planning terrorist attacks that could have been more deadly than those carried out in Madrid (2004) or London (2005). Bavaria's Interior Minister Günther Beckstein adopted a harsh tone, telling the daily *Handelsblatt* that when "security forces learn of a conversion, they should establish whether it involves a liberal and humane form of Islam or an Islamist one." This suggestion of surveillance, however, was plainly rhetorical, as data about how many Germans convert to Islam are hard to come by. Commenting on the growing number of German citizens converting to Islam, the Federal Interior Minister Wolfgang Schäuble stated that it definitively had "something very menacing about it," and warned against the possible danger of "home-grown terrorism" among "us."[9]

The "us versus them" paradigm is a constant refrain in popular discourse on German encounters with Islam, both on "our" as well as on "their" side. The latest story assigned "breaking news" status happens to be that of a twenty-year-old German convert called Eric B. from Neuenkirchen in Saarland, who appeared in two short militaristic films on the Internet in which he calls upon his brethren to join the jihad. Having only converted in 2007, he tells the camera in German that no Muslim should stand by and watch while "the infidels shame our women in our countries and jail and torment our brothers."[10] One wonders which countries rank in his classification as "our countries" and who exactly are meant with "our women"? Would the countrywomen of the "Landfrauenkreis Neuenkirchen" fit into his category?

The recourse to the "us versus them" paradigm was also immediately enacted after a fire had killed nine Turks in the city of Ludwigshafen in February 2008. Turkish media jumped on the topic, speculating that the tragic incident was a xenophobic attack. Already deeply distrustful of Germans, many Turks were quick with their judgment, accepting the possibility of arson as a proven fact. When the Turkish Prime Minister Erdogan made a visit at the site of the burned apartment block on 7 February, some demonstrators waved banners, protesting dramatically against what they perceived as German "racism." There were placards reading "Gestern Juden, heute Moslems" (Jews yesterday, Muslims today), and "Hitler war nicht alleine, Koch auch nicht" (Hitler was not alone, neither is Koch, referring to Hesse's right-wing State Premier Roland Koch, who was accused by German Muslims of having waged an anti-foreigner campaign for reelection). Despite the stereotype of the Germans as eternal Nazis, however, investigators could not find any evidence that the fire was an act of arson.

Viewed against the negative image of Islam in Germany, where it is closely associated with violence and backwardness, most vividly illustrated at the domestic level by widely reported cases of forced marriages, spousal abuse, and honor killings, the question as to why Germans would adopt Islam is particularly vexing. There is no short answer, because people may choose to become Muslim for a variety of reasons. It has been claimed that most conversions to Islam in the West occur among women in the context of marriage to a man born into the religion. However, female conversion is a particularly sensitive issue. A Dutch female convert once complained that ever since her shift in belief she had become the target of aggression, being regarded by her "fellow whites" as "a traitor to the race."[11] Meanwhile, a considerable corpus of proud testimonies is readily available in both offline and online media in the form of all kinds of life stories, which as a rule are intended to be persuasive, fulfilling a missionary goal. These conversion stories constitute a specific genre with its own narrative structure.[12] Their blatantly homiletic message is, in short: "Islam is the answer!"

In scholarly literature attention is drawn to the important role converts can play as interpreters of Islam within Western societies.[13] In particular, intellectuals who have converted are seen as knowledgeable mediators. In the *FAZ* article of March 2007, mentioned above, the possibility is also briefly mentioned that German converts could function as so-called "Brückenbauer" or mediators, because they know both sides. This idea, however, was quickly dismissed by the *FAZ* journalist as, in his opinion, these converts had turned their back on the Western world. In this chapter this point will be discussed in a little more detail. Questions arise such as: how feasible is it to expect Western converts to be ideal informants for a Western audience? Do they indeed reveal anti-Western attitudes?

In Islamic Studies the primary sources are normally those texts written by "insiders," that is, people who profess to be Muslims. Only they are able to provide us with genuine Muslim perspectives. Over the last decades, however, some Western academics who have converted to Islam have claimed a position for themselves as "insiders." Perhaps "initiated" is a better word choice here, because we are dealing with intellectuals who have entered Sufism, the mystical path of Islam. Well-known names in this field are the two German Swiss, Titus Burckhardt (1908–84) and Frithjof Schuon (1907–98), and the French metaphysician René Guénon (1886–1951). The teachings of the latter, in particular, have greatly influenced Western Sufis. These neophytes share a common disenchantment with rationalism and technocracy in the modern, industrialized Western world, emphasizing the importance of sacred traditions, which are regarded as manifestations of a perennial philosophy. All ancient esoteric teachings from around the globe are believed to be merely variant expressions of a single perennial philosophy that is basically one and eternal. Numerically, adherents of Perennial Philosophy belong to the margins of Europe's encounter with Islam, but the series of books on Islam and religion produced by members of this school have found a receptive audience and can readily be found in any ordinary bookshop in Germany and other Western countries.

This chapter will focus on the story of one German female academic who sees herself as a modern Western Sufi, namely Michaela Mihriban Özelsel, whose narrative of her pilgrimage to Mecca was brought out in 2005 by the Roman Catholic publishing house Herder in Freiburg.[14] The factual title, *Pilgerfahrt nach Mekka*, is an appropriate yet not exactly colorful depiction of the book's subject, but the subtitle *Meine Reise in eine geheimnisvolle Welt* functions as the real appetizer. It suggests that her account will give "us," the intended non-Muslim readers, a rare glimpse into the "mysterious world" of Islam. The opening sentence of the preface confirms this:

> Das vorliegende Buch gewährt Einblicke in die dem Westen fast gänzlich verborgene, geheimnisvolle Welt der sakralen Riten des Hadsch, der Pilgerfahrt nach Mekka. Also eine Reise in das innere und äußere Herz des Islam, gesehen durch die Augen einer Frau. Es ist ein Erfahrungsbericht, der in großer Offenheit Einblicke gibt in einen Prozess spiritueller Bewusstwerdung. (*PM*, 9)

Although it is true that non-Muslims are not permitted to enter Mecca by Saudi law, there is nothing really hidden about the outer aspects of the hajj. There is abundant information on this ritual, which is easily available and certainly not restricted to believers only. Furthermore, a large body of Islamic travel literature on this topic is accessible in Western languages.[15] It is the inner perspective that for us will be the most enticing part of the book.

Perhaps because Özelsel's hajj account is primarily intended for non-Muslims and also needed to be intelligible to non-Islamicists, remarkably little attention is paid to the intricate series of rituals that need to be performed by all pilgrims. We merely read that a pilgrim has to choose from three options, namely "hajj ifrad," "hajj tammatu," and "hajj qiran," and that Özelsel took the latter, described as the most demanding form (*PM*, 29). Nowhere, however, do we read about what these exotic-sounding alternatives entail or what the specific difficulties involving the choice of "hajj qiran" are. The back flap blurb informs us that the author in this travelogue describes her experiences with age-old rituals of the pilgrimage as well as "eine Reise ins eigene Innere—jenseits der Grenzen religiöser Tradition." The latter phrase, which alludes to some deep mystical experiences, indicates that we are dealing here with someone for whom Sufism transcends all religions. But if so, to what extent does Sufism still have to do with Islam?

So who is Michaela Özelsel? On the Internet she also features under the name of Michaela M. Özelsel-Heymann, but on her homepage (http://özelsel.de) and in the booklet about her pilgrimage she refers to herself as Michaela Mihriban Özelsel. She gives the following information about herself: she was born on 9 December 1949 into a German family in

Kiel, Germany, but mostly grew up in Turkey. After graduating from the German school in Istanbul, she studied psychology at the University of North Carolina, USA, and received her PhD in clinical psychology at the University of Frankfurt. Her dissertation was based on six years of research on psychosomatic disorders among Turkish migrant workers in Germany. On her homepage she calls herself "an Ethnic Minority Mental Health Specialist, doing Ethnotherapeutic Research on Methods of Healing in Islam and Sufism." Intriguingly, Islam and Sufism are separated here, as though Sufism is a form of universal spirituality that is only loosely connected to the "legalistic" religion of Islam. This is a typical Western view, often encountered today "in the freewheeling market of spirituality and New Age self-expression."[16] Apart from the pilgrimage account, Michaela Özelsel has a number of other publications to her name, of which her 1993 book *Vierzig Tage: Erfahrungsbericht einer traditionellen Derwisch-klausur* is perhaps best known.[17] It was translated in 1996 as *Forty days: A Diary of a Traditional Sufi Retreat; With an Accompanying Scientific Commentary.*[18] The emphasis on "Wissenschaft" or science is a recurrent theme in all her publications.

Pilgrims have written a plethora of hajj accounts in Arabic, Persian, Turkish, Urdu, Malay, and other so-called Islamic languages, which offer a wide variety of self-representations of their authors, but as they address a reading public of co-religionists, the Islamic affiliation of the authors in these descriptions is self-evident and never problematized. For a Western convert like Michaela Özelsel, whose target readership primarily consists of non-Muslims in Germany, the case is different. The unspoken question underlying her travelogue is why she willingly embraced such an alien religion, which, to put it mildly, is not very popular in Germany. A survey in 2003 found 46% of respondents agreeing that "Islam is a backward religion," while another survey in 2004 showed that 93% of Germans associated Islam with the "oppression of women."[19] Why, then, would a German woman holding a PhD degree enter Islam?

Michaela Özelsel's book can be read as a typical example of a "coming out story," justifying her option for Islam, but without a self-confident missionary appeal. Well over thirty and a convinced atheist, she first became seriously attracted to Islam after having had a sudden trance-like experience at the grave of the thirteenth-century Muslim saint Rumi in Konya, Turkey. To the utter astonishment of her travel companions, all of a sudden she completely lost contact with reality, standing stiff, tears flowing down her cheeks. It is not exactly clear what happened to her at that moment, but she informs us that as a "clinical psychologist" she knows that she may have been experiencing psychosis which, however, she immediately rules out as she was not psychotic (adding not unhumor-ously that all psychotics are convinced of not being psychotics). Özelsel does take great pains to explain that the bizarre hallucinatory experience was not the symptom of a severe mental illness but a genuine religious manifestation related to the renowned Islamic saint Rumi. In a long end-note of no fewer than three pages (*PM,* 148–50) she argues, by invoking "old writings from various traditions" and "contemporary scientific research," that something otherworldly had occurred to her.

This "awakening," as she also calls this event, marks her overnight conversion to Islam. The sudden shift from former atheism to Islam is thus presented as the result of an instantaneous, fully unexpected mystical experience, and it is this esoteric, gnostic tradition that appeals to her, and not the stern, scriptural Islam with its strict rules, as propagated in such austere countries as Saudi Arabia. At first she is a closet believer riddled with shame. Regularly we read that she's afraid of what others might think, what they might say, if they really knew about her "secret religious life." For example, after the crucial turning point at Rumi's grave, she writes that she did not want others to know about what she refers to as a "transcendental experience" (*PM,* 72), and her "conversion in the heart" (*PM,* 71), because of Islam's inferior status in Germany:

> Dennoch der Islam . . . In Deutschland, wo ich jetzt wieder lebte, sicherlich die am wenigsten angesehene, mit den meisten Vorurteilen behaftete Religion. Sich dazu zu bekennen, *als moderne westliche Frau, als Wissenschaftlerin,* war keine sehr angenehme Vorstellung. Aber, so damals meine Logik, selbst wenn all meine tief greifenden spontanen Erlebnisse anderer Ebenen bedeuteten, dass ich Muslima geworden war, so war das schließlich meine Privatsache. Die Konversion im Herzen, die mir unvermutet zugestoßen war, war ja die eigentlich gültige. Eine äußerliche Bestätigung erschien mir irrelevant, unnötig. (*PM,* 71, emphasis mine)

The parallels with sexual coming-out stories are striking. For instance, the British sociologist Ken Plummer, who discusses sexual stories around suffering and survival, writes about so-called "desire stories": "a story is told which recognizes a desire (often from a fairly early age) for some kind of satisfaction in a personal (emotional, erotic, intimate?) life which is persistently thwarted."[20] Compare this with what Michaela Özelsel has to say:

> Als ich zum ersten Mal in meinem Leben arabische Schrift sah, war es Liebe auf den ersten Blick. Ich war fasziniert, entschlossen, sie zu erlernen. Das war aber für ein Kind im Schleswig-Holstein der 50er Jahre nicht möglich. Später zogen wir zwar in die Türkei, aber dort war diese Schrift zu meinem Leidwesen schon in den 20er Jahren abgeschafft worden. Ende der 60er Jahre dann, als ich mit meinem ersten Ehemann in den USA lebte, ergab sich ebenfalls keine Möglichkeit. Der alte Kindheitstraum war schließlich verblasst, jedoch nicht vergessen. (*PM,* 72)

However, it is her love of Arabic script that finally will force her to break the silence. A year after her transcendental experience in Turkey, she learned about a course in Arabic script offered by the imam of the Turkish Muslim community in her part of Bavaria. The imam, however, excluded her from participating, on the grounds that the sole purpose of learning Arabic script is to read the Koran, "which none may touch except the purified."[21] Only if she converts to Islam will she be allowed to take part in the lessons. To the great astonishment of her (Turkish) husband, she decides to convert officially to Islam, arguing that she has already been a Muslim in her heart since the sudden experience at Rumi's grave. Her husband's stupefaction testifies to the deep secrecy in which Michaela Özelsel had held her newly found faith: hitherto no one could have known that she had become a Muslim. It is as if this were "the love that dare not speak its name."

Her husband wanted to dissuade her from this "absurd idea" (*PM*, 73), but she was determined, and went to the mosque in order to be officially converted. She informs us that after repeating all kinds of Arabic phrases, she was declared Muslim, and given the Islamic name Aziza Mihriban, after which she was allowed to enter the course on Arabic script. During the following nights she could hardly sleep, greatly worried that her German friends and acquaintances might find out that she was now officially Muslim. During the fasting month of Ramadan, however, she could not disguise her new faith any more, because her family, friends, and colleagues could not fail to notice that she refrained from food and drink every day from dawn to sunset, even though the summer temperature encouraged everyone around her to drink. To her relief, only a few people reacted negatively to her new status.

Michaela Özelsel admits that at this time Islam was still very new for her. She did not yet perform the obligatory five daily ritual prayers but started to abstain from alcohol and pork. She also read everything she could find on Islam, turning her attention especially to works on the inner path of Islam called Sufism. Mystical authors of all ages, however, insisted on the need for a master to guide the novice. Michaela Özelsel mentions the importance of having a sheikh (spiritual guide) who stands in a spiritual lineage (*silsila*) that leads from this master back through past generations to the Prophet (*PM*, 74). Surprisingly at first—but reflecting on her emphasis on "Wissenschaft," rather predictably,—she reveals that the master she found was a Western professor of psychology.

This person, whom she only mysteriously refers to as "Professor X.," suddenly comes into her life at an international congress in Phoenix, Arizona. Describing him as a brilliant orator, she immediately comes under his spell but does not at this time have the opportunity to meet him personally. She often thinks of him, and quite unexpectedly half a year later Professor X. knocks on her door in Germany. There is a congress in Heidelberg, and the organizers ask Michaela Özelsel to act as interpreter "für einen besonderen Referenten" (for a remarkable speaker; quotation marks in the original; *PM,* 76). She describes her co-operation with Professor X. as a trance-like experience. The following year she has further remarkable intensive trance-like meetings with him at seminars on their mutual "scientific" discipline, ethnotherapy, and one day she asks him spontaneously if he is her spiritual teacher. Professor X. reluctantly answers:

> In meiner Tradition nimmt man sich vier Tage Zeit, wichtige Entscheidungen zu treffen. Viele haben diesen Wunsch an mich gerichtet. Angesichts des inneren Beteiligtseins, das ein solches Abkommen erfordern würde, darf ich über meine Lebenszeit hinweg jedoch nur sieben Schüler annehmen. Diese Art des Lehrens erfordert so viel von meiner eigenen Substanz, dass ich bei mehr als sieben meinen anderen Pflichten nicht mehr gerecht werden könnte. Dieses Abkommen wäre ein Abkommen auf Lebenszeit. Und meine Erwartungen an den prospektiven Schüler sind absolute Aufrichtigkeit und ein starker Wille. (*PM,* 78)

Michaela Özelsel hears herself answering: "'Ich wäre bereit, mein Leben auf diesem Pfad zu geben. Ich weiß nicht, wie ich meine Aufrichtigkeit darüber hinaus beweisen könnte. Und für jemanden aus meiner Kultur ist mein Wille stark. Ich weiß nicht, wie er sich im Vergleich der Maßstäbe deiner Tradition bewähren würde'" (*PM,* 78). To this Professor X. merely responds: "Yes, your willpower is strong."

The next four days are torturous for her. Dramatically, she states that her entire life is dependent on his answer: "Nicht nur mein weiteres Leben, nein, auch mein bisher gelebtes. Sollte er "Nein" sagen, war alles, was ich bisher vollbracht hatte, sinnlos gewesen" (*PM,* 78).

Of course, the reader knows in advance that the answer will be affirmative, for otherwise we could never have had the account of this modern Western Sufi woman, but it must be said that Michaela Özelsel knows how to tell a story full of suspense. An ominous dream emphasizes the initiation, and a "spiritual osmosis" (*PM,* 81) between the two kindred spirits quickly evolves. In her opinion the intensive contact could be described as the start of a characteristic Sufi relationship—of a master and disciple type.

It is worth ruminating for a moment on what Michaela Özelsel is telling us here. An important aspect of Sufism, as she had stated herself (see above), is the "chain" (*silsila*), that is to say, the spiritual pedigree of masters going back to the Prophet Mohammed. Seen from a Sufi angle, there may be different individual paths to God, but all should somehow belong to the greater path, initially taught by the Prophet himself. However, the "Sonderweg" of Michaela Özelsel is not just another Islamic path. It should be remembered that her "master" is *not* a Muslim but belongs to an utterly different "tradition." Who is he, and why the vagueness about the congresses, which hamper verification, and the concealment of the true identity of "Professor X."?

The international congress in Phoenix, Arizona, where she first met her master, must have been the "International Congress on Ericksonian Approaches to Hypnosis and Psychotherapy," and most probably Terry Tafoya is our enigmatic "Professor X." In another publication Michaela Özelsel describes Terry Tafoya as an American citizen of Native American Indian descent who holds a professorship of psychology at the University of Washington, and who also acts as a shamanic healer.[22] She gives an example from a workshop, in which Terry Tafoya gave a "transcultural" treatment involving an Indian ritual to a married couple with strong roots in the "Islamic tradition."[23] However, the charismatic figure Terry Tafoya is quite controversial. In 2006, Ruth Teichroeb, an investigative reporter from the *Seattle Post,* wrote that Tafoya's claims are most dubious.[24] In the words of another journalist, "Tafoya's Indian blood is questionably thin, his academic record elusive, and worse his qualifications in psychology are troublesome."[25] The Taos Pueblo tribe of which he claims to be a member says that he is not enrolled with them, while in a legal deposition Tafoya admitted that he had only a 1974 Master's Degree in Education and a 1975 Master's of Communication from the University of Washington, not a PhD, as he has claimed for years.[26] Even if Tafoya is not Professor X., it should be sufficiently clear that this person is definitely not a Muslim sheikh, and, second, that whatever his true identity may be, we are not dealing with a very convincing representative of Western "Wissenschaft"—an anonymous ethnotherapist whose claim to fame rests on esoteric knowledge of ancient healing practices from his non-Western "tradition."

Michaela Özelsel's peculiar way of storytelling can be attributed to her (ethno)therapeutic background. On the back flap of her book she describes herself as a psychotherapist, academic, and Muslim, and the order of this triad is not coincidental. Somewhere else in her book she enumerates the many roles she has played in her life, opining that being therapist, mother, and wife have been the most significant. Now that her children have grown up and both of her marriages have broken down, she fully concentrates on her therapeutic work. This is for her a most rewarding job, helping people who are in pain and agony—God willing (*PM,* 94). Psychotherapy is a primary focus for her, and she locates it in the religious domain. In a seminar with Professor X. she likens the spiritual teacher-pupil relationship to the therapeutic connection between therapist and patient (*PM,* 79).

Michaela Özelsel rejects what she calls Cartesian dualism and propagates a "holistic worldview" that she assumes to be valid in all non-Western cultures. She interconnects "healing" and the "holy" by making the following etymological argument:

"Heilen" ist etymologisch gesehen verbunden mit "heilig" und "heil"—im Sinne von "ganz sein, heil sein," in einer von holistischen Sichtweisen geprägten Welt bedeutet dies, eingegliedert zu sein in die große Harmonie des Seins. . . . [27]

The cited phrase is from her article "Betrachtungen zu östlichen und westlichen therapeutischen Ansätzen: Ähnliches und Unterschiedliches" and is typical for her essentializing, dichotomizing view of Western and non-Western cultures. In another publication on "healing trance rituals" she posits: "Die alten Methoden unterscheiden nicht klar zwischen Therapie und spirituellen Handlungen, denn heilen, Heilung, heilig ist auch bei uns ethymologisch als eins erkennbar. In unserem Kulturkreis wurden Heilung und Spiritualität künstlich getrennt."[28]

Özelsel's psychology-cum-spirituality is rooted in a popular form of New Age counterculture. She divides the world into such general opposites as East and West, women and men, and traditional and modern. In her framework Islam is totally different from "us." For example, in her article about women in Islam she explains as her intention: "Zweck dieses Artikels ist es, einen Blick in die Stellung der Frau im Islam—und damit in ein *gänzlich anderes* Denksystem und Weltbild zu geben" (emphasis mine).[29] She also uses other related terms such as "grundsätzlich andere Sichtweise" and "andersartig."

For an analysis of her writings we may usefully invoke the resonant conception of "Orientalism." The latter term has become a household word because of the book *Orientalism* by the literary critic Edward Said (1935–2003), which was first published in 1978.[30] Said's central thesis, easily and briefly summarized, is that the concepts "West" and "Orient" as polar opposites have been created by Westerners (mainly in the context of Western imperialism) to provide a positive, strong image of the West with which Eastern civilizations could be negatively contrasted. The "Orient" is thus presented as lacking all active characteristics: it is effeminate, decadent, corrupt, despotic, and incapable of independent creative development. The Orientalist discourse, Said maintained, asserts that there is a mysterious "essence" that defines the East.

Now, Said's "Orientalism" is not without its flaws, as was inter alia pointed out by the Orientalist Malcolm Kerr, who criticized that "in charging the entire tradition of European and American Oriental studies with the sins of reductionism and caricature, he commits precisely the same error."[31] Nevertheless, the basic argument about the East as counterimage for the West still holds true for large parts of the Western media and popular culture today. In his 2006 book *For the Lust of Knowing: The Orientalists and their Enemies* the Middle East scholar Robert Irwin has sufficiently demolished Said's attack on academic Orientalists, but in a mocking review the British literary critic Terry Eagleton made the interesting point that the current Islamophobia would well seem to vindicate Said's general thesis.[32] As Eagleton put it, "all Irwin needs to do to recognize the broad truth of Said's thesis is turn on the television set."[33]

Intriguingly, Özelsel's approach to Islam could be seen as a variant of the Orientalist discourse in Saidan terms, but it is an Orientalism with a reversal of the standard stereotypical roles. It is not just Islamophilia, but an idealization of the entire non-Western world *tout court*, which is seen as homogeneous, a fascinating realm of the exotic, of the mystical, and, most importantly, of arcane ancient wisdom. She dichotomizes the world into "us" (Westerners) and "them" (non-Westerners), but thereby she intends to criticize the West, claiming that spirituality has been lost in the West, which has succumbed to materialism and other temptations of worldly wealth. As is typical of representatives of Perennial Philosophy, Michaela Özelsel confidently uses one tradition to explicate another. She talks, for example, about Islamic mantras, transcendental meditation, *yin* and *yang*, and the Kaaba as *yoni*. Esoteric concepts and techniques from all corners of the world are viewed as reflections of a higher reality.

The impression one initially gets is of an eclectic hotchpotch of beliefs, practices, and ways of life, enthusiastically embracing the broad- est possible range of esoteric non-Western traditions. Yet the apparent heterogeneity is not without any systematization: Özelsel's self-reflection is entrenched in a particular religious way of thinking which has been called "self-spirituality."[34] This "do-it-yourself" form of spirituality, which is obsessed with the self, shows a strong tendency toward what the Dutch expert on New Age and Western esotericism Wouter Hanegraaff has called a "psychologizing of religion" along with a "sacralization of psychology" that is typical for New Agers.[35] Key notions in New Age spirituality are "the quest within," "personal growth," or the development of "higher" levels of consciousness, and of course "healing." Özelsel's writings are suffused with this kind of terminology. Although she likes to call herself a Sufi, her form of self-spirituality is in fact the latest manifestation of Western esotericism. Her "holistic" worldview, stressing the transcendent unity of all non-Western traditions is rooted in the Western counterforce against Cartesian dualism and reductive materialism.[36]

The criticism of modern Western culture through a constant reit- eration of an essentialized opposition between "West" and "non-West" permeates Özelsel's whole hajj account (and other publications, for that matter). It can even be found at the most mundane level; for example, at the end of the hajj ceremonies she relates that she ate with relish slices of beef which had been dried in the scorching sun, described as a culi- nary procedure going back to the Prophet's lifetime. The exquisite taste reminds her of the "beef jerkies" from the United States, which she ascribes to the Native American Indian cuisine, and in her view the two delicacies are intimately related:

> Hier treffen sich Kulturen, die für mich Bedeutung haben, in ganz pragmatischer Art und Weise. Hier begegnen sich der Prophet (s.a.) und die Ureinwohner Amerikas im Bemühen der Achtung des Lebens, der Nichtverschwendung der Tiere, die ihr Leben für unseres hingegeben haben und mit denen wir verbunden sind im ununterbrochenen Kreislauf des Seins, (*PM,* 103)

In hadith literature (that is, the body of traditions relating to the words and deeds of the Prophet) the Prophet Mohammed is nowhere credited for a special beef recipe, but leaving this apocryphal attribution aside, Özelsel's parallel is intriguing. What is she hinting at? Is it just another example of her belief in the spiritual core that unites all non-Western traditions? Or is she perhaps alluding to yet another intrinsic connection between Native American Indian tradition(s) and Sufism? We have seen (above) that Terry Tafoya treated a married couple rooted in the Islamic tradition with the help of an old Indian ritual. If Tafoya is really Professor X., her spiritual guide, the phrase "Kulturen, die für mich Bedeutung haben" (cultures that have significance for me) would have a whole new meaning.

Being a therapist, Özelsel's account of her pilgrimage is a tale of intense suffering. She goes to Mecca as a way to find a solution for personal psychological problems. Her second marriage is about to end in a divorce, which very much upsets her. In the holy city she falls ill and finds it almost impossible to deal with so-called "third-world circumstances":

> Ich selbst habe mich schon seit gestern gehütet, etwas zu trinken, ist doch die Toilettensituation wirklich hoffnungslos. Aber wenn man Fieber hat und die Außentemperatur um 40°C im Schatten beträgt, wie sehnt man sich nach Flüssigkeit! Und nach einem Bett oder jedenfalls der Möglichkeit, sich auszustrecken, nach Ruhe und Geborgenheit und und und. . . . Was sind wir doch im Westen inzwischen hinsichtlich all solcher Annehmlichkeiten verwöhnt! Wieder denke ich, dass für so viele unserer Mitpilger aus den "Drittweltländern" diese Zustände nicht, wie für uns, zu den Ausnahmesituation zählen, sondern im Bereich der Norm liegen dürften. (*PM,* 88)

Apparently Michaela Özelsel is unaware of the fact that her fellow pilgrims from the "Third World" are not a bunch of beggars but belong to the affluent class who can afford this trip. It should be remembered that those who participate in the pilgrimage are typically from the more comfortable sectors of their societies, just like Özelsel herself. Predictably, lack of material comfort is juxtaposed with an abundance of spiritual richness: "Aus westlicher Sicht is es sicherlich eher einer der Tiefpunkte meiner Existenz, hier krank und absolut geschwächt im Straßenstaub Saudi-Arabiens zu liegen. Aus einer anderen Perspektive ist es ein Höhepunkt, eben eines der großen Rituale auf dem spirituellen Pfad, der Zweck und Sinn meines Seins geworden ist" (*PM*, 88).

The pilgrimage seems to be in her depiction a kind of seminar or workshop, a survival trip into the desert, with a spiritual bonus.[37] The voyage to Mecca, which Muslims like to call the journey of a lifetime, is done in exactly fourteen days. An elderly Turkish woman, a patient of Özelsel with her own problems, had invited Özelsel to travel along with her, and in a revealing episode we read that despite the prominence of spirituality and other-worldliness in her life Özelsel keeps a keen eye on material matters: "Wie um Himmels willen sollte ich es schaffen, für vier ganze Wochen von hier wegzugehen, ausgerechnet jetzt? Der Einkommensverlust eines ganzen Monats, während doch alle Kosten weiter liefen, . . . Und von all dem abgesehen, war doch allgemein bekannt, dass der Hadsch stressig ist . . . !" (*PM*, 19).

The compromise is a two-weekly "Kurz-Hadsch" or quick hajj tour. As the hajj proper spans only five days, Özelsel initially wanted more limited exposure to the mysterious world of Islam, but unfortunately there were no short city packages available anymore.

Özelsel regularly compares the hajj with the experiences she had had in 1991 as a recluse in Turkey, experiences about which she had written in her book *Forty Days: A Diary of a Traditional Sufi Retreat; With an Accompanying Scientific Commentary.* In 1990 her marriage to a Turkish man had ended in a divorce, and the forty-day Sufi ritual in Turkey was meant to be therapeutic. In 1996 her second marriage to a German man had broken down, and again an ancient ritual was to provide the much-needed psychological relief. The primary appeal of Islam, or rather its so-called Sufi variant, for her lies in healing. Sufism is designed to create a sense of personal well-being. Instead of presenting Sufism as an integral part of Islam, true because the Koran (God's word) and the Prophet Mohammed say it is true, Özelsel offers "Wissenschaft" or "science" as proof of its correctness.

But with all her talk of Western "Wissenschaft," Özelsel's sort of reasoning in fact rests on mistakes in logic. Non-Western healing techniques are said to be effective because they have been applied for centuries. This is the ludicrous *argumentum ad traditio* (appeal to tradition): a premise must be true because people have always believed it or done it. This is in tune with the thinking of New Age perennialists who believe in the existence of a "sophia perennis," that is, "a universal wisdom present, potentially at least, as the esoteric depth dimension *in* all great religions,"[38] except that Özelsel sees "true spirituality" as exclusively represented in non-Western traditions.

Another argument in her pseudo-reasoning is that non-Western esoteric traditions are true because they are in accordance with modern Western science. This is a fine example of circular reasoning, for what, after all, is this "modern Western science"? It appears to be just another word for ethnotherapy, the self-declared "scientific" practice of non-Western healing techniques. Ethnotherapy and modern Western science are constantly used interchangeably as synonyms. Her argumentation is topped off by an appeal to authority in the form of a Western PhD degree—on ethnotherapy. In other words: "Believe me, I'm a doctor. I know."

In reading Michaela Özelsel's account we learn a great deal about the inner journey of its author, but the story of her personal psychological problems refers to rather eccentric New Age views that cannot be said to be representative for large groups of other people who call themselves Muslims. To that extent her work provides a timely reminder that the encounter with Islam can be processed in manifold ways and that Islam is routinely misinterpreted or transformed in the process of reception, although perhaps not always as spuriously as appears to be the case in this text. At the very least, Özelsel's Orientalist strategy of "Othering" Muslims perpetuates old stereotypes, mirroring European fantasies about Islam that are far removed from the so-called mysterious world in which millions of Muslims happen to live. For "us" Westerners, and undoubtedly for non-Westerners also, Michaela Özelsel is not an ideal informant on Islam, because she is still very much one of "us."

Notes

[1] The article entitled "Ick bin ein Muslim," written by Christoph Ehrhardt, appeared in the *Frankfurter Allgemeine Zeitung* on Saturday, 17 Mar. 2007.

[2] Peter Finn, "Debate over a 'Defining culture' Roils Germany: In Statements of National Pride, Some Hear Nazi Lexicon," *Washington Post,* 2 Nov. 2000. Especially in German politics the Nazi bogeyman argument is the ultimate attempt to silence political opponents, but in this case the comparison is not wholly unfounded. As Arjun Appadurai makes clear in his thoughtful book *Fear of Small Numbers: An Essay on the Geography of Anger* (Durham, NC and London: Duke UP, 2006), the various ideologies of citizenship in Europe nowadays are not so "liberal" as they claim to be: "Are these majoritarianisms fundamentally different from the more 'totalitarian' ones that the Nazis installed in Germany in the 1930s and 1940s? My suggestion is that all majoritarianisms have in them the seeds of genocide, since they are invariably connected with ideas about the singularity and completeness of the national ethnos" (57).

[3] Rudolph Peters, *"A Dangerous Book": Dutch Public Intellectuals and the Koran* (Florence: European University Institute, 2006).

[4] Peters, *"A Dangerous Book,"* 11.

[5] Peters, *"A Dangerous Book,"* 11.

[6] The term "parallel society" is not exclusively German, but it seems to be reserved for Muslim communities in Western Europe; see, for example, George Thomas, "Muslims Create Parallel Communities," posted on CBNNews.com (the

Christian Broadcasting Network), 22 Feb. 2007, http://www.cbn.com/CBN-news/108405.aspx. Both citations are drawn from Thomas's worried article.

[7] The (German) text of Frits Bolkestein's speech entitled "Die Vielvölkerunion" can be found on his Web site, http://www.fritsbolkestein.com/docs/speeches/20040906_Vielvolkerunion_du.doc (accessed 16 May 2008).

[8] Frits Bolkestein, "Die Notwendigkeit einer Leitkultur," 19, http://www.fritsbolkestein.com/docs/speeches/20041018_Die%20Notwendigkeit_de.doc (accessed 16 May 2008).

[9] Aslan Khassan and Rizki Nugraha, "German Islamic Converts: Islam as an Alternative?" first published on 14 Feb. 2007, http://www.qantara.de/webcom/show_article.php/_c-478/_nr-569/i.html (accessed 16 May 2008).

[10] Mathias Gebauer and Yassin Musharbash, "Attacks Imminent? German Islamist Appears in New Jihad Video," *Spiegel Online International,* 29 Apr. 2008, http://www.spiegel.de/international/world/0,1518,550583,00.html (accessed 16 May 2008).

[11] Karin van Nieuwkerk, "Gender and Conversion to Islam in the West," in *Women Embracing Islam: Gender and Conversion in the West,* ed. Karin van Nieuwkerk (Austin: U of Texas P, 2006), 1.

[12] Van Nieuwkerk, "Gender and Conversion to Islam in the West," 4 provides useful references to secondary literature.

[13] See Van Nieuwkerk, "Gender and Conversion to Islam in the West," 5, for a discussion of different roles.

[14] Michaela M. Özelsel, *Pilgerfahrt nach Mekka: Meine Reise in eine geheimnisvolle Welt* (Freiburg: Herder, 2005). Subsequent references to this work are cited in the text using the abbreviation *PM* and the page number.

[15] For a popular anthology, see Michael Wolfe, *One Thousand Roads to Mecca: Ten Centuries of Travellers Writing about the Muslim Pilgrimage* (New York: Grove P, 1997).

[16] Carl W. Ernst, *Following Mohammed: Rethinking Islam in the Contemporary World* (Chapel Hill and London: U of North Carolina P, 2003), 166.

[17] Michaela M. Özelsel, *Vierzig Tage: Erfahrungsbericht einer traditionellen Derwischklausur* (Munich: Eugen Diederichs Verlag, 1993).

[18] Michaela M. Özelsel, *Forty days: A Diary of a Traditional Sufi Retreat; With an Accompanying Scientific Commentary* (Brattleboro, Vt: Threshold Books, 1996).

[19] Information from "Country Profiles: Germany" on the Web site Euro-Islam.info.

[20] Ken Plummer, *Telling Sexual Stories: Power, Change and Social Worlds* (London and New York: Routledge, 1997), 59.

[21] Koran, 56:79. The translation is taken from N. J. Dawood, *The Koran* (Harmondsworth, UK: Penguin, 1980), 112.

[22] Michaela M. Özelsel, "Die "andere Mentalität"—eine empirische Untersuchung zur sekundären Krankheitssicht türkischer Mitbürgerinnen," 12, http://www.praxis-kling.de/links/Oezelsel_die_andere_Mentalitaet.pdf (accessed 16 May 2008).

[23] Özelsel, "Die "andere Mentalität," 10.

[24] Ruth Teichroeb, "Masking the Truth: False Claims on Tribal Ties, Degrees Tarnish Counselor," dated 21 Jun. 2006. http://seattlepi.nwsource.com/local/274666_tafoyamain21.html (accessed 16 May 2008).

[25] Ron Franscell, "Terry Tafoya and Ward Churchill," dated 21 Jun. 2006. http://underthenews.blogspot.com/2006/06/terry-tafoya-and-ward-churchill.html (accessed 16 May 2008).

[26] Ruth Teichroeb, "Counselor Credentials Investigated: UW Registrar Ready to Take Action against Tafoya," dated 23 Jun. 2006. http://seattlepi.nwsource.com/local/275076_tafoya23.html (accessed 16 May 2008).

[27] Michaela Mihriban Özelsel, "Betrachtungen zu östlichen und westlichen therapeutischen Ansätzen: Ähnliches und Unterschiedliches," 2, Internationale Gesellschaft für Musikethnologische Forschung und Musiktherapie, spring 1993; http://www.ozelsel.de/files/6.pdf (accessed 5 May 2009).

[28] Cited in Jaan Klasmann, "Heilsame Trance," *Esotera* 2 (1998), 32.

[29] Michaela Mihriban Özelsel, "Frauen im Islam—in der Tradition und heute: Betrachtungen aus kulturanthropologischer Perspective," 1. This article first appeared in the journal *Dialog der Religionen* 2 (no year mentioned), 154–73, but I used the version on the Internet, http://www.fro.at/sendungen/islam/mihriban.html (accessed 16 May 2008).

[30] Edward W. Said, *Orientalism: Western Conceptions of the Orient* (London: Routledge & Kegan Paul, 1978).

[31] Review of Edward Said, *Orientalism,* by Malcolm Kerr in the *International Journal of Middle Eastern Studies* 12 (Dec. 1980): 544.

[32] Robert Irwin, *For the Lust of Knowing: The Orientalists and Their Enemies* (London: Allen Lane, 2006).

[33] Terry Eagleton's review appeared in the *New Statesman,* published on 13 Feb. 2006.

[34] On "self-spirituality" see Paul Heelas, *The New Age Movement: The Celebration of the Self and the Sacralisation of Modernity* (Oxford: Blackwell, 1996).

[35] Wouter Hanegraaff, *New Age Religion and Western Culture: Esotericism in the Mirror of Secular Thought* (New York: SUNY, 1998), 224–29.

[36] Cf. Hanegraaff, *New Age Religion and Western Culture,* 515–17. See also Carl W. Ernst, "Traditionalism, the Perennial Philosophy, and Islamic Studies" (review article), *Middle East Studies Association Bulletin* 28 (1994): 176–81.

[37] Cf. Heelas, *The New Age Movement,* 58–61 on New Age seminars and workshops.

[38] Hanegraaff, *New Age Religion and Western Culture,* 328.

12: Intimacies Both Sacred and Profane: Islam in the Work of Emine Sevgi Özdamar, Zafer Şenocak, and Feridun Zaimoğlu

Margaret Littler

There is a new wall rising in Berlin. Looking over that wall, one sees the parallel world of the Islamic suburbs. It's a world in which women, unlike some Muslim women in Europe who have risen to expansive lives, are still subject to arranged marriages and the control of their families.

T HESE ARE THE WORDS of novelist Peter Schneider, published in the *New York Times* on 4 December 2005, in an article that warns of the recent rise of radical Islam in Germany.[1] The author of *Der Mauerspringer* (1982), whose protagonist fantasized away the Cold War division of Berlin, now fears the development of another parallel world, of unassimilable, alien Muslim communities. And he is not alone in this anxiety. Despite significant changes to German citizenship legislation since 2000, which now acknowledges territorial as well as ancestral affiliation as the basis for German identity, the countermanding force of increased national security and decreasing tolerance of dual citizenship since September 2001 are signals of the troubled state of German multiculturalism today. Such antagonistic scenarios and fears of the emergence of a "Parallelgesellschaft" render all the more important the imaginative labor of Turkish-German authors in envisaging new kinds of German community, and in overcoming simplistic and homogenizing ideas of Islam in Europe.

Contemporary perceptions of Islam like Schneider's continue to rely on a tradition of dichotomous thinking in terms of global versus local, traditional versus modern, where Islam belongs immutably on the side of authentic local cultures and is pitted against global modernity. Scholars such as Yildiz Atasoy, by contrast, view Islam as part of the cultural complexity that is globalization, a view nowhere more aptly illustrated than in today's Turkey, where since 2002 a pro-Islamic, pro-Western party has had a majority in government.[2] As Atasoy points out, the strategic location of

Turkey between the West and the Islamic world, its position as an important player in NATO and applicant to join the EU, makes Turkey the only Muslim country that is integrated into Western political, economic, and cultural structures. It is also, in her words, the only one to have achieved "a political compromise between secular and Islamic political elites by incorporating Islam into the secular state structure."[3] Both a Muslim and a Western country, Turkey offers a unique and complex perspective on Islam, one inadequately understood in terms of tradition versus modernity, and local versus global dichotomies.

This seems an important and urgent context for understanding the work of Turkish-German authors today, despite Leslie Adelson's claim that "references to Islam are few and far between in this literature," usually occurring only with reference to Atatürk's secularization policies.[4] By emphasizing the European orientation of Turkish-German writers, she is resisting the tendency to locate Turks outside Germany and outside modernity.[5] But implicit in this is an assumption that *Islam* is outside modernity, whereas one could argue (with Atasoy) that Islam in Turkey can *only* be understood as a modernist project, in the context of the social, economic, and political development of the secular nation state. Moreover, as we will see, it can be a source of poetic inspiration and a site of transformative intensity in the texts under discussion here.

The aim of this chapter is to explore the complex ways in which Islam *does* figure in writing by Turkish authors in German, not in order to fix them in a culturally essentializing way, but rather to show how Islam is internal to the modernity of their works. This is also part of a project to read this literature as "minor literature" in Deleuze and Guattari's sense: not merely "representing" predictable images of minority or Muslim identities, but unsettling such images by means of their deterritorializing textual dynamics.[6] Thus in my reading, *all* intensities, both sacred and profane, can function as destabilizing of existing identities and creative of what Adelson has called a kind of "postnational intimacy."[7] Moreover, I see these texts as unsettling the very distinction between the sacred and the profane, so that spiritual encounters can be simultaneously intensely erotic, and the meeting of bodies productive of profoundly transformative affect. The porosity of boundaries between the religious and the secular may well be rooted in a tradition of mystical Anatolian Sufism for these writers, but it also has far-reaching and anticipatory implications for rethinking both individual and collective identities in dynamic terms of becoming, rather than fixed categories of being.

This chapter explores German encounters with Islam in texts by Emine Sevgi Özdamar, Zafer Şenocak, and Feridun Zaimoğlu. It will highlight their evocation of what Azade Seyhan has called "Islam with a Turkish accent,"[8] rooted in a rich tradition of Ottoman poetics and in the "mythic" dimensions of the Arabic language.[9] The focus here will be on the erotic encounters in Özdamar's story "Großvater Zunge" (1990) and in *Die Brücke vom Goldenen Horn* (1998), in which sexual and religious intensity are ambiguously linked. In Şenocak's novel *Der Erottomane* (1999), even the title suggests a link between erotic experience and Ottoman aesthetics.[10] These texts pose a cognitive challenge to Western perceptions of Islamic puritanism and frustrate any search for recognizable Muslim identities. Instead, Islam functions as a dynamic moment in the assemblage of the text, generating transformative intensities that resonate with unpredictable and anticipatory force. This is most evident in Zaimoğlu's story "Gottes Krieger" (in the volume *Zwölf Gramm Glück*, 2005), which treats both the latent violence in fundamentalist belief and the Islamic critique of capitalism, while confronting us with the disquieting possibility of the suicide bomber as a force of absolute deterritorialization.

Özdamar's short story "Großvater Zunge" (1990) can be read as an exploration of the differences between a mystical Turkish tradition of Islam and the orthodox Sunni teaching of the Koran.[11] It is the story of a Turkish woman's attempt to learn the Arabic script from an Arab teacher, Ibni Abdullah, in West Berlin, in order to reconnect with the Turkish of her grandparents' generation. As the relationship between pupil and teacher becomes one of passionate mutual desire, a tension emerges between Ibni Abdullah's view of "oriental" femininity on the one hand and the narrator's expectation of sexual autonomy on the other. But a further incongruity arises between his teaching of the Koran and her everyday understanding of Islam through Turkish folk tradition. This can be attributed to two things: first, the syncretic nature of Ottoman Islam, built on a foundation of earlier shamanistic traditions of nature worship, and second, the relegation of Islam to the status of personal faith in the early years of the Turkish Republic.[12] The Kemalists sought to show "that ancient Turkish culture was congruent with Western modernity,"[13] whereas Islam was averse to instrumental rationality and capitalist economy. Nonetheless, it remained an accepted, even encouraged, aspect of everyday life, and a tool of social cohesion. As David Shankland puts it: "Islam has been throughout the Republic at once an enemy of the secular state, and yet a tool of social order, excluded from the legislative apparatus of government, yet administered by the civil service."[14] In fact, he designates the state's insistence on secularism and its use of Islam to appeal to national sentiment a case of "parallel worlds" (33). Given the ambiguity of the republic's relationship to Islam, it is hardly surprising to find it reproduced in Özdamar's text. Her narrator is a Turkish Muslim, but unmistakably a product of the secular republic.

Of interest in this context are the sacred connotations of the sexual encounter between the narrator and her teacher, expressed in terms of a splitting of the beloved, who becomes both her sexual partner and an embodied part of herself: "Ich lief einen Monat lang mit Ibni Abdullah in meinem Körper in beiden Berlin"; "ich sprach zu dem Ibni Abdullah, der in meinem Körper ist."[15] Indeed, the voice of the Ibni Abdullah within distracts her with his love songs from her reading of the Koran, eliciting from her in response a passionate love song:

> Ich lernte die Schrift schlecht, weil ich immer mit dem Ibni Abdul-lah, der in meinem Körper war, mit anderen Wörtern sprach: "Du Seele in meiner Seele, keine ist dir ähnlich, ich opfere mich für deine Schritte. Mit deinen Blicken schautest du mich an, ich gebe mich zum Opfer deinem Blicke. Verwahrlost, Haar gelöst, fortwimmern will ich, mit einem Blick hast du meine Zunge an deine Haare gebunden. Ich bin die Sklavin deinen [sic] Antlitzes. Zerbrich nicht diese Kette, lehne mich nicht ab, Geliebter, ich bin die Sklavin dei-nes Gesichts geworden, sag mir nur, was tue ich jetzt, was tue ich jetzt." "Du bist ungeduldig, unkonzentriert," sagte Ibni Abdullah. "Die Schrift verzeiht es dir nicht." (29–30)

This bodily incorporation of the beloved may be derived from the Sufi desire to overcome the painful separation from God, resulting in an effacement of the sense of self.[16] But this dissolution of self may also arise from the intensity of an encounter that is not purely religious (or not in the sense of an appeal to a transcendent being), and can thus be read as an instance of Deleuzian becoming, an overriding of subjective boundaries in Özdamar's work, which occurs precisely where mutual understanding breaks down.

Todd May has described the erotics of desire in Deleuzian terms as just such a porosity of boundaries, rather then simply communication or a kind of "exchange."[17] This is based on Deleuze's ontology of immanence, where becoming is a continual creation, not reducing experience to the knowable but instead seeking "to palpate the unknowable."[18] The Deleuzian self is defined not by an unchanging center but by its margins, where it enters into relations with others, which are themselves seen as multiplicities. Here becoming is not simply the idea of the self being in flux; becoming is "an objective zone of indistinction or indiscernibility that always exists between any two multiplicities, a zone that immediately *precedes* their respective natural differentiation."[19] The objective and embodied nature of the one-ness with the beloved in "Großvater Zunge" suggests to me such a zone of material indistinction, and its corporeality is underlined by the narrator's finally resorting to the sensory deprivation of a night in the "Bahnhofsmis-sion" in order to drive Ibni Abdullah out of herself: "Ich brauchte ein sehr hartes Bett. Das Bett müßte mich so beschäftigen, daß ich nur an das Bett denke . . . Ich wollte Ibni Abdullah, der in mir ist, in Ohnmacht bringen. Ich aß nicht, ich trank nicht" (42–43).

This same trope—an intense erotic encounter followed by a solitary night in the station mission—is repeated in the later novel *Die Brücke vom*

Goldenen Horn. Here motifs of doubling also recall the earlier text, and although the encounter is not explicitly religious, there are unmistakable structural similarities. The novel is narrated by a young Turkish woman who goes to Berlin in the mid-1960s as a migrant laborer, becomes politicized in the escalating student movement, and returns to Istanbul in 1967. There she trains as an actress and experiences the much-more-serious political conflict between the political left and the state. In a lyrical passage about halfway through the novel, the narrator travels from Berlin (where she has been working in a factory) to Paris, where she encounters a Catalan student named Jordi. They share only a few words of broken English, but on the basis of their brief time together she identifies him as the love of her life. Shadow imagery plays an important role in the bodily encounter, as her first awareness of Jordi is of his shadow's overlapping with her own. The shadows in the park of the Cité Universitaire have a characteristically concrete presence, seeming much more substantial than an effect of light:

> Ich lief zwischen die Schatten der Bäume, als ob ich diese Schatten nicht stören wollte. Die Erde zeigte mir meine Beinschatten, sie waren sehr dünn, sehr lang, dann lief ein anderer Beinschatten neben meinem her, ich schaute nur auf die Erde. Dann lief der andere Bein-schatten durch meine Beine hindurch. Wir liefen und liefen.[20]

Their shadows become intimate before they even have eye contact, and as he follows her into the student canteen and stands with his tray in the queue next to her, the trembling of their two bodies is visible first in the water in her glass: "Als ich mit meinem leeren Tablett vor der Kantinenfrau stand und zeigte, was ich essen wollte, stieß ein anderes Tablett an meins, und das Wasser im Glas auf meinem Tablett zitterte."(129) This exteriorization of desire is more than metonymy and is a characteristic feature of Özdamar's writing, in which affect is frequently detached from individual subjectivity. Similarly the shadow motif can be read via Deleuze as a zone on the edge of the subject that affords knowledge, though not of a cerebral, conceptual, or even spiritual kind. Indeed, the soul/body distinction implied in the sacred/profane dichotomy has to be suspended, or at least questioned, when dealing with Deleuze's ontology of immanence.

Deleuze associates the shadow with a Spinozist notion of meaning that emerges at the level of matter rather than circulating in a system of signs. In an essay on Spinoza's *Ethics* he writes: "Effects or signs are *shadows* that play on the surface of bodies, always between two bodies. The shadow is always on the edge. It is always a body that casts a shadow on another body. We have knowledge of bodies only through the shadows they cast upon us, and it is through our own shadow that we know ourselves, ourselves and our bodies."[21] Frank Krause has interpreted the shadow motif in this novel as signalling a discontinuity in understanding in the cross-cultural encounter, and he links it to the Anatolian shadow-puppet theatre tradition of Karagöz and Hacivat, with its play on the cacophony of mutually incomprehensible dialects in rural Anatolia.[22] In terms of the present argument, however, the shadow may be viewed *positively* as an alternative kind of knowledge, akin to the material, affective language described by Deleuze, and not simply as a metaphor for a gap in understanding:

> The kind of knowledge they constitute [i.e. signs or affects] is hardly a knowledge, but rather an experience in which one randomly encounters confused ideas of bodily mixtures, brute imperatives to avoid this mixture and seek another, and more or less delirious interpretations of these situations. Rather than a form of expression, this is a material and affective language, one that resembles cries rather than the discourse of the concept.[23]

This is, after all, a delirious encounter between bodies in which almost no verbal communication takes place.

Connected to the idea of pre-subjective knowledge, a knowledge not communicated by language, and sharing the erotic/religious intensity of "Großvater Zunge" is the image of doubling that accompanies the encounter with Jordi. Very early in the encounter the narrator is split between an observing and an acting self: "Es war, als ob ich als ein zweites Ich neben mir lief" (130), and after a visit to the Hall of Mirrors at Versailles Jordi himself is also split, so they walk around Paris in a foursome. At other times there is a merging: as they lie together in his bed, they appear to the observing self "wie ein einziger Körper" (136), his beard seeming to grow into her face (137), and the embracing couple levitates in a surreal scene, viewed first from below ("Das Mädchen und der Junge flogen langsam hoch oben im Zimmer"; 136), then from the levitated position ("über unseren Körpern gingen kleine Feuer an"; 137). Their bodies are surrounded by inextinguishable flames, which reignite when dampened by their own sweat. This echoes the love poetry of "Großvater Zunge," where the hellfire threatened in the Koran appears less menacing in the face of the consuming fire of the lovers' passion and indeed is conflated with it. The doubling/multiplication of selves is augmented when the lovers address each other in different languages in the mirrors at Versailles, and when she leaves Paris on the train, Jordi's double, like Ibni Abdullah, initially accompanies her (144).

These passages of materialization and doubling are potentially both rooted in a Turkish tradition *and* point beyond a dualistic model of thinking, with their projection of affect outside singular, subjective experience. Victoria Rowe Holbrook has described a specifically Turkish understanding of "imagination" derived from Ottoman poetics, where imagination is not a product of the mind alone but an intermediary between the abstract and concrete realms, subsisting in its own realm, anticipating actualization: "Imagination is a realm of non-corporeal yet sensory comprehension, where its comprehension occurs; a realm interiorized as part of the human microcosm and objectified as part of the cosmos. This intellectual habit of objectifying a point of view, at once the place where it occurs, what is seen there, and the act of viewing, is something yet to be considered as a fundamental of Ottoman thought."[24] This is highly suggestive, both in relation to the shifting perspectives in the levitation scene just cited and to Özdamar's very "corporeal" style of writing in general, but it is also compatible with Deleuze's view of the virtual, as the unactualized potential within the real, for which art and literature provide possible worlds. A remarkably similar idea is captured in Holbrook's account of originality in Ottoman poetics: "Original poetry would not be an imitation of material reality, but a participation in bringing material reality to be" (453).

If Özdamar's writing evokes a premodern poetic tradition that seems compatible with a Deleuzian reading, in which erotic and religious intensities have transformative power, a similar tendency may be observed in the (stylistically very different) work of Zafer Şenocak. In an essay entitled "Das Schweigen der muslimischen Kultur" Şenocak has lamented the loss of a rich intellectual tradition in contemporary Muslim cultures, which have lapsed into prudish dogmatism. Despite the achievements of writers like Salman Rushdie and Orhan Pamuk, there is a whole erotic tradition of Islamic culture that has been lost without trace:

> Dabei bleibt vor allem die erotische Komponente der islamischen Kultur fast unangetastet, dort, wo sie vor ein paar Jahrhunderten begraben wurde. Das Spannungsfeld von Homosexualität und Heterosexualität war in der Blütezeit der muslimischen Kultur zwischen dem 8. und 13. Jahrhundert die eigentliche Triebfeder der geistigen Erneuerung. . . . Erst die Wiederentdeckung des muslimischen kulturellen Erbes in all seinen frommen und häretischen Strömungen, seinen rationalen und irrationalen, seinen skeptischen und euphorischen Geisteswelten kann eine wirkliche Renaissance der islamischen Kultur einleiten.[25]

Moray McGowan has shown the transgressive force of Şenocak's construction of masculinities, which challenge all kinds of polarized gender norms, but sees this as a feature of his postmodern, post-national credentials rather than linking it to a tradition within Islamic art.[26] We can, however, allow both to be true, and read the novel as Şenocak rendering a long forgotten cultural heritage dynamic for the present.

Similarities with Özdamar's prose in *Der Erottomane* include "Doppelgänger" figures that destabilize individual subjectivity (Robert, Tom, narrator), and characters who are driven by desire and the erotics of physical encounter rather than volition. This episodic novel opens with a letter to the narrator from his friend Tom, a lawyer, about the discovery of the dead body of Robert, a writer (and "der Erottomane") whose "Nachlass" appears to be collected in the chapters that follow. But it soon becomes apparent that both Tom and Robert might be alter egos of the narrator himself—they are all naturalized Germans of Turkish descent, polyglot cosmopolitans, in pursuit of sexual experience and creative inspiration—identities are interchangeable in the fragmentary narrative that ensues. However, cultural, geographical, and historical reference points, such as the notion of mapping a new Silk Road, point to investments that are global and political, not just personal or familial.[27]

The only explicit reference to religion in the text is in the provocatively titled chapter "Fridaynightfever"[28] which draws parallels between the rituals of religion and sex. The narrator (who is both Tom and Robert) attributes his heightened sex drive on Friday evenings to a residual, unconscious proximity to Islam (70). The erotic appeal of his Friday-night fantasies, which are described in terms reminiscent of collective worship, lies in their collective and ritual dimensions:

> Der Freitag ist der Tag des Höhepunkts, ein heiliger Tag. . . . In der Paarkonstellation definiert sich der Eine durch die Kontrolle über den Anderen. Bei der Gruppe dagegen konzentriert sich alles auf ein Zentrum, das variieren kann. Spiele um die ständig wechselnde Balance in der Gruppe sind Quelle ungeahnter Lust. Wer den Spaß in der Gruppe entdeckt, verliert jede Hemmung, fühlt sich geborgen und unkontrolliert, verteilt seine Lust und Aggressionen auf mehr als nur eine Person. Er gibt weniger und empfängt mehr. Wichtig ist, daß man vorher gründlich duscht, als ginge es darum, eine andere Person zu werden. Nachher wird man dasselbe tun. (72–73)

Of interest here is both the merging of erotic and religious rituals (and the possibilities of intensity generated by both), and the focus on collective dynamics, the dispersal of desire across and between bodies in contact. This again recalls a Deleuzian view of eroticism, which is as much a matter of surfaces and body parts coming into contact as it is about a relating of individuals. As Todd May puts it: "Love's erotics is a matter between individuals, but it is not only that. It is also a matter between body parts, between surfaces that come in contact. And the individuals to whom those surfaces belong are a product of that contact at least as much as its subject."[29] That is, the lover is as much a product of her erotic investment as the faith community is a product of its investment in prayer. Instead of prayer being the expression of a collective identity, the investment in the collective act of worship produces the collective religious identity. This is borne out by the interchangeable narrators of

Şenocak's text, who are produced by their language and certain shared characteristics, as described in a self-referential comment at the end of the book: "Der Leser muß sich an den Figuren orientieren, die immer wieder auftauchen. Es sind dieselben Figuren, wenn auch mit unterschiedlichen Namen, Berufen, Lebensorten und Situationen. Trotz ihrer unterschiedlichen Identitäten erkennt man sie anhand ihrer Eigenschaften und ihrer persönlichen Sprache wieder" (123).

A pre-personal focus on body parts characterizes many of the sexual encounters in Şenocak's text, which suggests the indeterminacy of self associated with both erotic and religious intensity. In "Der Antiquar" the narrator, who has taken over a secondhand bookshop in an unnamed coastal town, describes himself as "ein Reisender. Genaugenommen ein Durchreisender. Einer, der seinen Körperteilen nachreist. Mal ist es der Kopf, der mich führt, mal die Hände" (35); "Ich war dieses Mal meiner Zunge nachgereist" (38). The tongue has multiple connotations in the novel; it is synomymous with language (the narrator describes himself as a "Doppelzüngler" (15), implying both his bilingual and unreliable status); the tongue, rather than the hand, is the organ that enables writing (38); and Robert's lover Alexandra wields a "siebenzüngige Peitsche" (63), with which *she* inscribes her thoughts on his body. It is she who calls him "der Erottomane"; he experiences ecstasy in subjugation to her will and feels "impregnated" by her long after she has left him. This could well be a parodic reversal of Mediterranean machismo, or, as McGowan suggests, a play on "the orientalist image of the sensual Turk."[30] But it also invites reflection on the body/mind dualism, privileging the former as the site of greater intensity: "Der Geist ist nur ein Randbezirk des Körpers. Wenn man einmal im Körper Platz genommen hat, verweilt man nicht mehr gerne am Rand. Man muß zuerst fühlen, bevor man sich wohlfühlt" (66). Sexual intensity releases creative energies but can also lead to ritual murder, as in the last chapter of the book, where the victim "R" fails to emerge from an appointment with a prostitute. Death, it would appear, is a transformation, not an end; the narrative is picked up by another narrative voice and the story continues. This brings me to the last aspect of the treatment of Islam, that of its association with violence and terror.

In a chapter of Şenocak's earlier novel *Die Prärie* (1997), entitled "Phantasie eines Jägers," the narrator describes a "clash of civilisations" between North America and the Arab world, in which the Arabs use Islam mainly to distance themselves from the passionless, computer-controlled predictability of globalization: "Die Araber . . . pflegen ihre sinnlosen Rituale nicht, weil sie an sie glauben, sondern weil sie damit Distanz zur übrigen Welt aufbauen wollen."[31] The narrator, hired by the Arabs as a contract killer, shares their contempt for the complacent culture of his victims and has cynically converted and agreed to circumcision to take up his post. A more serious and lengthy treatment of the theme of Islamist opposition to Western imperialism is found in Feridun Zaimoğlu's short story "Gottes Krieger" in *Zwölf Gramm Glück* (2005). The text gives us a young Islamist's thoughts on returning to Turkey, leaving behind the extremist organization in Germany in which he had been trained as a committed anti-capitalist and "warrior of God." His thoughts are interspersed with italicized passages of the leader's own words, which afford insights into the grooming of young suicide bombers. It is unclear whether he has left the organization to go in search of the "Herzprediger," who has disappeared, or because of disillusionment at revelations of the man's sexual hypocrisy. The complexity of the story lies in the young man's incomplete detachment from the Islamist mindset, even after he has seen through the danger of the leader's rhetoric and finally broken with the organization. Moreover, set in a coastal resort of southern Turkey, the story reflects something of the political complexities of Islam in today's republic. The volume is divided into two sections, the first seven stories set in Germany and entitled "Diesseits," the last five set in Turkey being "Jenseits," already signaling (with considerable irony) Islam's relationship to the West as a central theme.

The young man is horrified by the sexual license all around him in the Turkish seaside resort, though he does also begin a discreet affair with his landlady, a considerably older divorcee and widow. Attending a rural wedding with "die Witwe," he is overwhelmed by desire for her at the very moment when a folkdance reaches a stage of frenzied acceleration. As in Şenocak's work, there are ambiguities between sexual desire and religious fervor:

> Die Männerkette schließt sohlenklatschend einen perfekten Kreis und tanzt immer schneller, immer wilder, ich atme aus dem offenen Mund, ich kann an nichts anderes denken als an die Frau an meiner Seite, die mich begehrt und die ich begehre, ich sehe die Krieger, und ich bin glücklich: glücklich darüber, daß diese wehrtüchtigen Männer sich jedem Barbarenheer in den Weg stellen werden, daß sie zurückschlagen, bis der Feind Blut und Galle kotzt. Ein Gott. Ein Gottesheer.[32]

The extent to which he is still the product of the discourse of his former leader emerges in the italicized quotations from his former leader, which speak in terms of the opposition between "Fleischmaschinen" and "Gottesmaschinen," and the need to combat the "West-Amerikanischer Judasstaat" (139) and "Byzanz-Babylon-Europa" (131). So even when he has shaved off his beard and started to watch celebrity TV shows, he cannot help but abhor the power of global capitalism to manipulate the poor with false, unsatisfiable desires: "Mir ergeht es wie allen Abtrünnigen: Ich bin müde, die Ruhe eines bloßen Zivilisten bekommt mir nicht" (144). He tries to explain his past to his lover (who is suspicious of sects and horrified by his revelations), the young Islamists' love of their leader and their belief that their self-sacrifice would bring them closer to God: "Ich bin kein Mörder. Ich war ein präparierter Sprengkörper. Ich glaube immer noch, daß die Judaslämmer den Erlöser nicht loswerden, Gottes Sturz haben sie umsonst gefeiert" (150). That is, he retains his belief and deplores secularization, even defending the position of the suicide bomber.

To understand the narrator's position it is not enough to see him as "cured" of his extremism by romantic love, settling for a "moderated" form of religiosity and pragmatic benevolence.[33] The text's insistent machinic metaphors, the power of the priest's rhetoric, and the ambiguous ending suggest a reading of the story in terms of the Deleuzian war machine, as a counterforce to the state's centralized and hierarchical apparatus. The war machine is one of the intensive processes, described in *A Thousand Plateaus*, which open up the potential of becoming and mutation in actual, steady state, or stable systems. The war machine's goal is emphatically not war but transformation and becoming. It only results in war when its energies are appropriated by the military state apparatus, the army being the reterritorialized residue of the war machine. Deleuze and Guattari attributed an ambiguous status to the universalizing religions such as Christianity and Islam, which could also be war machines, liberating deterritorializing and nomadic energies, just as much as they could fulfill their sedentary, regulatory function as state religions. This is particularly pertinent to today's Turkey, where a secularist, nationalist state ideology exists in increasing tension with the religious party in government:[34]

> For monotheistic religion, at the deepest level of its tendency to project a universal or spiritual State over the entire ecumenon, is not without ambivalence or fringe areas; it goes beyond even the ideal limits of the State, even the imperial State, entering a more indistinct zone, an outside of States where it has the possibility of undergoing a singular mutation or adaptation. We are referring to religion as an element in a war machine and the idea of holy war as the motor of that machine. The *prophet*, as opposed to the state personality of the king and the religious personality of the priest, directs the movement by which a religion becomes a war machine or passes over to the side of such a machine.[35]

A similar ambiguity infuses the end of Zaimoğlu's story, in a confrontation between the narrator and one of his former "brothers," who is the epitome of an ascetic urban guerrilla: "gestählt, wachsam, angriffsbereit" (154). This young man refuses to be known by his "Heidennamen," Karl, and has his own, personal reasons for hating the West. He sees the narrator as a traitor and declares the impossibility of worshipping God in modern Turkey, where the "Judaslamm-Demokraten" are plunging the country into ruin.[36] The narrator retorts that he is still a believer, but no longer a "Herrengläubiger," and walks out of the house, his mind no longer on the priest's hyperbole but full of the words of the Prophet. In an interesting twist at the end of the story, his intention in walking out in front of cars remains ambiguously open. He is perhaps no longer part of the de-individualized "Gottes Kriegsgerät" (149) in thrall to a charismatic leader and an oppressive transcendence, but his thoughts are now focused on the fine membrane that separates heaven and earth, soul and matter. Indifferent to the danger of death as he steps out with the sleepwalker's certainty into the traffic, he has abandoned the identity of the terrorist, setting off on a nomadic line of flight.

These three writers all bring German culture into contact with Islam in different and unpredictable ways. Özdamar's prose is informed by secular, leftist values, yet she draws on a cultural background that has accommodated Islam as a personal relationship with God, and she owes a debt to a poetic tradition in which sacred and profane are shifting and overlapping categories. Şenocak sets out explicitly to revive a tradition of erotic Islamic art, while retaining a cynical distance from political Islam. He has written of how the translation of the thirteenth-century Anatolian poet Yunus Emre's work helped him to reconcile the cultural clashes within his own upbringing. Emre's poetry afforded him "einen sinnlichen Raum, eine Existenzform des Geistes," and a fluid, non-individualistic awareness of difference, reminiscent of the decentered, multi-perspectival Ottoman aesthetic described by Holbrook: "Die Grenzen zwischen Glaube und Unglaube und zwischen den Religionen waren durchlässig, der Blick auf den Anderen war nicht durch die Rhetorik des Eigenen getrübt, vielmehr ein befremdeter Blick auf das Eigene."[37] Zaimoğlu's attempt to present the mindset of a young Islamist from within also unsettles a polarized understanding of religious versus secular values, while showing how a terrorist can be produced by discourse. The story's ambiguous ending, like many of Zaimoğlu's more recent texts, leaves open the possibility of a transformative, creative force of spirituality, offering an alternative to the familiar figure of the Muslim terrorist. The aim of this chapter has been to present these writers not *only* as referring "back" to an originary religious culture, however, but to read them as writers whose works unsettle our tradition of thinking in fixed categories of identity, whether religious, ethnic, national, or even gendered. The materialization of emotional states, the liberation of affect from its anchoring in individual subjects, and the notion of an affective, corporeal language can all be read in terms of Deleuze's view of literature, not as a representation of lived experience, but as traversing both lived and livable worlds. Or, to return for a moment to Ottoman Poetics, minor literature is "a participation in bringing material reality to be."[38]

Notes

[1] Peter Schneider, "In Germany, Muslims Grow Apart," *New York Times,* Sunday 4 Dec. 2005. www.iht.com/bin/print_ipub.php?rile=/articles/2005/12/02/new/islam7/php (accessed 10 Apr. 2006).

[2] "The AKP [Adalet ve Kalkınma Partisi] supports Turkey's military alliance with the United States, promises to advance Turkey's claim to European Union membership, and pledges to build a rapprochement with Greece. Yet it is at odds with Turkey's powerful military bureaucracy and the official state ideology of secularism." Yildiz Atasoy, *Turkey, Islamists and Democracy: Transition and Globalization in a Muslim State* (London and New York: I. B. Tauris, 2005), 6.

[3] Atasoy, *Turkey, Islamists and Democracy,* 8. The success of this compromise is, admittedly, debatable, in view of nationalist opposition to the AKP.

[4] Leslie A. Adelson, *The Turkish Turn in Contemporary German Literature: Toward a New Critical Grammar of Migration* (New York: Palgrave Macmillan, 2005), 13, 178.

[5] Adelson, *The Turkish Turn,* 22.

[6] It is important in this context to distinguish between "minority" writing (with which the authors in question may or may not identify) and "minor literature," which is a designation applicable to any writing that challenges the majoritarian norm.

[7] Adelson, *The Turkish Turn,* 20.

[8] Azade Seyhan, *Writing outside the Nation* (Princeton, NJ: Princeton UP, 2001), 146.

[9] I refer here to Deleuze's distinctions between the vernacular, vehicular, referential, and mythic types of language. Having lost its referential power in these texts, Arabic is now a purely mythic language, referring to a spiritual, religious domain. But in Özdamar's work it also functions performatively, no longer "naming" a world, but producing material effects. See Daniel W. Smith, "Introduction: 'A Life of Pure Immanence': Deleuze's *Critique et Clinique* Project," in Gilles Deleuze, *Essays Critical and Clinical,* trans. Daniel W. Smith and Michael A. Greco (London: Verso, 1998). xi–liii; here xlvi–xlvii.

[10] See Margaret Littler, "Erotik und Geschichte in Zafer Şenocak's *Der Erottomane,*" *Akten des XI. Internationalen Germanistenkongresses, Paris 2005: Germanistik im Konflikt der Kulturen,* vol. 6, ed. Jean-Marie Valentin and Stéphane Pesnel (Bern: Peter Lang, 2007), 267–72.

[11] See Margaret Littler, "Diasporic Identity in Emine Sevgi Özdamar's *Mutterzunge,*" in *Recasting German Identity: Culture, Politics and Literature in the Berlin Republic,* ed. Stuart Taberner and Frank Finlay (Rochester, NY: Camden House, 2002), 219–34, and Brigid Haines and Margaret Littler, *Contemporary Women's Writing in German: Changing the Subject* (Oxford: Oxford UP, 2004), 118–38. Adelson also acknowledges the importance of Islam in this story (*The Turkish Turn,* 155), noting in addition the ambiguity of color symbolism in the story, where "green" connotes both Islam and environmental thinking (157).

[12] Atasoy notes that the 1937 Sun-Language Theory saw the shamanism of the pre-Ottoman Turks as foundational for Turkish culture, whereas Islam was an ethnic religion of Arabs, associated with Arabic language and traditions (*Turkey, Islamists and Democracy,* 40). But at the same time the foundation of the Directorate of Religious Affairs in 1923 ensured complete state control of the religious practice of the Turks, at home and abroad, leading to a further "Turkification" of the practice of Islam. See David Shankland, *Islam and Society in Turkey* (Huntingdon: Eothen P, 1999), 28–32.

[13] Atasoy, *Turkey, Islamists and Democracy,* 40.

[14] Shankland, *Islam and Society in Turkey,* 44.

[15] Emine Sevgi Özdamar, *Mutterzunge* (Berlin: Rotbuch, 1990), 19 and 28. Subsequent references will be to this edition and will be given in the text.

[16] Littler, "Diasporic Identity," 228–29.

[17] Todd May, *Gilles Deleuze: An Introduction* (Cambridge: Cambridge UP, 2005), 167–69.

[18] May, *Gilles Deleuze,* 171.

[19] "The self is a threshold, a door, a becoming between two multiplicities," Smith, "Introduction: 'A Life of Pure Immanence,'" xxx.

[20] Emine Sevgi Özdamar, *Die Brücke vom Goldenen Horn* (Cologne: Kiepenheuer & Witsch, 1998), 129. Subsequent references will be to this edition and will be given in the text.

[21] Gilles Deleuze, "Spinoza and the Three Ethics," in *Essays Critical and Clinical,* trans. Daniel W. Smith and Michael A. Greco (London: Verso, 1998), 138–51; here 141.

[22] Frank Krause, "Shadow Motifs in Emine Sevgi Özdamar's *Die Brücke vom Goldenen Horn,*" *Debatte* 8.1 (2000): 71–81; here 77.

[23] Deleuze, "Spinoza and the Three Ethics," 143–44.

[24] Victoria Rowe Holbrook, "Originality and Ottoman Poetics: In the Wilderness of the New," *Journal of the American Oriental Society* 112.3 (1992): 440–54; here 453.

[25] Zafer Şenocak, "Das Schweigen der muslimischen Kultur," in *Zungenentfernung: Bericht aus der Quarantänestation* (Munich: Babel, 2001), 75–78; here 78.

[26] "Şenocak's work is one of the most strikingly original examples of a dialectic whereby, out of a process set in train by Turkish migration to Germany, writing is emerging which has long left these origins behind it." Moray McGowan, "Odysseus on the Ottoman, or 'The Man in Skirts': Exploratory Masculinities in the Prose Texts of Zafer Şenocak," in *Zafer Şenocak,* ed. Tom Cheesman and Karin Yeşilada (Cardiff: U Wales P, 2003), 61–79; here 76.

[27] It is, however, interesting to note that Batumi was the birthplace of Şenocak's maternal grandmother, whose family were Muslim Adjars from present-day Georgia.

[28] Zafer Şenocak, *Der Erottomane* (Munich: Babel, 1999), 69–73. Subsequent references will be to this edition and will be given in the text.

[29] May, *Gilles Deleuze,* 169.

[30] McGowan, "Odysseus on the Ottoman," 68.

[31] Zafer Şenocak, *Die Prärie* (Hamburg: Rotbuch, 1997), 94.

[32] Feridun Zaimoğlu, "Gottes Krieger," in *Zwölf Gramm Glück* (Cologne: Kiepenheuer & Witsch, 2005), 122–56; here 138. Subsequent references will be to this edition and will be given in the text.

[33] This is Tom Cheesman's interpretation of the story in *Novels of Turkish German Settlement: Cosmopolite Fictions* (Rochester, NY: Camden House, 2007), 79.

[34] This tension was most recently visible in the vote in parliament that sought to lift the headscarf ban in Turkish universities (Jan. 2008), and in the failed attempt to ban the ruling AKP party as unconstitutional (Jul. 2008).

[35] Gilles Deleuze and Félix Guattari, *A Thousand Plateaus: Capitalism and Schizophrenia,* trans. Brian Massumi (London: Continuum, 2004), 423.

[36] It is worth noting that although the Democratic Party that ruled Turkey in the 1950s was pro-USA and accelerated Turkey's Westernization, it was always the Republicans who were the most determined secularists, and it is actually the development of democracy that has produced the resurgence of political Islam in Turkey.

[37] Zafer Şenocak, "Zwischen Koran und Sex Pistols," in *Das Land hinter den Buchstaben: Deutschland und der Islam im Umbruch* (Munich: Babel, 2006), 29–33; here 31, 30.

[38] Holbrook, "Originality and Ottoman Poetics," 435.

13: Encountering Islam at Its Roots: Ilija Trojanow's *Zu den heiligen Quellen des Islam*

Frauke Matthes

WHILE MUSLIMS HAVE INCREASINGLY BEEN MOVING to Europe and not least Germany over the last few decades, bringing with them various denominations of their faith, another journey is at the center of every Muslim's life: the hajj, the annual pilgrimage to Mecca and Medina in the month of Dhu al-Hijjah. This journey constitutes one of the five pillars of Islam; the others are the *shahada* (witnessing the oneness of God and the prophethood of Mohammed), *salat* (regular observance of the five prescribed daily prayers), paying *zakah* (almsgiving), and *sawm* or *siyyam* (fasting during the month of Ramadan).[1] Like the other pillars of Islam, the hajj is part of every Muslim's duty as a religious individual and has to be carried out at least once in his/her lifetime, if sufficient finances and good health allow it.[2] This journey is a particularly Islamic way of traveling, as it celebrates Muslim belief in Islam's "homeland" and reinforces the pilgrim's feeling of belonging to the Muslim community, the *umma*. The pilgrimage is justified historically: the Prophet Mohammed emigrated from Mecca to Medina in 622 because he had to flee persecution by the Meccan aristocracy; this event is referred to as *hijra*.[3] In Medina he established the first Muslim community, which, from then on, was to be known as the *umma*. Although the pilgrimage to Mecca and Medina is an essentially communal form of traveling, it also makes each traveler reflect upon his/her individual identity as Muslim.

Ilija Trojanow, one of the most successful German writers of the last few years, traveled to Mecca and Medina in 2003 and later brought the experiences he had on his hajj to life again in his travel account *Zu den heiligen Quellen des Islam: Als Pilger nach Mekka und Medina* (2004). He went to Saudi Arabia as both a Muslim and a writer, and so his text makes explicit the journey of the traveler-writer as a form of self-exploration both during the journey itself and the subsequent act of writing about it.

Trojanow, who was born in Sofia, Bulgaria, in 1965, moved to Germany with his family in 1971. He has traveled widely and has lived in many places throughout his life. The writer-journalist-publisher has—in his own words—always aimed at "nicht von der Heimat in die Fremde und wieder zurück zu reisen, sondern die Fremde in Heimat zu verwandeln, sinnlich, sprachlich."[4] Between 1998 and 2003 he lived in Mumbai, and it was here that he rediscovered his Muslim roots; this led to his decision to go on the hajj. Like many others before him, Trojanow portrays in his account of his hajj his individual experiences of Islam among other believers. As a Muslim, he performs the hajj not only as part of his religious duties but also as the fulfillment of his longing for the unique experience of being a member of the *umma* that celebrates its unity in its original "homeland." Yet Trojanow also travels as a writer, specifically as a potential author of a *rihla*, the traditional account of traveling for learning and other purposes. He writes:

> Dieser Bericht steht in einer alten Tradition. Seit mehr als tausend Jahren existiert der literarische Typus einer Reiseerzählung über die Hadsch, auf arabisch Rihla, auf persisch Safarnameh genannt—Zeugnisse einer Pilgerschaft als Kulmination aller Sehnsüchte, als einzigartige Aus-Zeit, so reich an Mühsal und Zermürbung wie an Belohnung und Beglückung.[5]

The correlation between traveling and learning as it is emphasized by the *rihla* does not end at the journey's destination but continues as reflection on the trip, which enables the writer to relive the experience of the pilgrimage. The physical journey thus becomes a spiritual journey of the mind. Trojanow prefers to be seen as part of the Muslim tradition of writing about the hajj, reflecting upon what it means to be part of the *umma*, rather than as indulging in pure self-exploration in opposition to an "Other."[6] He even places himself in opposition to what he regards as Western travel writing. He wishes to distance himself from Western travel writers who construct the countries they visit in order to foreground their personal attitudes.[7] He writes: "Der Reiseerzähler, der die Welt um seine Physis und Psyche kreisen läßt, ist ein neueres, westliches Phänomen, das wesentlich dazu beigetragen hat, die Reiseerzählung als literarische Form zu diskreditieren" (8). It remains to be seen whether Trojanow as an individual travel writer is able both to avoid this trap and to meet his objective of capturing the collective experience of the hajj in *Zu den heiligen Quellen des Islam.*

One should therefore also keep in mind that Trojanow's journey is, after all, the journey of a professional writer, even if he does not bring this significant factor to the fore: in contrast to many of his fellow travelwriters, he rarely mentions taking notes or writing down his encounters and experiences immediately after they have happened. Yet books—and *Zu den heiligen Quellen des Islam* is not an exception—are always published with an eye to the market. Despite stating that the question of audience is insignificant for him (he claims to be writing for "anyone who can read"),[8] Trojanow also travels "in order to write," a phenomenon Michel Butor has explored.[9] Yet Trojanow makes his readers believe that his hajj primarily took place for a different reason, one identified by James Clifford, who argued: "The displacement [caused by the journey] takes place for the purpose of gain—material, spiritual, scientific. It involves obtaining knowledge and/or having an 'experience.'"[10] We can trace this "purpose of gain" in Trojanow's account of his journey, and it seems that it is the act of writing that enables him to enhance the spirituality and solidarity with fellow believers experienced on the hajj: "Als Ramadan erneut begann . . . , las ich meine Notizen durch und war fast überwältigt von der intensiven Vergegenwärtigung. Ich sehnte mich nach der Hadsch zurück, und ich wußte von einem Weg, wie ich die Reise noch einmal begehen konnte. Das war die stärkste Motivation, dieses Buch zu schreiben" (165–66). The writing of the book appears to be the "real" pilgrimage, the "pilgrimage of the mind," and yet it is also the pilgrimage that brings Trojanow's personal experiences to public attention. His journey is therefore both an intensely intimate encounter with Islam as he sees it and a public transmission of a particular aspect of religious life to Muslims, who can share Trojanow's emotions, as well as to non-Muslims, who will never be able to go on the hajj.

Trojanow employs distinct techniques to transfer his religious encounters to his diverse readership. Most importantly, he makes his readers believe that he went on the hajj for religious, not research purposes; he traveled primarily as a Muslim, not as a writer. Being a Muslim, he knows all the rules he needs to follow, but he acquires a more conscious understanding of the meaning of the religious rituals when he performs them in the land of Islam's origin. As he points out: "Jede Reise beginnt vor ihrem Antritt, auf die Hadsch aber, die Pilgerfahrt nach Mekka, bereitet sich der Gläubige ein Leben lang vor" (14). This sentence summarizes the significance of the Muslim pilgrimage as opposed to other forms of traveling. The perpetual awareness of the existence of Mecca and of one's religious roots (maintained by, for example, praying facing toward this city) and the constant knowledge from a very early age that one has to go on this pilgrimage to fulfill the duties of a devout Muslim have prepared the believer for this journey. Trojanow also uses the verb "sehnen" (14) for this kind of mental preparation; it is an indescribable, mystical desire to experience his faith at its roots. The pilgrimage starts long before the actual boarding of the plane. It starts and continues as a journey of the mind for the believer, although "die Hadsch ist nicht nur eine individuelle Pilgerschaft, sondern auch eine Versammlung Gleicher, eine Beschwörung der Umma, der muslimischen Gemeinschaft" (15). It is precisely this unique relationship between the individual Muslim and his/her role in the community of believers that Trojanow explores and that provides the basis for the creation of his own form of Islam.

Throughout his travel account Trojanow describes his relative inexperience in matters religious, though encounters with other Muslims help him find even more immediate access to his religion than he currently has. He finds himself, nonetheless, fully embraced by the more experienced Muslims. He had already sought advice from experienced Muslims while preparing for the hajj in India (37–40), and in referring to these "mediators" or "translators," Trojanow stresses the importance of teachers and education in Islam:[11]

> Badrubhai betete, als ich das Zelt betrat. Sein Kopf schwang rhythmisch von einer Seite zur anderen, die Worte wurden heftig gesetzt, rasant betont, die Stimme schien aus der Brust zu brechen.
>
> Zeige mir dieses Gebet, bat ich ihn, als er sich aus der Sitzstellung gelöst und auf seiner Decke ausgestreckt hatte.
>
> Ich kann es dir nicht beibringen, du bist dafür noch nicht weit genug fortgeschritten, sagte er, erklärte es mir dann aber doch: Das Gebet fängt im Herzen an. Du mußt alles aus deinem Herzen verbannen außer Allah. (114)

Although prayer is part of a Muslim's everyday life, it is also part of his/her lifelong learning process. Despite the fact that the act of prayer is an individual one, it is with the help of teachers (in the company of other believers) that a "real" spiritual experience can be achieved. This interaction between the "student" and the "teacher" is a significant experience for the Muslim Trojanow, who is searching for deeper spirituality and for a more profound understanding of his religion on his hajj.

Trojanow meets his fellow pilgrims in a "contact zone" of (spiritual) equality:[12] it is a space for all Muslims. This notion is already externally emphasized by the *ihram,* the seamless two-piece white garment covering the upper and lower parts of the body that all (male) Muslims have to wear on the hajj. It symbolizes both the mental state of purity and the equality of Muslims. Each pilgrim has to reach this form of inner immersion (mental cleanliness) before performing the rituals of the hajj. Mecca and its Great Mosque, the Masjid al-Haram, as the focal point of Islam are at the center of every Muslim's consciousness:[13] by facing toward the Ka'ba (the cube-shaped "House of God," which contains the Black Stone), and also by remembering the Muslims on the hajj by slaughtering an animal at exactly the same time as the pilgrims do in Mina, the places of Islam's origin are part of every Muslim's life. Yet Trojanow's "contact zone" reaches beyond a physical space: he approaches people's minds without trying to predict what they think, partly because he feels he is one of them:

> Die heulenden Stimmen . . . erklangen aus allen Richtungen. Was als Strohfeuer begann, wuchs sich zu einer Feuersbrunst aus. Je rötlicher der späte Nachmittag sich färbte, desto dichter wurde unser

Flehen. Keiner der zwei Millionen stand in dieser Stunde außerhalb des Gebets. Wir nutzten die Zeit . . . , um noch einmal um Vergebung zu flehen. . . . Hadsch Mabruk. Die Hadsch galt mit dem Ende dieses islamischen Tages als erfüllt. Unsere Sünden waren vergeben, wir waren wie neugeborene Kinder, und wir durften uns von nun an Hadschis nennen. (97–98)

Trojanow identifies with his fellow pilgrims (he uses the collective personal pronoun "wir"): as pilgrims, they are all in the same position and, physically, in the same space. They are united in the religious rituals and have the same aim, the fulfillment of the hajj. Trojanow seems to show that his interest in his travel companions is about his self-definition as part of an Islamic collective, which supports his case that he is trying to leave Western travel-writing practices behind. His use of the pronoun "wir" is particularly striking for his (Western) readers, who might never have come close to such a spiritually uniting experience. He simultaneously attempts to form a linguistic bond between his fellow pilgrims and his readership, whether Muslim or not.

Non-Muslims often superficially associate Islam with a strong sense of tradition and a focus on the past and the Prophet Mohammed: they think that ancient rituals, rules, and customs are not adjusted to the conditions of the present. Islam is the youngest of the three "religions of the book"; its self-consciousness arose out of the *hijra* and is reflected in the hajj as a Muslim's conscious engagement with his/her religious roots, and yet Western Christians often perceive it as a religion that looks back to its origins as a means of justifying or explaining the present. Trojanow is interested in Islam's origin for a particular reason: the individual Muslim travels to the roots of Islam in order to celebrate the unity of the *umma*. Yet the meaning of this concept is expanded at a time when migrations are taking place all over the world, and Islam's cultural roots are merging with other cultural influences.

Many of the hajj rituals Muslims practice are based on an awareness of their religion's origin, its history, and its ancient land. They are followed by all Muslims throughout the world, though with individual, often culturally determined variations, and have the same implications. Yet Trojanow also establishes a strong link between the religion's development and how this is expressed in culture such as architecture, particularly the architecture of the mosque. This, in turn, is connected with the believers who celebrate belonging to the Muslim community by worshipping in the sphere of the mosque.

For any Muslim, but particularly for a pilgrim who is going to Mecca, the origin of his/her religion is primarily symbolized by one place: the Ka'ba, which is the physical center for every Muslim believer. As a place of worship that goes as far back as Abraham, it carries a great sense of history.

As well as being the focal point for Muslim belief, Mecca provides each pilgrim with a unique spiritual experience in the aura of its history.

As all Muslims pray toward the Ka'ba, they create a strong sense of unity among themselves, even if the act of prayer is an individual one. The sense of the collective is particularly strong when worshipping together, which then creates a joint experience, particularly on the hajj and in Mecca, when pilgrims are closest to the Ka'ba. Trojanow writes: "Das Gebet, eine Struktur aus geraden und ungeraden Zahlen . . . , vervollständigt die angelegte Symmetrie. In keiner anderen Religion ist dem Gebet ein so fester Rahmen vorgegeben, für den einzelnen wie für die Gemeinschaft" (55). The notion of a symmetry that determines the believer's behavior, such as in prayer, can imply an idea of facelessness: the individual conceals him/herself behind the masses that form a human structure in worship.[14] However, this extreme concept of Islamic prayer as structured human form does not have any room in Trojanow's view of symmetry as part of Muslim worship, and he gives the idea of symmetry a more positive connotation: it becomes a metaphor for powerful communal belief and beauty. Trojanow returns to the idea of symmetry when describing Islamic architecture, which frames the spaces of both individual and communal Muslim worship. It enhances Trojanow's awareness of the beauty of Islam and is part of his feeling of being a Muslim, which is arguably increased in and by the mosque. This place even becomes a "Heimat" (139) for him, a home with deep emotional roots. Art as something divine, particularly in Mecca, is a means of connecting to Islam's past; art establishes a direct relationship between those who created it in the past and those who now worship in its presence.[15] Trojanow explains:

> Die Gänge, die Bögen, die Kuppeln, die Galerien [der Masjid al-Haram, der großen Moschee zu Mekka], sie sind imposant, aber ohne die Kaaba, eindrucksvoll ob ihrer Einfachheit, wären sie wirkungslos. Die goldene Stickerei auf dem schwarzen Stoff erscheint einem fast ein Zuviel an Ornament, eine Ablenkung von der reinen, kubisch gefaßten Idee. Das Symbol wird fortwährend bestätigt durch die Pilger, die zu jeder Tages- und Nachtzeit wie Planeten diese Sonne umkreisen (oder wie Elektronen den Atomkern) und mit jedem ihrer Schritte das rechteckige Objekt menschlich aufladen. Aus dieser Wechselwirkung entsteht erst das Bayt Allah, das Haus Gottes, und die Umma, die Gemeinschaft der Gläubigen. Es ist wie mit dem heiligen Text: Er benötigt die Hingabe, die Moralität des Lesers, um lebendig zu werden. Die Offenbarung ist in ein menschliches Gefäß gegossen, die Sprache, und somit abhängig von der Kraft und der Wirkung, die ein jeder aus ihr schöpfen und ihr verleihen kann. (41–42)

The pilgrims are united by their religion's past, which is embodied in Mecca and is also expressed by the architecture of the Masjid al-Haram. Their past is a living past, a past revived through themselves, because they must continue to relate back to it in their consciousness, whether through the act of prayer toward Mecca or through the actual journey to the original sites of Islam. Thus for Trojanow the believers form a spiritually powerful unity. This unity, the *umma*, is a historic concept that reaches into the present and points toward a Muslim future: it was formed by movement (the migration to Medina), a journey that led to the self-recognition of the believers as a community.

It seems that movement, migration, is still an important factor in the formation of Muslim identity: for centuries Muslims have moved to many originally non-Muslim countries. During the last few decades Muslims have increasingly made European countries their home, and Islam has influenced European cultures and contributed to the questioning of their largely Western-oriented characteristics. When the adherents of the faith visit the original sites from their distant homelands, then the pattern of Muslim migration can be seen to have come full circle. Throughout his travel account Trojanow celebrates the unifying force of Islam, the religion that all pilgrims—no matter where they come from and how they live their individual form of Islam—have in common, and yet he makes it clear that this celebration of the *umma* does not deny the significance of the individual pilgrim and his/her individual experience of being a Muslim, despite the vast numbers of pilgrims encountered.

Not only is migration a Muslim experience, but it is also something deeply personal for Trojanow: he was born of Bulgarian parents, grew up in Bulgaria, Germany, and Kenya and has lived in a number of countries, including India at the time of his pilgrimage. This peripatetic lifestyle reinforces the question of (Muslim) "origin," which serves as a leitmotif throughout his journey. Certainly Islam seems to operate as a more effective home-place for Trojanow than any state or nation. This is expressed in various answers to the question of where Trojanow is from, which vary according to his conversation partners. He never replies definitively, but leaves deliberate gaps:

> Bruder Ilias, warte! Ich habe von dir gehört. Ich wollte Dich unbedingt kennenlernen. Endlich jemand von meinem Kontinent!
> Ein knochiger Mann meines Alters stand vor mir und stellte sich auf englisch als Arif vor.
> Welcher Kontinent mag das wohl sein? fragte ich.
> Er war verunsichert. Stammst du nicht aus Deutschland?
> Doch, sagte ich, ein wenig.

Na, also, ich meinte Europa, ich bin aus England. Dort geboren und aufgewachsen.

. . .

Arif träumte davon, nach Indien heimzukehren (er sagte "heim-kehren," obwohl er in England geboren war), sobald seine Kinder erwachsen seien, auf eigenen Beinen stünden. Aber er hatte keine Antwort auf die Frage, ob das reine islamische Leben sich in Gujarat, woher seine Familie stammte, um so viel leichter verwirklichen ließe. (89–91)

Later on Trojanow tells us: "Ich erklärte ihnen, daß ich aus Indien stamme und daher keine Ahnung hätte von Fußball, aber wenn sie sich über Kricket unterhalten wollten . . ." (151). Trojanow makes it clear that the question of origin is a secondary issue for him: in the first quotation, it seems to be the continent of Europe that connects these two Muslims who have completely different backgrounds; in the second quotation, Trojanow perceives himself as an Indian, probably on the basis of his current place of abode. His and other people's perceptions of origin constantly change according to background and culture. However, this instability does not seem to create a longing in Trojanow for a place of origin, a "home," as it does for Arif in the first passage. Trojanow does not share this aspiration, which raises the question of whether he has the same notion of "origin" as many of his fellow pilgrims. For Trojanow, the experience of migration challenges such (often artificially created) categories such as state and nation, and migration—the literal as well as metaphorical crossing of national, linguistic, and cultural borders—has, he reminds us, always been part of the "human condition." Indeed, communicating this idea to his Western readers has been Trojanow's concern in numerous of his publications.[16]

Thus it is one of Trojanow's aspirations to show that despite their diverse backgrounds, their migrations and journeys, what unites Muslims on the hajj is their common belief. During his hajj, Trojanow appears to come closer to the Muslim community, a process emphasized by the actual movement of the pilgrimage. He also travels imaginatively, toward and simultaneously with his fellow believers as he talks to them. He experiences what Dale F. Eickelman and James Piscatori single out as the lasting effect of the hajj: a "heightened identification with Islam and fellow Muslims."[17] Yet Trojanow also makes us aware of the heterogeneity of Islam. He perceives a transnational or transcultural dimension in Islam. He does not see a clear-cut differentiation between "real" Muslims from an Arab background and Muslims from non-Arab or "colonized" countries.[18] Trojanow's religion is one lived through the experience of the *umma:* that does not mean that a Muslim gives up his/her individuality, but rather that his/her sense of being Muslim is strengthened by worshipping with "Others" who share the same religious background while keeping their "personal faiths." Trojanow develops a stronger feeling of community by going on this pilgrimage—with Muslims and with other hajj-writers (even reaching beyond religious boundaries): "Ich spürte eine Brüderschaft . . . mit den Muslims, die Zeugnis abgelegt, und mit den Christen, die Bericht erstattet hatten" (159). His travel account reaches beyond an Orientalist experience of Saudi Arabia. He recognizes "the Other" as part of himself: religion, for him, serves as a way of connecting to people.

Going on a journey, and a pilgrimage in particular, implies a sense of literal as well as metaphorical movement. The traditional hajj as a spiritual experience particularly reinforces this twofold meaning of traveling as change and transformation.

Trojanow constructs a communal form of Islam on his journey, yet he also perceives Islam in relation to himself—as peripatetic traveler and writer who has encountered a variety of cultures throughout his life. Thus he simultaneously creates his own form of Islam, which is an "image of a flexible Islam."[19] Iain Chambers suggests that on migratory journeys there is "no fixed identity or final destination."[20] This idea coincides with the reading of the hajj as a celebration of Muslim diversity in unity: Islam appears as an extremely culturally diverse religion. Although the pilgrims perform the same rituals that have been practiced for centuries, they are able to keep and constantly change their individuality by primarily focusing on cultural, non-religious differences. However, the successful completion of the hajj does not imply a final destination either: it seems to continue after the journey itself (in the mind) and is an ongoing process, which is possibly expressed though a changed lifestyle and changed perceptions of Islam. Furthermore, Trojanow's experience of both his individual spirituality and the celebration of the *umma* seem to have strengthened his sense of being part of a whole while discovering diversity in unity and symmetry.

In this sense, Islam stands for particular ideals that can be lived anywhere and are not tied to an "original" place. They can also be relived through the act of writing; Trojanow hopes to reexperience the feelings evoked by the hajj through the mental and creative journey of writing. Thus not only the literal movement of the physical journey but also the metaphorical movement of the mind as the pilgrim later reflects (both before and while writing) upon his journey—the places he visited and the people he encountered—contribute to a pilgrimage as a unique, enduring experience.

Notes

[1] This chapter was written as part of my PhD research, which was kindly supported by The Arts and Humanities Research Council. I am grateful to the council for its support. I would also like to thank Professor Sarah Colvin (University of Edinburgh) for her insightful reading of an earlier version of this chapter. For references to the five pillars of Islam see John L. Esposito, entry on "Pillars of Islam," in *The Oxford Dictionary of Islam*, Oxford Paperback Reference (New York: Oxford UP, 2004), 247–48.

[2] John L. Esposito, entry on "Hajj," in *The Oxford Dictionary of Islam*, 103–4; here 103.

[3] John L. Esposito, *The Islamic Threat: Myth or Reality?* 3rd ed. (New York: Oxford UP, 1999), 27.

[4] Ilija Trojanow in Christoph Bock, "Ortswechsel: Interview mit Michael Ebmeyer und Ilija Trojanow," *Parapluie: Elektronische Zeitschrift für Kulturen, Künste, Literaturen* 19: *Worte, Worte, Worte*, http://parapluie.de/archiv/worte/ortswechsel, para. 29 of 53 (accessed 8 Dec. 2004).

[5] Ilija Trojanow, *Zu den heiligen Quellen des Islam: Als Pilger nach Mekka und Medina* (Munich: Malik, 2004), 7. Subsequent references to this work are cited in the text using the page number.

[6] This technique is widespread in Western travel writing. See Patrick Holland and Graham Huggan, *Tourists with Typewriters: Critical Reflections on Contemporary Travel Writing* (Ann Arbor: U of Michigan P, 1998), xiii. See also Edward W. Said, *Orientalism: Western Conceptions of the Orient*, repr. with a new afterword (1978; repr., London: Penguin, 1995), 197.

[7] See Peter J. Brenner, *Der Reisebericht: Die Entwicklung einer Gattung in der deutschen Literatur* (Frankfurt am Main: Suhrkamp, 1989), 27 and 30.

[8] Ilija Trojanow made this statement in an interview I conducted with him on 14 Nov. 2006 in Glasgow prior to his reading at the Goethe Institute.

[9] Michel Butor, "Travel and Writing," trans. John Powers and K. Lisker, *Mosaic* 8.1 (1974): 1–16; repr. in *Temperamental Journeys: Essays on the Modern Literature of Travel*, ed. Michael Kowalewski (Athens, GA: The U of Georgia P, 1992), 53–70; here 67.

[10] James Clifford, *Routes: Travel and Translation in the Late Twentieth Century* (Cambridge, MA: Harvard UP, 1997), 66.

[11] See Ziauddin Sardar, *Desperately Seeking Paradise: Journeys of a Sceptical Muslim* (London: Granta, 2004), 209: "Thus, Islam does not only make the pursuit of knowledge obligatory but also connects it with the unique Islamic notion of worship: *ilm*, the term for knowledge, is a form of *ibadah* (worship)."

[12] See Mary Louise Pratt, *Imperial Eyes: Travel Writing and Transculturation* (London: Routledge, 1994). I borrow Pratt's term of the "contact zone" in order to describe a space where the traveller and his "subjects" come into contact, and not to refer to "the space of colonial encounter" (6), which does not hold true for Trojanow.

[13] See Gerhard Endress, *Islam: An Historical Introduction*, trans. Carole Hillenbrand, 2nd ed., The New Edinburgh Islamic Surveys (Edinburgh: Edinburgh UP, 2002), 84.

[14] This idea is strongly emphasized by V. S. Naipaul in his first travel account to non-Arab Muslim countries: *Among the Believers: An Islamic Journey* (1981; repr., London: Picador, 2003). Here Naipaul states that "facelessness had begun to seem like an Islamic motif. . . . Individualism was to be surrendered to the saviour and avenger" (28).

[15] For further details on the aesthetic experience of Islam, see Oliver Leaman, *Islamic Aesthetics: An Introduction*, The New Edinburgh Islamic Surveys (Edinburgh: Edinburgh UP, 2004).

[16] One of his latest publications is Ilija Trojanow and Ranjit Hoskoté, *Kampfabsage: Kulturen bekämpfen sich nicht—sie fließen zusammen*, trans. Heike Schlatterer (Munich: Blessing, 2007).

[17] Dale F. Eickelman and James Piscatori, "Preface," in *Muslim Travellers: Pilgrimage, Migration, and the Religious Imagination*, ed. Dale F. Eickelman and James Piscatori (London: Routledge, 1990), xii–xxii; here xii.

[18] This differentiation relates back to the Arab expansion and subsequent incorporation of other cultural influences into Islam.

[19] Eickelman and Piscatori, "Preface," in *Muslim Travellers*, xiv.

[20] Iain Chambers, *Migrancy, Culture, Identity* (London: Routledge, 1994), 25.

14: The Lure of the Loser: On Hans Magnus Enzensberger's *Schreckens Männer* and Ian Buruma's *Murder in Amsterdam*

Monika Shafi

IN MARCH 2006 HANS MAGNUS ENZENSBERGER, one of Germany's most prominent authors, critics, and intellectuals, published an essay, entitled *Schreckens Männer: Versuch über den radikalen Verlierer*, in which he developed the psychological profile of a "radikaler Verlierer."[1] This is a male figure whose isolation and desperation can turn deadly when co-opted by powerful and violent ideological forces. According to Enzensberger, the only violent global movement left today is Islamism, and after briefly surveying Islamism's history and current mission of terror he describes its lure for radical losers of Muslim background. While the essay is Enzensberger's first full-scale engagement with Islamism, it continues his long-standing commitment to confront some of the most current and most controversial problems facing contemporary European societies. The essay also takes up and modifies earlier insights into globalization and its effects on the latecomers to modernity, specifically ideas developed in his previous essays *Die Große Wanderung* (1992),[2] an inquiry into global migration and state responses, *Aussichten auf den Bürgerkrieg* (1993),[3] an essay on the perils of endemic violence in civic societies, and "Hitlers Wiedergänger" (1991).[4] In this last one he compares Saddam Hussein to Hitler, and the Iraqi regime to fascism. *Schreckens Männer*, too, focuses on what is arguably *the* defining issue in global politics today: the explosive mix of globalization, political Islam, and terrorism.

These are hugely complex problems requiring the intense scrutiny of current European and Muslim societies and the history of Muslim empires and Islam, as well as the role and perception of the United States as one of the chief globalization forces, and the scholarly and journalistic literature on these questions rivals its topic in breadth and global reach.[5] Enzensberger was, indeed, criticized by many for overstating and oversimplifying these highly intricate matters yet, by the same token, also applauded for his audacity in presenting them in such a condensed

manner.[6] By presenting his ideas in an essay, a genre in which Enzensberger has achieved supreme mastery, and providing it moreover with
the caveat "Ein Versuch," Enzensberger allowed himself to deal with this
enormously complex subject matter in a brief, poignant, and provocative
manner, thereby circumventing what he calls the expert's need to stake
out and to explore fixed subject territory.[7]

This essay's strengths as well as its shortcomings are thus intricately
linked to Enzensberger's interpretation of the genre as well as to his intellectual positions, which are known to be shifting and flexible. According
to Alasdair King, "it is notoriously difficult to try to attribute to him a
stable position or ideological perspective on any issue, as his statements
often seem to be contradictory."[8] *Schreckens Männer* in its taunting simplicity seems to take an almost populist approach, rich in bold assertions
and short on ambiguity, by depicting Islamism in a global binary populated by (Western) winners and (Arab) losers. At the same time, Enzensberger's intellectual self-perception has always included an ethnographic,
anthropologic stance that concerns itself with the everyday and the ordinary and is weary of ideological certainties and prophesies.[9] How then
does this ethnographic approach play out regarding Islamist terrorists?
To better understand Enzensberger's formal and thematic take on this
topic, this chapter will compare his account to a related exploration of a
radical loser turned assassin, namely Ian Buruma's reportage, *Murder in
Amsterdam: The Death of Theo van Gogh and the Limits of Tolerance,*[10]
published only a few months after Enzensberger's essay. Taking his cues
from the crime fiction suggested in his title, Buruma engages in a kind of
ethnographic detective work following the paths of both killer and victim
and their oddly intertwined fates.

In 2004 the Dutch filmmaker and outspoken critic of Muslim culture Theo van Gogh was murdered by Mohammed Boyeri, a 26-year-old
Dutchman of Moroccan descent. Boyeri, as Buruma's study makes amply
clear, is a text book case of the radical loser, a disenfranchised migrant
lost between cultures, who found recognition and a sense of community in Islamic extremism.[11] Buruma approaches his topic from both a
personal and a political perspective. Born and raised in the Netherlands,
but having lived abroad for many years, he returns to the country of
his youth because "there was something unhinged about the Netherlands in the winter of 2004, and I wanted to understand it better" (*MA,*
10). In seven chapters he provides a nuanced and detailed account of
contemporary Dutch society, chronicling colonial and postwar history,
portraying both well-known and ordinary Dutch citizens, and offering
multiple perspectives on the status of Muslim citizens and the challenges
of migration. In his lengthy reportage Buruma also adopts an ethnographer's gaze, since he observes the effects of social changes, specifically
as they regard Muslim immigration. Engaging these two authors and

their distinct thematic and formal takes on the lure of violence and terror allows one to explore their perception of Islamist terrorists and of Muslim minorities living in Europe.

In his essay "Nomaden im Regal" Enzensberger defines the essay as the outsider genre *par excellence* or as the nomad among literary forms, because it resists exact classification, boundaries, or limits (9). Essays eschew certainties and thoroughness, indulging instead in ambivalence, contradictions, and provisional arguments. A truly democratic form, open to all topics, approaches, and explorations, the essay by its very nature encourages critical responses. Essayists thus do not claim to get it right; they do not even aspire to this goal. On the contrary: "der Essayist will nicht unbedingt recht behalten. Kaum hat er geendet, schon räumt er das Feld und überlässt es den Anderen, in der Hoffnung, sie würden den Faden aufnehmen, die Sache weiterverfolgen, ihm widersprechen, ihn nach Belieben korrigieren oder ausplündern" (15). The essay, one could summarize Enzensberger's witty and delightful reflections, give both author and reader *carte blanche*. Arguments are not to be mistaken for truth claims, pronouncements not for expertise, and the rhetorical skill in exploring a topic trumps affirmative knowledge and somber erudition. As one of the most playful literary forms, the essay also demands, one could conclude, a reader who is familiar with and enjoys the rules of the literary game and who knows how to balance bold language and daring hypothesis against facts and judgments. But how is one to square the essay's preliminary, self-undermining quality with Enzensberger's penchant for razor-sharp verdicts, self-confident assessments, and outright provocations? Is this really an invitation to the reader to challenge cherished assumptions, to think critically, and to engage more profoundly with a topic? Or do hard-hitting arguments claiming to be only a preliminary approximation to, in this case, Islamism, provide a convenient mask to hide authorial authority? Does the essay, in other words, cover Enzensberger with a fool's cap allowing him both to assert and to play with the very truths he claims the essay circumvents qua genre? Irony, one of Enzensberger's favorite weapons, can, as Buruma reminds us, "be a healthy antidote to dogmatism but also an escape from blame . . . a great license for irresponsibility" (*MA*, 112). Does Enzensberger then use irony to battle doctrines, be they of liberal-multicultural or fundamentalist provenance, or to showcase rhetorical pyrotechnics?

The strength of Enzensberger's essay *Schreckens Männer* lies, one could argue, in its drawing attention to the destructive potential of powerful *emotions* such as loss, insecurity, lack of recognition, and above all humiliation, much of it caused by the forces of global capital. Yet by the same token his very focus on individuality and subjectivity, in short, on psychology, sidelines the historical, economical, and political powers informing the loser's particular profile. By paying attention to the

"Drama des radikalen Verlierers" (*SM*, 8) that empirical analyses cannot grasp, Enzensberger underestimates, as a number of critics have pointed out,[12] the specifics of the loser's socioeconomic milieu, particularly as it affects Muslim immigrants to Europe. As the comparison with Buruma will show, Enzensberger's mix of sociopsychological categories, select historical outlines, and anthropological essentialism yields a rather narrow view, which, however, claims to offer a comprehensive analysis. Moreover, Enzensberger's very argument, namely the murderous dynamics of humiliation, is in itself one-sided and flawed, because he highlights the *effects* of humiliation and downplays its causes as well as the role of those who engage in humiliation.

Enzensberger's two essay titles describe both a plurality ("Schreckens Männer") and a prototype ("den radikalen Verlierer"). The focus is on character and emotion, not on causality, since it does not specify what forces turn radical losers into men of fright. "Schrecken" connotes surprise and disruption; one is frightened by an unexpected, sudden event, and the combination "Schreckens Männer," a grammatical and semantic neologism, further emphasizes the exceptional, unsettling quality. Reminiscent of a warrior caste, a select band of fighters, it also alludes to heroism, albeit of a destructive kind, for those men obviously set themselves apart from the ordinary life from which they nevertheless originated. By emphasizing the generic and gender quality of these figures and their intent—the production of fear—Enzensberger underlines the fact that religious or ideological motivations are rather insignificant for them. The radical loser did not originate from any political community; he only finds it in the company of men of terror, as the singular in the subtitle indicates. The emotive quality of terms such as "Schreckens Männer," "radikaler Verlierer," intensified by the red of the title page, has a foreboding, apocalyptic tone that puts readers on alert and is carried over into the first sentence: "Es ist schwer, vom Verlierer zu reden, und dumm, von ihm zu schweigen" (*SM*, 7). This powerful opening statement, with its contrasts and juxtapositions, has an urgent ring to it and positions the author as one who is not afraid to take up a challenge others may have avoided. It bestows responsibility as well as courage on the speaker and sets him apart from the complacent others. This initial statement also establishes a clear-cut opposition between correct and incorrect approaches, a duality that will structure much of the essay.

Schreckens Männer is divided into nineteen brief segments, which total fifty-three pages. The first seven parts are devoted to the radical loser, and the remaining twelve sections focus on Islamism, an arrangement that reflects Enzensberger's inductive way of reasoning. Enzensberger defines radical losers as people who do not manage to integrate themselves into a collective, be it family, school, or work (*SM*, 12). What separates the radical loser from the simple loser, who has also experienced intense misery and defeat, is the latter's complete acceptance and internalization of the winner's view: "Der Versager mag sich mit seinem Lose abfinden und resignieren . . . Der radikale Verlierer aber sondert sich ab, wird unsichtbar . . . und wartet auf seine Stunde" (*SM*, 8). Like his antipode, the "radikale[n] Gewinner" (*SM*, 8), the radical loser is a product of the global economy. In his emphasis on the decisive role of global market forces, Enzensberger takes up arguments from *Die Große Wanderung* (1992) and *Aussichten auf den Bürgerkrieg* (1993), essays in which he delineated the unprecedented scale of human surplus produced by globalization. For the project of modernity, as Enzensberger writes in *Aussichten auf den Bürgerkrieg,* has failed in the sense "daß die 'Zurückgebliebenen,' wo immer sie sich auch finden mögen, in einer aussichtslosen Lage sind. Aus den ökologischen, demographischen und wirtschaftlichen Gründen wird das Modernisierungsgefälle nie mehr auszugleichen sein; die Niveauunterschiede nehmen im Gegenteil mit jedem Jahr zu. Jeder weiß es."[13] Latecomers to modernity, this argument claims, are doomed to fight a hopeless battle.

Having fallen to the very bottom of society, radical losers still need to make sense of their situation and will thus ask themselves who or what is responsible for their decline. Interestingly, Enzensberger does not assume that losers might try to change or try to escape their lot. Once a radical loser, always a radical loser. In this sense they are static figures, figures without hope, frozen in the universe of their failure. The only energy the radical loser will expend is in trying to find the person, the forces responsible for his downfall. Since this mission invariably leads him to face his own shortcomings and thus intensifies the pain, the radical loser is even more intent on blaming others for his misery. It is the fault of the boss, the wife, the noisy kids, or the bad neighbors. The only way out is through a "Fusion von Zerstörung und Selbstzerstörung" (*SM*, 16). The triumph of death—the death of others, or his own—is heightened by the, albeit short-lived, recognition the media will accord him. Enzensberger does not detail the economic, social, or political conditions leading to the feeling of radical loss, so that one could subsume under this category figures as diverse as a US teenager turned Rambo, a German postal clerk who runs amok, or university-educated Egyptians morphing into terrorists. Yet only Muslim radical losers can find a powerful community, Islamism. This is the point at which Enzensberger connects the radical loser with a movement, Islamism, the only violent movement capable of operating globally.

In focusing on the psychological profile of the radical loser and the Islamist terrorist, Enzensberger claims to pay attention to the personal, the emotional, that is often overlooked. However, as Talal Asad pointed out in his study *On Suicide Bombing* (2007), inquiring into the motivation of suicide bombers is typical of Western commentators, who tend to see them "as being in some way pathological. Or as being alienated—that is, as not properly integrated into Western civilization."[14] Yet the focus on motives, be they rooted in personal disenfranchisement or religion, Asad continues, reveals more about "liberal assumptions of religious subjectivities and political violence" (42) than about the act of terror itself. According to Asad, the horror at suicide terrorism stems from many causes, such as the sudden and public killings, the fracturing of everyday life, unregulated warfare, and a violent challenge to the liberal institutions, which are themselves based on "coercive violence" (92). This raises the question of whether "one can say that suicide terrorism (like suicidal nuclear strikes) belongs in this sense to liberalism? The question may, I think, be more significant than our comforting attempts at distinguishing the good conscience of just warriors from the evil acts of terrorists" (92). By interrogating possible connections between Western institutional and political principles and the rationale of suicide terrorists, Asad questions the validity of setting up strict epistemological and cultural dichotomies, whereas Enzensberger emphasizes the differences between Western modernity and premodern thinking.

Enzensberger certainly draws a sharp distinction between the religion of Islam and the political movement of Islamism—the latter abusing the religion for its terrorist purposes. Islamism, Enzensberger argues, is intimately connected both to Western technological supremacy and to the historical decline of former Muslim empires, and he particularly takes the Arabic world to task: despotic and corrupt governments, widespread discrimination against women, and centuries of deficit in cultural capital have produced a dismal national record (SM, 35). While this, by his own admission, sweeping assessment does not reveal anything about the abilities of individual Arabs, Enzensberger proceeds to describe all Arabs' complete dependence on Western technology: "Alles, worauf das tägliche Leben im Maghreb und im Nahen Osten angewiesen ist, jeder Kühlschrank, jedes Telefon, jede Steckdose, jeder Schraubenzieher, von Erzeugnissen der Hochindustrie ganz zu schweigen, stellt daher für jeden Araber, der einen Gedanken fassen kann, eine stumme Demütigung dar" (SM, 38). This is indeed powerful language. Vivid images, concrete examples, made even more compelling by hyperbole and repetition, create a seemingly credible line of argument, which Enzensberger backs up with select citations from scholarly literature and empirical data from the Arab Human Development Report. Its bleak statistics on literacy rates and the widespread emigration of Arab professionals help to further augment Enzensberger's thesis. However, the very persuasiveness of the link between Arab daily life and daily Arab humiliation also marks the essay's prime weakness, a generalization that is based on translating historical developments into collective psychological profiles. To suggest that *every* Arab, specifically every *thinking* Arab, cannot use a screwdriver, phone, or refrigerator, let alone a computer, a car, or a plane, without feeling disgraced or embarrassed suggests a uniformity of psyche and mind for millions of people across diverse nations and a huge geographical realm that even the garb of irony cannot account for. By focusing on Arab Muslims and the decline of their culture, Enzensberger in a roundabout way also seems to equate Arabs with Muslims, thereby further simplifying a complex global world into monolithic blocks of either progressive or premodern cultures.

Moreover, this assessment is based squarely on Western interpretive schemes and thus restores well-known oriental and colonial paradigms. It negates individual or national profiles, denies differences between classes, gender, generations, or ethnicities, and conceives of all Arabs as the negative and inferior counter-image of Western modernity and supremacy. To be an Arab means to be on the losing end of history and progress. Yet whereas in *Aussichten auf den Bürgerkrieg* Enzensberger conceded that the latecomers to modernity are disenfranchised and defenseless vis-à-vis economic forces beyond their control, he now seems to imply that the Arab nations have only themselves to blame for their decline. The effects of Western influence and colonization are not taken into account.

In addition, the Arabs' religiously based belief in their own moral supremacy stands, according to Enzensberger, in stark contrast to a reality of political and economic inferiority and weakness, which further fuels Islamism's furor. He depicts Islamism as a collective of losers unable to face their own shortcomings and failures. This collective of radical losers features all of the loser's well-known traits, namely "die gleiche Verzweifelung über das eigene Versagen, die gleiche Suche nach Sündenbökken, der gleiche Realitätsverlust, das gleiche Rachebedürfnis, der gleiche Männlichkeitswahn, das gleiche kompensatorische Überlegenheitsgefühl" (*SM*, 45). This register suggests that Islamism is an exclusively Arab problem, in which indigenous failures are projected onto to the West. It also leaps from individual to national profile, equating subjectivity with a collectivity that is driven primarily by emotions, namely despair, resentment, rage, and revenge.

Yet, in the same manner in which Enzensberger extracted the specifics from the radical loser's personality and milieu (age, profession, ethnicity, and so on) and thereby derived an anthropological prototype, he now extracts the specifics of politics, history, and economy of Arab nations and subsumes them under a collective. Islamism, to name only one of the most glaring omissions, is not an exclusively Arab problem, but it is fueled by foreign policies, by conflicts in the Middle-East, by Afghanistan's Taliban, or in the madrassas in Pakistan's North-Western provinces, and it is financed by the very same Arab nations Enzensberger could only perceive of as backward. The problem with Enzensberger's arguments is not that they are outright wrong—scholarly literature supports his focus on the effects of centuries of national humiliation—but that they are one-sided and facile. One could claim that the very point of his essay is to provide an unusual, perhaps even provocative focus, but such choices do not justify deceptive and self-serving conclusions. As Gerhard Fischer pointed out in the context of the earlier Enzensberger essays, this author's "global-anthropological perspective"[15] is prone to generalizations and, most importantly, it supports a Western bias that becomes particularly evident in his brief depiction of Muslim immigrants to Europe.

Muslim immigrants find themselves in a long-term culture shock, in which the "double bind von Attraktion und Ablehnung, und die fort-während Erinnerung an den Rückstand der eigenen Zivilisation" (*SM*, 47) can easily become intolerable. But the tipping point, when frustrated desires turn into terrorist action, is again connected to Islamism's lure: "In dieser Lage stellt das Angebot der Islamisten, andere für das eigene Ver-sagen zu bestrafen, für viele eine starke Versuchung dar" (*SM*, 47). While Enzensberger's thesis of the double bind is widely shared in scholarly lit-erature on migrants and integration,[16] he completely fails to acknowledge the extent to which the Western milieu, the Western view, and the West-ern treatment of the Muslim migrant will influence whether he/she will interact in a peaceful or violent manner with the Western nation.

Mohammed Boyeri, Theo van Gogh's murderer, for example, per-fectly fits the Islamist radical loser's profile. A hardworking though shy and ill-at-ease schoolboy, he struggled to adjust to mainstream Dutch secular culture, a struggle that expressed itself most clearly in his rela-tionship to authority, both parental and social; after a series of personal and professional setbacks he searched for and found solace in radical Islamist propaganda. Buruma describes this development and its underly-ing logic within a painstakingly drawn portrait of contemporary Dutch society. The strength of Buruma's argument lies precisely in providing a *spectrum* of native Dutch and Dutch Muslim immigrant perspectives and voices that range from right-wing and liberal positions to the outspo-ken critic of Islam, Ayaan Hirsi Ali, whose provocative film "Submission" Theo van Gogh had directed. In detailing the multiple pressures that turn a lost immigrant into an Islamist—and this includes many of the same factors Enzensberger lists—Buruma emphasizes not only the belated modernity of Muslim nations but also the lack of recognition Muslims so often experience in Europe. He also tries to view liberal Dutch culture from the perspective of deeply religious observers. Strolling, for example, through Amsterdam's red light district with its window prostitutes, porno shops, and sex shows, Buruma wonders: "Perhaps Western civilization, with the Amsterdam red light district as its fetid symbol, does have some-thing to answer for. Maybe these streets are typical of a society without modesty, morally unhinged. . . . For people whose faith is predicated on modesty and whose code of honor prohibits any display of female sexu-ality, every single window along that Amsterdam canal is an intolerable provocation" (*MA*, 234). This is an important, indeed, crucial moment in the text because Buruma deliberately switches perspectives and cultural location. By positioning himself as a member of the minority, he both questions the mainstream point of view and tries to comprehend a traditional interpretation of gender and sexuality.[17] According to Buruma the Muslim view is not premodern, inadequate, or false but a justifiable and valid perception. In this instance then, cultural difference is recognized and accepted, though not necessarily endorsed, as the probing tone of his observations indicates. By accepting the other's point of view as legitimate, Dutch majority and immigrant minority meet on equal terms. Seeing the red-light district not as a normal, acceptable part of the West's urban entertainment industry but as morally offensive, Buruma practices the kind of self-critical cultural assessment that according to Birgit Rommelspacher is key to a successful integration policy: "Die Anerkennung des Anderen bedeutet auf der symbolischen Ebene, *die Grenzen der eigenen Deutungsmacht anzuerkennen,* die Grenzen des eigenen Wissens und Verstehens, auf der Ebene gesellschaftlicher Praxen heißt es, in erster Linie den Zugang zu den gesellschaftlichen Ressourcen und politische Macht für all gleichermaßen zu öffnen" (206, italics mine). This is precisely the approach Buruma follows, for he advocates that democratic European societies must embrace plurality and learn to accept difference and to share power and resources.

Profiling different Muslim interlocutors, Buruma thus engages with their most pressing concern, namely "how to be a Muslim in a secular society" (*MA,* 239). Whether Muslims will embrace Islamism partly depends, Buruma argues, on whether nations like the Netherlands "accept an orthodox Muslim as a fellow free citizen of a European country" (*MA,* 261). In contrast to Enzensberger, who links Muslim radical losers to the lack of progress in Arab countries and argues from an exclusively Western perspective, Buruma pays equal attention to the experiences of individual Muslim immigrants and to those of Dutch native-born citizens, and he critically examines the different ways in which both immigrants and natives cope with the *common* challenge posed by their postmodern environment.

According to Enzensberger, when the two sides are faced with terror and murder, dialogue reveals itself as "Selbsttäuschung" (*SM,* 43) and only tough responses from the police and the courts will be adequate and effective. He continues that liberal societies like the Dutch, and he might be alluding here to van Gogh's murder, had to recognize that "die Taktiken der Verharmlosung und Beschwichtigung die Konflikte mit feindseligen Migranten nicht eindämmen, sondern verschärfen" (*SM,* 43). Not only does this statement equate dialogue indirectly with the down-playing and negation of conflicts, but it also holds dialogue to be incompatible with forceful actions and sees it, moreover, as contributing to the escalation of dissent. Postulating an either–or scenario, Enzensberger consolidates entrenched divisions of "feindselige Migranten" versus "liberale

Gesellschaften" (*SM*, 43) whereas Buruma asks whether liberal societies played a role in turning migrants into enemies and what it would take to stop this process. This is the question that, as René Aguigah pointed out, is most conspicuously absent from Enzensberger's deliberations.[18]

Both Enzensberger and Buruma also refer to Islamism's allegiance to Western products and concepts, but whereas Buruma traces the "deep current of European anti-liberalism" (*MA*, 219) in Boyeri's thoughts and thus acknowledges a conceptual overlap, Enzensberger mentions Islamists' use of high-tech weaponry, media-savvy propaganda, or terrorist tactics. He also points out that the majority of their victims are other Muslims, whose deaths are not decried by other Muslim nations, revealing the hypocrisy of the *ummah*, the global Muslim community. Killing fellow Muslims underscores, according to Enzensberger, the political void of Islamism, for it is not interested in solving the problems of the Arab world, nor does it have an action plan: "Es handelt sich um eine im strengen Sinn unpolitische Bewegung, da sie keinerlei verhandelbare Forderungen erhebt" (*SM*, 51). Whereas Islamism offers no remedy to the "Dilemma der arabischen Welt" (*SM*, 50), the West's dependence on oil also blocks solutions, a stalemate which gravely harms all players.

Enzensberger's concluding summary that a global economy dependent on fossil fuels will continue to produce radical losers and terrorism and that all we can do is to get used to it comes as a surprisingly unspectacular finale. His conclusion does not suggest that Western mental and national attitudes need to be reconsidered, nor does it imply that Arab nations can change. It offers a strangely static assessment demanding no intellectual adjustment or public policy for migrants in such vital areas as unemployment, education, or housing. In sum, Enzensberger's essay appears to take up the infamous post 9/11 question "Why do they hate us?" to which he delivers a stylistically virtuoso but conceptually facile and self-serving answer: "Because they lost!" The arrogance and self-righteousness of the Western winner, magnified, moreover, by the complete lack of solutions or outreach to Muslim migrants firmly entrenches a dualistic, oppositional worldview and reasoning that was alluded to in the very first sentence of the chapter. This attitude and the discursive and material realities it propagates can contribute, however, to the very humiliation whose effects it so vehemently decries.

The issues raised by Enzensberger and Buruma, including suicide terrorism, Muslim migration to Europe, and the global flows of people, goods, and capital, continue to generate intense discussion. Since they touch on the very definition of national identity and by extension on personal privilege and power, debates are often highly contested and emotional. A case in point is Timothy Garton Ash's review of Buruma's reportage and Ayaan Hirsi Ali's *The Caged Virgin: An Emancipation Proclamation for Women and Islam,* in which he defended Buruma's position in *Murder in*

Amsterdam and called Ali "a brave, outspoken, slightly simplistic Enlightenment fundamentalist."[19] This comment and the perception of Enlightenment and Islam it implies unleashed an international debate in which Ali, Buruma, and Ash, as well as numerous other critics, participated and which focused on the universalism proclaimed in the Enlightenment, on different models of integration, and also on Islam's capacity for tolerance.[20] One could also relate these different approaches—which would be beyond the focus and scope of this chapter to describe in any detail—to what Arjun Appadurai aptly called the "fear of small numbers," or the difficulty the nation state in the global world has in accommodating those who by their very origin question and challenge the nation's foundational narrative and *raison d'être*.[21] Seen within this broad historical and political context, the ethnic cleansing of minorities, as well as suicide terrorists, are for Appadurai a violent expression of the new global economy of fear and uncertainty that, like its accompanying vast economic disparities, cut across all national and social spaces (88). Depicting suicide terrorists as the radical losers of the new transnational global economy in the manner of Enzensberger may illuminate some features of this figure yet, as Buruma's case study showed, only an account grounded in the specifics of social contexts and historical legacies can explain the origin and development of this type of violence and potentially offer ways to contain it.

Notes

[1] Hans Magnus Enzensberger, *Schreckens Männer: Versuch über den radikalen Verlierer* (Frankfurt am Main: Suhrkamp, 2006), 8. Subsequent references to this work are cited in the text using the abbreviation *SM* and the page number.

[2] Hans Magnus Enzensberger, *Die Große Wanderung: 33 Markierungen* (Frankfurt am Main: Suhrkamp, 1992).

[3] Hans Magnus Enzensberger, *Aussichten auf den Bürgerkrieg* (Frankfurt am Main: Suhrkamp, 1993).

[4] Hans Magnus Enzensberger, "Hitlers Wiedergänger: Mit einer Nachschrift," in *Zickzack: Aufsätze* (Frankfurt am Main: Suhrkamp, 1997), 79–88.

[5] Selected examples include John J. Donohue and John L. Esposito, eds., *Islam in Transition: Muslim Perspectives* (New York and Oxford: Oxford UP, 2007); Ami Pedahzur, *Suicide Terrorism* (Cambridge: Polity, 2005); Jamal Malik, ed., *Muslims in Europe: From the Margin to the Centre* (New Brunswick, NJ: Transaction, 2004); Michael J. Thompson, ed., *Islam and the West: Critical Perspectives on Modernity* (Lanham: Rowman & Littlefield, 2003); and John L. Esposito, *Unholy War: Terror in the Name of Islam* (Oxford: Oxford UP, 2002).

[6] Examples of critical reviews are Sven Hillenkamp, "Die Bombe Mensch," in *Die Zeit*, http://www.zeit.de/2006/20/L-Enzensberger; René Aguigah, "Der flüchtige Robert," in *Literaturen: Das Journal für Bücher und Themen*, http://literaturen.partituren.org/de/archiv/2006/07_0806/index.html?inhalt=

20070206150824; the essay was positively reviewed by Richard Herzinger, "Im Teufelskreis der ewigen Verlierer," in *Welt am Sonntag*, http://www.welt.de/print-wams/article141164/Im_Teufelskreis_der_ewigen_Verlierer.html; Ingo Way, "Ins Verlieren verliebt," in *Der Tagesspiegel*, http://www.wadinet.de/news/iraq/newsarticle.php?id=2433; Henning Ritter, "Die Zukunft der Selbstmordattentäter," *FAZ*,http://www.faz.net/s/RubC17179D529AB4E2BBEDB095D7C41F468/Doc~EA6F828B5E3BE44A883F08A4D8A6E0054~ATpl~Ecommon~Scontent.html. All were last accessed on 13 May 2009.

[7] Hans Magnus Enzensberger, "Nomaden im Regal," in *Nomaden im Regal: Essays* (Frankfurt am Main: Suhrkamp, 2003), 15.

[8] Alasdair King, *Hans Magnus Enzensberger: Writing, Media, Democracy* (Oxford: Peter Lang, 2007), 13–14.

[9] King, *Hans Magnus Enzensberger*, 337.

[10] Ian Buruma, *Murder in Amsterdam: The Death of Theo van Gogh and the Limits of Tolerance* (London: Penguin, 2006). Subsequent references to this work are cited in the text using the abbreviation *MA* and the page number.

[11] Buruma refers to Enzensberger's "brilliant essay" in a footnote (*MA*, 140).

[12] See, for example, Hillenkamp, "Die Bombe Mensch," and Aguigah, "Der flüchtige Robert."

[13] Enzensberger, *Aussichten*, 44.

[14] Talal Asad, *On Suicide Bombing* (New York: Columbia UP, 2007), 41.

[15] Gerhard Fischer, ed., *Debating Enzensberger; Great Migration and Civil War* (Tübingen: Stauffenburg, 1996) vii.

[16] For an excellent discussion from a German perspective, see Birgit Rommelspacher, *Anerkennung und Ausgrenzung: Deutschland als multikulturelle Gesellschaft* (Frankfurt am Main and New York: Campus, 2002), 99–113.

[17] In contrast to Enzensberger, Buruma discusses the issue of gender and Islam in great detail, particularly with regard to Ayan Hirsi Ali and her controversial film *Submission* (141–86).

[18] Aguigah, *Der flüchtige Robert*, 5.

[19] Timothy Garton Ash, "Islam in Europe," in *The New York Review of Books* 53.15 (5 Oct. 2006): 8, http://www.nybooks.com/articles/19371.

[20] The full debate has been documented in Thierry Chervel and Anja Seeliger, eds., *Islam in Europa: Eine internationale Debatte* (Frankfurt am Main: Suhrkamp, 2007).

[21] Arjun Appadurai, *Fear of Small Numbers: An Essay on the Geography of Anger* (Durham, NC: Duke UP, 2006).

Contributors

CYRIL EDWARDS is a Senior Research Fellow in German at the University of Oxford and an Honorary Research Fellow in the Department of German, University College London. His major areas of research are Old High German, the medieval German lyric, Arthurian romance, the supernatural in medieval literature, and cooking. Recent book publications as editor and translator include Wolfram von Eschenbach's, *Parzival and Titurel* (2006) and Hartmann von Aue's *Iwein or The Knight with the Lion* (2007).

SILKE R. FALKNER is Associate Professor and German Section Coordinator at the University of Saskatchewan (Canada). She is interested in the textual construction of identity; to that end, she has been investigating novels by the contemporary Swiss writer Gabrielle Alioth, as well as early-modern texts about Islam. She has published the following articles about *turcica:* "Images of the Other: The Gender of War in *Turcica* Iconography" (2008), and "'Having It Off' with Fish, Camels and Lads: Sodomitic Pleasures in *Turcica* Discourse" (2004).

DR. JAMES HODKINSON (editor) is Assistant Professor for German at the University of Warwick, UK. He is a specialist in the areas of German Romantic thought and writing, the intellectual and scientific history of the eighteenth and nineteenth centuries, literature and music, and literary representations of cultural and gender difference. He has also published *Women and Writing in the Works of Novalis: Transformation beyond Measure?* (2007) and is currently working on a monograph on Islam in nineteenth-century German-language writing across the disciplines.

DR. TIM JACKSON, Associate Professor of German and Fellow (Emeritus), Trinity College Dublin, has research interests in saint's legends, courtly romance, didactic and spiritual writings, and the mechanisms by which meaning is communicated in medieval literature. His recent work includes chapters on the saint, the knight, concepts of beauty, and the semantic function of rhyme (*Typus und Poetik. Studien zur Bedeutungsvermittlung in der Literatur des deutschen Mittelalters,* 2003). Dr. Jackson is currently working on article-length studies of romance features in Hartmann von Aue's *Der arme Heinrich* and the motif of the Resurrection of the Dead in medieval German literature.

260 ♦ Notes on the Contributors

Margaret Littler is Professor of Contemporary German Culture at the University of Manchester. Her principal areas of research are minority culture and women's writing in German and literary and cultural theory. She is editor of *Gendering German Studies* (1997) and co-author (with Brigid Haines) of *Contemporary Women's Writing in German: Changing the Subject* (2004). Her current project is on Turkish-German writing as minor literature (Deleuze and Guattari). Recent essays include: "Anatolian Childhoods: Becoming-Woman in Özdamar's *Das Leben ist eine Karawanserei* and Zaimoğlu's *Leyla*" (2007); "Cultural Memory and Identity Formation in the Berlin Republic" (2007); "Intimacy and Affect in Turkish-German Writing: Emine Sevgi Özdamar's 'The Courtyard in the Mirror'" (2008).

Rachel MagShamhráin is a lecturer at the Department of German, University College Cork, currently working in the areas of film, translation studies, Holocaust studies, and discursive constructions of German national identity. Her PhD thesis explored the precocious modernity of Heinrich von Kleist's writing. She has recently published a first English translation with critical apparatus of his 1808 drama *Die Herrmannsschlacht* to coincide with the 2000th anniversary of the defeat of Varus's legions in the Teutoburg Forest, and is completing a monograph on truth and lies in the works of Kleist. She is a co-editor of the *Germanistik in Ireland* yearbook.

Dr. Frauke Matthes is Leverhulme Early Career Fellow at the University of Edinburgh. Her research has focused on transcultural literature and culture, the outcome of which will be published as *Writing and Muslim Identity: Representations of Islam in German and English Transcultural Literature, 1990–2006* in 2009. Dr. Matthes has also published on German Turkish literature and migration and travel writing. Her current research focuses on constructions and discourses of masculinity in contemporary German literature. She is working on a monograph with the provisional title *New Masculinities in Contemporary German Literature*.

PD Dr. Yomb May studied at the Universities of Aachen and Düsseldorf, where he gained his doctorate in 1998. He specializes in modern German literature and history and was a research fellow at the Kaiserswerther Institut für Xenologie. Since 2002 he has taught at the University of Bayreuth, where, in 2008, he became *Privatdozent*. He has published on xenology, Georg Forster, Johann Wolfgang Goethe, fables of the Enlightenment, and Wolfgang Koeppen. Major publications include "Die Fabeldichtung zwischen Oralität und Literalität" (2000) and "Den Fremden gibt es nicht. Xenologie und Erkenntnis" (ed., 2004). His *Habilitationsschrift* "Die Südsee im Schatten der Aufklärung" is in print.

Dr. Jeff Morrison (editor) is a Senior Lecturer at the National University of Ireland Maynooth and specializes in the study of travel writing and German aesthetics. His publications include *Winckelmann and the Notion of Aesthetic Education* (edited with Florian Krobb, 1996), *Text into Image: Image into Text* (edited with Florian Krobb, 1997), *Poetry Project: Irish Germanists interpret German Verse* (edited with Florian Krobb, 2003), and *Prose Pieces: Irish Germanists interpret German Short and Very Short Narrative Texts* (edited with Florian Krobb, 2008).

Dr. Kate Roy (PhD, Manchester) researches contemporary literature in German and French by culturally Muslim writers. Recent publications include "Writing Back: Letters Home, European Impressions and Discourse Subversion in Emily Ruete and Zeyneb Hanoum" (2009) and "A Multiple Otherness: Beginning with Difference in the Writing of Leila Sebbar" (2009). Kate has recently begun a postdoctoral project on the phenomenon of new, commercially successful literary trends in Turkish-German popular literature by women writers. Kate is grateful to the Tertiary Education Commission of Aotearoa/New Zealand for funding, which enabled the research for her chapter in this volume.

Monika Shafi is Elias Ahuja Professor of German and Director of Women's Studies at the University of Delaware and has published in book form *Utopische Entwürfe in der Literatur von Frauen* (1989); *Gertrud Kolmar: Eine Einführung in das Werk* (1995); *Balancing Acts: Intercultural Encounters in Contemporary German and Austrian Literature* (2001); and *Approaches to Teaching Grass's The Tin Drum* (ed., 2008).

Prof. Dr. E.P. Wieringa is professor in the Department of Oriental Studies at the University of Cologne, where he teaches courses in Islamic studies with a special focus on insular Southeast Asia. He has wide-ranging interests in both literary and religious studies. Intrigued by narratives from pilgrims about the hajj, he has also written "A Tale of Two Cities and Two Modes of Reading: A Transformation of the Intended Function of the Syair Makah dan Madinah" in the academic journal *Die Welt des Islams* (2002). His most recent publication is an anthology of fiction by contemporary Indonesian writers, entitled *Duft der Asche: Literarische Stimmen indonesischer Frauen* (co-authored with M. Arnez, 2008).

W. Daniel Wilson is Professor of German at Royal Holloway, University of London, and taught at the University of California at Berkeley from 1983 to 2005. His research is in eighteenth- and early nineteenth-century German literature, particularly political, social, and gender aspects. His work on the political matrix of Classical Weimar has received widespread attention: *Geheimräte gegen Geheimbnde* (1991), *Unterirdische Gänge* (1999), *Das*

Goethe-Tabu (1999), and *Goethes Weimar und die Französische Revolution* (2004). He is working on a book on Goethe and "Greek love."

Karin E. Yeşilada wrote her PhD on German-Turkish Literature of the second generation and has published several articles on this topic. Together with Dr. Tom Cheesman (University of Wales, Swansea), she edited a study book on German-Turkish writer Zafer Şenocak: *Zafer Şenocak* (2003). From 2005–2008, she appeared as a literary critic for the radio program "Funkhaus Europa" broadcast by Westdeutscher Rundfunk. She is currently part of a research program on "Turkish-German Cultural Contact" established at Paderborn University and Istanbul University, and currently teaches at Paderborn University and Ludwig-Maximilians University, Munich.

Index

As this entire volume is devoted to matters Islamic within German speaking cultural contexts, every term contained in the following index is implicitly related to those issues. Consequently, the terms "Islam" and "Muslim," and "German," even when subcategorized, appear too often to index in a way helpful to the reader, and in many incidences would lead to unnecessary and manifold duplication of references. The editors would, therefore, direct readers to individual search terms: "Medieval" and "Middle Ages," for example, will automatically indicate sections of the text relating to German encounters with "Islam" or "Muslim(s)" in that period. As the volume's chapters are arranged chronologically and cogently titled, readers are also advised to use this fact, together with the introduction, to locate the material sought. For reference to specific forms of the Islamic faith, terms such as "Sunni," "Shia," "Sufism," are indexed below.